A DELICATE AGGRESSION

A DELICATE AGGRESSION

SAVAGERY AND SURVIVAL IN THE
IOWA WRITERS' WORKSHOP

David O. Dowling

Yale UNIVERSITY PRESS   NEW HAVEN AND LONDON

Published with assistance from the Louis Stern
Memorial Fund.

Yale University Press books may be purchased in quantity
for educational, business, or promotional use. For
information, please e-mail sales.press@yale.edu (U.S. office)
or sales@yaleup.co.uk (U.K. office).

Set in Scala type by IDS Infotech, Ltd.
Printed in the United States of America.

ISBN 978-0-300-21584-7 (hardcover : alk. paper)
Library of Congress Control Number: 2018950106
A catalogue record for this book is available from the British
Library.

This paper meets the requirements of ANSI/NISO
Z39.48-1992 (Permanence of Paper).

10 9 8 7 6 5 4 3 2 1

For my faculty colleagues and students in the School of Journalism and Mass Communication at the University of Iowa

CONTENTS

A photograph gallery appears at the end of Part 1

ACKNOWLEDGMENTS

This project benefited from many who generously contributed their aid and wisdom. Among them, my faculty colleagues at the University of Iowa School of Journalism and Mass Communication have played a crucial role in the conception, development, and funding of this book. They include Stephen J. Berry, the Pulitzer Prize–winning investigative journalist, who read an early draft and provided valuable comments; Travis Vogan, a longtime co-author and collaborator who lent sage advice and useful feedback on key chapters from the beginning; and David Ryfe, who supplied essential administrative and financial support. Stephen Bloom's insight and encouragement have been invaluable. Our many conversations about the finer points of preparing a manuscript of this scope were inspirational. Subin Paul, my research assistant, made a profound contribution to the book by tracking down leads and scouring hundreds of boxes of archival material. This project would not have been possible without his vital presence at every stage of its research and writing. Subin toiled in the trenches beside me from the onset; he deserves much of the credit for this achievement.

Brooks Landon, former English department chair, kindly shared his voluminous knowledge of many of the figures discussed in this book as well as the larger institutional history of the Workshop's relationship with the English department. In the Special Collections department of the University of Iowa's main library, archivist David F. McCartney deserves special recognition for his professionalism, advocacy, and compassion. It was a privilege to have worked with an archivist of his caliber, especially one whose mastery of University of Iowa and Iowa City history is unmatched. He was a beacon of light throughout the entire journey. He and Kelly A. Smith, Iowa Writers' Workshop curator of the Glenn Schaeffer Library at the Dey House, were instrumental in arranging access to important materials.

My friends and colleagues in the International Association for Literary Journalism Studies, Bill Reynolds, Joshua Roiland, John J. Pauly, William Dow, Norman Sims, and David Abrahamson contributed vital suggestions and encouragement that enriched the manuscript. I am grateful to Connie Brothers for sharing her candid memories and decades-long experience in the main office of the Iowa Writers' Workshop. Her reflections brought to life many of the scenes depicted in this book. The many Workshop staff and graduates who graciously accepted my requests for interviews, from Tracy Kidder to Marilynne Robinson, deserve acknowledgment. I thank Paul Ingram of Prairie Lights Bookstore in Iowa City for insisting that a new history of the Workshop—by a non-affiliate of the program—needed to be written. Paul's recollection of the many distinguished figures Prairie Lights hosted over the decades sparked my full commitment to this project. Sarah Miller, my Yale University Press editor, has my deepest appreciation for her care and professionalism. I also owe a deep debt of gratitude for the meticulous work of Yale's senior manuscript editor Phillip King and publishing assistant Ash Lago. Their compassion, patience, and wit made for a productive and delightful process.

Immersion in this vast undertaking would not have been possible without author and professor Caroline Tolbert and our children, Jacqueline, Eveline, and Edward, who backed this research through all its stages with their love and strength. I owe the world to them.

TIMELINE

Author	Years at IWW	Major Works Linked to IWW
Flannery O'Connor	1945–1948	*Wise Blood*
W. D. Snodgrass	1951–1953	*Heart's Needle*
Robert Shelley	1949–1951	"Harvest"
		"Evening in the Park"
		"On My Twenty-First Birthday"
R. V. Cassill	1946–1952, 1960–1966	*Clem Anderson*
		In an Iron Time
Marguerite Young	1942–1943, 1955–1957	*Miss MacIntosh, My Darling*
Robert Lowell	1950–1951, 1953–1954	*Life Studies*
Dylan Thomas	1950	*Collected Poems, 1934–1952*
John Berryman	1953–1954	*Homage to Mistress Bradstreet*
Kurt Vonnegut	1965–1967	*Slaughterhouse-Five*
John Irving	1965–1967, 1972–1975	*The World According to Garp*
Sandra Cisneros	1976–1978	*The House on Mango Street*
Rita Dove	1975–1977	*The Yellow House on the Corner*
Jane Smiley	1973–1978	*Barn Blind*
T. C. Boyle	1972–1977	*Descent of Man*
Marilynne Robinson	1991–2016	*Gilead*
		The Givenness of Things: Essays
Anthony Swofford	1999–2001, 2007	*Jarhead*
Ayana Mathis	2009–present	*The Twelve Tribes of Hattie*

Introduction

On a drunken evening in the winter of 1954, renowned Pulitzer Prize–winning poet John Berryman groped for his mangled horn-rimmed glasses. Phil Levine, one of Berryman's star MFA creative writing students at the Iowa Writers' Workshop, had just landed a savage punch in his instructor's face, sending him reeling in pain. Recently hired on the recommendation of his world-famous predecessor, Robert Lowell, Berryman filled his classes on the basis of his esteemed literary reputation. But many fled once exposed to his "blow-torch approach" to conducting his graduate seminar in poetry writing. Levine ironically was among the thirteen out of forty students brave enough to remain in Berryman's course and "hang in there against John's special mix of crankiness, brilliance, and cruelty," as Robert Dana recalled.[1]

Although Berryman's tenure would end after one short semester—a tumultuous affair punctuated by a fall down a flight of stairs through a half-glass door that left him "happy to be alive" in the hospital after an evening drinking with his Princeton friends—Levine's punch in the eye established a lifelong friendship with his mentor.[2] On the strength of student recommendations such as Levine's, Berryman might have remained on the faculty at Iowa much longer had he not been fired when faculty discord boiled over into an ugly public incident. In the wake of an intense liquor-ridden dispute with a colleague at Kenney's, the Workshop bar of choice, Berryman's landlord refused to let him into his apartment. His unspeakable protest on the porch led to his arrest for disorderly conduct.[3] Despite what was perhaps the most bizarre exit by a faculty member in Workshop history, one that momentarily transformed this elite program into a theater of the absurd, Berryman's followers were undeterred. Unlike other students who either abandoned Berryman's seminar or chafed under his acerbic methods, Levine would remain his most loyal and vocal advocate, penning "Mine Own John Berryman" in support of his mentor as late as 1993.[4] "No hanging back," Levine recalled Berryman saying in class. "One must be ruthless with one's own writing or someone else will be." Such high standards meant "everyone who dared hand him a poem burdened with second-rate writing tasted his wrath, and that meant all of us." Levine found himself transformed by such advice, which "wakened a dozen rising poets from their winter slumbers so that they might themselves dedicate their lives to poetry."[5]

The Berryman-Levine brawl embodied the risks inherent in the founding principle of the Iowa Writers' Workshop built on contention and public criticism, a volatile cocktail of ego and competition that pervaded life in the world's most powerful and prestigious creative writing program since 1941. Workshop founder Paul Engle, a backslid Methodist minister who rejected mystical understandings of professional development rooted in epiphanies and divine callings, had drawn on Iowa English professor Wilbur Schramm's workshop method. In 1936, Schramm originally had classmates provide feedback on each other's writing to foster the "process of constant self-criticism" in which "a writer teaches himself to write."[6] Engle, the son of a horse trainer who regarded teaching as another form of athletic coaching, transformed the peer criticism component of Schramm's method into a blood sport.

Under Engle, students would provide copies of their creative work to their peers in a classroom ritual of dissection and criticism, some constructive and some damaging. Workshop sessions eschewed gratuitous praise and superficial compliments for brutally honest feedback that more often humiliated than ennobled young writers to harden them for the real competition of the literary marketplace. Designed to simulate the intense pressure of publication, workshop sessions subjected creative writers unaccustomed and averse to the business world to a highly professionalized approach to their craft with a sense of urgency most had never encountered. Many had been acculturated to view creative writing as developing under opposite circumstances characterized by growing the good rather than beating back the bad in one's work. Repercussions of this intense classroom environment could be felt in the student body's social dynamic. Some of the most significant authors in the history of American letters, such as Sandra Cisneros, would look back in anger at their alienating Workshop experience. But they also acknowledged that their opposition to the program helped spring their boldest experiments and innovations.

Competition can indeed breed community, and often did, according to Engle's plan. Some, like the famous alumnus T. C. Boyle, who encouraged his own children to enroll in the Workshop, swore by the method. Others found it hostile to their own cultural understandings of community formation. Engle's approach to bonding through preparation for a common enemy—in this case the publishing industry's legions of potentially hostile critics and editors—grew out of a Cold War mentality. Many writers rebelled against this model built on opposition and defense, seeking alternatives rooted in mutual understanding and affirmation. "Say yes to everything," the mantra Cisneros adopted as the key to creativity, developed as an alternative to Engle's legacy of rigid disapproval and negation.[7] Others embraced that vision. One of his most obedient students, Flannery O'Connor, articulated Engle's approach that later generations of writers rebelled against when she said, "Everywhere I go I'm asked if the universities stifle writers. My opinion is that they don't stifle enough of them."[8]

In its broadest sense, this book examines the impact of the Iowa Writers' Workshop on literary culture and the publishing industry through the careers of our most important contemporary authors who coursed the program from its origins to the present. Arranged as a series of critical biographies, it details the imprint Workshop members left on the institution's official narrative it has chosen to publicly identify with, while also investigating the program's influence on their professional development. With special attention to the institutional rituals and administrative leadership conditioning the program's fraught negotiation of the writer's role in mass culture at the nexus of art and commerce, it offers a glimpse into creative writing pedagogy and the enigmatic, often bruising, relationship between teacher and student. Now-famous authors appear in their formative years taking their first tentative steps toward professional careers, forming alliances and rivalries among intimidating world-renowned faculty and high-powered peers. Their struggles to survive the institutionalization of writing instruction deliberately designed to intensify the pressure and competition are etched in their successes and failures. This was an environment teeming with talent and ambition, a powder keg of emotion and creativity that exploded into bizarre controversies, unlikely bonds, turgid tensions, and frothy confrontations that shaped the course of literary history. At the Workshop, innovation and breakthroughs flourished in manuscripts that seemed to write themselves alongside others locked in the soul-killing anguish of writer's block, an affliction that seemed contagious in this atmosphere of heightened self-consciousness. Publication was the gold standard from the beginning of the program, designed to professionalize rather than coddle young creative minds. Pragmatic and strategic works would emerge from the workshop crafted to fit the demands of the industry.

But the Workshop was notorious for subjecting students and faculty alike to its own insular arbitrary standards. A student received a C– for a novel that was published by a renowned New York press; his fame later ostracized him socially, and he left the program.[9] Tennessee Williams's best friend at the Workshop, the African-American playwright Thomas Pawley, nearly dropped out due to the alienating and coarse bigotry of the place. "I could not eat in the restaurants of the student union, and I was told I could not stay in the dormitory," Pawley, the author of the play Ku Klux, testified to an environment totally hostile to accommodating his bare necessities much less providing a setting to inspire his creativity.[10] Decades later, Rita Dove also pointed to social segregation, "how everything ran by clique," as "one of the worst things about Iowa."[11]

Such repressive features persisted during Dove's era of the 1970s despite the Age of Aquarius being a time of liberation and rebellion against old repressive standards. Iowa's sexual renaissance was in full bloom then. Workshop student Allan Gurganus recalled porn films being made in the apartment adjacent to his. With a hyperactive erotic imagination worthy of Philip Roth's Portnoy, Gurganus fantasized that he might be recruited as an extra. He wrote amid the sounds of these productions taking place through the walls, glimpsing traces of the actors' body makeup left in the apartment's shared bathroom.[12] Cisneros talked openly of her affairs and her sexual awakening during her creative development; Curtis Harnack slept with his instructor Hortense Calisher, who was in the process of divorce, igniting passion in the unlikeliest of places— Iowa City, which "was surprisingly accommodating, with no comments or any awkward social complications," an environment "perfectly sophisticated."[13]

Too Much Blood

Paul Engle's singular ambition that developed the Iowa Writers' Workshop into the world's most powerful creative writing program significantly correlates with a scene at the end of F. Scott Fitzgerald's The Great Gatsby. In it, the father of the deceased Jay Gatsby reveals his son's well-thumbed copy of Hopalong Cassidy to narrator Nick Carraway. In the back pages is a list of mental and physical activities for self-improvement, from physical fitness and personal hygiene to studying before and after work. The list headed "GENERAL RESOLVES" would appear innocent enough and even heartbreakingly naive in the youth's raw desire to build himself into a success through a "bath every other day" and to "save $5 (crossed out) $3 every week." But more calculating plans to "study electricity, etc." and "needed inventions" calibrated down to the minute reveal the eye of the financial speculator he would become.[14] Franklinean invention blends with a Protestant work ethic in the list that appears in a book celebrating the life of the outlaw bandit Hopalong Cassidy. This telling volume, Fitzgerald suggests through Carraway, may provide the key to Gatsby's character.

Engle also had a well-thumbed copy of *Hopalong Cassidy*. And like Gatsby, he harbored the larger-than-life ambitions of a humble midwesterner. Born in Cedar Rapids, Iowa, in 1908, he trained to be a Methodist minister and preached briefly in a church on the edge of town, but "Heard no call," according to his curriculum vitae. When he abandoned the ministry, he also lost faith in mystical understandings of vocation and professional development.[15] After earning his M.A. in creative writing from the University of Iowa in 1932, Engle dedicated himself to a more systematic method of professional development, in defiance of both the divine calling his earlier religious training demanded and the visionary epiphany required of authors. Rejecting romantic notions of authorship and creative writing came naturally to Engle, because he had just renounced the ministry's mystified sense of professional attainment based on being "startled by a voice speaking from heaven," as he sneeringly described it in 1961.[16]

The man of letters, Engle insisted, must necessarily also be a man of business, as William Dean Howells also imagined. Engle's delicate aggression was equal parts genteel grace and opportunistic capitalism. Like a college coach recruiting young talent, he lured some of the best creative writers out of the bohemian culture idealized in Greenwich Village, Parisian cafés, and City Lights Books, the haven of Allen Ginsberg and the Beat Generation, where literary circles defined themselves in opposition to formal institutions and bureaucracies. In doing so, he offered not only aesthetic but also professional development, primarily measured in the Workshop through publication, fame, and the ultimate prize of earning a living as a professional author through the production of fiction and/or poetry. Engle tirelessly solicited funds for his fledgling program from Maytag and Amana, as well as a Chicago ice cream manufacturer he once persuaded to help finance a festival on Baudelaire.[17] The Workshop's glittering prestige is the result of his chameleonic politics—he backed Kennedy's Cold War and the Communist party at various intervals—and his relentless promotion of the program, which took place in a hog shack in his backyard that he converted into an office where he conducted business, attending to correspondence and finances for hours every night. His dedication to building a financial base for the program was consonant with its pedagogical emphasis on development through accretion rather than sudden visionary enlightenment.

The workshop method according to the legacy of Engle's pragmatic Darwinian principle refused to coddle the egos of young romantic visionaries. Stand-ins for the potentially dismissive professional publishing industry's editors and critics would be the students themselves. Engle's model of training through the delicate aggression of harsh critique in workshops rankled students raised on alternative models and understandings of artistic creativity according to more communal models drawn from ethnic feminist approaches. The legacy of Engle's whip that lay beside his typewriter as a symbol of the martinet authoritarianism of the older era began to crumble beneath pressure from students like Cisneros and Joy Harjo. Criticisms of the Workshop from the earlier era by such reputable figures as Robert Lowell also signaled an underlying discontent with the prevailing ethos of the Workshop despite its spectacular results in the way of publication records, awards, and celebrity careers it produced. Engle's Gatsby-like raw ambition, therefore, would not necessarily translate to all students, as the beginning of a more communal and mutually supportive model of writing began to take hold.

Engle's resistance to the notion of a divine calling as the catalyst for career development provided the foundation for his own professional advancement as well as the establishment of the Iowa Writers' Workshop. Both came at a time when bureaucratic efficiency, rather than mystical belief, ruled the business world. Engle would transform himself into the impresario, bureaucrat, agent, promoter, and publicist of the Workshop and its students into industry-savvy professionals with a tenacity and business acumen rarely seen in the literary world. Trading "the abrupt and ecstatic experience of Saul on the road to Damascus" for "steady development at the University of Iowa" was his radical anti-visionary model.[18]

Engle recognized that writing increasingly made its home with free market enterprise and thus depended on large sources of revenue outside of the academy, which itself offered aspiring writers at least minimal shelter from the rough seas of the free market. Gertrude Stein fed the starving Ernest Hemingway in Paris just as Ralph Waldo Emerson provided the real estate and financial backing for his protégé Henry David Thoreau's experiment at Walden Pond. The University of Iowa and a dizzying array of sponsors would supply similar patronage and protection from the ravages of the competitive market, while Engle would assume the role of literary agent and publicist relentlessly promoting the program and its students in the publishing industry with dogged, sometimes shameless determination.

The deliberately anti-romantic setting on the shores of the muddy Iowa River amid the drab and hopelessly mundane architecture of Iowa City was the antithesis of literary inspiration. A set of army barracks left over from World War II served as classrooms, their corrugated steel roofs radiating stifling heat during the hot months, silencing discussion with the drumming of loud rain, and freezing with ice and snow in Iowa's cold seasons. The workshop method itself took many aback. Robert Bly remembered being stunned by the bureaucratic sterility and military efficiency of its rituals, particularly that "it seemed beneath the dignity of art to mimeograph poems" and circulate them for critical feedback during class. Others shared Bly's sense that a poem should, of all things, exist outside the circuits of bureaucracy and business, and should never take on the corpse-like quality of so much paperwork embodied in "that strange thing, blue dittoed poems."[19]

The setting and materials reinforced the anti-romantic approach toward creative writing Engle's Workshop had in store for its students. To "workshop" a poem or story meant subjecting one's writing to the scrutiny of the entire class. Collectively, Bly recalled, "we didn't attack the teacher . . . in general, the aggression went against each other."[20] This was according to Engle's design, and according to his assumption that the work of writing and development of a professional literary career was rigorous and acutely painful, a free market enterprise far removed from the lavish luxury of pre-industrial artistry produced under the protective enclave of a single patron with commercial or political power. The workshop was intended to replicate the ruthless, often savage, rigors of editorial and critical scrutiny of precisely the sort that devours so many neophytes with fragile egos and lofty ideals. By throwing each student "into competition with those around him" who operate with the understanding that writing "is a difficult art not only worth an absolute commitment of faith, time, and energy, but demanding it," Engle sought to simulate "the imperatives of the marketplace." According to the workshop method of instruction, the aspiring writer "finds that the students around him are alert to his faults" while pitted in a hostile environment designed to provide "a manner of publication without losing too much blood."[21] The army barracks on the east shore of the Iowa River hardened young writers for the battlefield of the publishing industry. Engle's bullwhip curled beside his typewriter is richly symbolic of "the delicate and imaginative aggression" he felt was essential to literary production.[22] Demystifying romantic notions of literary production through the hard glare of peer criticism fostered a climate of envy, paranoia, and ruthless competition.

A Delicate Aggression explores students' diverse methods of enduring Engle's Workshop without the loss of too much blood. During Engle's era, from 1941 to 1966, students congregated at Kenney's and other local watering holes to commiserate about their struggles, often wondering who among them would emerge from the pack. Irene Kenney, the pub's proprietor, was a round-faced matron who would dispense wisdom for the down-and-out gambling-addicted Philip O'Connor and others. She often played the role of mother, sister, friend, and adviser, providing the sympathetic ear and universal acceptance missing from the incessant sparring and defensiveness of the classroom workshop environment. Other refuges of communal relief from the tension of the classroom-barracks known as the Quonset huts included a paperback bookstore run by graduate students called the Paper Place, the Renaissance II Coffee House, and Dave's Fox Head Tavern. Alcohol-fueled softball also provided self-medication and escape, as students divided themselves into teams of Poets versus Fiction Writers in games that alleviated the strain of the literary competition that dominated their lives.

Those who did achieve a measure of literary success were often maligned as sell-outs or deemed unworthy of their accolades. Many students directly benefited from Engle's vast connections in the publishing and entertainment media industries while others slipped through the cracks. Some found stories they had written for class published in high-profile and lucrative journals like *Life* and *Esquire*, thanks to Engle's negotiations on their behalf. Others wrote screenplays for the *Hallmark Hall of Fame* television series, all gigs arranged by Engle that paid handsome financial and professional dividends.

Legitimate literary achievements, such as W. D. Snodgrass's *Heart's Needle*, led to gossip and envy. Legend had it that Bly "regularly brought a snake to class with me in a gunnysack, and whenever someone began to criticize a poem of mine, I would take the snake out and lay it on the table." Although he denied the story, he allowed that its very existence made one "feel several kinds of fear" that characterized life in the Workshop classroom.[23] Social groups that formed in response to the isolating and individualistic classroom dynamic included ones spearheaded by more eccentric faculty members who enjoyed playing the role of magnetic guru. Marguerite Young's innovative novel *Miss MacIntosh, My Darling* attracted her own coteries of students, exhorting them

to model her fanciful embellished style, self-described as "on the side of angels."[24] Faculty members who subscribed to a more linear approach to teaching writing harbored resentment toward Young. Engle himself drew fire from
regular English department professors for running his program as his own
fiefdom bankrolled with scholarships and housing stipends from deals he independently brokered with fanciers and corporations. One English professor
made a habit of pausing on his way to university football games to shout a litany of profanities at Engle's front door.[25]

The Workshop evolved from Engle's original vision to adapt to an increasingly diverse literary culture, and toward alternative models of literary production that would still cater to the interests of industry. The contentious ecosystem
of the Workshop persisted throughout later generations, as some tension
boiled over into controversies that brought scandal, particularly during the
Engle era. Much of that controversy derived from the Workshop's historic
ambivalence toward the writer's role in mass culture, despite its production of
scores of careers in popular media industries such as journalism, TV, and
film. The careers of the figures of this book speak to the Workshop's influence
over literary and mass culture from the early 1940s to the present. Like no
other creative writing program, Iowa both shaped the course of literature and
set the terms for its migration into popular culture.

The Iowa Writers' Workshop in Literary History

The Iowa Writers' Workshop has dominated its peer creative writing institutions in higher education since 1941 and has maintained its status as literature's most potent producer of fame to the present day. As the Workshop's
status rose after World War II, the famous writers gathered. In the past quarter century, Iowa MFAs have published more than three thousand books,
compared with most programs, where the volumes by their creative writing
graduates number in the hundreds.[26] In one five-year span, the program produced two Pulitzer Prizes, won by Marilynne Robinson in 2005 and Paul Harding in 2010. Creative writing programs emulating the Workshop have
proliferated, with more than three hundred now in existence, growing from
the original five established in the 1940s, including at Iowa, Stanford, Johns
Hopkins, Cornell, and the University of Denver.[27] Their numbers rose from a
mere half dozen to forty-four by 1970, followed by a massive surge that topped
one hundred by 1980.[28] The growth was exponential, a kind of "pyramid
scheme," as the Workshop faculty member Donald Justice described it,

whereby Iowa-produced MFAs in turn founded new graduate programs in creative writing.[29] Iowa graduates established at least twenty-five new programs, including those at high-caliber institutions such as Stanford, under the direction of Iowa alumnus Wallace Stegner in 1947.[30] Iowa's "structure of the program of worksheets, open discussion seminars, and flexible credit is excellent and widely copied," according to Workshop graduate Edmund Skellings, who admitted to "using it myself for three writing programs of my own founding."[31] The Iowa effect was all too apparent for one survey respondent, asked to name the degree of his program's founder, in this case James Crumley of Colorado State University in 1967.[32] "How coincidental," he quipped, "he took his MFA from Iowa Writers' Workshop."[33]

Historian D. G. Myers has compared this proliferation of creative writing programs to an "elephant machine," a phrase drawn from American industrial parlance of the mid-twentieth century referring to a machine that makes a machine.[34] Iowa was the Ur-elephant machine of creative writing. But did it function only as a mechanism for reproducing itself, where the graduates would simply go on to establish more institutions like Iowa's where they would concentrate on teaching? Myers focuses on how educational features of creative writing programs replicate themselves, whereas my concern is the curriculum's extramural impact on professionalization into the publishing industry. Myers concludes that "the elephants teach." But Workshop graduates were not trained to teach—no course in pedagogy has ever appeared on the Iowa curriculum—but to write, publish, and become powerful figures in mass culture. Echoing Iowa's central mission of producing professional authors, as opposed to teachers or administrators, the first line of the creative writing program curriculum description for the University of California, Irvine, reads, "Aim: To aid the development of students into professional writers."[35]

This book is the cultural and industrial history of the Workshop told through the dramatic events that shaped the writing careers of its students and faculty. The key to the program's success from its origin has been the maintenance of an active and intimate relationship with the publishing industry. Engle was not just an academic entrepreneur, busy raising funds and writing press releases for his program to compensate for receiving no state financial support in the first twenty years of its existence. He was also a media entrepreneur, actively creating publishing opportunities to advertise the Iowa brand, support students financially, and initiate them into the literary marketplace. Starting in the 1940s, Workshop faculty and students have fostered a culture of literary production focused on results measurable by publication through emphasis on the importance of writing for a discriminating audience. This meant faculty and administration mentored as much as they marketed their students, performing the dual function of instructor and career counselor/literary agent. Lucrative funding in the form of scholarships and tuition assistance had never been instituted in creative writing programs with the zeal of Engle's Workshop. Historians of modern authorship point to the postwar era as a period of intense professionalization of the trade that necessitated authors' dependence on agents and intermediaries because the old patronage system had yielded to an increasingly competitive free market. The rise of corporate capitalism and conglomeration across the media landscape meant the small publishers and unconnected independent authors alike were extremely vulnerable to economic ruin in the literary marketplace.[36] Enter the university creative writing program, which at Iowa covered financial burdens during two-year residencies in which young writers could market their wares with the sparkling veneer of the Iowa brand. But how did Iowa develop that prestige from Wilbur Schramm's obscure Program in Creative Writing?

In a word, Engle poached it. Using an analogy he himself was fond of, Engle recruited talent like an athletic coach—with a missionary's zeal—to fill the ranks of his faculty and flesh out the student body. The mythic luster of reputation is difficult to parse; but in Iowa's case, it was the result of deliberate construction. Tactics like robbing other programs on campus of their skilled writers—Flannery O'Connor was originally enrolled in the School of Journalism when she arrived on campus—were not enough, however. Acculturating students to the publishing industry was essential. The workshop method in which writers offered their work for group discussion had long been in use by amateur clubs at Iowa, such as the Zetagathian, Erodelphian, and Hesperian Societies. But these dilettantish rhymers' clubs and literary cliques would give way to a more professional and competitive—often hostile and contentious—model in the corrugated cold steel of Engle's Quonset huts.

The imperative to produce market-ready publishable prose faced Workshop members with the conundrum of reconciling their artistic vision with the demands of the industry, a dilemma that has vexed writers at least since the Industrial Revolution. Many authors since that time have successfully navigated this tension. Washington Irving, Charles Dickens, Henry Wadsworth Longfellow, and Harriet Beecher Stowe were all bestsellers who also enjoyed critical canonization. Irving freely embraced what he called "the romance of trade," approaching the literary profession with a notorious "nose for gold," in the words of his jealous literary rival James Fenimore Cooper. Less charitable was one twentieth-century literary historian who described Irving's publicity engine as a "literary pimpery."[37] But Irving was revered rather than reviled by his contemporaries, mainly since authorship as a profession had yet to exist except as an ancillary activity to one's main occupation.

When authorship became a sustainable occupation, certain commercially successful writers found themselves isolated from the literary community. Stephen King succumbed to this truth in his emotional acceptance of the Distinguished Contribution to American Letters award from the National Book Award Foundation in 2003. King saw this lifetime achievement award as a token recognition of his decades-long dominance of the genre fiction market and an unmistakable sign that none of his works were worthy of the highly esteemed National Book Award itself, regardless of his various attempts to write literary fiction of that caliber. Authentic acceptance among the ranks of the elite literati permanently eluded him, he realized. The stigma of genre fiction writing that prevented him from joining the ranks of great American authors "was still hurtful[;] it's infuriating and it's demeaning," he confessed. King has long held a grudge against the establishment occupied by figures like Martin Amis and Michael Chabon, leaving him "bitterly angry at writers who were considered 'literary.' " Chabon, who won the Pulitzer Prize for his novel *The Amazing Adventures of Kavalier and Clay,* is a graduate of the prestigious creative writing MFA program at the University of California, Irvine, and Amis is the son of the literary lion Kingsley Amis, whom *Time* named one of the greatest British writers since 1945. King, without a degree like Chabon's or a legacy like Amis's, complained that these writers "seemed to have an inside track."[38] He is not mistaken that Norman Mailer and John Cheever, among others whom King revered and emulated throughout his career, all coursed through Iowa City and joined forces with the Workshop during their careers, the former in various visits and conference presentations, and the latter as a faculty member. Had he been armed with an Iowa MFA, King (the King of *Shawshank Redemption* and *Dolores Claiborne* rather than *Cujo*) might have been a force to be reckoned with in the literary world.

American culture has been so disinclined to canonize popular writers because it deems that commercial success should follow rather than precede artistic greatness, mainly because of the persistent myth of the starving artist. To starve for one's vision and then attain wealth is acceptable, whereas the reverse is an execrable taboo. Most master narratives of literary history, especially those produced by the webmasters and memoirists of the Iowa Writers' Workshop, obscure the commercial concerns for promotion and publicity in order to highlight a mystified portrait of the literary artist's creativity, a vision of authorship ironically at odds with Engle's. But creative writing programs came of age when literature itself became show business, and Iowa was atten- tive to this shift. Resistance to or renunciation of that shift crippled fledgling programs such as Columbia's, which until recently offered limited financial support for its MFA creative writing students on the smug assumption that writing was the bastion of the independently wealthy.[39] Iowa, on the other hand, responded to the cultivation of consumer taste and the popularization of literature visible not only in the standard bearers of the *New Yorker, Harper's,* and the *Atlantic,* but in increasingly sophisticated popular postwar venues such as *Look* and *Flair.*

The program's intense dedication to commercial publication despite back- lash from its own students surfaced in an *Iowa Writers' Workshop Newsletter* from 1972. The heading, "ABOUT 'PUBLICATION': This is bound to enrage— so be it!" anticipated a firestorm on this sensitive issue. "We presume to be a professional body," the statement proclaimed, "and are thus largely concerned with professional publication. While it is hardly the function of the Workshop newsletter to determine which are professional publishers and which amateur, some standards must be applied or the word itself becomes meaningless." It then proceeded to rule out "Newspapers, vanity press, house-organ, public relations, one-shot or occasional magazine, and gratis publication," this time prompting rather than bracing against protest: "You want to disagree about it? Come ahead. But keep us informed." An impressive list of publications in high- profile journals and presses followed, featuring such students as T. C. Boyle, Robert C. S. Downs, and Dan Gleason. In the next issue, for spring 1973, a heading labeled "Angry" aired the dissenting views, suggesting that "if the Workshop has gone commercial, then where in America can there be any vir- tue left?" More outspoken ones claimed, "Once again profit and respectability are confirmed as a basis for professionalism, that touchstone of technology, as American as apple pie or Vietnam." The anticommercial romantic idealists of the Age of Aquarius had protested against allying the Workshop with the pub- lishing industry, which to them represented hegemonic rule, either through the director's vision of the program or the top-down definition of publication, a management method found reprehensible because "only institutions in the advanced stages of fossilization make definitions."[40]

Commercial definitions of professionalism, however, served to reinforce Iowa's solid alliance with the popularization of literature, a project historically contiguous with that of Horace Greeley and Margaret Fuller, who wished to bring literature to the masses a century earlier. Notable examples of Workshop literature that reached a mass audience include W. P. Kinsella's *Field of Dreams* franchise (based on his first novel, *Shoeless Joe*), Anthony Swofford's adaptation of his book *Jarhead* into a major Hollywood motion picture, and more recently Ayana Mathis's *Twelve Tribes of Hattie,* which earned an endorsement from Oprah Winfrey. Literature's intersection with popular culture in the broader culture appears in online group readings where classics from Dante to Melville receive serious attention alongside contemporary literary fiction such as *Saturday* and *The Line of Beauty.*[41] Through the agency of creative writing programs like Iowa's that are both steeped in literary tradition and dedicated to professionalization, Charles Dickens's achievement during the Victorian age of simultaneous popularity and critical acclaim becomes more accessible to aspiring writers today.

When assessing attempts to write the great American novel, which trace back at least to Herman Melville's *Moby-Dick* in 1851, one is struck by authors' profound struggle to align literary art in a fruitful way with mass culture. American literature blossomed during the height of the market revolution in the decades before the Civil War. Melville committed a sort of professional suicide in the pages of his strangest novel, *Pierre,* in 1852, when he realized that his magnum opus of *Moby-Dick* had failed miserably in its critical reception the year before. In *Pierre,* Melville savagely bit the hand that fed him, skewering literary intermediaries, including his own editor, Evert Duyckinck, as so many pretentious slaves to fashion in both attire and the printed page. In one passage, he drew out the analogy by imagining one publishing house doubling as a men's clothing store. The coupling of literature with commercial culture received similar flack from the Workshop students in 1972 who rebelled against their director's mandate for professional publications, a decree they said was as American as apple pie and Vietnam. But complete renunciations of commercial measures of authorial success had their own liabilities, as seen in Melville's illustration of the idealistic young author's role in derailing his own career. Without a market to check and balance the creative writer's ego, the Workshop student risked falling into Melville's trap (figured through the fictional Pierre), in which he "imagined himself as high priest charged by god to bring forth Truth."[42]

Workshop students subscribing to such a conception of authorship rooted in the myth of the solitary genius passively waited to be "discovered" at their own peril. Others searched in vain within the curriculum itself for answers. One former student, Barbara Spargo, suggested that beyond workshop sessions consisting of peer criticism of the writing itself, "more advice on how to publish" would be helpful, but not to teach students only "how to write what will sell" in a narrow sense. Formal guidance on publishing would be useful, perhaps in the form of a class dedicated to it, she argued, since eventually "many excellent writers are forced to learn" how to write for a mass audience, and "probably with no detriment to their career hopes."[43] Although no such courses would ever appear on the curriculum, the workshop method served in tandem with the program's well-connected faculty as vehicles of professionalization within the institution's larger culture, whose privileged inner circle Spargo had clearly not circulated in. An insider like T. C. Boyle would never ask that class time be dedicated to instruction on how to publish; such information was exchanged in the social networks between rather than in classes.

Creative writing program administrators have long faced the dilemma of whether and how to train students to pursue truth at the expense of professionalism and vice-versa. Truth seeking and professionalization, as Michigan professor Irving King claimed in 1908, do not need to be mutually opposed goals. "The truth seeker," he argued, "is really the person who chooses, definitely and habitually to abandon the careless attitude in the sphere of activity in which he is engaged."[44] Aesthetic truth, King contended, could be transformed into a deliberate undertaking rather than a "careless" one reliant on a purely intuitive process of conjuring insight. Interestingly, creative writing programs originally distinguished themselves from basic writing associated with introductory English composition courses and standardized vocational training of journalists. Both were considered too rigid and formulaic to accommodate the more wide-ranging experimentation and modes of expression of creative writing. Peter Elbow's contemporary concept of writing without teachers, the process-oriented "find your voice," nondirective approach to composition instruction that prevails today, is part of a longer history of resistance to commercial literary intermediation. King's emphasis on writing as deliberate truth-seeking set the stage for the entrance of more professionalized approaches diametrically opposed to Elbow's efforts to liberate writing from authority and institutions, both educational and commercial, figured in teachers and played out in his cornerstone activity of intuitive "free writing."[45]

Resistance to the forces that mediate writing proved quite marketable, ironically, in several notable instances throughout literary history. The increasingly commercial condition of literary publishing is the subject of a contemptuous satirical novel called *The Literary Guillotine* by William Wallace Whitelock. In it, editors take over control of contemporary literature. "Writers may be relatively important, but it's the editors, in the last analysis, upon whom literature depends," a well-reputed publisher proclaims.[46] In the nineteenth century, the publishing house of Roberts Brothers expressed the same sentiment with their No Name Series, which represented a backlash against the myriad editors, publishers, and agents creating and conditioning the reception and thus the reputations of authors.[47] The purpose was to separate the text from the industry and to cleanse it of any distorting filter or spin of intermediaries. The stated intention was to restore the pure, unsullied relation between author and reader, liberating literature from a reception dictated by marketing campaigns on behalf of authorial name brands. The literature, and not its promotion and meta-commentary by blurbers and publicists, they insisted, should carry the day. But such pretensions were a thinly veiled scheme by which to entice readers into guessing which of the well-known writers, such as Louisa May Alcott, recruited for the series had penned each title. Emphasis inevitably gravitated directly toward authorial identity as the fetishized literary commodity.

In this vein, Edward Bellamy's utopian novel from 1888, *Looking Backward: 2000–1887*, imagines a literary marketplace based on a disintermediated meritocracy. In it, authors succeed or fail based entirely on their capacity to win an audience through writings alone—that bear their names, yet are free of any promotional apparatus—rather than the power of agents and editors to market their reputations. Mark Twain and Ralph Waldo Emerson also detested interference between the supply and demand of literature, as both reserved their most acerbic venom for authors like Sir Walter Scott and his popular medieval romances, which they deemed more a function of fashion than literary quality. Edgar Allan Poe also inveighed against the corrosive effects of artificially manufactured literary fame according to the mechanical reproduction of popular conventions in "How to Write a Blackwood Article." Who's your agent? is the nervous question among Workshop students entering the market, rather than style or genre as a marker of the author's identity and status in the program. The intermediary—a devoted agent or editor/friend—deeply complicated if not overwhelmed definitions of literary success in the Workshop.

As a shaping force in the formation of the twentieth-century literary canon, Engle was perhaps the most powerful literary intermediary—a "middle man" of the Midwest—in the mid-twentieth century. In the nineteenth century, Melville's editor Evert Duyckinck had a similar effect on America's first literary efflorescence. His editing of Putnam's Library of American Books series and the *Cyclopaedia of American Literature* combined with his connection with the worlds of trade and politics to make him one of the primary architects of the American literary canon. The authors Duyckinck backed—Melville, Nathaniel Hawthorne, Edgar Allan Poe, Margaret Fuller, John Greenleaf Whittier—now represent the pantheon of great authors. Playing a similar role in the twentieth century, Engle would also mint young talent in the literary market. A preponderance of Workshop students and faculty members directly benefited from Engle's position as editor of the O. Henry Award from 1954 to 1959, most notably, Flannery O'Connor, R. V. Cassill, Hortense Calisher, Donald Justice, and John Cheever. *Life* publisher Henry Luce was an intimate business acquaintance of Engle's and thus offered his platform—glossy high-end journalism with an interest in capturing literary-minded audiences—for those connected to Iowa. With such media at his disposal, Engle turned the Workshop into a direct channel to the publishing industry and its mechanism of fame.

The literary canon was in part formed in the nineteenth century under Duyckinck's influence by catering to an expanding reading public receptive to literature as entertainment. In the twentieth century, however, the film and music industries directly competed with print. Engle publicized his authors and his program by reaching the masses through middlebrow magazines and TV such as *Reader's Digest* and the *Hallmark Hall of Fame,* for fiction writers, and the company's greeting card line for poets.[48] The greeting cards, interestingly, may appear an appalling concession to mass culture for the sake of promotion, until one considers that Maya Angelou, the great American poet and winner of numerous awards, including a Pulitzer Prize and a Presidential Medal of Freedom, wrote verse for the Hallmark Mahogany line of cards. Angelou's name may have aided in the company's effort to reach the untapped African-American market and bring poetry to a segment of the population otherwise alienated from the genre.

Engle's and Angelou's Hallmark deals represent an improbable alliance of high literary art and commercial culture. But the real traffic of the literary market has never abided by such strict divisions between art and commerce. Engle combated the anti-intellectual strain in mass culture, paradoxically deploying the University of Iowa's insulation from the mass market as a selling point to attract powerful authors who were already literary celebrities. Writing to Sinclair Lewis in 1951, Engle argued that his faculty authors didn't have "that financial dependence toward magazine editors and on publishers which the writer out bucking the market always has. In that sense, the university is a release, not a hindrance."[49] But Engle insisted that faculty were expected to continue to maintain their public reputations with a steady stream of publications. If publications were frequent, he demanded they be more calculated for greater impact. "Produce or get out" was Engle's ultimatum on one occasion to a faculty member who failed to live up to this standard.[50] A non-publishing professor, to Engle, was no longer an author. And he would only have authors, preferably famous ones, running his Workshop.

Creative writing programs of the 1980s and 1990s with less rigorous professional standards than Iowa's bred complacency inside the protective institutional enclaves of universities, and thus productivity suffered dramatically. Such declining productivity has been documented by Shirley Lim, who outlines how critics have noted that "creative writing programs have composed a system of patronage between universities and writers that has resulted in a mediocre literary culture and intellectual dereliction for creative writing students and faculty."[51] August Kleinzahler has correlated the sharp "decline in the quality of contemporary poetry with the spread of creative writing programs."[52] Dana Gioia also noted a link between the rise of creative writing programs and poetry's disappearance from "public view."[53] He has since advocated for more aggressive commercial engagement on the part of poets, actively supporting *Poetry* editor John Barr's attempts to commercialize the vocation through a kind of economic stimulus package funded by a windfall $200 million donation from a pharmaceutical heiress.[54] Lauding the comparative quality and quantity of American verse that attended authorship prior to the university's shelter from the free market, Gioia laments the passing of the era when financial pressure to produce "delivered the collective cultural benefit of frightening away all but committed artists."[55] Ironically, Engle's founding vision was to maintain that pressure through stressing publication among faculty and students in the Workshop.

Students indeed felt pressure to publish. There was "an intense jockeying for status and position within the program," mounting into "social pressure that formed over who could publish the most and the quickest," according to Edmund Skellings. The process was "a variation on the then accepted theme of publish or perish."[56] On at least one occasion, students found themselves writing for publication more than they desired, despite advantages Engle's connections to the publishing industry provided. Engle's own capacity to generate Workshop revenue through gifts and contributions was predicated on the quality of his students' published writing. He once dumped a pile of student publications on the desk of the dean to dramatize their worthiness of his resources. Student writing was his selling point for soliciting donations. There were allegations of "Paul's making use of his students, taking them with him to the firms he targeted and having them recite their poems in front of the company executives. 'We aren't in show business,' a girl in the group said." One particular student had "refused to play the role of the bard" but nonetheless became the eventual beneficiary of Engle's recommendation of her work to a prestigious literary journal.⁵⁷ On other occasions, Engle acted as a literary agent to his students. He once announced to his class "that he surreptitiously sent a story by one of us to *Esquire,* and that the magazine had bought it," theatrically "waving a check in the air as proof," according to Charles Embree, the student who originally wrote the piece as a course assignment.⁵⁸ For Workshop students, literature by then had irretrievably entered the realm of show business, for better or for worse, and Engle had assumed the role of their impresario with or without their consent.

Mass Culture and Professionalization, 1959–2019

Speaking in Iowa City in 1959 at a conference on "The Writer in Mass Culture" hosted by Paul Engle and the Iowa Writers' Workshop, Ralph Ellison considered the vexing question on everyone's mind. "We can't really separate the two" categories of high art and low art, he said, highlighting the elitist politics of those who denounce the mass media. Whereas the encroachment of mass media industries and audiences into the world of literature appeared as a direct threat to authors, Ellison assured, "It's not quite as dismal as it seems." The mass dissemination of literature may have a democratizing effect. "I don't believe that you can really in this country separate the political from the artistic," he added.⁵⁹ Ellison cited Whitman as a poet of the masses who nonetheless could not reach them very successfully, and Melville, who defied the market with *Moby-Dick,* but "really suffered for his position." Seated next to Ellison was Norman Mailer. He candidly admitted, "I'd like *everybody* to read my books," as did Ellison, who added an important caveat: "I personally would like to be read by as many people as possible but on my own terms."⁶⁰ That common object, inevitably, required a full engagement with the mechanisms of promotion and publicity in the literary marketplace.

The conference topic of "The Writer in Mass Culture" was not only a subject for Iowa creative writing students to reflect upon. It also was self-reflexive of Engle's own promotional powers to attract highly publicized literary celebrities recognizable to the wider public whose names had saturated mass media outlets. Ellison, Mailer, Dwight Macdonald, and Mark Harris were present along with Arnold Gingrich of *Esquire* magazine, a journal designed to bring political and literary topics of learned controversy, ones traditionally reserved for the educated elite, to a popular audience. The Workshop may appear to have built its prestige by separating itself from mass culture "to ensure the maintenance of a literary elite," as Loren Glass describes it.[61] Certainly the University of Iowa provided a protective bureaucratic shield from the immediate financial and professional risks of the free market, but not as a means of escaping the reality of the publishing industry. Rather, the university offered a way of strategically and effectively engaging that industry. *Esquire* was the perfect sponsor for a conference on "the writer in mass culture," since it shared the Workshop's aim to foster a highbrow reputation for acclaimed literature while also reaching as many readers as possible in the mass market. And of course, behind this impressive promotional apparatus that was the envy of most literary agents and publicists at the time, the Workshop's curriculum offered a training ground tailored to the rigors of the market. But since the training occurred in the context of the classroom, failure was cheap. A disastrous showing at a peer critique would not ruin a fledgling career.

The institutional shield of creative writing programs has provided an advantage plagued by unique drawbacks for ethnic writers. Although Engle's penchant for recruiting international students and faculty to the program would lead to his establishment of the International Writing Program in 1967, the Iowa Writers' Workshop was slow to accommodate such diverse cultural perspectives throughout the Frank Conroy era. The current director, Lan Samantha Chang, recalled being advised by Conroy to stop writing stories with Chinese-American characters if she did not want to be typecast. But like Cisneros during the 1970s, her own culture was her strong suit, the topic into which she could delve deeper than any other. "There was no way I could have written about anything else," Chang said. The stratospheric career of Workshop graduate Ayana Mathis, an African American from New York who came to the program with her gay Latino friend Justin Torres, began with considerable trepidation. Upon entering Iowa, both harbored serious reservations about the lack of cultural diversity in the place and the program. Mathis became famous for *The Twelve Tribes of Hattie*, her debut novel that was selected for Oprah's Book Club 2.0 in December 2012 ("I can't remember when I read anything that moved me in quite this way, besides the work of Toni Morrison," Winfrey proclaimed); she later accepted an invitation to return to the Workshop as a faculty member. From this position of power, Mathis spoke candidly about the flaws of the learning environment in Iowa. In at least one instance, she recalled being told her writing was somehow less powerful because it was about race. She openly wondered to what extent the cachet of the Workshop played into her success. "I would like to think that Knopf would have published my novel if I'd had a completely different experience and a completely different agent and never went to Iowa." She speculated to what extent, rather than if, the Workshop fueled her success, confirming that "writers of color [should be] able to take advantage of that kind of access" she benefited from, thus acknowledging Iowa's very real mechanism of fame.[62] Junot Díaz recently denounced his Cornell creative writing education for being "too white," part of a broader pattern whereby "nothing in creative writing programs begins to even equal the diversity not only of our country but of our readerships," despite "creating all sorts of opportunities" with their prestige.[63]

Students made other compromises in exchange for the professional advantages of a distinctive creative writing degree. The Naropa Institute, originally the Jack Kerouac School of Disembodied Poetics, was notorious for terrorizing its students. At Naropa, founded in part by Allen Ginsberg, one ritual was designed to shake new attendees out of the false sense of security that presumably went with joining an institution of higher education. Instructors would drive individual students high into the mountains above Boulder and abandon them alongside the road, telling them to find their way back to campus, a ritual solo journey into the dark night of the soul to inspire a discovery of their untapped reservoirs of creativity. Sam Kashner recounts such an experience at the hands of Herbert Hunke and Kerouac himself in *When I Was Cool* (2005). Kashner recalls the challenge being all the more horrifying because he was hallucinating on psychedelic drugs at the time and his mentors refused to furnish him with a map, instead telling him to rely on his spirit to find his way back.

Although several Iowa students reported that Engle put them to work on menial tasks at his Stone City residence in Cedar Rapids in exchange for special fellowships and financial aid, most could expect their baptism by fire to take place in the classroom pitted with the challenge of surviving the workshop method, the creative writing equivalent of the *Hunger Games*. The submission of an application to Iowa signified a ritual submission to bureaucratic constraints, a drab environment of Quonset huts, and the bland, often retrograde culture of the Midwest—local barbers refused to serve blacks in Iowa City as late as the 1960s, and the nearest town for an African American to get a haircut was Cedar Rapids—all for the glittering Workshop MFA.[64] It was a Faustian deal that young writers readily accepted.

Competing Programs

Were it not for the success rate of its graduates, the Iowa Writers' Workshop's rural isolation, intense internal competition, and stark army barracks classrooms should have sent prospective students flocking to competing programs such as those at Michigan, Virginia, NYU, Boston University, and Brown. The professional focus of master's level creative writing did not emerge until the 1960s, with the exception of Iowa, which embraced the mission of fostering authorial careers decades earlier. Although outsiders to the Workshop routinely tried to deemphasize the professional bent of the creative writing MFA—Malcolm Cowley once warned an incoming class at Iowa in 1950 that they should not expect their training to lead to publications that they could parlay into careers—this defeatist view was not shared by Engle.[65] Students from the Workshop were far more prolific than those from rival programs, outpacing them with a steady flow of books and articles.

During the postwar era, the earliest graduate programs shared New Criticism's objective of "seeing literature from its maker's point of view," as Myers describes it. This approach derived from an "attempt at critical understanding conducted from within the conditions of literary practice," a now largely abandoned method of teaching the function of the text from the perspective of a producer.[66] At Iowa, Wilbur Schramm's program that coupled criticism with creativity gave way to an entirely new perspective under Engle's guidance, which pioneered creative writing's professionalization. Iowa's MFA program was unique in that, from 1941 on, it never adopted a largely undergraduate model of teaching creative writing as a novel approach to understanding the function of literature, one totally disinterested in producing writers. "Creative writing reached its full growth as a university discipline when the purpose of its graduate programs (to produce serious writers) was uncoupled from the purpose of its undergraduate courses (to examine writing seriously from within)," Myers explains.[67] Iowa was the first to forge this template. The undergraduate model of using creative writing to enhance new critical approaches to teaching literature derived from Hughes Mearns, the most prominent proponent for the teaching of creative writing for students in kindergarten through twelfth grade.[68] His wildly popular and widely adopted course in creative writing emphasized process over product and the removal of outside pressures, such as teachers and peers, that might interfere with the child's discovery of the insight within that each already possessed, a view inherited from Emerson's democratized understanding of divine energy existing in all individuals, according to his concept of the infinitude of private man.

To Mearns, creative writing was a means of self-expression for its own sake, not for the sake of demonstrating mastery of concepts in English language and literature, and certainly not a means toward a career as a professional author.[69] Beginning with Mearns, whose model deeply influenced the goals of

most postwar MFA programs, there was a distinct movement away from competition and results, and toward aesthetic experience and process. But at Iowa,
this new partnership between criticism and creative writing was wedded to the
business of making professional writers, where competition and results came
to define both the culture of the Workshop and its curriculum, which fell short
of titling its courses "how to publish," but whose contents and methods were
readily transferrable to industry. Teachers at Iowa were candid with their students about the chances of forging a career as a writer. Kurt Vonnegut said he
would "pay for a plaque dedicated to the 90 percent of Workshop graduates
who don't go on to become writers," asking "Can you imagine if 90 percent of
the graduates of the Harvard Law School didn't become lawyers?"[70] But the
90 percent rule applied more to other, smaller programs whose publication
record among MFA creative writing students is a fraction of Iowa's. Further,
Vonnegut's comment, and others like it alluding to the long odds and steep
demands of the market, did not demoralize Workshop students and send
them fleeing for law school. Instead, it paradoxically inspired them to redou-
ble their efforts and fortify their resolve to become members of the successful
10 percent, especially given the privileged access to the publishing industry an
Iowa MFA offered.

In weighing their options among creative writing programs, most candidates, particularly in the 1970s, were well aware of the compromise they faced.
On the one hand, the Workshop's reputation for elite snobbery and the competitive culture among the student body suggested to many that there were
paths of less resistance toward a literary career in competing programs. The
other concern about Iowa was the allegation that the disapproving and highly
critical climate had a homogenizing effect on writing. Indeed, many brilliant
works were savaged in workshops for their deviance from the accepted workshop aesthetic that privileged the academic story and poem, usually steeped
in world literature, philosophy, and mythological allusion, over other models.
One victim was *Shoeless Joe* author W. P. Kinsella, whose style, which would
earn him world fame in popular and literary circles alike, met with a
hostile reception at the Workshop. Gordon Mennenga recalled how "Kinsella
would put up quite good stories, and people would fall on them with knives
because they were too 'light' maybe, or too 'effusive,' and Kinsella would
say, 'That's okay. I've already published it in Canada.' " Sandra Cisneros was
browbeaten for similar reasons. "Sandra fell into that trap too. If all her characters had died or thought philosophical stuff, she would have been a star,"
Mennenga aptly observed. "I felt that we were always being 'dampened,' not

encouraged to take any risks, because of the 'same think' that went on."[71] On at least one occasion, the Workshop rejected an application whose writing sample contained material that later led to a six-figure book deal, as in the case of Barbara Robinette Moss.[72] Showered with major awards and critical acclaim, Moss's *Change Me into Zeus's Daughter* was published by Touchstone of Simon and Schuster and became a national bestseller that reviewers compared to the best work of Frank McCourt.

More nurturing and accommodating environments tolerating and even encouraging literary experimentation were found in creative writing programs like those at Sarah Lawrence College and the University of Montana at Missoula. Iowa by comparison was "a colder harder unknown" to alumnus Don Wallace, who described it as "snotty and East Coast" from the point of view of the cohesive community of his own funky Santa Cruz scene. But Wallace chose Iowa, Quonset huts and all, over Missoula because of its high standards. All "the Santa Cruz writers would get into Missoula," but the more selective admission into Iowa would offer him a more powerful degree. Iowa's virtual monopoly drew spite from Montana's Richard Hugo and other faculty from competing programs. "Go to Iowa," Hugo advised a student, knowing his own institution paled in comparison to the sheer magnitude of its prestige and attendant professional advantages. "I hate the sons of bitches there." Students like Sam Kashner opted to attend Kerouac and Ginsberg's Naropa, a radical choice made in defiance of Iowa, which Beat aesthetes condemned for being rigid and formulaic. Beat writer Gregory Corso once caught wind that the rising star Jayne Anne Phillips was considering applying there. "He grabbed my nose and twisted," she recalled, telling her "Don't go to Iowa; you'll come out of there with your nose all wrong." Of course, she went.[73]

Marvin Bell noted that this younger generation "began to focus on their careers as we had not, and to publish while students, which was rare in my day. They had become professionals," he explained, "instead of the funky countercultural community of my student days."[74] But much of his nostalgia here is for a Workshop era that never really existed, given its students' unusually strong showing of publications from the earliest days. The result was the Workshop's training of market-ready professional authors in a highly selective environment dense with ambition and talent. The irony is that during the 1960s and 1970s, its successes during the Cold War era only expanded, since the countercultural rebels flocked to the program, politely filling out their applications and moving into their spartan Iowa City apartments and dorms. Despite its conformist and careerist reputation, attributes totally anathema to the anti-establishment counterculture of the Age of Aquarius, Iowa remained the first choice among America's best young writers willing to make such concessions for entrance into this fame factory. High professional standards for students trace back to Engle's original commitment to a program vigorously engaged with the publishing industry and a faculty stocked with successful practicing authors. His guiding principle, which had a lasting effect on the Workshop's reputation, for better or worse, was that "in an open society such as ours, writer, businessman, and university can join to make an environment which is useful to the writer, friendly for the businessman, and healthy for the university."[75] Indeed, Engle was innovating the business of letters—a sin many deemed unpardonable—by reimagining the social function of the creative writing circle in light of new developments in capitalism.

Proceeding through the three major generations of the Workshop, the following chapters focus on selected authors representing both faculty and students and their most significant projects. The biographical impact of works produced in the program considered here span a diverse spectrum of genres including fiction, poetry, creative nonfiction, memoir, and journalism. Part 1 details life among the cohort that operated under the leadership of Engle and his senior faculty, Donald Justice and R. V. Cassill. This era extends from the inception of the Workshop in 1936 through Engle's directorship, from 1941 to 1966, the year of his resignation. Part 2 focuses on the Workshop from the late 1960s through the 1970s, detailing the blossoming of the first powerful and diverse group of writers in the post-Engle era. Their forms of rebellion against the Workshop method would lead to alternative networks that expanded the range of expression, especially for ethnic and women writers, of Workshop literature.

Part 3 treats the Workshop from the Frank Conroy era (1987 to 2004) to the present. This period was dominated by Marilynne Robinson, who continued to win the lion's share of literary accolades for her deeply spiritual novels through her retirement in 2016. Anthony Swofford offers his unique perspective on his experience as a student during the Conroy era and as a faculty member at the beginning of Lan Samantha Chang's directorship, a transition marking a distinct shift toward diversity under her inclusive leadership. The epilogue reveals the city's and the university's ongoing efforts to brand themselves with the prestige of the Workshop in light of Paul Engle's controversial legacy.

Individual chapters on Tennessee Williams, John Cheever, and Robert Penn Warren are not included because these figures have received an overabundance of attention for relatively sparse contributions to the program made during truncated stays. Other celebrity faculty members who joined the Workshop with the intention of staying longer in more permanent positions who I discuss are grouped in chapters in pairs. Kurt Vonnegut mentored John Irving, so the two are dealt with in the same chapter. The ever colorful and whisky-drenched Dylan Thomas shares a chapter with poet John Berryman, whose writing and teaching were deeply influenced by Thomas. Thomas's Iowa City antics and international renown for his wit and singularity of character alone would justify inclusion in this volume. But Thomas was more than an itinerant celebrity, as indicated by his profound impact on the Workshop's faculty and students. It is to the first generation of students that we now turn, beginning with Flannery O'Connor—the first world-famous Iowa MFA—and the fruitful tension of her tutelage under Paul Engle.

PART I
COLD WARRIORS: WRITING IN THE ENGLE ERA (1941–1966)

1 • The Brilliant Misfit: Flannery O'Connor

At the Iowa Writers' Workshop in 1945, nothing horrified Flannery O'Connor more than the prospect of reading her stories aloud in class. One of only three women in the program, the abstemious southern Catholic and future National Book Award winner found herself in utterly alien—and often hostile—territory among her GI veteran classmates. Her friend Robie Macauley normally read for her, except on one notable occasion. Due to the sensitive nature of one particular scene, it seemed unconscionable to put him to the task; so with a quavering voice, she faced the scrutiny of her peers. Fresh from the European and Pacific theaters of war, her classmates were "a pretty riotous bunch, very hard-living people" who did not "fit Flannery's lifestyle at all," as former classmate Walter Sullivan recalled.[1] Unlike them, she believed "there is a great deal that has to be given up or taken away from you if you are going to succeed in writing a body of work." She modeled her own celibate life after the bohemian-turned-theologian Thomas Merton, who epitomized how abstinence could extend beyond the domain of priests and nuns to suit the life of an artist and devout worshiper. "There seems to be other conditions in life," particularly authorship, "that demand celibacy besides the priesthood," she explained.[2] It thus came as a shock to her instructor Paul Engle when the bespectacled, nunlike O'Connor regaled the room with the erotic encounter of Hazel Motes, later to become *Wise Blood*'s protagonist, and the oversized African-American prostitute, Leora Watts. Engle promptly called his star pupil into his office for a one-on-one conference, where she immediately froze.[3] The private confines of his car, he suggested, might provide a more comfortable setting for her to speak openly about her sexual experiences.

Engle and his protégée, the strongest of the first generation of writers to enter the Workshop in the 1940s, walked in awkward silence down the hall, crossing the parking lot flanking the Quonset huts that housed the program. It was with trepidation that O'Connor climbed onto the wide bench seat of Engle's car for an intimate discussion with her mentor about what constituted an effective sex scene. "There, I explained to her that sexual seduction didn't take place quite the way she had written it—I suspect from a lovely lack of knowledge," Engle recalled. Despite his efforts to transform his car into the functional equivalent of a confessional booth, a private place for the budding writer to fully disclose her sexual experiences to him, she refused to comply.[4] Her confession in this case was that there was nothing to confess. She had committed no personal sin, nor—in her humble estimation—had she committed a literary one in her fiction. Politely holding her ground, she swung the door open and stepped out of the car, bringing Engle's tutorial in literary erotica to an abrupt end.

Although it might appear that the "frank and gregarious Engle obviously intimidated her," as one O'Connor biographer suggests, the signal moment instead represented a bold statement of her editorial autonomy, the first of a series of firm stands that unleashed the full potential of her singular creative vision.[5] Engle retold this story on several occasions long after the incident to illustrate her sexual naivety, hardly aware of its gender politics that today seem like a scene straight from David Mamet's Oleanna. Notwithstanding 1940s gender ideology, to coax a shy, inexperienced student into the front seat of one's car is a dubious tactic to begin with, especially by a faculty member whose power in this case was magnified by his position as director of the program. O'Connor's refusal of Engle's creative sexual remediation prefaced the decisive stands against male editorial authority that established her aesthetic independence from her mentor and the Workshop.

Given her unique predicament as a devout Catholic whose spirituality drove her ungodly work ethic and justified her ascetic lifestyle, O'Connor paradoxically thrived in this aggressively masculine and militaristic environment, which otherwise might appear hostile to a sheltered postwar woman writer. The Workshop's regimentation and emphasis on writing by elimination provided her with the essence of her own writing practice. The process of what she called "writing for discovery" that established autonomy from Engle and her faculty mentors at Iowa was marked by a recursive rigor, a fierce dedication to revision, and a surprising willingness to promote her work to a broad audience.[6] But tensions with Engle and her male workshop peers were initially the least of the worries of this diminutive twenty-two-year-old with a heavy Georgia accent. Homesick the moment she stepped off the train in Iowa with her mother from Milledgeville, O'Connor felt a sense of displacement on campus among the burly GIs and female suitemates at Currier House dormitory, who routinely blasted their rumba records at high volume, that compounded an even more daunting concern—she had chosen the wrong major.[7]

"I Am Not a Journalist"

The arc of O'Connor's career at Iowa and beyond was determined in large part by her tutelage under Engle, as evidenced by the dedication of her MFA thesis, "To Paul Engle, whose interest and criticism have made these stories better than they would otherwise have been."[8] This expression of gratitude was prompted by Engle's unwavering support that began with his acceptance of her request to transfer from Iowa's graduate program in the School of Journalism. But like many creative apprenticeships, O'Connor's aesthetic development would not reach full fruition until she had figuratively killed off her mentor. As a journalism graduate student interested in pursuing a career as a political cartoonist—an early sign of her penchant for caricature and wicked satire visible in her best fiction—she had originally enrolled in Magazine Writing, Principles of Advertising, and American Political Ideas. Frustrated with the string of rejection notices she had received from the *New Yorker* in response to her cartoon submissions, she had determined that an advanced degree in journalism would lend insight into the magazine and newspaper industry while distinguishing her from competitors. Her interest in visual arts is evident in her paintings and illustration of two books for children.[9] Creative writing in Engle's Workshop struck O'Connor as a viable career option only after she had arrived on campus. The Workshop was not her original destination in part because it was not a household name in 1945. At that early stage, Iowa students had yet to enter the limelight, but certainly had begun to win notice in literary and mainstream journals.

William Porter's Magazine Writing, for which O'Connor's lackluster writing received a B, stands out in the journalism curriculum she abandoned for the Workshop. The mustachioed Porter, with his loud checked shirts and crime stories he brokered into Hollywood films, expanded her purview beyond her provincial experience as editor of *The Corinthian* at the Georgia State College for Women. The stage was set for a career in journalism, a vocation for which she seemed destined, as seen in a photo of her as a young editor staring directly through the camera with steely determination as her staff adoringly clustered around her. A decade later, editor Robert Giroux, who published *Wise Blood,* would be captivated by the imagination behind those "electric eyes, very penetrating. She could see right through you."[10] Even at this early stage, O'Connor was intensely focused on establishing a winning byline, using her middle rather than her first name. "Flannery O'Connor" rang with celebrity promise, whereas "Mary O'Connor" was a name hardly destined for fame. She jokingly asked, "Who was likely to buy the stories of an Irish washerwoman?"[11]

O'Connor's other journalism course in Principles of Advertising, perhaps more than Porter's, sent her fleeing for Engle's Workshop. Despite coming to Iowa with a desire to build on her journalistic background and learn how to reach a mass audience, she soon discovered that selling advertisements was a soul-crushing endeavor focused too narrowly on the bottom line of profit. Although O'Connor's practical side could respect Porter's knowledge and expertise in how to wring revenue from magazine writing, his commercial interest was excessive for her taste. His preferences and methods were garish and shared little with the category of literature for which she longed. On the other side of campus, Engle's Workshop carried the promise of professional training but without the loss of creative integrity. Although she "had earned a scholarship to the Iowa School of Journalism," O'Connor "crossed over to do shum storrowies," as she told her friend and Workshop classmate James B. Hall.[12]

While crossing campus in 1945 from Seashore Hall to the Quonset huts on the east shore of the Iowa River, O'Connor weighed how to make a graceful yet powerful first impression on the Workshop director. Her delivery, however, was anything but. In a trembling whisper she struggled to explain her desire to write fiction instead of selling advertising. Engle, unable to decipher her syrupy southern drawl, rendered unintelligible by her overwhelming anxiety, handed her a slip of paper and a pencil. "My name is Flannery O'Connor," she wrote, careful to suppress the dull washerwoman for her more dramatic authorial persona. "I am not a journalist. Can I come to the Writers' Workshop?" she scribbled.[13] Engle was unaware that this muted voice would blossom into the Workshop's first world-famous author.

When O'Connor transferred to the Workshop, it resembled nothing of its cozy domestic origins a few years before her arrival. For Wilbur Schramm, Engle's predecessor, creative nonacademic writing was more pastime than profession, an activity to be savored rather than endured as a means toward building a career. The Journalism School's focus on "selling stories to magazines," as described in Porter's syllabus, met its antithesis in Schramm's domestic idyll.[14] The earliest Workshop classes took place in Schramm's living room. Ensconced in overstuffed sofas with a giant bearskin rug at their feet, students sipped literature like tea before the crackling fire. Discord had no place on this tranquil stage. The only histrionics surfaced when Schramm's young daughter performed periodically to the students' delight. MFA Barbara Spargo reminisced about how student writing was just one component of a scene in which "his big dog, Shakespeare, snored by the fireplace [and] the very attractive Mrs. Schramm served coffee and cookies. We watched four-year old Mary Schramm showing off for guests and being loved, too."[15] The program's next home in the steely Quonset huts of Engle's Workshop seemed worlds away.

Students in the Workshop under Schramm's direction from 1936 to 1941 enjoyed an intimate atmosphere that evacuated all vestiges of institutional structure. These were the earliest days of the "workshop method," and sessions were "not held at regularly scheduled times, but took place perhaps once a month whenever several members had something 'ready' to present." Engle's postwar setting instead implemented with unprecedented regimentation the New Criticism that encouraged close scrutiny of texts. GI Bill veterans held forth at Workshop sessions, which transformed into literary war zones where peer feedback blasted away like artillery assaults. "Many sensitive young writers got shot down by the heavy onslaught of their critical fire," according to Iowa MFA Jean Wylder.[16] Although the rudiments of the workshop method certainly can be traced to Schramm's informal instruction, Engle's curt businesslike demeanor with students sharply contrasted with his predecessor's "very warm and human personality," through which he "seemed to regard himself as a friend of the would-be writers."[17] Soon after Franklin D. Roosevelt declared war against Japan on December 8, 1941, it was not the bellicose Engle who rushed to the front. The reserved Schramm instead requested a leave of absence to support the war effort in 1942, while Engle remained on the domestic front as interim director in his place, eventually taking over the program for the next twenty-four years. The cultural ascendancy of Cold War rhetoric during that time afforded ample ammunition for his quest to conquer the literary world.

Unlike Engle, who held two M.A.s, one as a Rhodes scholar at Oxford, Schramm had earned a Ph.D. in American literature, served on the English faculty, and went on to direct the School of Journalism at Iowa. Engle's distinction as the first to receive a graduate degree from Iowa for a creative thesis, an epic poem titled *The Worn Earth* written for his M.A. in 1932, initiated his career-long rivalry with literary critics. He routinely raised their ire with competitive taunts. At the Workshop "you can get an MA degree without counting commas in Shakespeare," he declared, mocking literary criticism's narrow pursuits.[18] Engle aimed to bring credibility to the program, a goal that demanded decoupling the creative writing MFA from its stereotype as an easily attained and intellectually lightweight degree. Engle wore his belligerence like a badge of honor. "You do not create new programs without driving hard and if you drive hard you're going to irritate people. Quiet people," he proclaimed, "don't offend."[19] Corn-growing Iowa quietism—from Grant Wood's *American Gothic* tableau to Schramm's living room—had never heard such a brash voice. Engle heralded nothing less than a literary revolution.

O'Connor's serious temperament was ideally suited to Engle's mission. Especially appealing to her was that creative writing constituted the program's primary subject rather than an ancillary diversion, as in the graduate programs in English and journalism. The Georgia State College for Women's student-centered pedagogy had left her rudderless and aching for direction, particularly in the form of carefully assembled readings designed to advance her craft. Although her journalism courses made no pretense of placing the development of her writing under close scrutiny, their emphasis on selling stories to magazines did indeed resonate with Engle's curriculum. Engle's course titled Writers' Workshop had even been cross-listed in both English and journalism. In the fall it appeared on O'Connor's transcript as journalism, and thereafter as English.[20]

Engle's Understanding Fiction course lived up to O'Connor's expectations for rigor and direction. Frustrated with her alma mater's haphazard curriculum that integrated "English literature with geography, biology, home economics, basketball or fire prevention," she was relieved to finally focus exclusively on fiction. In Engle's class, she found an environment that embraced specialization toward publication and professional career development, one diametrically opposed to her former college's demonization of vocational training.[21] Radical for its time, the Peabody method used at GSCW derived from Elizabeth Peabody's transcendentalist-inspired pedagogy, developed in the 1830s as an alternative to the rote learning and memorization that ruled classrooms then. But for a southern woman like O'Connor seeking skills necessary to launch a professional career first through cartooning and then through fiction writing, it left her empty. She found the curriculum and method of instruction favored "anything at all that will put off a little longer the evil day when the story or novel must be examined simply as a story or novel."[22]

A New Devotion

When she enrolled in Engle's Understanding Fiction course and purchased her copy of the required textbook of the same title (edited by the New Criticism figureheads Cleanth Brooks and Robert Penn Warren), O'Connor felt equipped to fulfill her aesthetic and professional ambition. The New Criticism was known for its highly specialized approach to the study of literature, which anatomized textual structure to the exclusion of biography and history. Although detractors objected to its narrowness, it liberated O'Connor from the phobia of specialization at GSCW. According to her former Georgia classmate Elizabeth Horne, she "was so disturbed about the trend of asking the children what they wanted to do" that she demanded "there should be a list of books that everybody should read. She felt there must be a basic knowledge within each discipline."[23] Embarrassed that her own self-selected reading included such works as "a book of Ludwig Bemelmans' about the hotel business," she "was very much upset about not having to read some things that everybody ought to."[24] Porter and the journalism faculty provided structure, but approached stories as if they were advertisements. The Writers' Workshop, on the other hand, allowed her to enter more decisively into the literary realm. Under Engle's direction, the category of literature sacrificed nothing of the specialized professional training she sought, nor was it disconnected with the publishing industry that drew her to journalism in the first place.

O'Connor was enthralled by Engle's energy and vitality, which became the signature features of his teaching and promotion of the program. In response to her friend Betty Hester's request for advice on how to develop creative writing skills, she recommended *Understanding Fiction*, "a textbook I used at Iowa." Her letter, written in 1959, reveals that the book held significance to her more than a decade after she completed the course. This foundational text became her bible of the craft. Although she could see its obvious liability as "pure textbook and very uninviting," she urged that "part of the value of it for me was that I had it in conjunction with Paul Engle who was able to breathe some life into it." Engle's role in animating this otherwise lifeless "how-to-do-it book" was clearly integral to its value for her at the time, as the personal impression of his teaching clearly resonated with her permanently. Ideally, the book should be read under Engle's guidance, she suggested, "but even without him, it might help you some."[25]

Engle's teaching of the otherwise dry textbook *Understanding Fiction* was a potent source of creative vitality for O'Connor, specifically through the models of short fiction it offered in William Faulkner's "A Rose for Emily," Nathaniel Hawthorne's "The Birthmark," and Caroline Gordon's "Old Red." Faulkner's voice of the community in "A Rose for Emily" exposed O'Connor to characters drawn as perverse outsiders with highly complex interiority, misfits compensating for profoundly frustrating missed opportunities—spiritual, social, economic—in their pasts. Interest in the spiritual psychology of outsidership captured her imagination in this early course, as evidenced in an exam essay she wrote for the class on Thomas Thompson's "A Shore for the Sinking." In it, she judged the story's central concern to be about "a man's realization that he has been 'left out.' " Engle marked an "A+" on the blue book filled with her rococo handwriting, describing it as "Admirable."[26] Understanding fiction, according to the logic of the course, was essential to writing it well. The assumption was that great literature could be learned from the masters without exclusive dependence on individual inspiration.

If O'Connor adored Engle for his Understanding Fiction course, the feeling was more than mutual. Her classmate Hank Messick, who published several nonfiction books and novels, described a hierarchy in the course that situated O'Connor at the pinnacle. Engle, he said, openly displayed favoritism on her behalf, creating a sense of jealousy and resentment in less gifted students such as himself. "We argued a lot about writing and the purpose of writing," Messick recalled. He knew that his "optimistic suggestion that man might improve himself by his own efforts" was futile since O'Connor was Engle's favorite. "She, of course, was a genius and was so recognized by Engle," he remarked, noting that "I was scarcely tolerated" by contrast. Engle's emphasis on suffering and self-denial in the creative process resonated with O'Connor's "morbid, obviously Catholic point of view," marginalizing Messick's romantic optimism. Obviously hurt by such treatment, Messick groused that "she was a bit arrogant," because Engle had endorsed her disdain for liberal Emersonian transcendentalism, with which she "disagreed angrily."[27]

The hostile classroom climate was designed specifically to raise such tensions. Engle described the strict procedure in 1947, the year O'Connor graduated, as "the reading of manuscripts by, customarily, two students, and the detailed criticism of the them, first of all by the staff of the writing program, acting as a critical panel, and then by the students themselves." Engle deliberately choreographed the dynamic to condition "the students [to be] quite merciless in criticizing each other's work, as well as in challenging the faculty before them." Literature was to be fought for, this pedagogy assumed, as modeled in the "severe disagreement among the staff, and sustained arguments as to the proper fictional or poetic manner of handling a given manuscript." Although dubbed a "workshop," no emphasis on the actual process of writing received much attention in these sessions. Instead, the focus was on how defensible the final product was in the face of an onslaught in which "No holds are barred."[28]

Engle's favoritism shielded O'Connor from the savagery of workshop sessions in Understanding Fiction, but in courses taught by other faculty members, she was battered into silence. In 1945, before her first publication, "her stories had not been well received and she had not tried to defend them."[29] Although she was never a vigorous participant in workshop sessions, they played a crucial role in her daily ritual, which she divided between attending class and writing in her dorm room at Currier House. She would rarely go out except for daily mass and Sunday services at St. Mary's; one of her closest friends, Jean Wylder, recalled seeing her in public in this tiny community on only one or two occasions. She once crept out of her room to buy a single bar of soap at Woolworth's Five-and-Ten-Cent Store. "I doubt if Flannery ever bought two of anything at that store," Wylder commented. Surplus of any sort represented distraction from her aesthetic and spiritual practice.

In her final year at Iowa, the room O'Connor occupied at 32 East Bloomington Street, in a house that was an annex of the Currier dormitory, embodied her abstemious devotion to the craft. Her former roommate, Martha Bell, described O'Connor during these days "as a quiet unassuming girl, totally introverted, with a deep religious conviction and a delightful sense of humor." Bell was acutely aware of what writing meant to O'Connor, since it "totally consumed her attention; nothing could distract her." By day, O'Connor shut herself in and "insisted on having the shades pulled, even in day-time, no doubt to prevent distractions." The dim room drew "artificial light from one unshaded bulb hanging by a long cord from the center of the ceiling."[30]

Wylder provided a similar account of O'Connor's daily life and habits rooted in incessant writing that took place in her spartan dorm room. The room contrasted sharply with those of the rest of the building that were crammed with sentimental tokens of home and popular culture. "There was nothing extraneous about the room except for a box of vanilla wafers beside the typewriter," her only indulgence. "She nibbled on the cookies as she wrote, she said, because she didn't smoke." The spare environment conveyed a "monastic simplicity" to Wylder, who remarked that "there was something of the convent about Flannery." In class, she typically sat "alone in the front row, over against the wall." The functional equivalent of a nun's habit, "her 'uniform' for the year" consisted of a "plain gray skirt and neatly-ironed silkish blouse, nylon stockings and penny brown loafers" with "a trace of lipstick" as "her only makeup."[31]

O'Connor displayed neither rosary beads nor crucifixes in her dorm or apartment rooms at Iowa. Instead, St. Mary's Catholic Church on East Jefferson Street in Iowa City became her refuge. She would walk the two blocks from Currier House in all weather, entering the sanctuary's ornate setting, decorated with stained glass windows depicting the Blessed Virgin Mary and the patron saints; a huge cross bearing a suffering Christ, head hanging, towered behind the pulpit. Vivid paintings and sculptures of Saint Boniface and Saint Patrick crafted during the nineteenth century animated this visual feast missing from her colorless residence and classrooms. The atmosphere alone was a refuge in which to genuflect and find spiritual sustenance, beyond anything the priests or congregation might offer. "I went to St. Mary's," she told Roslyn Barnes, a Workshop student in 1960, "as it was right around the corner and I could get there practically every morning." She recalled going "there three years and never knew a soul in that congregation or any of the priests, but it was not necessary. As soon as I went in the door I was at home."[32]

O'Connor had no need for the priests at St. Mary's because Engle more than filled that role in her life at the Workshop. Driven by salvation through suffering and the hard glare of self-scrutiny, she was an apt fit for the relentless Protestant work ethic of Engle's midwestern Methodism. The meeting of a Protestant midwesterner and a southern Catholic at the uncanny crossroads of the Iowa Writers' Workshop proved fruitful. O'Connor saw the path to spiritual redemption as a terrible and volatile process. Violence, which Engle spent his career justifying as a tool for developing creative writers, was engrained in his own upbringing at the hands of an abusive father.

"My Ex-Mentor"

Judging by his own writing, it is surprising that Engle—whom O'Connor referred to as her "ex-mentor" when she won the O. Henry Award in 1957 based on his nomination—could have such a profound influence on this towering figure in literary history.[33] He influenced O'Connor mainly through his function as advocate and literary agent rather than aesthetic guide. Engle's own writings from the period have been chided as treacle of the worst sort, sentimental nostalgia from his father-knows-best sonnets on raising his daughters to idyllic reminiscences of his childhood in *An Old Fashioned Christmas*, all regrettable popular Cold War domestic idealizations on one level. On another, his writings render insight into the origin of his colossal vision to build the Workshop into a literary empire, an ambition he confessed to University of Iowa president Virgil Hancher in a private letter on Halloween of 1963: "My interest has never been in simply having some modest writing courses inside an English Department. I want this to be the best in the USA, and I want it to be an international as well as national center for young writers." He did not intend the Workshop merely to contribute to literary culture, but to *become* literary culture. "My ambition is to run the future of American literature, and a great deal of European and Asian, through Iowa City. We are on the way."[34] Engle's annual salary was $2,400 for his first four years; after ten years, $3,791; and $11,000 after fourteen years, through 1963. He routinely funded his own travel to solicit donations and fellowships from wealthy patrons and massive corporations, facts presented to Hancher as evidence of the need for an increased financial commitment to the program from the university. Personal profit was clearly not his priority, but ruling the world of literature was.

Engle's ambition functioned in part as a mechanism by which to flee the demons of his abusive childhood. His frantic commercialization of domestic harmony in the publishing industry can be understood as his attempt to liberate himself from his impoverished upbringing. Early life for Engle consisted of a struggle for financial survival in which his father, "working hard from 6AM to 9PM seven days a week, never made enough money in any one year to pay income tax, but he fed and housed a hungry family of six without complaint."[35] His father's violence was interminable. "Father had a leathery voice and an instant temper," Engle recalled in his autobiography. His rage knew no limits; "Even injured, an invalid in bed, he was violent." Physical beatings were equally as brutal as the sting of his verbal assaults. "He dealt with us as he did with horses. If we did something wrong, it could be corrected by howling cuss words and giving us a smack (sometimes many)." Looking back at the horror of that abusive household at the age of seventy, Engle could explain if not excuse his father's beatings as symptoms of his frustration with taming and training recalcitrant young horses. "The horses kicked him, he kicked us." From a house "reeking with strong odors" of horse feces that "also rang with the noise of the howling of us children," an Oxford-trained Rhodes scholar would emerge, moving in the most elite circles of literature, culture, and politics. Engle's forte was fund-raising, a skill that required social grace and charm. This from the son of a brute, who "because of his sloppy eating habits,

Mother always put newspapers under Father's plate to protect the tablecloth and catch his drippings," and whose literary inclinations amounted to a bovine pastime of reading "the *American Horseman* with snorts of agreement and indignation."[36] Tom Engle died falling from his horse into young Paul's arms, fittingly, after suffering a heart attack during a particularly frustrating and enraged attempt to break a high-spirited colt. "He died like an Engle: swearing, in violence."[37]

Away from this toxic home life, Engle benefited from a public school experience that included art instruction from Grant Wood, the painter renowned for glorifying Iowa agrarians and their land. Wood is most famous for *American Gothic,* his iconic portrait of a farmer and wife staring ahead with determined and decidedly unglamorous grit. This combination of human oddity and imperfection—Wood's model for the painting was his dentist, whom he selected for the comic angularity of his facial features—is set against the majestic glory of the landscape. Wood's Edenic rows of corn are echoed in Engle's *Corn,* a Whitmanian ode to Iowa farming. Just as O'Connor had emerged from the South with the dark orchestral movements of Poe and Faulkner resonating through her, Engle had been cultivating his image as a poet who "sings with the full, long breath of a young Walt Whitman," as the *New York Herald Tribune Book Review* anointed him.[38]

When Engle accepted $250 to write a five-hundred-word piece on the American dream for a scholastic magazine on international cultures, he appeared not only the Cold War ideologue generating grist for the propaganda mill.[39] He was also a man eager to exorcise the ghosts of his impoverished past, plagued by memories of how his "Mother had to beg [Paul's father] for enough money for groceries so that he himself could eat. It was humiliating to see her ask," he recalled, and "to see how reluctantly he gave her a dollar."[40] Engle's television, magazine, newspaper, and film deals—along with others involving educational publishing giants like Britannica—suggest that his interest in expanding the Workshop into mass culture was precisely such a compensatory drive. This furious momentum propelled him to become the first to engineer consciously a literary empire by harnessing the simultaneous economic growth of corporate American and entertainment media industries.[41] The Workshop creates value for itself by entering the mass market with a literary brand designed to elevate it above trade publishing. Engle's mission was to signal to the world that all roads of contemporary literature pass through Iowa. To achieve that end, he would need to tap into the most advanced mass communication and marketing technologies available.[42]

Although O'Connor appreciated Engle's enthusiasm in the classroom and his powers of managing publicity, she was skeptical of his editorial judgment. In her view, he teetered perilously close to disingenuous salesmanship. Robie Macauley, O'Connor's friend, recalled laughing at Engle's "mannerisms and pretensions" as a mild rebellion against the knowledge that he ultimately held power over them as "the moving force behind the workshop." Macauley explained that O'Connor had the utmost respect for Engle as a teacher, but was unable "to take him very seriously as a critic." This was because "she thought that his suggestions for revision in *Wise Blood* were off the mark."[43]

O'Connor's "The Geranium," the first of the six stories that made up her MFA thesis, testifies to how "the men gave her a hard time" in class, especially in their objection to its suicide ending, which she was forced to excise. Her classmate Norma Hodges had read the story and was "flabbergasted" at its brilliance, and was left wondering why the men had disapproved of its dramatic concluding scene of a despondent old man plummeting to his death from atop a tall building. Hodges found the suicide "mythical," while "They all went, 'No . . . couldn't happen . . . it's too much,' and so on." Reading before her mostly male peers, "her broad Southern drawl" instantly elicited their disdain. "After a few lines, groans arose from the oval of chairs and the story was given to a man [Macauley] with more recognizable diction."[44] Her work often received "less attention than it deserved," because the mostly male World War II veterans showed an obvious bias toward their own tales of combat, as Kay Buford remembered.[45]

Engle imagined the Workshop fostering a sense of community in which it is "a heartening help where there are others facing the same problems and the same hopes."[46] This of course implies that such mutual support would take place outside of the creative process, between and after classes as a means of consolation rather than through collaboration and co-authorship. Engle originally made no pretensions that the program offered a space for collaborative creativity, the way many institutions have reimagined the Workshop's pedagogical model thereafter. He instead cast it as a necessarily painful bout of solitary production. Interestingly, as the program grew, not only did alternative collaborative approaches surface, but an understanding of writing as edifying addiction (much less excruciating labor) emerged as well.

If the Workshop faculty and student body provided the congregation and priests O'Connor never met at St. Mary's, the program primarily functioned as a social system to reinforce her deeply individualistic aesthetic practice. Indeed, O'Connor's cloistered process of production responded precisely as Engle had hoped all students would to the criticism of workshop sessions. The goal was not to drive students into isolation out of a sadistic desire to crush their individuality, as some have suggested, but to force a serious self-critical examination of one's work precisely to withstand competition in the publishing industry.[47] Publications, in this sense, set the standard of excellence not "as student work but as regular work in competition with that of professional writers." This Engle later argued was "one of the most forward-looking steps a university in this country has taken."[48] To that end, his colossal ambition grew, hinging on a deal with an opportunistic publisher and the promise of his star student.

The Rinehart Debacle

Students and faculty in the Workshop functioned as stand-ins for the editorial boards of the many publishers to whom they would submit their work. Training for publication, Engle insisted, was built into the workshops, because in them, "the manuscript is not treated as a theme, but severely as if it were being submitted to a professional editor."[49] If he could convince publishing companies that the program was serious, and that the writing it produced came from a systematic screening process in which "students are told that their writing is bad if it is bad," the Workshop would build prestige by offering its students an inside track to publication. Publishers found the program particularly appealing precisely because it functioned as a kind of talent agency that vetted the best writers. "As a result, we have kept a good many untalented people from thinking they were writers," a feature that "certainly spares editors many a weary hour," he quipped.[50] Only the strong survived, according to this Darwinian mentality, and Engle's strongest—and most publishable—was Flannery O'Connor.

The most impressive evidence of the effectiveness of the program's pedagogy, as showcased in "How Creative Writing Is Taught at University of Iowa Workshop"—an article (really an advertorial) Engle wrote for the *Des Moines Sunday Register* in 1947—was the awarding of the Rinehart & Company Publishers Fellowship to Flannery O'Connor in May that year. Engle had persuaded Rinehart to "offer two Fellowships a year, of $750 each, as an outright gift and not less than a further $500 when the manuscript is accepted for publication, to members of the Writers' Workshop here." The incentives in the deal were clear. Workshop students had access to a publisher with a vested interest in seeing their work in print, and for the sake of their own revenue, salable to a wide audience. Only a rigorous and severe program in which "the staff acts as a form of publication, giving the writer an objective critical view of his work" would be appealing enough for a publisher such as Rinehart to pay for access to the best of the program's students. As one might expect, Engle was not demure about heralding the Rinehart Fellowship as "the only example in the United States of a commercial publishing house offering such prize money to a single university class." Engle expounds on the singular achievement as one that pitted the Workshop itself in fierce competition against other creative writing programs, such as Stanford's, which at the time was far less interested in developing ties with the publishing industry and so aggressively channeling their students into print.

As the recipient of the first Rinehart Fellowship, O'Connor became the face of the Workshop, the embodiment of its potential to produce professional authors. But little did Engle know, when he boasted how "she is now completing her novel in the Workshop" under the Rinehart Fellowship, that his star student would come to a critical crisis with the publisher. His presumptive language, "*when* the manuscript is accepted," overlooked the conditional nature of editor-author relations as well as the manuscript's fit within the publisher's existing list.[51]

As the heir apparent to the new throne of literary glory, and as Engle's new selling point of the program, O'Connor faced immense pressure when she was awarded the Rinehart Fellowship that funded her for a third year, following her June 1947 graduation. The following fall, when O'Connor was as signed to work with editor John Selby, Rinehart & Company was riding high on two recent bestsellers, *The Lost Weekend* and *The Hucksters*, and wanted a new rising star to build on this mounting wave of success. But these titles hardly represented the sort of fiction O'Connor was writing. They consisted instead of mass market pulp with highbrow pretensions, whereas her work inflected Poe's dark humor with Faulknerian metaphysics, a heady cocktail of spiritual crisis and existential terror periodically inverted with an almost surreal slapstick humor anticipating Vonnegut. Thus, when Selby received her manuscript in progress, he "didn't think much of the 108 pages and didn't know what to say," as O'Connor confided in a letter to Engle. The response was "*very* vague and I thought totally missed the point of what kind of a novel I am writing." She worried "that they want a conventional novel," and that Engle might catch wind of Selby's contention that she was "working in a vacuum" isolated from editorial opinion. That opinion, however, was mitigated by that of "the ladies there [at Rinehart who] found it unpleasant (which pleased me)," she sardonically added. O'Connor could see clearly that Selby's

editorial taste was in his mouth.[52] The domineering Selby demanded a sum-
mary of the rest of the novel before proffering a contract. His sense of her as a
sheltered woman writer whose fiction suffered from a lack of Hemingwayesque real-world adventure was unmistakable in his rhetoric.

Selby had totally missed that her method of writing by discovery without
drawing on past events or preconceived plans was actually aided by her intensely private life. He thus scolded her by invoking the collective wisdom of
his Rinehart colleagues. "To be honest," he sniffed, "most of us have sensed a
kind of aloneness in the book, as if you were writing out of the small world of
your own experience, and as if you were consciously limiting this experience."[53] With her confidence shaken, she consulted Robert Lowell for validation, which he duly delivered. She knew as well as Lowell that imperfections at
this early stage would be corrected in subsequent drafts, given her persistent
process of revision. Selby's contention that she was "prematurely arrogant" in
her refusal to follow his command missed the importance of revision in her
process of production. "Believe me, I work ALL the time," she told Engle, "but
I cannot work fast. No one," especially not Selby, "can convince me I shouldn't
rewrite as much as I do."[54] She explained her writing habits in a letter written
later to Elizabeth McKee: "I don't have my novel outlined and I have to write
to discover what I am doing. Like the old lady, I don't know so well what I
think until I see what I have to say; then I say it over again."[55]

The dispute between O'Connor and Selby ended in a standoff. O'Connor
accurately diagnosed Rinehart as "interested in the conventional and I have no
indication that they are very bright." Enter Robert Giroux, of Harcourt, and in
1955 the famed publisher Farrar, Straus and Giroux. "Robert Lowell brought
her into my office late in February 1949," according to the editor. "After she
had obtained a release" from Selby, "I offered and she signed a contract for
Wise Blood."[56] Her break with Rinehart thus liberated her to find the true value
of the novel in the literary market, as evident by its eventual publication with
the more reputable FSG. Buoying her through the darkest moments of doubt
during the courtship with Rinehart was Engle, ironically the one who had
initially arranged it. Indeed, the man to whom she dedicated her MFA thesis
was her anchor tethering her to her vision and securing her self-confidence in
her refusal to bow to the unreasonable demands of Selby. His support was
instrumental in her courage to annul what was to be the Workshop's first
book published by a Rinehart Fellowship winner. Far from fearing the repercussions of refusing Rinehart's demands, she felt galvanized by his example
of drive and fortitude. "Now I am sure," she wrote Engle, who at this stage in

1949 was still very much her mentor, "that no one will understand my need to work out the novel in my own way better than you."[57] The Workshop had paradoxically taught her to stand up to criticism and trust her creative instinct, rather than taming it into submission.

Selby clearly misjudged the power of O'Connor's literary method of writing by discovery. One of the mysteries about O'Connor was her capacity to describe scenes she likely had never encountered firsthand. Her disapproving veteran classmates had also underestimated her talent by dismissing it in favor of their own superficial macho idiom. There was no substitute for personal lived experience, they believed, as the source of fiction. Instead she drew from news stories and cultural cues, using her memory and powers of observation to set her characters in motion and grapple with their anguished spiritual lives. "She never forgot any person she ever heard or the meaning of any small episode of the human comedy she ever witnessed," as one of her undergraduate instructors at GSCW observed.[58] Aspects of her characters Manley Pointer and the Misfit—both cracked criminals, the latter of whom coldly empties his revolver at point-blank range into a grandmother pathetically pleading for mercy in "A Good Man Is Hard to Find"—were drawn from a news report about an outlaw. She needed very little data to enter imaginatively into this world to chart the emotional terrain of her spiritually frustrated protagonist. "Why, she could just walk by a poolroom and know exactly what was happening just by the smell," her instructor Andrew Lytle recalled.[59]

At this phase in her apprenticeship, nearing the end of the Rinehart Fellowship providing her with a third year at Iowa to write her novel, she had made her most decisive step toward professional and aesthetic autonomy. Her rejection of Selby signaled a sea change from the obedient acolyte who had entered Engle's office trembling in the fall of 1945, her voice faint and unintelligible behind her lilting southern accent. Working intuitively without a preconceived plot outline, O'Connor enriched and expanded the initially flat embryonic fiction she had submitted for her MFA thesis in 1947. Soon it bloomed into the wakeful dreaming of her Poe-inspired allegorical tales that arrested even her closest friends like Robie Macauley, who found them "entirely original, strange."[60]

"The Least Common Denominator"

By 1952, *Wise Blood* was making its way from hardcover to paperback, and O'Connor could share a laugh at Engle's expense with her confidante Robie Macauley, only this time not as an underling but as an established author. In a letter to Macauley, she told of Engle's disapproval of the title and the ending of *Wise Blood,* in addition to the erotic scene between her wayward main character Hazel Motes and Leora Watts, the prostitute whose name he discovers on a restroom wall. This latter point she could only smile about, thinking of her meeting with him in his office and the awkward consultation in his car about the finer points of sexual realism in fiction. But what she found especially amusing was Engle's criticism of the cover, which lacked any promotional mention of the Workshop. Here again was the impresario, the indefatigable promoter of the program that O'Connor and Macauley had joked about as students. "From the jacket nobody would have known I had ever been at Iowas [sic] WHEREAS my book had really been 'shaped' there and this was a 'simple and honorable fact that I should have thought of myself.' " Not missing a beat, she related to Macauley how she wrote her ex-mentor back, alleging to have told Harcourt, which later published the paperback version, "that I had been to Iowa and studied under him but that I hadn't had anything to do with the jacket and didn't know how it would look until I saw it." She assured Engle that an even better opportunity to market the Workshop awaited in the forthcoming paperback edition, "the drugstore reprint that has been sold to the New American Library." Its design, she said dryly, would be especially memorable. "That would really be a jacket," she promised, "with Mrs. Watts on the front cover, wearing the least common denominator, and I would certainly see that everything about Iowa etc. etc. was on that one."[61] By imagining Watts sharing space with an advertisement for the Workshop, O'Connor rendered a scathing tableau worthy of her satirical political cartoons from the beginning of her career at Iowa. The visual counterpart of Watts in her "least common denominator" served as a fitting lampoon of the business tactics of her ex-mentor, one that Macauley, a sharp critic of Engle's shameless self-promotion, could appreciate.

Although Engle's insistence on advertising the Workshop struck O'Connor as ludicrous, especially when paired with the marketing of *Wise Blood,* she continued to promote her own work and name to the widest audience possible. That audience extended well beyond the *Esquire* and *Mademoiselle* readers Iowa MFAs typically catered to at the time. Indeed, O'Connor's unpublished correspondence with Engle subsequent to her graduation speaks to her marketing efforts and business acumen. If Engle no longer was useful for creative advice, he continued to provide invaluable support on the business side of her career, which came to define their relationship until her early death in 1964 at the age of thirty-nine. Writing in February 1955, she expressed her pleasure

with his "kind words in the O. Henry collection about my stories," which functioned as well-placed publicity on her behalf. Elsewhere in their correspondence she shared notes with Engle about her experience on the road promoting
her work. Undaunted by the oddity of being an intellectual in Milledgeville,
Georgia, where her "kin" assume she sleeps rather than writes while in her
room, she tells of her efforts to reach a popular audience. She touches on the
comic juxtaposition between high and lowbrow reading culture in her plan to
deliver an invited talk at a breakfast for the Atlanta Branch of the Penwomen.
That audience contrasted with the one attending her panel at a Greensboro
arts conference: "I figure the company will be more high-toned there." As
for her Penwomen engagement, and a similar speaking gig with the Milledgeville Book Club, she says she "goes wherever I am invited to see how the other
half lives," opening herself up to unusual interactions, many hilarious, for
an author of her caliber. At the book club, she notes, "one lady told me
that the kind of book she liked best was books about Indians."[62] O'Connor
knew Engle would appreciate hearing of such encounters with provincial culture, since he had experienced similar awkward moments during his countless lectures touting the powers of poetry to nonliterary audiences, from rural
schoolchildren to business executives. O'Connor was not above finding readers like the Penwomen of Georgia, just as Engle boldly brought literature,
for better or worse, to corporate America. Both were avid ambassadors of
literature.

Five years later, O'Connor herself was playing the role of publicist and literary agent to young talent. Her letter addressed to Engle in 1960 intended to
"recommend a Miss Roslyn Barnes for a fellowship in English out there."
Barnes "knows about as much about [writing] as I did when I arrived out there,
which is to say nothing," she joked. "I'd appreciate anything you can do for
her," adding a pitch on her own behalf. "You were supposed to be sent a copy
of my novel which I hope you got and will read some time."[63] By 1961, O'Connor
had considered Engle an extension of her own literary agent, whose contact
information she shared with him. "My agent is Miss Elizabeth McKee," she
reported with the witty aside that "she is happy to receive even small checks."
Engle had requested her agent's name and address in order to direct future
business, especially publishing contacts, toward her.[64] Their fond relationship
thus continued to develop over the years in this manner, as the two utilized
each other's considerable fame for the mutual benefit of their careers. Short of
emblazoning the image of Leora Watts with the Workshop name, O'Connor
clearly maintained her affiliation with the program almost exclusively through

the friendship and literary agency of Engle, the figure behind its peerless promotional engine.

From Workshop to *Wise Blood*

Rewritten as the first chapter of *Wise Blood*, "The Train" was one of six stories O'Connor submitted as her MFA thesis. The original story draws its descriptive details from her train ride from Iowa City to Chicago with Jean Wylder, where she also was struck by the kinetic and forceful manner of the porter. O'Connor would recreate the porter as the comic foil of her novel's protagonist Hazel Motes. Just as O'Connor had conformed to her Workshop peers' demand to suppress the gripping suicide ending of "The Geranium" during one particularly acrimonious critique, Motes was a character more in the mold of her classmates—a disoriented war veteran headed home—in her Workshop story than the spiritually wracked cynic who becomes an accidental questing agnostic in her novel. Early tension with Engle regarding her erotic writing method, interestingly, did not prevent her from placing her main character in bed with a prostitute as literally the first stop of his journey at the end of chapter two. Indeed, our introduction to Watts in *Wise Blood* is through Motes's first glimpse of her unglamorously trimming her toenails. Free of Workshop censors, O'Connor unfurls a mixed-race sexual encounter. When his cab driver warns, "She usually don't have no preachers for company," Motes replies, " 'Listen,' tilting the hat over one eye, 'I ain't no preacher.' "[65]

O'Connor's characters often exude a kind of reckless frustration at the elusiveness of a meaningful existence. According to the Misfit, if Christ "did what he said, then it's nothing for you to throw away everything and follow him, and if he didn't, then it's nothing for you to do but enjoy the few minutes you got left the best way you can—by killing somebody or burning down his house."[66] Hazel Motes annoys theatergoers by leafleting them to promote his Church of God Without Christ, a bizarre rebellion against the faithless and his own failure to achieve redemption. *Wise Blood*'s first chapter plunges into terror only hinted at in its early version written for the Workshop. In his cramped sleeping compartment on the train, Motes meditates on the coffins of his two brothers, recollecting how "One died in infancy and was put in a small box. The other fell in front of a mowing machine when he was seven."[67]

As a backslid minister like Motes's grandfather, Engle also ran from the ragged figure of Jesus, in the process racing into a commercialized form of selling faith in creative writing at the Iowa Writers' Workshop. Like Engle on his fund-raising trips, the grandfather would parade into town "as if he were just in time to save them all from hell."[68] Not surprisingly, neither the confrontational proclamation by Motes that "I wouldn't believe in Jesus even if he were on this train" nor the description of the circuit preacher appears in "The Train." Left to her own devices after operating within the confines of Engle's curriculum and Rinehart's publishing deal, O'Connor not only unleashed her grand apocalyptic vision of Motes's spiritual quest in *Wise Blood*. She responded to the Workshop's form of collective critical coercion by dedicating herself to what she called her "perennial service" of helping young writers in informal one-on-one meetings unmitigated by the strictures of institutional pressure.[69]

But O'Connor's career depended on that institution. It was Engle who selected "The Life You Save" for the 1954 O. Henry prize that helped spring her career. It was his ongoing support that sustained it. Her ex-mentor indeed proved instrumental in the renown she enjoyed up until contracting lupus, the disease she succumbed to long before her time. O'Connor was the first Workshop graduate to break through the rut of anonymous scattered publications and breach full bodied into the limelight of literary celebrity. Others after her achieving such status inspired both envy and admiration from their Workshop peers. The ascendance of W. D. Snodgrass illustrates such perils of literary success to which we now turn.

2 • The Star: W. D. Snodgrass

Given his extraordinary talent, students and faculty alike at the Iowa Writers' Workshop loved to hate W. D. Snodgrass, the confident, self-possessed free spirit who glided into Iowa City "resplendent in cast-off Navy costume, great head of hair and flowing beard, and properly abstracted poet's eye."[1] Effortlessly playing the part of poet both in appearance and habit of mind before attending his first day of classes, Snodgrass rapidly established himself as the program's prized prodigy. Everyone knew "that W. D. Snodgrass . . . had done something introspective and important in poems later called *Heart's Needle*." This meant he "had to be careful if he turned up, because knives seemed to be out for him," as his classmate Robert Bly explained.[2] Even small victories in this hotly competitive environment drew hostility, as the struggling majority of young writers were all too aware of "the easy confidence of someone whose story had obviously gone well in workshop that day." As soon as the triumphant writer was out of earshot, "when he or she'd get up to go to the bathroom, everyone would cut them down in a barrage of catty commentary." Desperate to discover their own creative brilliance, the jealous then would typically retrench in small groups, or individuals would retreat in isolation to a corner, "pull out some paper and commence to chew their pens and stare out the window."[3]

The success of William De Witt Snodgrass, known as "De" at the Workshop, might have been more tolerable to his classmates had he not done precisely what they had yearned to do—defy the New Critical convention of depersonalized writing by placing himself unapologetically at the heart of his poetry. " 'Snodgrass is walking through the universe'?" they protested. "Man, you can't get away with that."[4] But he did, and like a colossus. Along with Robert Lowell,

Snodgrass became known as a founder of the confessional school of poetry associated with Sylvia Plath, Anne Sexton, John Berryman, and Allen Ginsberg. His distaste for the term, like Anne Sexton's, stemmed from its evacuation of the possibility of artful expression in the verse. Snodgrass wrote in the preface of his collection of autobiographical sketches that "confessional" is "a term I heartily dislike," in part for its religious connotations as well as its association with "the lurid revelations of afternoon TV shows or of 'true confessions' publications." Personal and private matters were well suited to poetry, in his view, but with the caveat that they are not "broached for their own sensational sake, where they could damage people still living, or might lead to self-display or self-justification." The art should demand confession, rather than the individual's thirst for publicity or self-promotion, he urged, so that "autobiographical details, if they appear, should satisfy the poem's needs, not the author's hankering for notice or admiration."[5] The irony in this aesthetic is its disavowal of self-promotion embodied in the Workshop's unmatched mechanism for literary publicity, one that enabled *Heart's Needle* to attract the attention of aspiring young poets like Sexton to probe her suicidal demons, sex addiction, and repeated hospitalizations in the confessional mode.

In the context of the Workshop, Snodgrass's most audacious exploit was his brazen breach of the New Critical doctrine of depersonalized writing advanced by Cleanth Brooks and Robert Penn Warren. "When I started to write these poems," Snodgrass described in a personal letter to his friend J. D. McClatchy, "my teachers were concerned for me and didn't like the poems at all." Above all, his mentor Robert Lowell "was particularly distressed."[6] Depersonalized writing of the sort that leaves out the subjectivity of the author was sacrosanct; Snodgrass's "confession" in his poetry—complete self-disclosure that laid bare his anguish over losing access to his first-born child Cynthia Jean in the wake of his divorce in 1953 from his first wife, Lila Jean Hank—was considered taboo. Snodgrass, in his profound pain, had revolutionized poetry, wresting it from the grip of the Workshop model's systematized approach to writing based on pared-down minimalism and a disciplined refusal to obey introspective or highly subjective instincts. Surprisingly, three of the poems from *Heart's Needle* made their way straight from the worksheets to the Pulitzer Prize for poetry.[7] Even more striking, despite his grave concern for his pupil's introspective turn, Lowell himself "credited his Iowa pupil Snodgrass for showing him the way to *Life Studies*," a "major swerve" toward poetic autobiography, which won the National Book Award in 1960 and was named a "groundbreaking book" by the Academy of American Poets.[8]

Snodgrass's complete disclosure of his personal psychic state indeed flew in the face of the Workshop's "pedagogical and compositional method" that begins "in 'self' but ends in disciplined 'impersonality.'" That pedagogical method echoed James Joyce's insistence that "the personality of the artist, at first a cry or a cadence or a mood and then a fluid and lambent narrative, finally refines itself out of existence."[9] Workshop director Paul Engle had determined to shake young authors from "writing as the spontaneous outpouring of immediate feeling," to embrace a more methodical and technical approach. Snodgrass had all but desecrated the vision, especially in the runaway success of *Heart's Needle* and the confessional school of poetry. In *Midland,* Engle derided any association of psychotherapy sessions with the creative process, scoffing at authors who write "like a patient on the psychiatrist's couch, the sodium amytal in his blood dissolving his inhibitions . . . releasing the babble of language."[10] Interestingly, the culture of psychotherapy in the 1950s not only drove much of Snodgrass's greatest poetic innovations, but provided the template for poets like Anne Sexton to write in the same mode, as evidenced in poems such as "Said the Poet to the Analyst" and "You, Dr. Martin," where she reshapes her therapy sessions into verse. Sexton's *All My Pretty Ones* passed among Workshop students like literary contraband—Chuck Hanzlicek's copy made its way across the coffee tables of Iowa creative writing and literature students, including one notable undergraduate suicide—a forbidden aesthetic that squarely faced the fragile and often tragically broken psyche of the creative mind.[11]

When asked about Snodgrass's success in an interview published in the *New York Herald Tribune* book section, Engle elided any mention of the underground culture of psychoanalytic aesthetics that spawned it. Instead, he credited the Workshop curriculum for producing *Heart's Needle,* portraying it as the direct result of rigorous class criticism focused on elimination. "I think the criticism he had there—and not merely from me, but from, for example, Robert Lowell—was very useful to him" in producing these "finished poems." Revision and industry, not spontaneous confession, Engle asserts, were behind Snodgrass's success. Despite his pupil's bold resistance to these institutional protocols, Engle claimed that "Snodgrass adopted the attitude that is in the writing program—you work a poem until it is absolutely as good as you can make it," especially under the intense glare of constant criticism. "Almost all of those poems had been criticized in the poetry workshop," and thus "we were responsible, in part, for the fact that Snodgrass was so eager to go back and back and get them right," he said, ascribing undue credit to the Workshop.[12]

Engle spun Snodgrass's defiance of the Workshop into its crowning glory out of a stubborn consistency in promoting the program's distinct identity and brand rooted in the development of "self-criticism," enabling a young author to "put aside a manuscript he has written and then come back to it with a cold eye for its faults."[13] Engle's commentary pointed to the Workshop's many uses for and reactions to Snodgrass's newly minted fame. Maligned by envious fellow students, and willfully misapprehended by an administration seeking to promote the Workshop, Snodgrass epitomized the privileges and perils attendant to being the Workshop's star student.

Poetry Beckons

W. D. Snodgrass originally entered college to pursue a degree in music, but soon discovered he sorely lacked the background necessary to excel. He absurdly reasoned that his next best option was literature because it required no experience beyond the ability to speak English. After seeing an article in *Life* about the Workshop, he applied, and through the intervention of his mother, who had connections with the program, he gained admission. Snodgrass's initiation into the Workshop through playwriting was a baptism by fire. The instructor, who had been the bane of Tennessee Williams's existence when he attended the Workshop, disparaged Williams as "a one shot author" for the success of *The Glass Menagerie*, the first draft of which had originally been rejected as his master's thesis. Much to her chagrin, "the one shot author" received even greater acclaim when his second play, *A Streetcar Named Desire*, was produced just one month before Snodgrass's entrance into her class. Snodgrass recalled that she was "generally known as 'The Bitch' " and "was rumored to be the model for Blanche DuBois."[14]

While Snodgrass was enrolled in his first playwriting courses, his acculturation to the workshop method was anything but smooth. He learned quickly, as Workshop student Pete Hendley did in a later generation, that classroom critiques of manuscripts were forums for determining status within the program, for better or worse depending on one's performance. Hendley was stunned to learn that offering up an early draft of a story to a class for feedback meant "that my ability and my status as a writer were also on the line and that I could greatly impact whether I would eventually be able to get recommendations for fellowships or teaching positions."[15] A powerful showing at workshop, such as Flannery O'Connor's stellar reading toward the end of her second year, was often taken as a universal harbinger of a brilliant career. In

O'Connor's case, her classmates spontaneously gathered flowers "from people's yards as if they were public domain . . . taking only the most beautiful" as an outpouring of love for the author.[16] Alternately, manuscripts faring poorly at workshop could have the reverse effect, sending the student retching into reeds on the swampy banks of the Iowa River adjacent to the Quonset huts.

Snodgrass first sensed trouble when his playwriting instructor began one class by asserting that all leading characters needed to be likable. Snodgrass protested, citing *Macbeth* and *Medea,* to which his instructor responded, "you had to learn the rules before you could break them." Thereafter, "she and I were at war," he acknowledged, a very bad sign for his future as a playwright, but less obvious than her habit of parading about the classroom dangling his writing "between pinched fingers as if it were a dead rat's tail, meantime holding her nose with the other hand." When she assigned students to create scenes based on a plot sequence she provided them, Snodgrass instantly shifted into workshop mode, critiquing the quality of the given script. "I collected my nerve and said it was gawd-awful," an utterance that forever changed the course of his career. After class, a group of theater majors pulled him aside to reveal his galling error: "You idiot!—don't you know that play is in her doctoral dissertation!" Snodgrass, it turned out, was the only one who was unaware.[17]

Rather than leaving the program altogether, or flying south with the swallows, as in William Cotter Murray's escape fantasy, Snodgrass transferred to the poetry unit of the Workshop, where he pursued the MFA from 1951 to 1953. Although he published several poems during this early period, his efflorescence did not occur until the appearance in 1958 of *The New Poets of England and America,* which showcased a substantial five-section sequence reworked from his larger MFA thesis titled "Heart's Needle."[18]

Snodgrass's circuitous path to this lofty perch—one that veered from his initial aspiration to become a symphony composer into playwriting and finally poetry—began when he first laid eyes on Robert Lowell's *Lord Weary's Castle.* The surging energy and immediacy of Lowell's verse sparked a new sensation "after the dry, etiolated language and attitudes of Eliot." Having recently won the Pulitzer Prize for poetry, *Lord Weary's Castle* "had overwhelmed young readers" who were "ravenous for its vigor," a revitalizing force for the bloodless anatomies of the New Criticism. Lowell's book functioned like "some massive generator, steel jacketed in formal metrics against the throb of rhetoric and imagery." Such metrical formality barely containing bursting cadences of emotion became for Snodgrass's generation of poets the model they emulated.

"Even before we heard he was coming, I'd been writing like him," Snodgrass admitted.[19]

Lowell's cryptic syntax and dissonant images many found bewildering, just as the nonlinear digressions and shocking metaphors of Emerson's ecstatic language transfixed his followers. The bewitched admirers of *Lord Weary's Castle* were as baffled as they were dazzled by Lowell's indirection and jarring juxtapositions, so much that "I cannot say we understood them. I cannot say I understand them now—or even that Lowell understood them," Snodgrass revealed.[20] Lowell's much anticipated arrival at the Workshop preceded him in the buzz of gossip about his conscientious objection to the war, his madness, and his violent past. Tension eventually arose when Lowell admonished Snodgrass for excessive sentimentality. Pressing him for greater abstraction and less personal revelation, Lowell urged, "Look; you've got a mind. You mustn't write this kind of tear-jerking stuff!"[21]

The figure to disabuse Snodgrass from imitating his mentor was not Lowell, whose advice to avoid direct revelation in his poetry actually guided him closer to his own aesthetic. Lowell's brutality in workshop sessions stymied rather than encouraged individual creativity, especially according to his favorite method of highlighting how student work paled in comparison with classical masterpieces such as Milton's "Lycidas" or Tennyson's "Tithonus." Lowell and other faculty members "were teaching me to write learned, symbol-laden poems that any good poetry committee could write. They all thought I was wrong, and were really concerned for me."[22] Criticism of student poems in workshop sessions was thorough and violent, "as if a muscle-bound octopus came and sat down on" their manuscripts, as Snodgrass described it. Instead, it was visiting faculty member Randall Jarrell who held a mirror to Snodgrass's dysfunctional relationship with Lowell. With his signature outrageous aplomb, Jarrell observed what Snodgrass had been blind to for months. "Do you know, Snodgrass," he crowed, "you're writing the very best second-rate Lowell in the whole country? The only trouble is there's only one person writing any first-rate Lowell: Lowell."[23]

Known as a World War II poet dealing in dark subjects, Jarrell spurred Snodgrass to life when he arrived as a visiting faculty member at the Workshop. For as intensely intellectual as Lowell was, Jarrell's emotional and personal dimension "helped jar me out of that style" drummed into him by martinet instructors such as Andrew Lytle. Famous for mentoring Flannery O'Connor, Lytle "managed us as though we were blooded animals to be trained correctly," and "could make 'a federal case out of a comma.' "[24] In sharp contrast to such domineering teachers stood Jarrell: "Slender and graceful, with a pencil-line mustache, his manners and vocabulary [like] those of a spoiled but lively little girl." In stagey falsettos, he could make disarmingly glib comments like, "don't you just love Colorado? I think Colorado's simply *dovey!*"[25] Snodgrass appreciated Jarrell's panache. "It's fun to have a gee whizz critic now and then, after these austere visitors," Snodgrass remarked. Jarrell's aplomb as both a critic of his poetry and a conversationalist gave him license to mine the depths of his own complex emotions free from the conventional gender codes of New Criticism that called for impersonal approaches to subjects. With Jarrell's validation, Snodgrass expressed his personal anguish in the verse of *Heart's Needle,* and felt liberated from pressure to mute or excessively reconfigure his sentiment; if his voice ached with love for his absent daughter, it should carry the day. Jarrell's flamboyant personality and candid powers of observation formed an emblem of individualistic self-expression uncommon in the Workshop culture.

Snodgrass, like so many other Workshop students, found refuge from the stultifying air of the Quonset huts in places that invited rather than silenced self-expression. These included bars such as Kenney's and the Airliner "or wherever the main gossip was," according to his classmate William Stafford. The formalist paradigm predominated to the extent that spontaneous and passionate expression in literature was considered inferior, if not contraband. During one workshop led by Robert Penn Warren, a sartorial southern gentleman poet, the entire tradition of romantic poetry came under fire. During the assault, one woman leaned toward Stafford and whispered, "But I *like* Shelley." The reign of formalism had so taken control that when Warren peered at a sheet of a student's highly subjective spontaneous verse saturated in autobiographical details, the dean of New Criticism rocked back in his chair and sighed magisterially, "I do not understand these poems."[26]

The origins of *Heart's Needle* can be traced to Snodgrass's discovery, through Jarrell's astute observation, that the voice he was using was not his own. His acute depression in the wake of his divorce had prompted him to seek out professional psychotherapy. During therapy, he realized what Jarrell had highlighted to him in a professional literary context. "I noticed that of the two of us, the doctor and myself, one sounded like a psychiatry textbook; it wasn't *him.*" The sense of alienation was compounded by how "he—the doctor—wasn't *really* in the room at all because the whole thing was part of an experimental technique." Snodgrass had "gone into therapy because (partly) I'd not been able to write for two years. I recall that my doctor specifically asked me if that wasn't because I wasn't writing about things I cared enough about to get me past the resistance."²⁷ The suggestion led Snodgrass to treat his daughter as his next poetic subject, much in the way Dr. Martin Orne encouraged Anne Sexton to write poetry as a means of assuaging her demons.

The Workshop's effect on Snodgrass was unmistakable; it had undone his creative instinct and distanced him from the locus of energy nearest his heart. Instead of searching for poetic technique, method, or convention from the masters, whether in *Lord Weary's Castle* or classical poetry, Snodgrass trained his sights directly on the source of his pain. Indeed, the language he used during therapy sessions alerted him to the corpse-cold habit of self-expression innumerable workshop sessions had drummed into him. That language became his rally cry for aesthetic rebirth, his own *Howl* of Ginsberg-esque self-disclosure. A major influence was Robert Shelley. "We were all very fond of him," so to emulate his approach "seemed not only permissible but even a good thing." Snodgrass resolved "to take that style he'd only begun and go on to develop it."²⁸ This discovery, Snodgrass remarked, "led me to write markedly different poems, in particular a cycle of poems about my daughter which first brought me general notice."²⁹

As he later made clear in the preface to his collection of autobiographical sketches, Snodgrass was careful to avoid the impression that he was exploiting his own personal trauma for self-promotion. And as the critical and popular acclaim of *Heart's Needle* indicates, the culture sanctioned confession only if it emanated from the tortured soul of a previously unknown creative figure like Snodgrass, especially in the key of the suffering artist. In *Heart's Needle*, he suffers not for art, but for the broken relationships in his life. This struck a chord with readers ready for a human presence missing in the Eliot-Pound school advanced by Brooks, Warren, and Allen Tate.

Heart's Needle compelled readers with its rendition of the most traumatic chapter Snodgrass suffered in what Workshop alumnus James B. Hall called "the terrible emotional disarray of growing up artistically." Few, however, could channel that artistic turmoil into subjects that might render confessional poetry possible. Snodgrass could because "he was at the time living 'Heart's Needle.'" Like *Howl* before it, the poem is a powerful protest against the alienating effects of institutional repression, which Snodgrass feels most acutely in the restricted access to his daughter meted out by the judicial system. The slow death of his relationship with his daughter Cynthia was a symptom of the 1950s judicial system that typically placed children in the custody of mothers.³⁰ "Winter again and it is snowing;/ Although you are still three,/ You are already growing/ Strange to me," he laments, exposing the fractured nature of their relationship, artificially broken into distanced and painfully infrequent visitations. The girl is increasingly alien to both him and his neighbors. When she visits for Halloween, he notices, "How queer:/ when you take off your mask/ my neighbors must forget and ask/ whose child you are."[31]

Heart's Needle is in part a protest against the sterility and regimentation faced by the artist in a bureaucratic institution of higher education. But unlike Beat poetry, "the intimacy of its disclosure is distilled into variations upon some very old forms of English prosody." Specifically, "beautifully perfect" little stanzas are set in regular ABAB meter, neatly packaged according to the Workshop's obsession with formal precision.[32] The poem's power lies in its appearance of formal constraint belying its subject of unleashed inner anguish. "What might have become 'merely personal,' " Larry Levis observed, "is never idiosyncratic; it is representative not only of the pain of an absentee father but also of the entire impoverishment of the culture." Snodgrass locates that broader cultural impoverishment specifically in "cold war soldiers that/ never gained ground, gave none, but sat/ Tight in their chill trenches." In the fray, "It's better the soldiers live/ In someone else's hands/ Than drop where helpless powers fall," in places like rural Iowa, "On crops and barns, on towns where all/ Will burn. And no man stands." "Pain seeps up from some cavity" in the culture, entering the individual, so that "The whole jaw grinds and clenches."[33]

Much of the impetus for *Heart's Needle* is rooted in romanticism, both poetic and musical. Before entering the Workshop, Snodgrass "started taking voice lessons, first with an excellent speech teacher in Detroit, then with a series of fine singing coaches," which he acknowledged, "clearly . . . has affected the way I write. Influenced partly by the Beat poets, who gave so many readings, and by Dylan Thomas, I do compose for the voice—particularly my own voice."[34] His classmate Richard Stern confirmed that Snodgrass was the first "of us to break out of the Brooks-Warren-Tate world of the perfected piece, trying to open up," acknowledging Snodgrass's role in leading a kind of renaissance in poetry. "My two years—'52–'54—were big for poets."[35] The regular meter and well-mannered English prosody of *Heart's Needle* brought an ironic edge of control in a romantic torrent of emotion traceable to Thomas and the Beats.

"The Prodigal Son of New Criticism"

Snodgrass's political critique in *Heart's Needle* drew on campus countercultural figures like Morgan Gibson, a leading political radical and conscientious objector who established an "anti-war group on campus" that confronted "incredible opposition by the administration of the university." As an aspiring author, Gibson found that the Workshop's "formalistic approach to writing, inculcated by disciples of Eliot, Ransom, Tate, Brooks, and Warren," stultified his creativity, as the classroom climate left him broken and defeated. "I learned the art of poetry and fiction according to the orthodoxy of the New Criticism, which prevailed at the time; but the more I tortured my speech into forms that remained immortal only until dissected in the next workshop, the more discouraged I became." Gibson could not "remember anyone teaching a workshop who mentioned Henry Miller, Kenneth Rexroth, Paul Goodman, Kenneth Patchen, certainly not surrealism or dada." Thus he had to discover these writers for himself, just as Snodgrass did. He could rely on neither Engle nor Lowell to introduce them. "Certainly no one recommended, in any workshop, LEAVES OF GRASS for the young writer," whose only hope at such innovative models could be found in the English department curriculum. "Fortunately, up on the hill, John Gerber required CALL ME ISHMAEL in his Melville seminar," which buoyed Gibson, but only in a limited fashion since "no one indicated that Charles Olson was a formidable poet" from Black Mountain College.[36]

Thus the search for inspiration in the barren setting of the Workshop must have been a formidable one for a romantically inclined poet like Snodgrass with a musical background steeped in "the great Romantic composers— Beethoven, Brahms, Chopin, Schumann." The program's curriculum systematically denied him both English and American romantic traditions, and deemed his own contemporary Beats sacrilege.[37] Thus when one considers the notorious dust jacket blurb supplied by Robert Lowell for *Heart's Needle*, one often cited as a vicious swipe at the Workshop, it appears less a personal retort than an accurate assessment of the literary culture. Lowell, after all, knew better than anyone that Snodgrass had defied his own warning to avoid sentiment and steer away from personal self-disclosure in the poem. Despite this, Lowell still found power in the book, recognizing his protégé's unique contributions, leading him to declare, "Except for Philip Larkin, Snodgrass is the best new poet in many years." Lowell finds it remarkable that he "flowered in the most sterile of sterile places, a post war, cold war Midwestern university's poetry workshop for graduate student poets." Lowell's targets were not motivated by personal spite toward the Workshop. Instead, they are mainly political, as seen in his "post war, cold war" reference, and regional, in the "Midwestern university" allusion, reflecting his antiwar activism and New England roots. His comment that "most of the poems here have a shrill, authoritative eloquence" refers to the confessional mode of Snodgrass's poem. His distaste is apparent in the word "shrill," a quality hardly appealing in any poetic work. However, no such misgivings appear in his next statements. "It's the best parts of the sequence entitled *Heart's Needle* that I really want to go all out for," because "they are beautifully perfect and a breakthrough for modern poetry," according to Lowell. "Their harrowing pathos will seem as permanent a hundred years from now as it does now," he predicted.[38]

In *Heart's Needle,* the poem "Cardinal" reveals Snodgrass's process of production, as it depicts him searching for sounds to turn into poetry despite his barren surroundings. He begins in the confessional first person. "I wake late and leave/ the refurbished Quonset/ where they let me live./ I feel like their leftovers:/ they keep me for the onset of some new war or other," he writes, emphasizing his bizarre occupation as a government-issued artist. Equipped "with ink and ink eraser," Snodgrass describes how "I tromp off to the woods,/ the little stand of birches/ between golf course and campus/ where birds flirt." Despite being surrounded by tokens of the profane "inside this narrow compass" that is littered with "beer cans and lovers' trash," he persists "in search of my horizons/ of Meadowlark and thrush." With the acute sensitivity of the seeking poet, he carries "a sacred silence/ with me like my smell" that enables him to connect with nature despite signs of industrial mechanization toward war and the refuse of consumer gluttony. He miraculously finds music, reveling in "the insect noises" that make "The weeds sing where I leave," situating himself like a latter-day Thoreau to conduct his aesthetic business in the woods. "I've come to set up shop/ under this blue spruce/ and tinker with my rhymes." The poem validates Lowell's praise for his pupil's discovery of lyrical inspiration in an environment hostile to it. Snodgrass is careful to register the herculean effort demanded in this enterprise. "Though I strain to listen,/ the world lay wrapped with wool/ far as the ends of distance," he writes, noting the formidable resistance to hearing "Little that sounds like mine" in the cacophonous town of Iowa City "across the way" where "mill whistles squeal," and the "whine of freight car wheels" bombard his senses.[39]

Lowell aptly credits Snodgrass for discovering powerful art in an environment where the voices of the muse are wrapped in wool. Rather than simply venting his own personal disgust with Iowa, Lowell appreciates his pupil's flowering "in the most sterile of sterile places." Indeed, the dust jacket of his best student would have been an odd place for a full-throated condemnation of the Workshop. Instead, it reflects the depth of Lowell's bond with Snodgrass, and their mutual awareness of the unique ideological and aesthetic difficulties of being a Workshop poet at the height of the Cold War. In "The Campus on the Hill," Snodgrass renders a telling tableau of the setting, as he sees "White birds that hang in the air between/ Over the garbage landfill and those homes thereto adjacent." They hover over "the shopping plaza," "the backyards of the poor," and "the dead canal," a world of materialism, economic inequality, and environmental blight.[40]

Although journals such as the *Northwestern Tri-Quarterly* highlighted Lowell's hard words directed at the Workshop, Snodgrass's confessional aesthetic came as "something of a triumph," one that "at its calm, insistent best has both credo and style." Indeed, critics did not find Lowell's assault on the Workshop a troubling liability for *Heart's Needle,* but instead focused on the innovative poetic approach toward personal self-disclosure that came to define the confessional school. Almost Whitmanian in its emphasis on the musical dimension of poetry as a force of personal expression, Snodgrass claims a presence for himself in his writing typically denied in the depersonalized Workshop curriculum. His poetic voice acts on the world, rather than passively receiving it, so that "The world's not done to me,/ it is what I do." In lines that offer the clearest definition of confessional poetry in the verse itself, he declares, "I music out my name," brazenly "verbing" in violation of the grammatical rules of expression established in workshop sessions. "And what I tell is who/ in all the world I am," he boldly asserts, echoing Whitman's famous opening of "Song of Myself" in which he sings himself into existence, becoming both his own muse and announcing that the subject of his poem will be himself.[41]

Snodgrass's self-possession is extraordinary in light of the Workshop's active suppression of subjectivity. The program according to Engle derided introspective writing as a narcissistic form of talking to one's self, or worse, an indiscreet public method of resolving psychological problems that should otherwise remain private. Many graduates from Snodgrass's era simply stopped writing after enduring two years of the doctrine of depersonalized authorship. Ed Blaine, for example, located "the reason I haven't written" since earning the MFA from the Workshop "in the curriculum," particularly in the effect of "two years of concentrated criticism classes and workshops" that left him knowing "so much about technique that I was paralyzed." The program provided "too much opportunity to become completely absorbed in techniques," about which "everyone was so serious." Blaine was thus disgusted with his culminating short novel project for the MFA, which he admitted "was really shitty," pausing to point out, "See how I've loosened up? Twenty-five years ago I would have said, 'Execrable.' "[42]

Loosening up was difficult in a culture dominated by the New Criticism, but for many it was a process of growth through opposition, as in the case of Snodgrass's confessional poetry. Snodgrass's classmate Ogden Plumb "didn't realize it then, but in my rebellion against professionalism and the devouring influence of the Pound-Eliot-New Criticism, I was gradually finding literary values which have remained amazingly unsoiled." He thus became dedicated to "rescuing the sentimental and the rational from the hordes of dabblers." The dabblers, he notes, "were undergoing a population explosion along with the rest of us more-dedicated fellows sitting in that meager Quonset by the peaceful river, or mixing cheap beer and inconsequential brilliance at Kenney's Tavern on a barely remembered Iowa evening."[43] For his part, Snodgrass mixed plenty of cheap beer and banter at local bars, but in the process he did not waste his best insights.

Lowell's early resistance to confessional poetry led Snodgrass to the discovery of literary values rooted in intimacy and authenticity. Snodgrass brought rich emotional substance to poetry in such a way that rescued its human dimension from bloodless technical approaches. Writing in the *Prairie Schooner,* Frank H. Thompson took to task the Workshop for overemphasizing technique, chiding "the technically adept, empty poets that Paul Engle so complacently turns out." Lewis Turco took exception, arguing that "although readers are used to this sort of remark concerning the [Workshop], the hostility displayed by various writers . . . such as Robert Lowell is remarkable and largely unwarranted." Such dissent, Turco claimed, was largely directed at the legions of mediocre writers produced by the Workshop. Such weaker poets are inevitable products of the Workshop due to the law of averages in any student population ranging the gamut from stellar to abysmal. "Thus, the appearance every now and then of a Snodgrass . . . is expected and applauded" by critics such as Thompson. But "why must the rest be deplored—worse, vilified?" Turco asked. The Workshop is not an elitist star factory, he asserts, but endeavors to develop all writers to their full potential, regardless of their creative limitations. "If all our schools were to restrict their enrollments only to the potentially supreme," according to Turco's populist appeal, "we would have an unworkable society at best."[44]

Finding an occasion to deride the Workshop was relatively easy, since mediocre poets like Edmund Skellings had so far outnumbered the W. D. Snodgrasses. But what sustained the careers of weaker poets who were perennially envious of the success of Snodgrass—including a Guggenheim in 1972, nomination as Fellow of the Academy of American Poets in 1973, and praise as "one of the six best poets now writing in English" by 1987—was the vast net-work of Workshop graduates and faculty throughout the world. Engle cer-tainly did not focus his attention on remediating his less adept students. Instead he was actively engaged in expanding the scope and power of this network, scurrying to answer phones, constantly excusing himself from con-versation to handle his incessant flow of contacts. He often stopped class to answer a phone ringing in a nearby office. In one instance, a euphoric Engle reentered the classroom after handling a call to proudly announce the Iowa Natural Gas Fellowship in Creative Writing. The class erupted in laughter, the double meaning of gas in a room full of apprentice poets having escaped none. "Hurrying back to class, he would take a quick look at the poem under discus-sion and, without knowing what had been said so far, nonetheless wade in with remarks useful and to the point. And then, like as not the telephone would ring again," Marvin Bell recollected.[45] Engle's preoccupation with pur-suing "administrators, legislators, businessmen for the funds to support those students, their courses, the writers who taught them," meant Engle's criticism of student manuscripts "reverted to a sort of knee-jerk New Criticism," accord-ing to Snodgrass.[46]

Despite Engle and the faculty's resistance to Snodgrass's poetry, Lowell shared his pupil's basic temperament. James B. Hall astutely observed that "For one kind of absolute taste in poetry, Robert Lowell was a pure example: He was so sensitive, he trembled when he read to us." Snodgrass also recog-nized Lowell's special talent long after their conflict at the Workshop. In 1965, he affirmed his admiration for his old mentor with a ringing review of *The Old Glory* in the *New York Review of Books,* one of the most powerful critical plat-forms in the world. "In Praise of Robert Lowell" is at once a critical tour de force and an appreciation no one but Snodgrass could have produced, given his intimate knowledge of his craft, sources, and methods from hours of dis-cussion in the Quonset huts on the muddy shores of the Iowa River.

Although Snodgrass was grateful for both Lowell's guidance and Engle's willingness to admit him to the program, his treatment there was severe. Per-haps his harshest treatment came in the wake of his divorce. The hostile split left him wounded and virtually childless, removed from his role in the com-munity as the father of his little family that lived happily if unglamorously in a converted Quonset near "the garbage house."[47] Before the divorce, he was often seen downtown with his wife and cherubic daughter Cynthia at parades and festivals like the one held for the city's Fourth of July celebration. James Sunwall had fond memories of the Workshop in the 1950s, particularly its convivial community in which "our children had picnics by the river, while other husbands, such as W. D. Snodgrass, pushed their infants in strollers along the banks of the Iowa near Riverside Park." In addition to regular visits to the City Park Zoo, which makes an appearance in the final image of *Heart's Needle*, "all attended the Fourth of July Fireworks," as Sunwall described the cohesive community of Workshop families.[48]

It thus came as a devastating blow when Snodgrass learned that Engle had abruptly cut off his funding. The decision came in part as a punishment for Snodgrass's rejection of Engle's advice to pursue his Ph.D. But the larger factor was his divorce. Classmate Robert Dana speculated that "perhaps his divorce, in the buttoned-down 1950s, when divorce was not the conventional solution it is now . . . had put him in some special social category."[49] Engle blamed his decision on a lack of resources, although the program was actually well endowed. The news could not have come at a worse time. Snodgrass had been horribly blocked, failing to write anything substantial toward his MFA thesis in two years. This galling situation threatened his aspiration to make writing his main source of income. A tidal wave of debt and stress overwhelmed him in the form of attorney fees, alimony, and rental payments. Bills for his psychotherapy drove him deeper into debt and depression. His meager seven-hundred-dollar annual income from his teaching assistantship was not enough to cover his responsibility to his wife and child, so he was forced to take a second job "as an orderly at the V.A. Hospital, sometimes handling stiffs," according to Robert Dana.[50] During his expensive therapy sessions his doctor ironically steered him away from questions "about those things where I could sound impressive." His powers of poetic expression were stymied; "more often he asked me how I was planning to pay my rent."[51]

The transformation of divorce and financial crisis into world-class poetry demanded a recalibration of creative powers. Snodgrass's greatest creative achievement came at his most vulnerable personal and professional moment. He was at the nadir of his precipitous fall from family man to divorcé, from precocious prodigy to failed writer facing the prospect of dropping out of the Workshop, given Engle's withdrawal of financial support. This jarring psychological fragmentation appears in the poignant final image of *Heart's Needle*, in which he returns to the City Park Zoo with Cynthia on one of her rare court-ordered visits. Bears and raccoons in their cages metaphorically reflect his own aching isolation. "We've come around to the bears,/ punished and cared for, behind bars," echoing his own predicament. Snodgrass yearns for freedom like "the coons on bread and water" who "stretch thin black fingers after ours," taking solace in one slim fact he addresses to Cynthia: "And you are still my daughter."[52]

Snodgrass's escape from the captivity of his New Critical training demanded subtle tactics. "In working on an actual poem," he explained, "I almost always find myself starting it much the way we were taught at Iowa." After writing his first draft as a Workshop poem, he then stripped it of abstraction, laying bare its core meaning in direct language. He described the process as first making "a very compacted, intellectualized, and obviously symbolical poem with a lot of fancy language in it. But then, as I go on working at it, the poem happily becomes plainer and longer, and seems much more 'tossed off.' " The process of unpacking dense language and images to remove the appearance of technique was Snodgrass's systematic way of shoring his fragments against his ruin, as Eliot would say, of escaping the "labored and literary and intellectual" to land on "the final version, if I'm lucky, [that] will seem very conversational, and sort of 'thrown away.' "[53] He built upon the hard thinking he learned from Lowell with his unique blend of unlabored spontaneity. That dashed-off feel, however, masks his airtight symmetry and near perfect meter, which at second glance bears the unmistakable fastidiousness of an Iowa MFA. Those traces of Iowa remained in Snodgrass in the face of the administrative neglect he endured in an institution that, like the City Park Zoo, alternately punished and took care of its subjects.

Snodgrass's letters to Engle over the years since winning the Pulitzer in the early sixties reveal how the administrator who once forgot his name at an alumni fund-raising event transformed into his greatest promoter and publicist. One telegram in 1964 asked to arrange a speaking appearance on campus; the same year a handwritten personal cover letter for his poetry translation project on Yves Bonnefoy requested Engle's help in finding a publisher. Snodgrass also introduced to Engle "Walter Hall—my best student just now . . . very promising, I think," much in the way Flannery O'Connor recommended aspiring authors to him for admission and financial aid. Immediately after graduation, Snodgrass accommodated Engle's request for "several versions of the poem on what I recall as vivisection—known as Ph.D. study."[54] Engle wanted a variorum of one of the poems in the *Heart's Needle* series for the Workshop as a way of demonstrating the rigor of revision and self-criticism fostered by the program.

If he was blind to the value of Snodgrass when he was a student, Engle quickly became aware after his graduation that the program's greatest poetic success to date was ideal for promotional purposes. Engle thus sought to showcase how his process of production was shaped by the Workshop pedagogy emphasizing intensive revision against impressionistic inspiration. Despite Snodgrass's careful efforts to strip his poetry of any signs of the Workshop, Engle felt he could make the case that his poetry epitomized the program's method. Interestingly, Snodgrass complied. The series of exchanges for their mutual benefit testifies to the ongoing business of maintaining literary enterprise through the benefit of the influential Workshop brand.

For Snodgrass, like O'Connor before him, loyalty to Iowa brought privileged access to the Workshop network that ran mainly through the literary agency of Engle. MFA John Gilgun observed that Iowa Workshop alumni, unlike graduates of Grinnell and Columbia, remain in close contact in the manner of former students of the English public school system, except "We don't meet in the House of Commons or in The Foreign Service; we meet in the foyers of publishing houses." As with all Workshop alumni, Gilgun knew his most vital professional contacts grew out of the Iowa network, since "of the six or eight people I know in New York now, five of them I met at Iowa."[55] The lasting effects of a Workshop MFA, it would seem, are immeasurable, even for neglected stars like Snodgrass.

3 • The Suicide: Robert Shelley

In an interview published in *Look* magazine in June 1965, Paul Engle blithely bragged that "out of the nearly 2,300 men and women who have labored in his workshops, only one ever committed suicide on the scene in Iowa City." He claimed this was remarkable since "Beautifully balanced people do not become artists." In portraying himself as the "bill-paying daddy to more poets than any man in the history of letters," Engle carefully suppressed details about the deceased and their circumstances. Such information might have cast doubt on his impeccable record of care for so many creative characters. Thus he did not mention that the twenty-five-year-old Robert Shelley had shown clear signs that he might take his own life when he arrived at the Iowa Writers' Workshop in 1949, fresh from his B.A. in English at Washington University in St. Louis. Nor did he allude to how faculty and students mourned his passing on April 25, 1951, as the loss of perhaps one of the greatest minds to enter the program. He also withheld comment on the Workshop community's spontaneous outpouring of collective shame and guilt from the knowledge that Shelley's death was entirely preventable. Fourteen years later—looking for an irresistible promotional angle for the glossy *Look* magazine spread on his role as benevolent "poet grower of the world" in Iowa farm country—Engle rendered Shelley both the punch line of his tasteless joke and a nameless inevitable statistic.[1]

To those who knew him, Robert Shelley was uniquely gifted; faculty member Warren Carrier remembered him as "the student with whom I learned the most." Carrier reminisced about how "My course in modern literary criticism often turned into a dialogue with Shelley as we explored the intricacies and limits of criticism." More than just a memorable student, Shelley, "had he lived, would, I am convinced, have ranked with Justice and Snodgrass and Stafford as a poet."² W. D. Snodgrass himself acknowledged that Shelley's innovative verse cast the aesthetic blueprint for his own *Heart's Needle*, the breakthrough work that made his career. Indeed, Shelley was the figure behind Snodgrass's Pulitzer Prize–winning masterpiece and one of the founding visionaries of the confessional school. In a private letter, Snodgrass admitted Shelley was the real inventor of "exactly the sort of poem all the critics were saying you couldn't write because our age was too fragmented or complicated or something. He finished only half a dozen of those poems, however, before he committed suicide." Snodgrass then picked up where Shelley left off. "So all of a sudden, his style came onto the market" and was available for use.³

The community of poets at the Workshop soon followed, taking up Shelley's unorthodox approach to escape the New Critical standards dominating the program at the time. Prior to Shelley's experimental verse, most found themselves stuck in a derivative rut. Shelley himself was struggling to write imitation Hart Crane, while Snodgrass admits he "was writing imitation Lowell." Liberation from the depersonalized mode signaled a renaissance; Snodgrass recalled how Shelley's discovery "struck on a very simple, direct, lyrical style that really floored me."⁴ This became the new voice and form of the confessional poets—a disarmingly direct address divulging inner demons in fastidiously clad verses of almost nursery-rhyme prosody. The musicality and deceptively simple lyricism of confessional poetry was such a hallmark of the confessional school that Anne Sexton, one of its more celebrated practitioners, dedicated an entire volume titled *Transformations* to seventeen adaptations of Grimm fairy tales.

From 1949 to 1951, the Workshop's most celebrated poet with the widest range of publications was not Snodgrass but Shelley. Snodgrass proved the most adept of any in the program at building on Shelley's innovations, emerging as the one student capable of realizing the full potential of the revolutionary style represented in his half-dozen prototypes of confessional poetry. But beyond the new sensation he had created with these few experiments, Shelley had a dossier that suggested he was already an accomplished writer at the age of twenty-five. He may have imitated Hart Crane in a few derivative workshop manuscripts, but his original and haunting publications began to attract serious critical notice. Shelley had led the way; his classmates followed. Beloved by students and faculty alike, this powerful writer dreamed living nightmares in beautifully intricate verse, laying bare his tortured psyche in the process. To no one's surprise, he yielded to the demons that drove his greatest art. To everyone's dismay, no one in the Workshop community intervened. No one, Snodgrass and Carrier included, wanted to impede the surging momentum of this young talent that drew aesthetic power from being at war with himself. A tranquil, medicated Shelley, all were well aware, would never have produced such works as the Dante-esque "Le Lac des Cygnes." Was it fair to encourage aesthetic creativity that was clearly self-destructive? Or was poetry actually a lifebuoy on his sea of inner torment? Did other issues besides poetry lead him to take his own life, concerns such as "his inability to cope with reality and especially his homosexuality," as Carrier claimed?[5] Or further still, as the Korean writer Richard Kim claimed, was the shame attached to suicide merely an artificial construct of Western culture, a judgmental view lacking the compassion of more honorable understandings?[6]

Auspicious Beginnings

Shelley initially made himself known to the Workshop faculty through his play *Now Falls the Shadow*, performed at Washington University in 1947. This drama made headlines when it received the Wilson Memorial Award during Shelley's junior year. On the strength of its success, along with such poems as "Le Lac des Cygnes" and "The Homing Heart," both of which appeared in different issues of the *Western Review* in 1948, Shelley emerged as one of the nation's top undergraduate creative writers. Warren Carrier promptly offered him a place in the Workshop, luring this rare talent with a desirable position teaching advanced literary criticism, plus a generous stipend and tuition waver. Shelley's Dante-inspired poem appeared the first semester of his senior year in the journal edited by Workshop faculty member Ray B. West. West had brought the *Rocky Mountain Review* with him to Iowa City when he relocated from the University of Colorado at Boulder. The renamed *Western Review* became the standard bearer for poetry and criticism featuring influential figures such as Cleanth Brooks. Shelley was all of twenty-two when his poems were published, making him by far the youngest contributor in their respective issues.

Shelley epitomized the new turn in poetry heralded by West. At the beginning of the second half of the twentieth century, there were many "inescapable signs that writing in America has reached the end of an era." Shelley's 1950s generation left behind the "confused iconoclasm of the expatriates and Greenwich Village . . . followed by the uncertain orthodoxy of the Marxists and the pseudo-regionalist quarterlies of the Thirties," featuring the little magazine that "resided finally in the academic reviews (*Southern, Kenyon,* and *Sewanee*) of the Forties." West's aggressive recruitment of Shelley speaks to the passing of grassroots literary movements and their attendant niche journals of the prior decades. Interestingly, West finds no threat to the organic vitality of literature in its migration from niche Greenwich Village circles to MFA programs. Just the opposite, Shelley stood at the forefront of liberation from the earlier era that West claimed "will be best remembered for the critical battles it has fought out in the smaller magazines."[7]

Shelley's reputation preceded him. Workshop faculty members were impressed by the lyric gloom of Shelley's "Le Lac des Cygnes" that imagines Dante's eternally tormented "spirits, who came loud wailing, hurried on by their dire doom" from Canto V of *The Inferno.* The sky at the close of day above "The lake awry, a crumpled bedsheet of glass" fills with blood, "darkened by leaks in a rotting thigh" of the "murdered Odette." Trees beside the lake transform into grotesque agents of pain. He imagines how these "Willows drive forked arms down to water/ As if divining cortex-depth through pain," and swans "re-riding on hashing mesh of knives." Beneath the lake, the murdered Odette suffers eternal unrest, "Nudged unintelligibly by blind schools of fish,/ Upborne her green wings burn in naveled bight."[8] Although submitted well in advance of his death, the subject of an afterlife of perpetual torment reflects the psychological suffering he was already enduring before he had arrived at Iowa.

In the spring 1949 issue of the *Western Review,* West announced that Shelley would be joining the Workshop in the fall. Soon after Shelley accepted Carrier's offer to enroll in the program, he received an invitation from West to serve as an assistant editor of his journal. Shelley's formal application to the program lists several publications in monthly journals in addition to book and theater reviews for the *St. Louis Post-Dispatch,* the paper of his youth, originally established by media mogul Joseph Pulitzer.[9] Accompanying Shelley to Iowa City from Washington University at St. Louis was William Stuckey, who had also gained admission to the Workshop. With the security of a close friend from home as his roommate and an accomplished curriculum vitae in hand, Robert Shelley was ideally positioned to become the program's next rising star.

His first days in workshop did not disappoint. Shelley impressed classmates and faculty alike with his critical and creative gifts, especially his flair for weaving simple diction into complex syntax. Creative writing in university settings was all Shelley ever knew. Unlike so many of his classmates attending on the GI Bill, he had never been a veteran of war, or seen any walk of life other than literary labor under the auspices of a well-endowed academic institution. Shelley was not averse to the rigors of criticism; he tended to thrive in that arena. Indeed, his reviews for the *St. Louis Post-Dispatch* helped land his position as assistant editor of the *Western Review*, where he reviewed *A Fountain in Kentucky and Other Poems* (1950) by John Frederick Nims. Shelley's editorial eye was already adept at pinpointing rising new voices in poetry, as Nims would later go on to earn a nomination for a National Book Award in 1960 for *Knowledge of the Evening*. Since Shelley's established professional credentials extended to editing and reviewing for a powerful literary journal, Engle's intimidating curriculum simulating the rigors of publication did not present an obstacle for Shelley. The workshop system designed to professionalize aesthetes instead stimulated his creative growth.

Engle's *Look* magazine interview casts the Workshop Shelley encountered as a kind of "boot camp" for young writers, a phrase used to describe one intensive course in creative writing advertised on the walls of the English-Philosophy Building at Iowa as late as 2012. "At Iowa there has always been a bit of a boot camp mentality. Real Writers can take the heat," Workshop graduate Robin Hemley commented. But all too often "the student whose piece is being critiqued receives conflicting and confusing reactions" and the student emerges "deflated and no longer able to see her work clearly." In terms of professional attainment, similar results can occur. When he was a student in the early 1980s, Hemley, who went on to become director of nonfiction creative writing, "saw talented writers so discouraged that I never heard another peep from them after graduation."[10] This competitive climate intended to transform students into an army of "America's relentless young writers" often crushed ambition. As in the military, boot camp is a matter of survival, a rite of passage that proves one's fitness for the real battlefields that await. Attrition—in the form of failures and dropouts if not suicides—made the challenge of retention a daunting task for the faculty, given Engle's commitment to cleaning up and shaving down sensitive creative artists. Faculty member R. V. Cassill was known for going to great lengths to persuade faltering students to persevere and remain in the program. In one case he made a personal visit to an at-risk student at 5:30 in the morning, knocking at his apartment door "with a simple message: 'Don't be yellow.' The two took cups of hot tea out on the grass to watch the sun rise." According to the boot camp mentality, Engle expected students to "sweat ink-blood in his workshop," in the process forcing those with "self-conscious beards" evoking romantic narcissism to "shave down to clean professionalism."[11]

Unlike many of his classmates, Shelley was not one of the "long-hairs" who chafed against the emphasis on published work and professionalism. But where the program misread him and underestimated the depth of his psychological instability was in the expectation that sanity would emerge from the no-nonsense regimentation of workshop sessions. In 1947, the year Shelley was making his name known to faculty for his powerful publications, Engle promoted the program as a place for creative writers with "no long-hairs," one that rejected the assumption that "a poet is an unstable creature (if he wasn't unstable, or even slightly cracked, then why would he write poetry?), who does not belong in the disciplined work of a university." According to this formulation, Shelley never presented a problem to the faculty; he never received a 5:30 A.M. knock at the door from an instructor intending to exorcise his demons. Indeed, Shelley's string of successful publications and prestigious awards signaled that he was already well on his way toward becoming a professional writer. Engle and most of the faculty besides Carrier, whose knowledge of Shelley was the most intimate of any instructor at Iowa, assumed him to be the antithesis of a precious and fragile idealist, the poet as "long-haired object with a nest of robins in their hair."[12] Yet what they terribly underestimated was the fallacy that productivity somehow equaled sanity. Heavy doses of Protestant work ethic and Cold War militant regimentation yielding steady publication made one immune to mental illness, so the thinking went.

Engle insisted that only productive citizens and no free spirits could be found among his ranks. "Our experience is that poets today are so serious and, on the whole, stable, that their very stability is a worry," he joked. Such an antiseptic condition, like that mentioned by Lowell in his blurb for *Heart's Needle*, could be construed as a detriment to inspiration, to the wild flights of the imagination integral to creative pursuits like poetry. "Where is the frenzy? Where the eye rolling to heaven?" Engle asked rhetorically, affirming that the assiduous "poet in Iowa City works hard at his poetry and does his job as any other student does his." With his frenzied visions kept neatly on the page, Shelley immediately fit into this system as a productive citizen capable of teaching his own courses in cutting-edge literary criticism and holding forth during workshop sessions with the authority of a faculty member. In this sense, he arrived as a finished man never to be confused with the neophyte "aesthete who wants to come and dabble his delicate fingers in the valley of the Iowa River."[13]

Engle's formulation presumed that professionalization—through acculturation to productive literary labor—in a university setting stripped the specter of suicide from the program. Like the husbandry his own father practiced as a horse trainer in Cedar Rapids, Engle was convinced that authors could be broken of their unstable temperaments and that their creative energies could be tamed and directed toward productivity. But such productivity in the form of published work, which was Engle's favorite measure of the Workshop's success, was not a panacea for the very real illnesses that plagued its members, fractured lives, troubled careers, and ruined marriages. Medical research "is confirming the long-held suspicion that there is a clinical link with important psychosocial implications between creativity and mental illness." In particular, eighty percent of a sample of thirty Iowa Writers' Workshop members studied by Nancy Andreasen "suffered from affective disorder compared to thirty percent of a matched control sample whose occupations ranged from lawyers to hospital administrators and social workers." Shelley was not in a small minority, as Engle liked to suggest. Among the thirty Workshop members of Andreasen's study, "Forty-three percent of writers had suffered from bipolar disorder in comparison with 10 percent of the controls." Two of them committed suicide, totaling six percent of the sample, a number thousands of times greater than the one suicide, Shelley, out of 2,300 Engle estimated in 1961.[14] In 1947, Engle refuted the link between creativity and mental illness on the evidence of his students' long list of publications, prizes, and grants that included pieces in "Atlantic Monthly, Harper's, Mademoiselle, Harper's Bazaar, Saturday Review of Literature, New Yorker, Esquire, Poetry, Kenyon Review, Sewanee Review, Accent, and the annual collections of short stories, The Best Short Stories of each year, and the O. Henry Prize Stories of each year."[15] According to the *Look* feature in 1965, he admitted the connection and thus presented the program as an institution that might serve as a corrective influence on imbalanced artists. In this vein, he touted the Workshop's function as caustic medicine.

"Our Richard Cory"

Richard Cory was a well-acculturated professional man, a productive citizen to all who knew him—or thought they did. What troubled him remained closeted from view, discreetly hidden beneath a mantle of respectability that passed through society unquestioned. Edwin Arlington Robinson's haunting poem, "Richard Cory," depicts "a gentleman from sole to crown" who "fluttered pulses" and "glittered when he walked." He was universally admired and even envied for his manifest material success and regal bearing that bore no ostentation. "In fine, we thought he was everything/ To make us wish that we were in his place." Laboring to acquire his prestige, his admirers "worked and waited for the light,/ And went without the meat, and cursed the bread." But, to their astonishment, "Richard Cory, one calm summer night/ Went home and put a bullet through his head."[16]

The professional success and social graces of Robert Shelley were appearances that belied the severe mental illness exacerbated by his closeted gay identity. "He is always cordial, always neatly attired," notes Richard Bode of Shelley's poetic counterpart. "But what he presents is not himself but a counterfeit picture of himself, a carefully composed disguise to impress those he encounters along the way," he explains, noting that "the world is full of Richard Corys." Like Shelley, repressed homosexuals "are dying slowly, dying inevitably, because, whether they admit it or not, they despise the person they pretend to be and lack the courage to become the person they are." Only on rare occasions did figures like Randall Jarrell, who dared to reconfigure gender identity, pass through the Iowa Writers' Workshop in the late 1940s and early 1950s.[17] Coming out to a community dominated by macho heterosexual combat veterans would have taken an extraordinary feat of courage. Shelley was thus "one of many who would sooner die than remove his mask and stand barefaced before the world."[18]

Heterosexual normativity was etched into the public life Shelley encountered at Iowa. The cultural climate at the workshop was replete with nuclear families, including that of Shelley's mentor Warren Carrier. Carrier lived with his wife and children among "the young married students in the trailers, Quonsets and barracks" provided by university housing. "The hot summer of 1950" was filled with "the sound of clacking typewriters" that "vied with the cries of children," a symphony of literary labor and domestic clamor. Ambition was paramount; "We would all be famous, and we would all have famous children. Yes." But the students "were equally uncertain, whether authors or parents." As the GI Bill funding began to run out, many scrambled to make ends meet for their young families "with part-time jobs to pay for cans of Gerber's baby food and Carnation milk." For men in the program, "the writing went slowly," Shelley's classmate James Sunwall notes, "and I fear we were only part-time husbands and fathers as well."[19] Tethered to his roommate and longtime companion William Stuckey from St. Louis, who had enrolled in the Workshop with him, Shelley was neither husband nor father. Those roles both dominated the cultural climate of the postwar Workshop and dictated the subject matter of student and faculty poetry. Engle's own *American Child: A Sonnet Sequence*, published in 1945, was written for his daughter focusing on his trials of fatherhood, and Snodgrass's *Heart's Needle* also takes up the theme of fatherhood, only from the point of view of loss and estrangement from his daughter in the wake of his divorce.

On the rare occasions when Shelley treated domestic subjects in his poetry, fatherly love is conspicuously absent. The most notable instance depicts children at a playground in "Evening in the Park." In it, they "Seemed adrift on a darkened excursion" as evening closes in, cast as "ghosts in a sea of debris." Opposite Engle and Snodgrass, the antithesis of sentimental and caring parents hurry them "to waiting cars and could have slapped/ Their children whose hands smelled of crushed fireflies" and, death-like, "shone with a greasy green light in the dark." The alienation of the wives of MFA students was indicative of the heterosexual-male-centered locus of activity. "One young mother couldn't stand pushing a cart through the abundance of a supermarket." That sacrifice of family combined with a dedication to craft, Engle urged, was essential to the work of writing. "A writer is a monster with character," he claimed, presuming the writer typically was a father compromising his family's immediate well-being for long-term literary success.[20] This formulation of authorship in effect evacuates the situation of the gay writer who ostensibly is not a father at a time predating married gay families by more than a half century. Shelley faced such trying circumstances in which he began to forge confessional poetry—a form that dropped masks and peeled labels to lay bare identity—within a veritable boot camp predicated on the systematic removal of identity from writing.

Although everyone close to Shelley agreed that his death could have been prevented, there was no consensus about what finally drove him to the act. Carrier suggested his student's inability to cope with his sexuality in this environment precipitated his suicide. Sunwall, on the other hand, cited undue pressure to achieve literary prestige. Shelley may have had a series of powerful publications that preceded him, Sunwall argued, but he was not immune to how "there was always a doubting of talent" at the Workshop. The seeds of his destruction were sown in the inherent dangers of the creative process itself, because "when you plumb around in the deep womb of the unconscious, anxiety and disturbance results. Such was the end of Bob Shelley, our most brilliant and best at the time." In this sense, "He was our Richard Cory." The drive for literary fame "in the midst of youth" epitomized in his singular "talent and publication—suddenly ended." Sunwall attributed the response to how "we took too narrow a view, but our lives were caught up with writing and creativity which demand life and survival." Students such as Snodgrass rushed in to occupy the newly vacated creative territory Shelley had discovered. But had the student body moved forward beyond his death with too much alacrity? Had his death merely operated like everything else at the Workshop—a justification for more literary production?

According to Shelley's classmate and fellow Workshop poet James B. Hall, too much sacrifice was made for the pursuit of publishable writing, an obsession that totally overshadowed the mental health of the students producing it. "Our wide reading, our commitment to the arts, our interest in criticism and theory, the often informed care that went into conceptual matters now seems to me to represent one overwhelming thing," Hall concluded: "I think we cared too much." Workshop students poured themselves into the creative process at the expense of their personal lives and social well-being. His accounting of the damaged and destroyed lives tells a different tale than Engle's boast of only one suicide occurring on his watch as the program's director. Hall could count "at least three workshop members [who] destroyed themselves." Shelley stood out as "one marvelously talented poet [who] wrote 'And chunks [sic] of snowmen tumbled from the sky,' and thus foretold his own suicide." Others with only a modicum of the talent Shelley possessed, who "seemed never to have attained literary—or perhaps emotional—maturity most surely killed themselves over things close to literature." Self-destructive behavior was rampant in the vicious cycle of drinking and divorce. Many "lapsed into silence, disappeared, failed to reregister, drifted off into something else." The dropouts and suicides mounted into a "process of elimination" that many saw "as tragic, as wasteful." Those who "moved happily to something else" could rest assured "their leaving was for the best." Praise was hard won in this environment where writers could expect their work to be received with skepticism and opposition. "False encouragement at Iowa City, there was none."[21]

Authorized histories of the Workshop have carefully muted any such insinuation that the students may have been overzealous in their pursuit of literary esteem to the point of neglecting the well-being of themselves and others. Hall's original testimony, according to its appearance in the Iowa archive, was heavily excised and censored for *A Community of Writers: Paul Engle and the Iowa Writers' Workshop*. Without Hall's dark commentary, the volume maintains its commemorative appeal in honor of Engle's memory. Two decades earlier, Engle himself hurried across campus when he heard that Stephen

Wilbers's history of the Workshop was headed into production at the University of Iowa Press. Similarly, Engle wanted to add key details to polish his historical memory. He supplied new passages that alluded to his own contribution to the study of criticism in the program to refute dissenters in the English department claiming the curriculum lacked theoretical substance. In particular, he insisted that the manuscript should mention how "He introduced, and himself taught—the first course in Contemporary Literature on the campus; the first Seminars in such major individual writers as James Joyce, W. B. Yeats, Proust, etc."[22]

Any gaps in the area of literary criticism within the curriculum Shelley covered by developing his analytical expertise in the advanced theory course he taught and the sophisticated reviews he published. Had he lived to see the publication of *Poetry* in February 1952, Shelley would have been gratified that he was proclaimed the unofficial poet laureate of the Workshop. He had single-handedly revitalized poetry at Iowa, which had come under fire for its stale standardized curriculum and factory-like production of MFAs. His death in late April of 1951 indeed came precisely at the moment the literary establishment had made preparations not just for his introduction as a young new phenomenon, but also for his canonization in the pantheon of great contemporary literature. If the Workshop students cared too much about their professional development, as Hall suggested, it was in large part because such powerful and accomplished writers as Shelley had been poached by Carrier and Engle, who groomed them as future Workshop faculty members.

Shelley's grooming into the literary profession was perhaps no more apparent than when he made his debut in *Poetry*, which was engineered by Engle and the journal's editor Karl Shapiro. At the time, Shapiro had dedicated a series of issues to trending topics such as Activists for the May 1951 issue and the translated poetry of Juan Ramón Jiménez for July 1953. Between the two issues, he prominently positioned an issue recognizing the high quality and quantity of work crossing his desk from "colleges and universities and from the poetry workshops and summer writing conferences of America." For February 1952, *Poetry* thus divided its pages between the world's two most powerful graduate creative writing programs. Shapiro had chosen Engle's Iowa Writers' Workshop on the strength of its brilliant showing in a variety of high-end literary journals. What struck him most was a thirty-three-page booklet published by Prairie Press that had appeared the previous spring, in 1951. Shapiro found the work showcased in the slim volume so impressive that he conscripted Brewster Ghiselin, then director of the MFA program in creative writing at the University of Utah, to review it in the back pages of the issue. His dedication of the issue to such a great deal of Workshop writing was in many ways a foregone conclusion for Shapiro, given the manifest success of Engle's young poets. Shapiro had also served on the Workshop faculty before taking over as editor of *Poetry* in 1950.[23] The only difficult consideration for him was which of the Workshop's peer institutions to feature in the issue. He settled on the University of Washington, not because any of its students particularly struck him as the face of poetry's future, but because its director, Theodore Roethke, had achieved a luminous presence in the literary world. Roethke, along with Lowell, was *the* standard for aspiring poets. In Lowell's creative writing course at the Boston Center for Adult Education, Anne Sexton began to model her work after Roethke. Together with Randall Jarrell and Sexton, Roethke defined the middle generation of mid-twentieth-century American poets.[24]

Of the many MFA students from Iowa and Washington featured in the February 1952 issue of *Poetry*, Shelley received the lion's share of attention. Saving the best for last, Shapiro selected his Shakespearean sonnet "Harvest" for the prized closing position in the collection. The one piece Ghiselin chose to reprint in its entirety from *Poems from the Iowa Poetry Workshop* in his review was Shelley's "Evening in the Park." Whereas all other contributors were limited to one poem each in the issue, Shelley had two and was spotlighted in Ghiselin's glowing review. Indeed, Ghiselin reprinted "Evening in the Park" less as a means of illustrating the volume's prowess than as a way of showcasing Shelley, whom he named the best of the top three poets in the volume, along with Peter Hald and James B. Hall. But in praising Shelley, Ghiselin's words seemed to prophesy the young writer's suicide. He wrote that his technical skill reinforces "thematic" effects of "slack integrity" and "imminent disintegration." Shelley's impeding self-destruction saturates "Evening in the Park." "Paper boats soon sank" on this playground as "balloons went limp" and the sky darkened. Ghiselin highlights how "in the second section of the poem the park itself becomes a boat washed on a journey brief and digressive like a pleasure trip, in every sense 'darkened'; and in the last line the 'sea of debris' shows to baffled ghosts a green light of passage that suggests grave-gleam and sea phosphorous." As the children gather their belongings, they "Had expected too much probably," signaling a despondent note of resignation that refuses to determine the symbolic meaning of the poem's details of balloons, "*crackerjack* icons," and the sunken paper boats. This results in an eerie detachment from embodied presence, a kind of evacuation of humanity focused instead on an image of the park after death, occupied only by "ghosts in a sea of debris."[25]

Just weeks before the publication of *Poems from the Iowa Poetry Workshop* that featured his work so prominently, Shelley brought his life to an abrupt end. His poems in that volume, particularly "Evening in the Park," earned him recognition that even Engle had not anticipated. Engle's preface to the Workshop's half of the special *Poetry* issue dedicated to MFA poets points out that "The Iowa poems are not the selected best of a year or two," as was the case for his rivals at Washington, "but those available this autumn. In the spring of 1951, the best poems of the season were published in a booklet, *Poems from the Iowa Poetry Workshop*, and various others from the class have been eliminated by acceptance for *Poetry*, *The Kenyon Review*, and other magazines."[26] Engle, the master of publicity, spun a liability into an asset by promoting the sale of the booklet and arranging for its review in the same issue. He also covered for his overexposure of his students' work in a cheap publication by a local press—the booklet appeared under the imprint of Iowa City's Prairie Press and was priced at $1.00—by boasting that his students could produce enough quality verse to fill an entire thirty-three-page volume plus half an issue of *Poetry* in addition to assorted other single publications. What he overlooked in the process of touting the quantity of his program's aggregate literary production was the quality of his singular greatest talent, Robert Shelley. Indeed, the previous publication of "Evening in the Park" in the booklet should have disqualified it from appearing in *Poetry*. But on the strength of its writing, it breached the editorial chasm and found its way into the pages of *Poetry* by way of Ghiselin's positive review. "Though success of this kind depends primarily upon insight, it is impossible without technical skill of the kind Shelley" displays in the poem, he raved.[27] Shelley did not live to see the greatest accolades he would receive from the literary establishment during his short career. He did not even live long enough to see his poems in the spring 1951 booklet, which appeared just three weeks after his death.

Living Death

The afternoon of Wednesday, April 25, 1951, seemed just like any other at the Iowa Writers' Workshop. Engle was busy checking proof sheets for *Poems from the Iowa Poetry Workshop*, while students were busy preparing their final projects for the end of the semester. Shelley had wowed his classmates with the new forms he had discovered in his metaphorically rich lyricism, emerging as the first of the Workshop's lyrical confessional poets. His work confirmed that "there was always either a sense of direct surface narrative or else a musical and lyric thrust to carry you through the poem." Based on his innovations, "most of us there at Iowa" began to "put the subrational up on the surface of the poem" due to Shelley's influence, Snodgrass recollected.[28]

As graduation approached, Shelley faced a moment of truth, in both a personal and a professional sense. His stellar record at Iowa made him a highly sought-after candidate for faculty positions in creative writing programs such as at the University of Utah, which was primed to extend him a job offer given his ringing endorsement in *Poetry* from its director Brewster Ghiselin. The prospect of entering professional life, however, plagued him with self-doubt. Engle's edited booklet of Workshop poems and the special issue of *Poetry* were in progress but had yet to materialize by late April. The appearance of these publications bearing direct evidence of his imminent success would have alleviated his stress. Compounding his anxiety was concern over the professional impact of disclosing his homosexuality. His faculty mentor Warren Carrier acknowledged that Shelley was struggling with making his sexual orientation publicly known.

With the exception of Shelley's roommate, William Stuckey, no one was aware that he had sought medical help for his condition. After his suicide, "Friends of Stuckey said they knew no reason for his action." Few realized that "he had been taking treatment at the Psychopathic Hospital" at the university during "the last week" before his death. Most were stunned to learn "he was a patient at the hospital last year, police said," and that he had received treatment for his mental illness dating back to his first two semesters at the Workshop.[29] Whereas Workshop members were surprisingly oblivious to his ongoing medical treatment, they were all too aware of Shelley's inner pain, because it was etched in his verse. If students knew anything intimate about each other, it was primarily through their writing, the object of their obsessive pursuit of literary success.

"Harvest" clearly signaled Shelley's impending suicide. Morbid images of "last year's ash" combine with visions of death as "the scraps of summer were all hauled away/ To shifty piles out back and left to rot," corpse-like, as remnants to be removed.[30] Carrier spoke for many when he confessed that Shelley's death was "a sad event for which all of us who knew him felt guilty."[31] The collective guilt was inescapable because no one had cared enough to intervene despite widespread intimate knowledge of his personal pain through his writing. James Sunwall conversely felt faculty and students, himself included, were the equivalent of the admiring "people on the pavement" in Robinson's "Richard Cory" who "looked at him" with admiration, yet were blind to his colossal inner struggle.[32] Shelley "carved" his verse "to portray/ The fire within, the sickly grin without." Alternative perspectives on conventional understandings of gender unambiguously blazed through his writing. "We recognized high heels and cast-off dress;/ Nudged each other, laughed at masks they wore—/ The very things we'd tried to dispossess." Struggling with these forbidden identities, Shelley sought solace in a rifle blast.[33]

On what seemed to all a routine Wednesday at the Workshop, after attending class in the barracks on the banks of the Iowa River, Shelley quickly withdrew to his apartment at 1209 Kirkwood Avenue in Iowa City. He knew the apartment would be empty, since his roommate Stuckey had a seminar in the early afternoon every Wednesday. Shelley fumbled for his key and unlocked the door, his mind racing. The act itself would have to be quiet and discreet; no onlookers, no witnesses, no drama. But the effects, he knew, would have the entire campus staring in amazement, blinking their "eyes/ At pieces of snowmen falling from the skies."[34] Practicality struck him as something of a curse. Would Stuckey's .22-caliber gun be powerful enough? It was a rifle no less, making the act that much more difficult to pull off. A weak gun could work anyway, especially through the temple rather than the roof of the mouth, the method Hemingway would use ten years later with a much more powerful shotgun in his new home in Ketchum, Idaho. Shelley rose and opened Stuckey's closet, peering on tiptoes at the top shelf. Like a good midwestern boy, Stuckey had brought his beloved boyhood hunting rifle with him to college at Washington University, and did not fail to remember it on making the move to Iowa City. Iowa's rural locale would certainly bring opportunities to hunt deer and turkey, and at the very least squirrels and chipmunks. The last thing he imagined it would do was to provide his roommate and closest companion with the instrument of his own destruction.

Reaching up, Shelley pulled the gun off the shelf and removed it from its case. Stuckey kept the rifle clean, locked, and never loaded while in storage. Shelley remembered from his own youth the procedure for loading the rifle. He methodically broke the barrel and dropped the ammunition into the chamber. His movements by now were unwavering and even precise. This was the tool. He felt its power in his hands as he headed into the bathroom, conscious of the mess he was about to make and Stuckey's horror at its discovery. Seated on the edge of the sink in their cramped bathroom, he anchored the heel of the gun on his instep, resting the end of the barrel against his right temple. He reached down and eased his thumb onto the trigger.

No neighbors reported hearing the loud crack of the gun's report. Stuckey, returning from campus, found the door unlocked and assumed Shelley was at his desk poring over his work as usual. Discovering his typewriter standing silently at attention, Stuckey called out instinctively. Pushing the bathroom door open, he shuddered and recoiled from the catastrophe before him. Blood pooled on the floor beside the dropped gun as Shelley lay grotesquely contorted against the edge of the tub. Stuckey, now fully aware of what had happened, reached for his roommate, his feet slipping on the blood-slick floor. He could immediately see that "the bullet entered his right temple and went completely through his head, emerging from the left temple," as the student newspaper, the *Daily Iowan*, reported the next day.[35] The steady crimson streams had been flowing for hours from both sides of his head. What he took to be the lifeless body of his roommate, to his horror, moved almost imperceptibly. Shelley's chest was gently expanding and contracting in shallow breaths; he was very much alive. The .22, it turned out, was not powerful enough after all. Struggling to maneuver him into a more comfortable position, Stuckey winced and gagged at the soaked clothing—spongy to the touch—that clung from his friend. Frantic efforts to revive him were to no avail; Shelley was totally unconscious, his face slack and eyes firmly closed, caked with drying crimson. Without the capacity to speak, he was trapped in a body that cruelly would not die, sentenced by his own hand to the living hell of a botched suicide. Sensing a chance for survival, Stuckey sprang out of the room to dial for an ambulance, his trembling fingers barely able to make the call.

After making the call at 3 P.M., Shelley's distraught roommate greeted the ambulance that soon arrived with lights flashing and sirens blaring. By 3:20, neighbors and onlookers gathered, curious about the commotion. Whispers and downcast eyes immediately spread through the crowd as Shelley was carried on a stretcher into the waiting vehicle, his face hideously matted with fresh and half-dried blood from the hours-old bullet wounds. The ambulance sped away to the university hospital, where Shelley was rushed to the emergency room and prepared for surgery. Stuckey paced in the lobby as police and journalists from the *Iowa City Press-Citizen* and the *Daily Iowan* student paper peppered him with questions. During surgery, Shelley's faltering vital signs persisted late into the night. Doctors labored nonstop for over seven hours to repair his shredded brain tissue, their efforts hampered by his excessive blood loss and fluttering pulse. Shelley drew his last breath at the staggeringly late hour of 11 P.M., when his body finally released its ferocious grip on life. The Johnson County coroner's autopsy report indicated that he had pulled the trigger sometime around 1 P.M., two hours before Stuckey encountered him, protracting his torturous last day to an agonizing ten hours total after receiving the self-inflicted wound. "It was this lingering" that Carl Hartman, who had worked with Shelley as an editorial assistant on the *Western Review*, "still recalled painfully."[36] Here, finally, was the "dark bird with a bleeding breast/ Returning to his lair," the death Shelley foretold in "On My Twenty-First Birthday." Staring "with my brain's furrowed eye/ To the long limbed boy I left behind," Shelley sees himself in his youth with eyes "Bright with madness, in which I stripped him naked/ And so unmanned myself." The stark realization of his madness, and his "unmanned" sexual identity, had perpetually sent him back to poetry to "make my music with help/ Of new beasts rushing up a bone-dry stair."[37]

The coroner described the death as "a suicide due to ill health," and the *Press-Citizen* reported that Shelley had been a patient "for 30 days last year" at the University of Iowa's psychiatric hospital.[38] The *Daily Iowan* described the incident starkly in a front-page headline, "Student Kills Self with Hunting Rifle," tastelessly positioned next to a voluptuous actress preening full-bodied on stage in a bikini and high heels. Staff reporter Charles Nickell had taken the photograph at MacBride Auditorium during opening night of a student comedy series of short productions called Kampus Kapers. Shelley's pulse stopped less than an hour after the curtain lowered on the raucous show. The frolicsome performance took place about a mile from where the shot rang out at 1209 Kirkwood Avenue earlier that afternoon. Ironically, the skit pictured on the front page of the paper next to the story of Shelley's death bore a significant relation to the Workshop. It was "a satire on authors and publishers who turn out midget books at the rate of 100 an afternoon," a thinly veiled spoof of the Workshop's increasing commercialization that the literary accomplishments of Shelley ostensibly contradicted.[39] No mention of Shelley's peerless record and high standing in the program appeared in the adjacent article reporting the news of his death.

In Memoriam

If the *Daily Iowan* and *Look* magazine had missed the significance of Shelley's brief literary life, the poetry establishment had commemorated its full value with deep appreciation. Shelley's biography was in his poetry; he seems to have written his epitaph in his lyrics. Ten years after his death, Shelley held a prominent place in Engle's collection of the best writing of the first twenty-five years of the Iowa Writers' Workshop. As with his powerful showing in the *Po-etry* issue of 1952 and the booklet of Workshop poems in 1951, Shelley received due acclaim that he never lived to see. He bears the honor of having three po-ems in the volume, "Harvest," "Evening in the Park," and "On My Twenty-First Birthday," a distinction shared by only a few authors. Following Shelley in the anthology with three of his own poems is Snodgrass. The accident of alpha-betical order that positioned him after Shelley in the volume could not have been more fitting, since it was Snodgrass, after all, who carried on the legacy of Shelley's signature style. "On My Twenty-First Birthday" signals another death, this one of his old self, the "long limbed boy" left behind in his youth. His pro-tracted struggle for sanity appears in his realization of "how long I have tried to clear the stables of his heart." Writing for him was a release of the madness on to the page, the source of his art voiced when "now I turn the key and hear and await the roar . . . of new beasts," metaphors for his never-ending parade of demons.[40]

While he was alive, Shelley inspired Workshop poets like Snodgrass, intent on bringing his new mode of self-disclosure to their own verse. Shelley in-fused new life into a cadre of young writers, whose sporadic attempts at branching out from routine modes had been systematically stymied by often brutal remediation in workshop sessions. Insights tended to be funneled into a uniform style. "We had all been writing in a neo-Symbolist, neo-Metaphysical style," Snodgrass admitted, noting, "it is very strange to marry the Metaphysi-cals and Symbolists, but that is what we were trying to do."[41] To distill such a highly abstracted approach into intimate direct expression as Shelley had done was entirely novel, breathing new life into the program, and setting the course for the confessional school of poetry.

In his death, Shelley was also an influential source of inspiration. He left a distinct impression on classmates such as Donald Petersen. Petersen wrote a seven-poem ode to Shelley, printed in *Poetry* in December 1953, as a tribute to his beloved classmate. The sonnet sequence is written with a fierce directness that Shelley would have admired. Shelley had already published in all the right places associated with refined literature on his arrival at the Workshop, par-ticularly in such journals as the *Western Review*. His work therefore did not bear the stigma of "being published in the 'wrong' places" that were routinely shunned at the Workshop. Although he had written journalism and produced a popular play, Shelley was immune to having his "new workshop manu-scripts . . . worked over very carefully by the experienced people in the back rows," students who took it on themselves to keep up standards. "The most

damning criticism of any manuscript," according to Hall, "was, 'It's slick,' "
that is, "commercial by calculation, or—worse—by a fault of authorial mind."
The paradox that faced students was that while "everyone understood one *was*
to publish—of course," a tidal wave of resistance pushed against that urge in
that "We seriously questioned the point at which a manuscript was 'ready.' "
Shelley himself was an arbiter of such standards for poets. Most upstarts eager
to send out a manuscript for publication after a favorable showing at workshop would be told, "Ace, it's not ready. Work on the last scene some more."
In this context, "Rewriting was a fetish. It was well known that one now-
famous author [Flannery O'Connor] did at least 25 versions of the first page of
every story."[42]

Unscathed in a minefield of struggle and contention, envy and resistance,
Shelley seemed untouchable. Immune to assaults on his literary integrity and
prolific publication record that could have raised questions about his commercial leanings—and to Engle's belief that any good creative writing program
"should be a place where the too sure poet can be knocked down a few times"—
Shelley remained, in the eyes of admirers like Petersen, a voice and vision out
of time.[43] "The Stages of Narcissus," written by Petersen "to the memory of
Robert Shelley," aptly describes how he was admired and sought after in the
highly contentious market for new poetic insight. "He might go on/ Pretending he did not know," but he was "considered a thing of some refinement,
sought/ For all his wit or common sense alone,/ While in their secret cells
they railed and fought/ Like stray dogs yapping over a choice bone." But his
inner turmoil came from precisely this scrutiny, especially in "how the eyes
peered out at him and made him dread/ The will to live which terrorized the
dark." His confessional introspection is evident in how in "the still pool he
had his second birth/ Studying his imagery in fateful springs," leaning in
"more closely, hunching his thin spine." The seeds of his destruction Petersen
aptly captures in his tortured sexual repression and fear of public derision,
leaving him "With no fair love, no marriageable heart." Misunderstood like
Richard Cory, "By day the world pursued him and he fled/ To its dark night
where the pure waters start," drowning in his own pain.[44]

Close Quote

Although official histories and memoirs by affiliates of the program tend to
skirt the topic, suicide was a concern at the Workshop.[45] One remarkable case
in Shelley's cohort was the death of poetry Workshop graduate James Cox.

James Sunwall described the loss of his classmate Cox as a particularly tragic incident after Shelley's passing. Sunwall reconnected with Cox after graduation, reminiscing about the compromised employment they were forced to endure for the sake of their young families. Cox supported his wife and three boys by shelving his dignity and working as a "bellboy at the Jefferson Hotel" in Iowa City; Sunwall swallowed his pride and accepted a position as an orderly, as did Snodgrass.

The sacrifice seemed entirely worthwhile, given the comfortable faculty positions Sunwall and Cox secured after both had returned to the Workshop to earn their Ph.D.s. With Sunwall at the University of Florida and Cox at nearby Florida State, "We got together and talked frequently of the Workshop, our friends, our teaching and writing." Sunwall described how "our last all-night session centered around the recent suicide of Hemingway." They concurred that it made no sense. "What a thing! No author, we agreed, could be more renowned in his own time, honored to the very limit possible for a writer in America. And yet?" Like the unknowing and astonished people on the pavement stunned by Richard Cory's suicide in Robinson's poem, they were nonplussed. "Such was the tenet of our talk," Sunwall remembered morosely. "I have remorsefully gone over it again and again in the years since." Sunwall, echoing the guilt Carrier felt for failing to intervene on behalf of Shelley, wondered if "there was something more I could have said or should not have said?" Following their last discussion about the curious case of Hemingway's self-destruction, "one week later, at the hour of the first meeting of his class that fall, Jim Cox joined Bob Shelley and Ernest Hemingway." Sunwall commemorated his friend by referring to a decade punctuated with such tragedy, mourning the passing of these powerful creative minds. "The decade of the Workshop for me," as he understood that passage of time, "was marked by Bob Shelley and Jim Cox, those two echoing rifle shots like quotation marks enclosing it." This occupational hazard specific to creative writing—despite the rewards of "the birth of literature" through the assistance of "such skillful midwives as Ray [B. West], Paul [Engle], and Verlin [Cassill]"—came in the "warning . . . that creativity must always carry a mortal risk."[46]

Sunwall's reminiscence came at the request of Workshop historian Jean Wylder in the early 1970s. Wylder was so struck by his touching eulogy that she asked him to elaborate, but he demurred. "Frankly, I do not want to write more than I did, on the last months of his life. It was too sad," he explained. "Jim, indeed, got very disturbed, ill, and depressed," and sought psychiatric treatment. But, "he was released too soon," meaning that, in effect, "the doctors killed him," in Sunwall's estimation. He reported that "Jean and the boys," Cox's surviving immediate family, "must have felt Jim's death as a terrible and final rejection." Wylder shared Sunwall's letter with John Leggett, the Workshop director at the time. She attached a handwritten note to the letter, mentioning that James B. Hall had referred to Cox's suicide as an event that haunted faculty and students alike. "Everyone in the late 40s and early 50s felt that same nagging guilt he talks about here—could we have done something or said something to have kept it from happening?" Leggett wrote back at the bottom, "*Very* interesting—we'll have to *tell* that" in the project that Wylder would never complete, a story that also went untold in the history Stephen Wilbers compiled in the late 1970s and published as *The Iowa Writers' Workshop: Origins, Emergence, and Growth* (1980).[47]

Sunwall's recollection of Cox's sad end speaks to the profound guilt suffered by Workshop members following the loss of their classmates and colleagues to suicide. There was an awareness among them that the culture of creative industry inhered a perilous set of risks. The acute sense of responsibility in Shelley's loss came directly from the way in which the lines of his poetry foretold his own self-destruction, staring back at his survivors in the aftermath as a clear warning they could have heeded. But the relentless culture of literary production inculcated at the Workshop disinclined them to intervene. What Richard Stern, an Iowa MFA from 1954, called "the ferocious gamesmanship of the Iowa Fifties" had meant that "we weren't much in the world," preoccupied with the latest manuscript in progress, worrying over the scansion of their sestina for Lowell or series of sonnets for Justice, and polishing their post-symbolist syntax and neo-metaphysical conceits for Carrier. Such immersion could yield an appalling blindness to the suffering of others. Stern noted this capacity for barbaric insensitivity when he hurried up the hill with others after class to the requisite gossip sessions over drinks at Kenney's, the Airliner, and the Mill, oblivious to the chalk outline of a body they passed over, the victim of a shooting recently removed from the crime scene only hours before.[48] Stern's image describes a Workshop culture so self-absorbed that no one stops for the dead. Worse, little is done to prevent them from dying.

This was a group that looked after one another intellectually and aesthetically, if not in terms of their mutual physical and mental health. Mutual aid often took the form of "passing annotated texts to each other" and savaging shared enemies both in workshop and behind the scenes. Workshop students of the early fifties—Shelley included—"lived day to day: the provincial enchantment of narcissism, relieved by the lyric narcissism of your friends, collaborators, semblables-presque-freres [similar-almost-brothers]." He too was "flipping through two-hundred books a week to pass exams," he too "partied, wrote, worked on the WESTERN REVIEW," maintaining a frenetic work schedule in which he rarely stopped to notice that he, like his classmates, "seldom left Iowa City."[49] By placing his demons in plain view inside the space of his poetry, the mask concealing his suicidal impulses proved all too effective. In this environment his anguish was less a cause for alarm than for a celebration of the brilliant art it produced. Shelley—the true inventor of confessional poetry, whose main confession was his desire to end his life—in the end, never left Iowa City. Like his writing, Shelley's death was inextricably woven into the cultural fabric of the Workshop, a community capable of creating and conditioning its own Richard Cory.

4 • The Professional: R. V. Cassill

In 1948, Ronald Verlin Cassill built his house in Iowa City with his own hands. At under two thousand dollars, it was more economical to construct a home in late-1940s Iowa City than to rent an apartment near the University of Iowa's campus. He did it much in the way he wrote his twenty-four novels and seven collections of short stories—with steely resolve and textbook precision, combining Hemingwayesque craftsmanship and Thoreauvean economy. When he began construction, Cassill was enrolled at the Iowa Writers' Workshop, attending class in "old army fatigues and GI boots with mud on them—before it was fashionable to dress that way." He meticulously managed every detail himself "from his own architectural design—building it board by board, digging the foundation, pouring the cement, laying the roof, putting in the furnace ducts and electrical wiring." Since he had barely enough money for furniture, the house felt empty and cavernous except for his paintings, "his second art: delicate watercolors of the Iowa countryside and oil portraits of his friends." The works he had no room to display he gave to classmates like Jean Wylder, who cherished her watercolor depicting "a field of wheat gently blowing in the summer wind seen from his window." As an Iowa native, Cassill was in his element, living for little else besides literature and art. But as Wylder recalled, "Iowa traditionally has not been kind to its own."[1]

Cassill published his first short story at the age of eighteen before entering the University of Iowa as an undergraduate art student. He drew recognition for his technical mastery and spare economy of style, earning an Atlantic First Award. He steadily built upon this auspicious beginning, eventually establishing himself among the literary elite as editor of the *Norton Anthology of Short*

Fiction and later the *Norton Anthology of Contemporary Fiction.*[2] It was not by coincidence, then, that when facing the most threatening crisis of his career, during which his credibility as a faculty member of the Iowa Writers' Workshop hung in the balance, the consummate craftsman vowed to "take a hammer" and "personally destroy" the local establishments he was convinced were harboring conspirators bent on destroying him.[3]

The dispute that shook the very foundation of his academic and authorial integrity during the spring semester of 1963 was just the beginning of the turmoil precipitating Cassill's permanent withdrawal from the Workshop and deeper renunciation of his birth state, alma mater, and employer. The break was permanent and irreversible, severing all ties to the forces that had built his personal and professional identity. He did not go quietly, instead venting his disdain in a 1965 *Esquire* piece later expanded into "Why I Left the Midwest," the closing essay of his 1969 collection, *In an Iron Time.*

Parisian, Artist, Novelist

Cassill never envisioned his Iowa MFA as training for a faculty appointment at the Workshop. "When I first came to the State University at Iowa," he explained, "I had no good reasons for registering there, but the good reasons emerged—as if they had been the basis of my prior decision—in the course of time."[4] After four years of teaching at the Workshop, from 1948 to 1952, a period during which his works focused on serious literary fiction, Cassill went to Paris to pursue training in art at the Sorbonne. Throughout the 1950s, as he focused his creative energies on art, Cassill's writing took a distinct turn toward popular trade fiction. The sexually liberated environment of France encouraged Cassill to venture into popular erotic fiction with such titillating titles as *The Wound of Love* (1956), *My Sister's Keeper* (1961), and *Night School* (1961). His pace of production increased to an average of more that one novel per year, a rate more reflective of a purveyor of pulp than a serious literary artist. These works represented a vast departure from "New Mexican Sun and Other Stories," his MFA thesis at the Workshop directed by Engle and Wilbur Schramm. To support himself and his growing family, he spun out racy yarns like *Left Bank of Desire* and carnal tarts such as *Taste of Sin* and *Lustful Summer* that made use of his immediate surroundings.

The move into the mass market, however, was not entirely mindless, nor was it a renunciation of his aesthetic for the profit motive. Instead, it reflected his desire to converge the popular novel with the novel of ideas. Great literature, Cassill believed, could sell on a large scale and appeal to broad audiences, leveraging recognizable structures and tropes for deeper, more nuanced meanings. Even in his literary works such as *The Eagle on the Coin*, about a coalition that seeks to appoint an African American to the school board of a small midwestern town, we see Cassill intellectualizing popular idioms, like jazz, from urban and African-American culture. He freely ventures into settings such as "a dive . . . with people whose minds swung like reeds gracefully in any direction—music, sex, art, politics—while they got drunk." His artist's attention to detail reveals an unmistakable erotic dimension that he later developed in his popular novels. One sees this in his description of his character's seersucker suit, "colored but transparent like an oil film on water above the stream bed," creating "an illusion" whereby "the pucker of the ripple on the surface reflects the sky and hints, too, the guessed shape of the stone underneath."[5] *Clem Anderson* similarly renders a complex character study of a self-destructive writer modeled after Dylan Thomas, perhaps the most recognizable and charismatic literary figure of the 1950s to have simultaneously won both critical and popular acclaim. The novel renders addiction, alcoholism, and the antics of the mad poet in living color, but not at the expense of probing the fatal nature predisposed to some creative minds. Similarly, *Dormitory Women*'s subject of the gradual decline of a young woman into total insanity is much more serious than the one suggested by the lurid cover promising "an explosive novel of sex on campus."[6] Through both literary and popular elements, the narrative's attention to the character's disturbing interiority anticipates the tortured unraveling of Toni Morrison's protagonist in *The Bluest Eye*.

Such experimentation in Cassill's aesthetic was certainly a factor of his Parisian environment, in which genre divisions between high and low culture were far less ossified than in the U.S. market. This more liberating artistic environment combined with the economic necessity of supporting his wife and two children to reshape his writing. No longer was he reticent about sex and crime blending with psychological and social realism, or about intrigue and sensationalism giving way to incisive cultural critique. In Paris, Cassill was free to engage these forms as he had never done before, without heed to the cultural stigma attached to the commercialization of literature. So when he returned to Iowa to resume his post at the Workshop in 1960—just then entering its halcyon days of commercial solvency by way of lucrative publishing fellowships—the severe culture shock of a far more rigid and disapproving Iowa climate awaited.

Workshop Payola

The Workshop Cassill departed in 1952 was a shadow of the one he encountered upon his return from Europe in 1960. Cassill had just arrived when Engle secured a fellowship from Harper and Brothers, for $2,500, designed to harvest publications from Workshop students and faculty. Engle had used the same formula as when he negotiated a similar contract with Rinehart & Company, whose first fellowship went to Flannery O'Connor. Rather than investing in just one talented student per year, Harper instead spread its financial resources to ten different Workshop members, offering the awards based on merit, regardless of student or faculty status. Cassill rejoiced at the opportunities that awaited him in Iowa, a place flush with publishing options and financial support for his writing, not to mention a steady salary for teaching. The Workshop had transformed in his absence into a powerhouse of literary production, a fortress of institutional security. This financial backing was precisely what Paris—despite its aesthetically stimulating environment—was lacking.

In a 1960 letter to Engle, Evan Thomas, the director of general books for Harper and Brothers, explained the carefully designed terms and incentives of the prestigious fellowship. "We will give twenty-five $100 options to the first twenty-five college faculty members (or really accomplished students) who come to us with an outstanding piece of material, either fiction or nonfiction," he noted, stipulating that "student material submitted will first of all have faculty approval," and can come in the form of "either a short story, or a chapter of a book, or an article." This contract guaranteed Harper a virtual monopoly of exclusive rights to first refusal over Workshop material, since "The $100 will not be returnable, but it will constitute part of whatever sum may be later agreed on as an advance against earnings in a book contract." The nonbinding contract came with the incentive to land a project with the peerless publisher for instant status among the literary elite. The prize would "obligate the recipient to give us the first chance at his or her first (or next) book project," ostensibly for a lucrative advance contract, with the built-in incentive that "if the book project turns out to be a novel and comes along in time for our Novel Contest, it can also be in the Contest." This arrangement is a much more sophisticated corporate strategy than the one Engle established with Rinehart publishers immediately after taking over the Workshop. Thomas promised that "in attracting attention to Harper's anxiety to get closer to the new young writers—or to so far unpublished faculty members—it will be more than worthwhile."[7] The spread of the award across the best twenty-five works produced by faculty and students of the Workshop in any given year cornered the market for fiction, but not on poetry or instructional material.[8]

After signing what amounted to a collective advance contract with Harper and Brothers for Workshop members, Engle had entered into a new set of negotiations with Dodd, Mead and Company, "to discuss any kind of general trade editorial advisory relationship with book publishers."[9] By 1960, thanks to Engle's relentless marketing campaign, publishers were courting him. Within a week they struck a deal. The appropriately named R. T. Bond offered the Mead Fellowship in Creative Fiction "on a three year basis at $1500 a year, as you suggest. We should like to assign $500 of this amount to an outright gift and $1000 to an advance against royalties earned by the award winner." But unlike the Harper deal, the terms of the Mead contract moved into potentially unethical territory, anticipating precisely the Britannica conflict in which Cassill would become embroiled by 1963. Sensing an opportunity to capitalize on the rising value of Workshop manuscripts in the publishing industry, Engle demanded personal compensation for each fellowship. Bond agreed, "As to the $500 for each fellowship book, payable to you, that, too, is satisfactory." Engle's request for direct payment to him built in a cash incentive making him the functional equivalent of a one-man talent agency much less the director of an academic unit. "But we have one note of caution here," Bond warned, wary of the appearance of bribery, "perhaps unnecessary—namely, that we don't want to involve you in anything resembling payola. This, as we say, is probably unnecessary since, in return for the payment of this amount we may easily expect editorial work on the books beyond your academic duties."[10] Bond rationalized the direct $500 payment to Engle, rather than the Workshop, for each fellowship book as a quasi salary incentive, making him an unofficial employee of Dodd, Mead and Company.

Engle was ostensibly being paid off directly for fellowship books, similar to the payola scams record labels used to bribe underpaid radio disc jockeys to increase the air time received by their clients. Bond's awareness of the unlawfulness of the arrangement did not, however, prevent him from discovering a way around it. He thus suggested that his payments to Engle should be framed as compensation for "editorial work on the books" beyond his "academic duties." Of course, the process of teaching creative writing already involved editorial work, often of a much more rigorous sort than that performed in the publishing industry, thus making the suggestion a facile cover for a clearly underhanded deal. With Harper already committed to twenty-five fellowship books per year, Engle was in an especially powerful position when Mead approached him, and thus did not hesitate to profit personally on his unprecedented bargaining power. The other way to cover up the bribe, Bond suggested, was to call it a royalty. In the case that "there still might be a suggestion of payola here," he proposed to Engle, "we can make the payment as an overriding royalty of 2 ½ percent against the books payable as a total sum of $500." This would function as an effective cover for any appearance of payola, since "such a [royalty] formula has been sanctioned a thousand times in the textbook field, although at a lower guarantee."[11] The Dodd, Mead–University of Iowa fellowship in fiction thus came to fruition through a self-justifying allusion to royalty schedules typical of the textbook market, a field of the publishing industry Engle and the Workshop had yet to capitalize on at this point.

MFA by Mail: The Britannica Scandal

Cassill's paltry Iowa salary was not enough to recover from the massive debts he had accrued from a decade of expensive Parisian living, Sorbonne tuition for his art training, and the sustenance of his wife and two children. All of Engle's efforts to increase Cassill's wage from the university were stymied by the administration, mainly because of the openly hostile attitude of John Gerber, chairman of the English department, toward the Workshop. Engle's 1963 financial report to Gerber highlighted the injustice of Cassill's status as the lowest paid of his full-time faculty members despite his prolific output. Sharing notes from his meeting with the regents "about the present and projected needs of the program in creative writing," he reported to Gerber that his expanding program consisted of "300 graduate enrollments in the writing program courses this year, of which 126 are actually in writing courses, 86 in fiction. For many years there were 35–40 students in fiction, with four staff members to look after them," he explained. "Now we have twice as many students, and one less faculty member." Cassill was his lowest paid faculty member, at $8,500 per year. Despite publishing scores of articles "in most of the good magazines," five novels, and a textbook, he earned less than his former student James B. Hall, who "now receives $11,500 at Oregon, although he has published less than his teacher."[12] Such humiliation and injustice Engle would not tolerate.

Cassill's popular fiction written in France relieved only a fraction of the financial pressure, which became acute by 1963. Turning to the commercial publishing industry made perfect sense. Enter Britannica Schools, which offered a variety of correspondence courses for a fee. Engle agreed to undertake "the servicing of students enrolled through Britannica Schools" for poetry, playwriting, and fiction courses, while Britannica would "acquire the students through mutually acceptable advertising," and the two entities would "split the proceeds down the middle." The company's affiliation with the Workshop was intended to "add luster to the Britannica Schools roster of offerings."[13] The Workshop in turn could enjoy the advantage of added exposure to increase enrollments through the correspondence course's marketing campaign while bolstering sales of Cassill's textbook to answer to his acute financial straits.

But while Engle was abroad on a visit to Hong Kong funded by the Rockefeller Foundation, details of the deal with Britannica were published in the *Daily Iowan* on March 19, 1963—and it could not have come at a worse time. It appeared that a student-writer, Peter Huyck, had seized upon his routine assignment to review Cassill's latest publication, *Writing Fiction*, as an occasion for revenge. Faculty member Donald Justice, in a letter to Engle, added a marginal comment identifying the author of the article as "a former student of Verlin's who'd been given a 'C'—now a philosophy student & a hanger-out at Kenney's." Justice's conclusion was that, snubbed by his own treatment in the Workshop, Huyck had eviscerated Cassill for irresponsibly advising budding authors "to adopt the writer's lifestyle, to 'Go in debt as a writer,' or 'Choose writers' illnesses,' or (I like this one) 'Drink like a writer.' " Engle also came under attack in the piece for pursuing funds through commercial channels and trafficking in "the slick magazines" instead of growing "serious talent."[14]

Although Huyck allowed that "the new [correspondence] program seems at first to be a boon since it will obviously provide a great deal of money for additional graduate students and staff," he argued that this method of fundraising corroded the program's literary integrity. "For although the only legitimate purpose of the workshop may be the dissemination of funds," he observed, "few if any students are initially attracted here for that sole reason (this, however, is conspicuously not so in the case of some staff)."[15] Perhaps most stinging was Huyck's own investigative journalism: "To convince myself that the new program is offensive enough to discourage talented young writers from coming to Iowa City in the future one need look no further than the advertising ballyhooing it." He sent in the advertisement coupon for a "ten-day trial examination" of the course titled "Writing Is for Readers" that Britannica offered, which was "given for no credit, but you will receive an individual certificate of completion," a faux diploma bearing the Workshop seal.

Particularly devastating was the brochure's shameless cover art "in montage: GI with machine gun, small boy fishing, man shooting grizzly bear, mechanic and race car, private eye and prostitute." Under the heading "THE GREAT CHALLENGE" is a scene "of some Greeks talking on the Acropolis" that inexplicably includes "some women in Roman orgy dress" and begins with the words, "From Homer to Hemingway . . ."[16] Huyck predicted a dire fate from this Faustian deal: "I doubt that even the thriving SUI Art Department could survive the establishment of a correspondence course in conjunction with Britannica Schools."[17] In a lengthy typed letter to Engle detailing the calamity, Justice scrawled in pencil on the last page the cause of the publicity crisis in his view: "The illustration on the cover of the Britannica brochure, for instance (machine gun, lady of the streets, etc.)." He insisted, "We ought to take steps to correct any commercial implications of the Britannica association, I'm sure."[18]

The scandal positively unhinged Cassill, who watched in horror as a public inquisition ignited the editorial pages of the *Daily Iowan*. Some rushed to his defense, such as David Roberts, who groused that although the student newspaper had chosen to publish a lengthy assault on *Writing Fiction*, it would not "condescend" to review *Clem Anderson*, Cassill's most ambitious novel. "The only mention this fine novel merited" in the campus paper "occurred two and one half years after its publication in the form of a couple of letters," he sneered, "by snot-nosed blurb quoters who seemed more interested in book jackets than in literature."[19] The next day, Norman Peterson blasted the "editorial irresponsibility" of the paper for printing the piece by Huyck. In defense of Cassill, he predicted that "at least one of his books will be considered a literary masterpiece," arguing that he is an authority in his field "whose character cannot be attacked with impunity."[20] Three days later, a rebuttal criticized Cassill's textbook and the "*means* by which the Workshop wishes to take culture to the masses," highlighting "shortcomings in Mr. Cassill's *text* book" rather than his novel, and questioning "the value of the venture with which it is connected."[21]

With the editorial page ablaze, Justice reported to Engle that "all this was unbearable, especially to Verlin who very naturally flew into a rage which has not subsided since." Justice admitted, "I myself still smolder and I am tamer than Verlin." Cassill responded by contacting everyone who might aid his plot for revenge. He "got in touch with various people, wrote letters to Gerber & Hancher [president of the university], and managed to have the publisher of the Iowan print a substantial correction of some of the misrepresentations." Predictably, the unsympathetic Gerber "was of the opinion . . . to let the whole thing drop." But his indifference only intensified Cassill's fury, causing him to jump "to the conclusion, partly on intuition, partly on the basis of conversations with Gerry Stevenson, and partly (as I suggested to him) out of incipient paranoia, that a sort of conspiracy existed in Iowa City against the workshop," Justice wrote. Cassill was convinced "that its headquarters were the Paper Place [bookstore] and Kenney's and that one of the ringleaders was Stevenson; that, further this ring had a direct line to the Iowan somehow." Although initially skeptical of Cassill's theory, Justice allowed "that there are a number of disaffected ex-workshop students who don't much like us" and "wanted to do some mischief." Justice noted that if such a cadre of conspirators had not existed before, Cassill's fiery crusade essentially willed them into existence, "hardening their views" collectively as "an organized conspiracy of malcontents." This all distilled into a commitment to vengeance. "It is now for Verlin practically a vendetta."[22]

The *Daily Iowan* expanded the scope of the scandal by sensationalizing the firing of recent Workshop graduate Edmund Skellings from his faculty position at Frostburg State College for teaching *Lolita*. As word of his firing spread, Skellings immediately dashed off a letter to Engle, begging for support. "Old faculty thought you were vulgar, same with Snodgrass and Langland," he told Engle, hoping the director would sympathize with his own casting as "a dirty old man, contributing to the delinquency of students' morals, which everyone knows the Commies are mixed up with and other liberals."[23] The newspaper claimed—and with more than a hint of schadenfreude—that Skellings taught for the Workshop. Despite holding a Workshop MFA, however, he had never been an instructor for the program. Cassill took the misidentification as further evidence of the *Daily Iowan*'s conspiracy against the Workshop, which for him "was the last straw."[24]

Leaping to defend the Workshop's reputation, Cassill made it his first order of business to send a letter to the paper explaining that the shamed graduate had never taught at the Workshop. Next, he called Frostburg's president to say that Skellings "had disgraced the U of I while in the Workshop, and that the Workshop washed its hands of [him]." The rampage provoked the incredulous Skellings to ask, "Why would Verlin spew this gratuitous venom?" Skellings consulted Gerber to find a deeper motive, discovering that "Verlin was having personality problems and acting strangely." Skellings then learned that Cassill's strange behavior was directly linked to his vendetta against Gerald Stevenson, the alleged leader of the Kenney's conspiracy and perceived mastermind of the Huyck review. According to Skellings, at Cassill's lowest point, he had "threatened Gerry physically and libeled him publically in the workshop (Gerry is deciding whether to sue) and said he would take a hammer and personally destroy Kenney's and the Paper Place."[25]

Stevenson posed a major threat to Cassill primarily because of his powerful position as an editor of the underground press in Iowa City at the time. Stevenson had originally taken the reins of the *Iowa Defender* from Stephen Tudor, a disgruntled *Daily Iowan* editor bent on revenge against his former employer. Stevenson reinforced Tudor's vision for the *Defender* as an anti-establishment countercultural alternative to the *Daily Iowan*. Its initials *ID* symbolized its oppositional stance—and lack of restraint—toward the *DI*. Cassill was well aware of the radical anti-corporate bent of Stevenson's paper, which appeared weekly throughout the school year from 1959 to 1969 (except for 1966). A former special collections curator at the University of Iowa library, Stevenson held perhaps even greater power as proprietor of the Paper Place bookstore and the Qara Press. Combined with the *Iowa Defender*, these radical outlets formed the underground press of Iowa City, providing a potent liberal progressive critique of the university's policies and practices, especially as they became intertwined with corporate financial interests.[26]

Although Cassill was convinced Stevenson was the mastermind behind the Huyck attack, Skellings aptly diagnosed that the real source of the upheaval was the perception that Cassill had prostituted the Workshop for his own profit. Still worse, he had compromised his own standards to do it. "The Brit. Deal," he remarked, "was a commercialization of the University and Workshop name." The most damning evidence against Cassill was the deal's violation of his own conviction that "it was impossible to teach writing without personal contact," as Skellings pointed out.[27] Cassill's role as textbook author of the correspondence course enabled this faceless distant pedagogical arrangement that was totally adverse to the ideal he touted. How seriously would Workshop faculty really take the mission of educating correspondence students who would earn neither actual university credit nor a valid MFA? This was a clear case of not just compromising principles for money, but obliterating them. It was also the grain of truth in the criticism that nearly drove him to the brink of insanity.

By now beside himself in Hong Kong, helpless to save his sinking ship with each incoming tale of the worsening disaster, Engle finally received Cassill's testimony. In his letter, Cassill described Stevenson as "a local crank" trained in library science "who deeply loathes all Britannica enterprises." Although rife with paranoia and indignation, Cassill's account does acknowledge Huyck's noble aim of encouraging the program to return to original principles that might attract rather than discourage serious writers. Cassill discovered this after calling the disgruntled student into his office, where he girded himself for a volcanic confrontation that threatened to boil over into raised voices, frank invectives, and even fisticuffs. To Cassill's surprise, Huyck was operating less out of a personal vendetta than a desire to rescue the program from excessive commercialization. The student "eagerly asked if we weren't changing plans as a result of his intrusion. I told him no."[28] If Cassill's letter to Engle was any indication, it would appear that Huyck had achieved his agenda of initiating institutional reform specifically designed to tone down the promotion of the Workshop from its current shrill pitch.

Whereas letters from Justice, Skellings, and Cassill on the home front to Engle were frantic and desperate—all sent within weeks of each other representing a dizzying constellation of views of the controversy—damage control at Britannica was cool and collected. Britannica executive Gordon Dupee sent a letter to Engle in July, months after the smoke had cleared, in which he resolved to replace the scandalous brochure cover with a more dignified group portrait of the Workshop's principal faculty members. "The photo would be the one taken of Cassill, Justice, and yourself, rather than the one originally indicated by the advertising agency people" who had devised the pulp montage evoking sensational rather than literary fiction, much less poetry.[29] Engle was relieved to reach this resolution, which nonetheless failed to address the deeper problem of profiting from the sale of faux Workshop degrees by mail.[30]

Look Back in Anger

In this Cold War climate of government surveillance and suspicion, R. V. Cassill fell prey to his fear of a conspiracy in Iowa. His free gravitation between popular culture and literary art in France was a recipe for disaster at the Workshop in the early 1960s. This is mainly because Engle's work to bridge the gap between literature and commerce—spanning the deeper chasm between art and money, which the culture understood as mutually exclusive— had come to a head with the Britannica correspondence course. In 1951, Engle was actively promoting himself in precisely this manner through an aggressive campaign spearheaded by his publicity agent at W. Colston Leigh, Inc. The company compiled quotes on Engle's lecturing in a series of full-page magazine advertisements with the explicit objective of showcasing his vision for both academic and business audiences. Engle's marketing of his own speaking engagements positioned the Workshop as a viable partner with commercial trade and for-profit enterprise. Advertisements identified Engle as a friend of business appropriate for both academic and popular audiences.[31]

Cassill's sense of the state of literature reflects his paradoxical bitterness toward the mindless commercialization of "the short story and who is writing it in 1962." Engle had sounded Cassill on the topic for a magazine piece he was commissioned to write shortly before the Britannica scandal. Cassill took it as an opportunity to weigh in, ripping J. D. Salinger and the *New Yorker*. He groused that "one of the great disasters of the last fifteen years was the promotion of Shirley Ann Grau as a writer, just because some of her idiot notions of what the short story ought to be (perhaps given an assist by Martha Foley through Rita Smith and them) very superficially resembled the departures from realism of Eudora Welty and Flannery O'Connor." He fumed that "this is part of a larger pattern" in which "bad money drives good money out." Commercialism taints literary art, he ranted, pointing to how "Tillie Olsen's stuff resembles what certain 'serious' frauds in decades of writing classes were too often turning out." Reserving his deepest cut for the author of *The Catcher in the Rye*, he says, "then there's Salinger, who turns out to be an artist 'after all' in somewhat the same way Buster Keaton, the Marx Brothers, W. C. Fields, and even Laurel and Hardy turned out to be artists making important contributions to the 'development of film.' " Under the category of "minds I have loved [that] have prospered little of late," Cassill reserves praise for "George PE, Jim Hall, Flannery O'Connor, Florence Gould, Herb Wilner, Robie Macauley, J. F. Powers . . ."[32]

Cassill's bitterness toward the literary market's advancement of writers he considered superficial was just as intense as his spite toward university bureaucracy. He found particularly hollow the University of Iowa's administrative promise to increase funding for creative writing: "since the legislature was getting more 'liberal' they could now buy for Iowa a better place in the cultural sun."[33] Such spite is not surprising since Cassill was so grossly underpaid. More pressing still was the fact that John Gerber had sought the hiring of Oregon faculty member Robert Williams with tenure at the rank of associate professor in January 1965. Such a lucrative offer came as a direct affront to the perennially underpaid Cassill, and a breach of authority to Engle who was out of town when the hire was made. Cassill immediately demanded that he too be considered for promotion and tenure, but was denied. After he submitted his resignation, which had been looming since the Britannica incident, the committee on appointments and promotions (which included Engle) persuaded him to remain for a one-month "cooling off" period, during which he might reconsider carrying on in his former position.

Cassill withdrew his resignation, although he did anything but cool off during the ensuing month. Instead he marshaled an army of supporters who rained hellfire on Gerber and the university's new president Howard Bowen, circulating petitions to protect his place on the Workshop faculty. One former student, Andre Dubus, arranged a protest march on the Pentacrest, the main square of Iowa's campus, but was dissuaded by Engle, who feared the public display would destroy the program. Hardly a gesture of diplomacy, Cassill's vitriolic campaign was clearly the wrong tactic for securing lasting employment. Instead the assault functioned as a wild form of self-immolation. "Almost immediately," Gerber recorded in a department memo he stapled to Cassill's file, "he and his friends began a steady attack, orally and in letters, on certain individuals and groups within the Department." Now under pressure, Gerber suggested that the English department would "review Mr. Cassill's claims to tenure but not while subject to duress which is both unjustified and unjustifiable."[34] Convinced that Gerber had been "disarmed by the ploy" to withdraw his resignation, Cassill, in a last desperate act, made "a tactical offer to assume the directorship" during the spring of 1965.[35] No one, including himself, took it seriously. By the following fall, Cassill had begun a writer-in-residence position at Purdue University. On leave during the upheaval was Donald Justice, who returned to the Workshop in the fall. Engle requested a salary increase for Justice, but was denied because the administration had allocated the necessary finances for a new secretary. The Williams hire, the abuse of Cassill, and now the refusal to support Justice, his next strongest faculty member, combined to break Engle's spirit. He submitted his resignation, effective at the close of the spring semester in 1966, after which he immediately founded the International Writing Program.[36]

In his bitter diatribe "Why I Left the Midwest," Cassill blamed a climate in which young talent cannot thrive. To know finally that in Iowa "young writers are unthinkable" is the instance in which "one realizes the reality of his exile." Worse yet, Iowa is ignored in New York City, Cassill complained. "In the distorting mirror that the Midwest offered me in recent years, I saw reflected the pig who had been, not very gloriously, after all, to the culture market in New York, valued or ignored on the basis of his market value, his voice lost somewhere on the wind." A "sign painted on the wall of one or another of the public buildings" near the Iowa State Fair in Des Moines, reading, "*Where there is no vision the people perish,*" captured Cassill's attention. He read it "as a warning with a very personal application. Coupled with my instinct for survival," he recalled, "the sign said, '*Homo fugit.* Get out while you can!'" From that moment on, Cassill "made arrangements to move and withdraw [his] manuscripts from the University of Iowa library," transferring them to Brown University, where he accepted a visiting lecturer position, replacing the novelist John Hawkes in 1966.[37] Just one year before this epiphany, signs of his imminent departure were evident in his spirited invective, "Must Be Trouble in River City," published July 1965 in *Washington Post Book Week*.[38]

In his final meeting with President Bowen, Cassill charged that "expediency, political maneuvering, jockeying for personal advantage had prevented any clear articulation of the issues most important to the students and the concerned people of the state." The administrator simply replied that Cassill should "understand how that happened," since so much of his own fiction dealt with it. Leaning back in his chair, Bowen lit a cigarette and ran his fingers through his hair. "Then with a flick of his wrists and impatience in his tone, he said, 'If you feel the way you do, why don't you take your manuscripts and just GO-oooh!'"[39] So Cassill left, never to return to his birth state that had shaped and nurtured his personal character and professional identity.

Cassill's achievements at the Workshop were considerable. Among the most notable was the success of his student Margaret Walker, the first African-American woman writer from the Workshop to win critical acclaim. Originally written as her MFA thesis under Cassill, her novel *Jubilee* (1966) initiated a movement dedicated to contemporary aesthetic treatments of the slave past that would eventuate in Toni Morrison's *Beloved*, a work many regard as the greatest novel in the history of American literature.[40] In his sweeping dismissal of Iowa, Cassill clearly failed to appreciate his accomplishments with students such as Walker, and the progress he made with them. Not to be underestimated is his work with Raymond Chandler, whose writing embodied the principle of elevating popular forms to the level of literature that Cassill advanced throughout his career. This conviction was visible in Cassill's comment on Jim Thompson's *The Killer Inside Me* (1952) as a representative of how "the mode of the paperback original, husks and all, turns out to be excellently suited to the objectives of the novel of ideas."[41]

Cassill's notorious habit of disowning and defacing his own significant contributions to American literary culture did not end with the Iowa Writers' Workshop. In dramatic fashion rivaling his public rejection of all things Iowa, Cassill attempted to destroy a decade and a half of professional development in one speech. The speech took place at the fifteenth annual meeting of the Associated Writing Programs he had founded in 1967. Disgusted with its current trajectory, he declared the association irreversibly flawed and urged it to disband immediately, much to the horror of its loyal constituents. Capitalist corruption, he claimed, arose when faculty began "using other people's money—grants from their universities and arts agencies—[and] devised ways to get their own and one another's work into print, and then converted those publications into salary increments," as Louis Menand explains.[42] His stunned audience listened in disbelief as he pontificated on how "We are now at the point where writing programs are poisoning, and in turn, we are being poisoned by, departments and institutions on which we have fastened them."[43]

Greener pastures, it would seem, awaited Cassill at Brown University in Providence, Rhode Island, the location of his self-exile. But controversy followed him even there. Once again the university newspaper proved to be his nemesis. The staff of Brown's newspaper had caught wind of an *Esquire* article by Cassill, "Up the Down Co-Ed," a racy treatment of sex on campus reprising his previous fictional foray into the topic. "Verlin Cassill: Another D. H. Lawrence, or Just a Dirty Old Man?" the headline ran. Humiliated, Cassill decided to retreat rather than retaliate as he did with the Britannica controversy. Robert Day, his successor as head of the AWP, recalled his first meeting with Cassill. Due to the *Esquire* scandal just then hitting the headlines, "Verlin was having a bad day." Cassill handed Day a shoebox of three-by-five index cards. "These are the names and addresses of all the creative writing teachers and graduate programs in the country. This is AWP. It will need to be many things to many people, but at its soul it should always be for our students to find their life as writers, and less for us to establish our academic careers," he said warmly.[44]

The ruptures and fissures in the arc of Cassill's career occurred at the juncture between literature and commerce, forces in tension arising from Engle's larger vision of forging an alliance between business, art, and higher education. Ironically, the corporate third-party interests Cassill found so reprehensible in the university infrastructure at Iowa were exactly those he had fully engaged for the sale of his textbook *Writing Fiction* with the Britannica Workshop course. Just as he had pursued avenues toward elevating conventional popular fiction into novels of ideas, Cassill also transgressed into the forbidden territory of journalism and advertising for his methodology. In particular, "the form of the story (which owes much to McLuhan's analysis of the logic in advertising layout and the composition of a newspaper front page—and, therefore, by extension, owes much to ads on front pages) ought to indicate that character here is a product of cut-paste-and-paste editorializing, mine and the imperial ad-men's," he said in describing his work, making explicit the parallel between commercial marketing and his approach to short story writing.[45]

Cassill mined his Workshop experience for his best material. His career clearly benefited from his association with the program. His first collection of short stories, for example, appeared in a volume co-authored with the former Workshop teachers Herbert Gold and James B. Hall in 1957. Iowa provided the settings and characters of his stories that appeared in the collections *The Father and Other Stories* (1965) and *The Happy Marriage and Other Stories* (1966). "And In My Heart," which Clarence Andrews describes as a "thinly disguised *roman à clef*," features a writing student named Steve Forest who dreams of becoming the next Dostoyevsky. Forest finds himself embroiled in academic turf wars, mainly between older and younger faculty with divergent aesthetic approaches. Cassill's commentary on campus sex among co-eds again enters the scene, as Forest's love interest, a charismatic and alluring sorority girl, happens to also be a nymphomaniac.[46] Embedded in his stories are scores of references to Iowa, not the least of which is the literary pretense of its poets "trying to extend the Whitman catalogue of American goodies." He skewers the belief that the rural setting is fertile for the country idyll, and the feeling "that coming west of Chicago is, in itself, qualification of a poet." He writes, "the smell of horse dung does not automatically make it literature."[47] Cassill dismantles the myth just as surely as he helped construct it as an Iowa author. Ironically, Cassill believed his problems were in Iowa, when they were really in himself, as controversy followed him to Brown. The Workshop and Iowa nonetheless continued to influence his writings, which "carry with them a certain air of the creative writing class; even if they weren't produced in one," Bernard Bergzorn observed. One can "readily imagine these well-made pieces being put on the seminar table and opened up for examination."[48] The finish and technical brilliance of his work helped inspire a generation of writers who "can turn out a product that is as mechanically ingenious as the latest television set," as James Laughlin commented in 1957.[49]

Cassill idolized the aesthetic freedom and innovation of "the little magazines." He admired such outlets as *Perspective* in St. Louis, *Epoch, Accent*, and sophisticated literary quarterlies like *Kenyon* and *Hudson*. Little magazines arose in opposition to the allegedly standardized and uniform "*New Yorker* rule book" of conventions that transform writers into mere reporters of "points of sociological interest" who "reproduce with the utmost authenticity—the points of view, the tags, the mannerisms—and the customers love it, because often they can recognize themselves and get a self-appreciating laugh."[50] The backlash aligned with the anticommercial mission of graduate creative writing programs. But Cassill saw regionalism as the barrier separating Iowa from the aesthetic credibility associated with the little magazines. "The collective denial of the very concept of an Iowa writer" to Cassill limited the state's authors to such categories as "yokel poets" in the tradition of Edgar Lee Masters.[51] Cassill's venom toward this label surfaces in a telling passage from his early story "And in My Heart." In it, his character pinpoints Masters as the cause of the Iowa curse, demonizing him "for delaying the building of literature." "He shook himself and hissed, 'I do blame it on Masters. If the sonofabitch were here I'd hit him in the face. *I'd hit him in the face.*' He struck his knee with his fist." The fictional professor confesses, "Once I went to the trouble of finding out where Masters was buried, and I made the pilgrimage there to spit on his grave. Pork-barrel poetry is killing us," he proclaims, forecasting Cassill's own exodus to Rhode Island, never to set foot in Iowa again.[52]

5 • The Guru: Marguerite Young

Resplendent in her black woolen cape despite the stifling ninety-degree heat of late August, Marguerite Young cut a charismatic—if not downright eccentric—artistic presence at the Iowa Writers' Workshop. "I thought she was crazy," her student Bruce Kellner confessed. He quickly learned what her dedicated "sub-flock of young writers" knew.[1] She dwelled in fictional worlds that spawned sprawling manuscripts running thousands of pages long. The most conspicuous of them was the capacious novel *Miss MacIntosh, My Darling*, her greatest achievement, which won her the spotlight she had always yearned for. The project was two decades in the making. Virtually invisible by comparison was her other gargantuan effort, an eclectic 2,500-page biography of the radical Socialist Eugene Debs, which she never finished. At Iowa, her runaway popularity among students sparked jealousy from professors like Robert O. Bowen, who once brandished a large butcher knife menacingly at her during an Iowa City party. Trying to shake off his hard glares during conversation, Young whispered to her interlocutors, "Bob is going to kill me." Bowen's knife drew blood that night, if only his own. In his drunken rage he accidentally sliced his hand, bleeding "all over the countertop, the floor, himself." The wound was so severe that he was carted off to the emergency room, on the way screaming, "Goddamn! Goddamn Bruce Kellner!" in frustration that his star student had migrated to Young's cohort.[2]

Young's magnetic appeal to Workshop students, which drove other teachers like Bowen mad with envy, was overwhelmingly obvious to all present during the first fiction workshop meeting for fall 1956. Poised before the incoming class in flamboyant bohemian attire that made her colleagues appear staid by comparison, "she looked every bit the literary artist."[3] Forty new students crowded into the baking Quonset hut that day to select a mentor. Only a slim minority of the class opted to sign on with Ray West and Curtis Harnack, while the rest flocked to Young. Much of her allure derived from her reinvention of the novel in a project of colossal ambition and experimentation not seen since Melville or Proust. Many elite and influential journals had published portions of it, drawing attention from posh literary audiences, much to the consternation of her colleagues such as Bowen. His own stilted war novel *Bamboo* was largely ignored by both critical and popular readers.[4] In addition to her literary prowess, Young's supportive teaching style also clashed sharply with the harsh methods of faculty members such as John Berryman.

By her second year teaching in the program, Young had established a devout following of young writers dedicated to her belief in "using a fuller language for an imagination of plentitude."[5] This approach defied the program's overriding emphasis on condensed prose produced through a halting composition process rooted in negation and depersonalization. Much of her appeal came from her curiously nineteenth-century bearing and attitude toward creative expression, one bizarrely anachronistic in this era of New Criticism that placed a premium on curtailing and pruning imaginative flights, much less surrendering to them with wild abandon. Her intimacy with her coterie, whom she took on research outings in the dead of night to observe passengers disembarking a midnight bus and filing into a sad downtown café, alerted Workshop student William Murray to "the fine line between mentor and apprentice." Although he "would have liked it if she had asked me to sit with her," Murray, who was not included in this silent "coterie ritual," knew he would have been intruding and potentially calling attention to himself as an outsider.[6] Years later he recalled rushing from class to retch into the reeds beside the Iowa River after his story "Goats" had been destroyed by his classmates, when moments later he felt Young's consoling hand on his heaving shoulders.[7]

Achieving access to Young's inner circle promised nothing less than total liberation from the strictures of the workshop model and tyranny of New Critical creative methods. Young's refreshing tolerance of subject matter selection invited experimentation. "Oh, the subject matter doesn't matter!" she sang out. "I was having a romp letting my imagination go and not worrying too much about realism," Murray wistfully reminisced. Rather than Young herself, "who made you feel special aesthetically," the student body posed the greatest threat to creativity as a collective force capable of meting out lacerating criticism.[8] Young focused primarily on students' aesthetic growth.

Although her work as literary agent was far less conspicuous than Paul En-gle's, her deep concern for the reception of their writing in class carried over into the public realm, where she played an instrumental role in initiating their authorial careers.

Young's most famous student, John Gardner, Jr., the author of *Grendel* and *October Light*, which won a National Book Critics Circle Award in 1976, flour-ished under her literary tutelage. Gardner discovered his distinctive voice un-der her guidance, as he recalled in a 1971 interview, because "I was writing something different from what the other people in the Workshop were writ-ing." Like Young, he was averse to the damage of unproductive negative criti-cism and the stultifying conformity fostered by workshop sessions. "I didn't want any comments because some writers want to learn how to write correctly. What that really means is that they write exactly like everyone else." As one of the first serious writers to connect with Gardner, Young struck him as "so 'Left Bank' [that] I simply fell head over heels." Like so many of her students, Gard-ner benefited enormously from "the writerly validation" she instilled in him, all through her unique subversion of the workshop method of instruction.9

Parallel Universes

Stalking campus in the Iowa dusk like a figure out of Edgar Allan Poe's imagination, Marguerite Young's "presence was in her cape." Her mystique had a magnetic appeal to budding novelists and short story writers in the pro-gram, whom she commonly invited to her home. Once inside, they could see signs of the parallel universes she occupied. Her quirky blend of antebellum Gothic mysticism and Virginia Woolf stream of consciousness appeared in the form of a huge Civil War diorama. Figurines on horseback and tiny bugle boys populated "a plaster of Paris replica in living color of some battle scene or another," as Murray remembered.10 Perched menacingly on a hill in the miniature scene was a stuffed raven. In the mid-1950s, she was "about forty-five and with a face like a friendly basset hound, lank hair chopped off in a long Buster Brown or Prince Valiant bob," favoring "wide skirts and crisp blouses and often some eccentric necklace or brooch." Under the tutelage of Gertrude Stein, Young carried "a massive handbag over her shoulder always stuffed with food and manuscripts," Kellner observed.11 Although her tastes in attire and writing deviated from Stein's, Young had sat at her feet in Chicago working toward a master's degree in 1936, drawing confidence from the ex-ample of her radical individualism and unbridled creative expression.

Besides Stein, the other figure at Chicago who had the greatest impact on Young was Minna K. Weissenbach, whom she called "the most remarkable person I've ever known in my life."[12] Young had contacted the employment office at the University of Chicago in search of work to help with her finances, since her fellowship did not cover accommodations, and Weissenbach, known as "the opium lady of Hyde Park," hired Young to be her secretary. To Young's delight, Weissenbach was one of the first patrons of the university to support Edna St. Vincent Millay's career by providing her with free room and board during a key phase in her development. Millay went on to write what Richard Wilbur and other critics called "some of the best sonnets of the century," which earned her the Pulitzer Prize for poetry in 1923.[13] Young recalled how "the idea of sleeping in Millay's bed seemed to be the most marvelous thing that could ever happen to any young person."[14] The employment office, however, neglected to tell Young that the wealthy heiress who had financially underwritten Millay's spectacular career spent the majority of her days in alternate universes, hallucinating fantastic dreams.

In order to make these dreams as lyrical as possible, the aging matron requested that Young read Shakespeare to her, thereby accompanying her opium-fueled visions with the sounds of the greatest dramatic verse ever written. At first shocked, Young soon warmed to the only task Weissenbach set for her as personal secretary. "I'm looking for someone to take a vacation with me away from the modern world. Would you like to come?" With some trepidation, Young replied with a guarded, "Yes." Her only instruction was, "If I am passing into an opium dream," she said, "pay no attention. Just go ahead and read—or go home."[15] Young proceeded to read, soon growing comfortable and by degrees exhilarated at providing the verbal passport for the old woman's journey to another time and place, setting the keynote for her hallucinogenic experience. This was precisely the role she wished to play as a novelist leading readers into parallel universes. Like the fiction Young aspired to write, every detail of the Opium Lady's house exuded allusive literary wonder, especially "a silver drinking cup" on the night stand "which had belonged to John Keats, a little mosaic Persian letter set, and a beautiful bird with a seashell."[16]

When Young remarked on how "everyone fell under the spell of the opium lady" of Hyde Park during her graduate apprenticeship at the University of Chicago in 1935–1936, she could have been describing her own effect on the Workshop student body when she served on the faculty from 1955 to 1957.[17] She transfixed students with a combination of close journalistic scrutiny of human behavior and a penchant for lofty flights of ethereal mysticism. Unlike the perpetually high matron of Hyde Park, who depended on chemical stimulus, Young's passport to her fictional worlds relied on no foreign substances. "She drank little or nothing alcoholic" and took no drugs, according to her protégé Kellner. This was because she had naturally inhabited another realm, even as a girl growing up in Indianapolis. There, "she had known a doctor who delivered imaginary babies" and "a virtuoso violinist who played without strings on his instrument," as well as an electric-chair factory with a garden whose flowers wilted with every execution.[18] Right out of high school, Young accepted employment with a chair manufacturer, which she recalled was "the most interesting, strange, horrifying experience." Her friend Carson McCullers, the southern gothic novelist, "thought it would be smart to tell everybody that I used to work in an electric chair factory." She used to imagine that "Indiana apples fell up as easily as they fell down if you held them the right way."[19]

Young's historical imagination was also uncanny. "On occasion she saw Edgar Allan Poe hurrying along the street in Greenwich Village," Kellner said.[20] "Once I dreamed that I was in Iowa City at my house," she recalled. Present in the dream was Henry James, "sitting in a corner pouring whiskey into his high silk hat." The frequency of his visits rose when she was in the throes of writing Miss MacIntosh, My Darling. His muse-like presence spurred her on, infusing her with the courage and confidence to continue with the unwieldy, increasingly amorphous manuscript constantly on the verge of slipping from her control. "He would come to me in my dreams . . . and read what I had done," she recalled. "Sometimes I was typing, and sometimes I was writing in long hand beautiful pages." "That's beautiful," the apparitional Henry James whispered gently, gazing at her with kind, loving eyes, "go right ahead . . . go right ahead. You're the late twentieth-century development of what I was doing."[21] She used precisely this assuring parental hush with her students, never hesitating to say, "that's beautiful," when their writing warranted it.

In class, Young would startle her pupils by alerting them to the presence of impossible visitors. "When I'm teaching, I often say, 'Come in, Mr. James . . .' My students love this. I will stop . . . 'Oh, how do you do, Henry James, won't you be seated.'" Her classroom full of creative writers, obsessed with configuring fictional characters and worlds of their own, were invariably transfixed: "they all look, [thinking] he's really there." A parade of select literary luminaries made cameo appearances in Young's class. "Boswell will come; Cervantes, I spend a great deal of time with him. I entertain: I see Emily Dickinson, quite often, Virginia Woolf and Dickens." Poe was a favorite. She would see him not just as a novelty to enliven the drab teaching environs of Iowa's corrugated steel army barracks, but "all the time. I see him on misty nights on Sheridan Square, when the rain's falling; he's going into that little cigar store to get a cigar. I am on very close terms with Poe."[22] While living in Greenwich Village, the literary past surrounding her was palpable. "Oh, how I love our contiguity to the sacred past!" she effused in a letter to Engle. "I am right around the corner from Melville, Henry and William James, E. A. Poe, Whitman, Elinor Wylie. Would you believe these ghosts could mean so much to me?"[23]

Despite such conjurings, Young's journalistic bent grounded her in reality. A vast portion of her writings appeared in the *New York Times Book Review*, *The Nation*, *Vogue*, *Mademoiselle*, *The Kenyon Review*, and *The Conscientious Objector*. Although the complex interiority of the characters in her fiction seems otherworldly, she maintained that all of them "are recognizable, true to life." They provided an imaginative entrance into the subjectivity of real people such as those disembarking the midnight bus in downtown Iowa City she and her students silently observed. In addition to such observation of strangers and intimates in her life, "I get my characters from the daily newspapers, and from biographies and medical histories and thousands of sources." The journalist in her proclaimed, "I believe, like Browning," whose poem "The Ring and the Book" is based on an actual murder in Rome, "that the poet is a reporter."[24] In this sense, she tied her fantastical flights to lived events and human history according to her insistence that "I do not believe in inventing characters." Kellner later confirmed that "Under every fantasy there was a hard truth; under every illusion, there was a reality." Crucially, these were "not always the same reality, and nobody else's but hers."[25] The opium lady of Hyde Park, for example, was integral to the formation of Young's Catherine Cartwheel, a drug-addicted heiress living in a cavernous mansion on the Atlantic, a stormy coast that serves as a creative extension of Lake Michigan's windy shore.

The two-room Iowa City apartment Young occupied overflowed with the accouterment of her imagination. "In what should have been her kitchen," Kellner observed, "stacks of typing paper in various stages of completion crowded a trestle table for space with her typewriter; books spilled over shelves into stacks against the walls." With the air of a used bookshop, the other room in the apartment contained a myriad of assorted models, gadgets, and figurines, "a remarkable collection of gimcracks and doodads, including a lot of toys and ornaments" crowding every surface. Throughout the apartment were books of all varieties amid ubiquitous stacks of manuscripts. Sleeping and eating seemed secondary, if not entirely unnecessary, to the life of creative imagination that sustained her. None of her friends recall her ever preparing a proper meal; nor could they discern what served as the bedroom. "I don't know where she slept," Kellner said.[26]

"That Well of Energy"

Among Young's special gifts was the capacity to defuse hostility. This attribute served her well when tensions ran high during group workshop sessions at Iowa. Young's own experience as a professional writer had taught her that the publishing industry, populated by potentially disapproving editors and critics, could be devastating to an author in the early stages of a career. She therefore made every effort to mollify, and in some cases preempt, critical resistance to her students' writing. In the process, she avoided bland universal approval that might have washed out the diverse continuum of responses to literature represented in the mid-twentieth-century reading public. Instead, she intended to generate supportive feedback in place of savage attacks that euphemistically passed as "constructive criticism." She identified with Virginia Woolf's predicament as a woman writer who faced profound resistance from the male-dominated critical community. Woolf dramatized such resistance in *To the Lighthouse* through the character of Lily Briscoe, an artist struggling against "Mr. Tansley whispering in her ear, 'Women can't write, women can't paint.' "[27] Young's predilection for rescuing writers from unfair criticism appears in her review of Woolf's posthumous *Haunted House*. In it, she "resurrects Virginia Woolf from the dust which has been thrown on her by a number of critics who think, like Dr. Johnson and Bishop Berkeley's nonmaterialism, that material is real because one cannot walk through a closed door or who feel that such a view of life is precious or exclusive."[28] The impulse came from her desire to remove rather than erect barriers to the creative process. She believed the elaborate world of her ornate imagination, like those of her students, was worth defending.

The sort of critical resistance embodied by Woolf's Charles Tansley left Young humiliated at the hands of an unfair review in *Time* magazine. Fortunately, she had been buoyed by praise from the far more reputable *New York Times Book Review*, which was a major arbiter of literary taste. *Time* magazine's assault on *Miss MacIntosh, My Darling* represented the sort of destructive criticism she tried to protect her Iowa students from. The worst critical abuse she endured consisted of sexist slurs that left her the "victim of some brutal male reviewers. 'If she had gotten married, she never would have *done* this,' they would write," as she recalled in an interview.[29]

The highest praise of her career came from Nona Balakian, one of the four original founders of the National Book Critics Circle. The Nona Balakian Citation for Excellence in Reviewing was known as "the most prestigious award for book criticism in the country."[30] At a celebration in honor of Young held by the American Professors of Creative Writing in 1983, Balakian delivered the keynote address, affirming that in *Miss MacIntosh, My Darling*, "with all its dirgelike moments, there is a salutary, nourishing quality about this book that links it to the great classics of American literature." "Only an American could have written it," she claimed, describing Young as "a remarkable woman of wide vision, humor, compassion and enduring strength."[31] In an earlier essay, Balakian lauded the novel as "the crystallization of an historical evolution in the novel form and of the shake-up of the notion of reality that has occurred in our life-time."[32] Anaïs Nin, Young's longtime friend and fellow novelist, claimed the book spoke with a collective conscience, representing "nocturnal America, just as Don Quixote became the spirit of Spain, and Ulysses that of Ireland."[33]

Young's acute concern for literary reception originally mounted with the publication of *Angel in the Forest*, a novel that began as a collection of sixty interrelated ballads she first crafted in blank verse in 1940 as a Ph.D. candidate at the University of Iowa. There she met Paul Engle, who alerted her to the professional potential of her poetry. After a brief stint teaching with the Indiana Writers' Conference at Indiana University and Shortridge High School in Indianapolis, Young returned to Iowa City in 1942 on a creative writing fellowship arranged by Engle in conjunction with a lecturer position in the English department. By transforming *Angel in the Forest* into prose under the influence of the Workshop students and faculty, she began to master the style that made her famous, eventually honing it into the byzantine circuitous prose poetry that became the signature of *Miss MacIntosh, My Darling*. Her mention in *Angel* of "being tired of the Sinclair Lewis view of middle America as a continual Main Street" led to an unexpected encounter years later at the Algonquin Bar, where she "was accosted by a red-faced man who told me he was Sinclair Lewis." She recalled how Lewis was "so grateful that I was seeing the Middle West from my own point of view and not as an imitation of his."[34] Concurrent with *Angel in the Forest* was her work on a book of poetry titled *Moderate Fable*. Combined with teaching responsibilities as a lecturer and doctoral study, these projects made for a life in Iowa City fully immersed in literature. The stacks of typewritten manuscript pages sprouted and mushroomed, gradually taking over her apartment as the fruits of her playful creative spirit and hard-won literary labor. She loved those stacks, as can easily be seen in the most well known photograph of her, embracing four thick bundles of manuscript pages, resting her head lovingly on the massive heap. Her face bears the unmistakable look of an author's simultaneous relief and joy at the offspring of her creative mind.[35]

The first major break of Young's career came when Engle brought her in contact with Frank Taylor, an acquisitions editor from the New York publisher Reynal and Hitchcock. As she headed home on an empty street in Iowa City during a midnight snowstorm, a stranger in a trench coat emerged from the shadows. She wheeled around, darting in the opposite direction. "Miss Young?" Taylor called in a cosmopolitan tenor. She glanced over her shoulder at her future editor gliding toward her. He smiled broadly, extended his hand to introduce himself, and breathlessly explained that in his attaché case was the book contract that would spring her career.[36] Angel in the Forest earned Young an American Association of University Women fellowship for 1943–1944, an award that prompted her temporary leave from her lectureship and doctoral studies at Iowa. She was on her way to Bleecker Street in Greenwich Village, the heart of literary bohemian culture in New York City. Her ascendance into the powerful inner circle of American letters was imminent. The next five years would bring a Guggenheim fellowship and inclusion in a group of twenty-seven of the nation's most prominent authors, led by the Nobel Prize winner Sinclair Lewis. New York began to look and feel like home to her, as she rapidly made herself a prominent figure in Greenwich Village. "In the Village I seem to be known as that 'well of energy,' " she wrote in a letter to Engle in February 1945. Unmarried and without children, her outpouring of production had more than filled that void in her solitary life. Writing made her life rich with the wild opportunity of radical independence. "My aim is to support myself by writing," she told Engle, admitting, "though that may be a rather foolish aim." The romantic in her could not resist. "Who knows, I might swing it?" she said, peering into her future, "especially as I have neither chick nor child?"[37]

In a densely typewritten single-spaced letter to Engle from New York, with her signature coffee stains in half circles at the corners, Young referenced her emergence into professional authorship as a sort of literary maternity. Writing weeks before the publication of Angel in the Forest, she realized that her book of poems, Moderate Fable, was to appear simultaneously with the novel. "All of a sudden, I was rather overwhelmed. It's like being the mother of twins!" Ecstatic, she could see how suddenly "everything doubled, and you hardly realize the full significance of the fact."[38] She intended not only to receive strong reviews, but also "fat sums" to realize her dream of economic autonomy, in the spirit of Woolf's *A Room of One's Own*. She therefore charged Engle with the task of lobbying on her behalf for a Guggenheim fellowship. Both *Angel in the Forest* and *Moderate Fable* "have earned high praise from critics, which fact pleases me more than anything," raising her expectations. "I am so anxious that it sell! They predict that it will, but you know the old saying—many a slip betwixt the cup and the lip, etc." In this mood of self-advocacy—justifiable on behalf of her literary children she was sending out into the world—she turned the subject to Iowa. Her matriculation toward the Ph.D. there had slowed due to a new classical language requirement instituted by Norman Foerster, one of the founders of the Iowa Writers' Workshop. "Can't you get Foerster to let down the restrictions as to the Greek and Latin?" she demanded. "I hate to think of myself as memorizing verbs when I could be writing." Writing was her highest priority. Despite her insistence that "I am going to get the Ph.D.," she never did. She made true on her other plans. "I don't want to teach for years to come. I am planning on returning to New York" after a trip to Europe.[39] Engle had wanted her to return to Iowa City to take on a faculty position at the Workshop, but at this stage in her career, New York, Naples, and Rome occupied her through the early 1950s. She finally landed in Iowa City in 1954 after being lured to the Workshop on a Rockefeller Foundation Fellowship secured by Engle.

Despite holding off Engle's invitation to return to Iowa City and join the Workshop faculty, Young maintained close contact with him, utilizing his network of connections and financial resources for career advancement. Her solicitation of Engle's support for the Guggenheim in her letter of December 1947 had the desired effect, as she received the fellowship the following year. Her surprisingly direct request revealed a commercially savvy side of Young that understood the system of rewards and advancement in the literary market. That business sense belied her otherwise detached appearance. "If you have the inclination ever," she implored him, "I wish you'd do me a favor! Write to Mr. Moe and beg him to give the Guggenheim to me for *Miss MacIntosh, My Darling*—won't you—and tell him as specifically about you and it as you can."[40] Her tone lowered to a conspiratorial whisper. "Paul," she wrote, "you are responsible for all my good fortunes—you are the one who started me off on the right road."[41] She needed him now.

Engle delivered. He both published a glowing review of *Angel in the Forest* and stirred support for her Guggenheim award. "That was a beautiful review," she gushed, "and I thank you. It will undoubtedly be quoted in the advertising," she added, knowing that his intention was to provide commentary on the book with an eye toward its commercial promotion. She catalogued the journals that favorably received the book, "*N.Y. Post, Sun, World-Telegram*, Chicago papers, *Saturday Review*, etc.," lamenting that the *New York Times* "panned it." Engle's review proclaimed that Young wrote like an angel, an assertion that also appeared in the *Saturday Review* in a notice by Ben Ray Goodman. "He couldn't have seen yours," she said, basking in the glow of their nearly identical expressions of praise, which captured precisely the ethereal quality she had hoped to convey. Complimenting Engle's review "for its discernment and balance," she chided a notice on the work by Orville Prescott, who, in his bombast and trumpery, "blew his head off" in her estimation. Plans for promotion were firmly in place, she reported with resolve, to bring this book to the literary community and beyond, to the masses. Speaking engagements at the Boston Bookfair were to follow a week in New Harmony, Indiana, dedicated to "*Life* magazine which will do a picture essay on 'Angel.' " Fame was upon her, and she adored the adulation. "I've been wined and dined and beflowered until my *knees* groan."[42] She dressed the part to promote the work. The poet Amy Clampitt remembered her angelic ensemble of "a coronet of primroses to match an improbably mod dress of the same color" at a party celebrating the publication of *Angel in the Forest*.[43]

The following fall of 1945, Young returned Engle's favor with what she called her best "commercial review" for his book of poetry *American Child*. She dashed off a letter to him after she had "just mailed to the *Chicago Sun* my three-page review," assuring him that it was designed to reach a mass audience. "I deliberately evaded literary criticism" in order to establish "some value for you in the practical realm—a commercial review, suggesting the book as a Christmas gift, for example." Buoyed by a healthy advance on *Miss MacIntosh, My Darling*, Young was in a position to repay the favor of Engle's earlier positive review. She felt secure in her new identity as a "Scribner's author with Max Perkins as my editor." Her literary success had a financial measure, an equation that had always resonated with Engle. "I received a huge advance from Scribner's, one which assures my independence for at least another year or so." She allowed that "the novel progresses, but slowly," estimating not "to be finished for at least another year."[44] In fact it was another two decades before the novel finally appeared, under Scribner's imprint, in 1965, making it one of the most ambitious works in the history of American literature. The *Nashville Banner* heralded *Miss MacIntosh, My Darling* as "the most important work in American literature since . . . *Moby-Dick*."[45] The compari-son was apt, since Young's tome, like Melville's, and Proust's for that matter, "is too long for general consumption now." Melville's admirers, who included Pablo Picasso, did not surface until seventy years after the publication of *Moby-Dick*, and Nona Balakian predicted that "just as it took fifty years for Proust's work to reach public accessibility," Young's universal recognition would have to wait, since "*Miss MacIntosh* is to our era what Proust's work was for an earlier one."[46]

Iowa lacked the literary legacy of New York, but it held a distinct advantage in the sustained aesthetic collaboration between faculty and students built into the institution. With no students or close colleagues in New York, the gloomy past of places like Fire Island, by contrast, could haunt her with its transfixing energy. She regretted, for example, not sharing her visit to Fire Island with Engle, "a beautiful, desolate place—off the coast of which, as you remember Margaret Fuller drowned with a cargo of marble statues." Fuller, an author possessing a similar mystic bent grounded in journalistic powers of observa-tion, epitomized the romantic intensity of Young's ambition. She saw author-ship embodied in "the ocean there [that] is wild and fierce and transcendental," a force that generates creativity. "I find my novel flourishes best in a salt world!" Young effused, only to realize that, in Greenwich Village, "Alas, there is no salt here." Europe beckoned as an escape from her narrow confines. "My orbit is a small one—I hardly ever go above Fourteenth Street—and when I do it's a great adventure," she explained to Engle. Flashing a wild urge to "go far, far away—maybe to Judea," she joked, "Maybe I'll become a citizen of Judea. What do you think?"[47]

Although Judea did not make her itinerary, Rome did. There she met the magisterial Marguerite Caetani, Princess di Bassiano. Young was enamored with Caetani and her literary journal *Botteghe Oscure*. She later capitalized on the connection to secure the publication of her story "The Opium Lady" in its tenth issue. Young further utilized Caetani's blessing on returning from Eu-rope to Iowa City on the Rockefeller Foundation Fellowship that Engle ar-ranged for the completion of her novel. Playing the role of literary agent, Young made certain to promote the best of her students' work for publication in Caetani's journal. One of them, Peter Merchant, recalled how Young's workshop method brought about the unexpected result of his being published in the *Botteghe Oscure* and other literary periodicals, despite that pedagogical method's defiance of the program's more conventional approach to profes-sional development.

Although it was not Greenwich Village, the Workshop that Merchant encountered included a clear sense of togetherness. "The closer one approaches
the Workshop itself—its offices, its students—the more concentrated this
sense of a truly literary *community* becomes," as critic Andrew Levy observed.
In the main offices, Merchant was overwhelmed with signs of this insular
enclave on bulletin boards showcasing the famous writers and their
children—"Workshop babies"—born or conceived in Iowa City; the phone
ringing with calls from Nobel Prize winners; bookshelves loaded with volumes penned by Iowa alumni and faculty. But unlike Young's prior residence
in Greenwich Village, in the heart of one of the world's most diverse and
densely populated urban centers, Iowa City's tiny population magnified the
insularity of the creative writing collective represented at the Workshop. Without the distractions of New York City's endless boroughs and neighborhoods
full of culture and commerce, Iowa City's rural isolation intensified the intimacy of students and instructors alike, distilling and concentrating both camaraderie and competition. Students were well aware of the futility of the
workshops themselves as learning experiences. They understood that "if [they]
wanted constructive criticism of [their] work, the last place to go would be a
community of recent college graduates all wanting to be writers, all competing
for the same slender perks."[48] No one understood this paradox better than
Young, whose workshops conformed to protocol in form only.

Not Killing Your Darlings

Peter Merchant's tutelage under Young typifies how the construction
of creative community at the Workshop cracks under the pressure of "an urban planner's equivalent of the ambivalent rejection of the romance of
the artist, and the uneasy embrace of literary professionalism," as Levy notes.
"The dream of authorship is so strong that it moves the landscape."[49] Young
firmly believed that the path to that dream was not through depersonalized
writing obsessed with omission. As in her advice to Merchant that he
should expand rather than condense his writing, guidance that was also
integral to Murray's and Kellner's creative development, she instead felt
the dream of authorship was rooted in the depths of the psyche. There,
she believed, the writer must surrender conscious control of narrative
convention. "Stop being afraid of yourself," she advised Merchant. "Let go.
Explore the phantasmagoric below the surface. Allow your unconscious to
take over."[50]

Merchant had been trained from the beginning to "cut your darlings—you have to prune your rosebush ruthlessly." After doing just that with his first assignment, he handed it to Young marked up, with line after line crossed out. He offered to retype it, but she said she could read it in its current state. Next to every omission, Young wrote, "As was." "I tried to cut all the dead wood, and you want me to keep it?" Merchant asked, exasperated that she would have him undo his painstaking pruning. She retorted, "You've crossed out the best parts of your writing." His rational mind had interfered with his most probing insights. He had cut the line, "She saw the sun glittering on the hot-house roofs and wondered why they didn't crack from the heat," claiming it was "nonsense. Hothouse roofs don't crack from sunlight." Young would have none of this, asking him rhetorically, "Her fear of sex has nothing to do with her fantasy about glass shattering? Come, now." Merchant then went about implementing her suggestion to "put back all those fantasies. You can cut the logistical realities—they don't matter and they're dull."[51] In less than a month, the manuscript swelled beneath his hand to three hundred pages.

Merchant's manuscript was the subject of a mini-workshop of three students, Bruce Kellner, Carl Van Vechten (who would later become Gertrude Stein's biographer), and Richard Kim, selected by Young. The group gathered at his house and listened as he read deep into the night, finishing at 2 A.M. The consensus was that it was a beautiful story, but the denouement was lacking. "You will suffer, and then you'll find it," Kim said, in a prophecy that came true. The concluding chapter had been rejected by Merchant's publisher and proved troublesome. Then, Merchant wrote, in a rush of creative energy fueled by Young, "suddenly and effortlessly, I typed the last chapter in about two hours, and that was it." The key was the discovery of his unconscious that unlocked the fantasies of his characters. Merchant was now aware that his training under Young was not without its professional and financial rewards. "By the end of the first year, I sold my story . . . to a British publisher," a feat that made him "wild with excitement and pride."[52]

Much to the surprise of others in Merchant's workshop class, publication flowed freely from Young's unorthodox approach to teaching. One of Merchant's classmates (unnamed in his account), "a wiry tough Iowan with a caustic wit," arrived in the class deeply skeptical of Young's methods, openly smirking at her mystical flights. He secretly showed Merchant a scathing parody of Young he had written that cruelly mocked her fascination with the "phantas-ma-goric."[53] After receiving his work, Young calmly invited the abrasive youth to her home to discuss ways of improving the story. After "a long session with her," they went for a beer at Kessler's. Leaning on the bar, he stared straight ahead. "I've changed my view," he said, his once mocking voice now earnest and full of resolve. "There's more to my story than I'd thought," he realized, tacitly acknowledging that there was also more to Young than he had thought. After deep revisions, under her expert guidance, the piece landed in the pages of *Botteghe Oscure*, the aesthetic purveyor of precisely the "phantas-ma-goric" fiction he had sent up. The journal paid him "what seemed to us all an enormous sum." To Merchant's astonishment, the satirist "was the first of our group to be published."[54] Young's acumen for literary business also enabled her to realize, in retrospect, that her 1,200-page magnum opus escaped her intended audience, because "*Miss MacIntosh, My Darling* would have sold many more copies had I published one volume at a time."[55]

In addition to understanding the pragmatics of establishing a viable literary career, Young knew the motivation to write drew from a well of deep psychological need. In one workshop, she asked "Why do you all write?" One student paraphrased Samuel Johnson by saying, "Anyone who doesn't write for money is a blockhead." Another cited Milton's maxim that "Fame is the spur" driving all authorship. Others rendered more personal motives. "Because my father never listens to me," one confessed. Immortality was the reason another student took up the pen, who proclaimed, "Before I die, I want to leave behind, 'one poem as cold/ and passionate as the dawn,' as Yeats said." Young leveled her eyes at them. "You all write," she said, "because you want to be loved."[56]

Young herself wrote to be loved; she taught as a form of expressing her love. Merchant was astonished by the time and energy she committed to her students, especially since the "professional survival" of faculty "depends little on their teaching, and a lot on their own publication."[57] Her encouragement to Iowa students like Murray to "try on a style," was rooted in her belief that "style is thinking." She refused the assumption shared by many elite writers at the Workshop that talent was innate. Like Emerson's concept of the infinitude of private man, she instead believed in a radically democratic notion of creative power that is "almost a commonplace, something that almost everyone shares—and most people dream." The difference between Merchant before he encountered Young and after his tutelage followed the pattern of the hundreds of students she mentored at Iowa. They first approached her as "dully neutral" writers, each with "a very active tollkeeper, turning many things back," a symptom she diagnosed as a fear "of writing what he really thinks and feels."[58] The Workshop culture, in her view, tended to play on such inhibitions. Working against this institutional norm, she propelled her students to new levels of creative achievement.

Young suggested to all of her students that, as D. J. Enright said of Thomas Mann, "it takes a sound realist to make a convincing symbolist."[59] Powerful creative writing, she urged, is "based upon a close observation not only of the inner world of sleep and dreams, but of the outer world of contemporary and historical event which saves the writer from mechanical fantasies."[60] Reportorial observation of her contemporary world, such as the weary passengers stepping off the midnight bus in Iowa City, provides access to the interiority of the characters in *Miss MacIntosh, My Darling*. "The bus-driver was whistling, perhaps in anticipation of his wife." She envisions him driving "erratically, perhaps because of the heavy mist" and veering "off into a ditch," a scene unmistakably drawn from the endless sea of farmland surrounding Iowa City, where he "and his three passengers would be killed, our dismembered heads rolling in a corn field of withered corn stalks."[61] Her overstuffed apartment brimming with tokens of her imaginary life bespoke the bus driver's real identity as a "bachelor, perhaps even some mad Don Quixote chasing windmills."[62]

In Iowa City, her closest friends Gustav and Leola Bergmann kept up a vigorous correspondence with her for decades beginning in the 1950s. As late as December 1983, long after Young had left the Workshop, she revealed to Leola a secret desire she would never act on, but one that speaks volumes of her affinity for the community of academic life. "I always thought I wanted to write an academic novel," she confessed, "but know that without limitless years ahead and other commitments, I never will." Too deeply committed to her biography of Eugene Debs, and nearing the end of her life, she knew this dream was out of reach. The works she had read in this genre convinced her she could do better. "Have you read Katherine Shattuck's Narrowest Circle? Or did you read Elizabeth Hardwick's novel about that tuxedo murder?" she said, alluding to *The Simple Truth*.[63] It alerted her to how one "can do better than the latter which evoked perception in favor of abstraction and generality," areas she considered her strong suit.[64] Instead she pressed forward with her Debs project, which took on a life of its own, exceeding in manuscript pages and notes her gargantuan project of *Miss MacIntosh, My Darling*. In the absence of a novel of ideas to write, the Debs manuscript was a nonfictional substitute, a capacious intellectual journey through history and culture, indicative of that seemingly unlimited "well of energy" her neighbors in Greenwich Village identified nearly a half century before. Although she passed away in 1995 before completing the epic three-volume history, *Harp Song for a Radical: The Life and Times of Eugene Victor Debs* appeared posthumously under the editorial care of Charles Raus. As she lived out her final years in the Village, she became something like a literary Rip Van Winkle—a figure from a bygone era, beloved and endearing, flush with fascinating tales from the past. After first meeting her on Bleecker Street, the Iowa-born poet Amy Clampitt aptly remarked that Young "was and still is, part of the neighborhood, a lingering monument to a literary bohemia that has all but vanished."[65]

6 • The Turncoat: Robert Lowell

One muggy afternoon during a workshop session on campus at the Iowa Writers' Workshop, James B. Hall received a particularly thorough savaging at the hands of his instructor and peers that left him a beaten and broken man. "I went home limp, with a headache," through the sponge-humid late August heat. "It's a terrible thing to be twenty-five, to have survived other things for so long," including five years of live combat in World War II, "and not be able to hold back the tears when your poems and stories got what they deserved."[1] Receiving criticism from literary lions on the Workshop faculty like Pulitzer Prize and National Book Award winner Robert Lowell could reduce even the most grizzled of veterans to tears. Lowell "was both aggravating and helpful," according to his former student Robert Dana. "In conferences, his strategy seemed to be to give with the right hand and take away with the left." Had he been uniformly cruel, Lowell might have been easier to handle. But his chameleonic nature meant "if he complimented one aspect of your poem, he was sure, in the next breath, to comment adversely on another."[2] While he found hope in "a spiral notebook full of failed drafts" by Dana, proclaiming, "I expect you will be publishing soon," he frowned upon other students with great promise like Philip Levine. Detecting Lowell's Boston Brahmin bias against his Detroit Jewish immigrant background—his father sold used auto parts for a living—Levine knew "I could write nothing that pleased Lowell, and when at the end of the semester he awarded me a B, I was not surprised." He confronted him, demanding an explanation. " 'You have come the farthest,' Lowell drawled, which no doubt meant I had started from nowhere." Levine, a future poet laureate of the United States, pressed him, asking "Then why the B?" Lowell averted his eyes and muttered absurdly, "I've already given the A's out."[3]

Workshop students faced profound difficulty reading the mercurial Lowell, who taught at Iowa for three semesters on two separate faculty appointments in the early 1950s. Even harder to decipher was precisely where Lowell stood on Iowa and its famous writing program. Today's Workshop public relations materials even admit, "it is almost impossible to pinpoint exactly how the poet [Lowell] regarded the early literary hub."[4] Workshop members have been obsessed with the question of Lowell's estimation of the program, due to his stature as "the unofficial poet-laureate of post-World War II America," on the path to becoming, "by something like a critical consensus, the greatest American poet of the mid-century, probably the greatest poet now writing in English," according to critic Richard Poirier.[5]

Since he had received only lukewarm treatment as Lowell's protégé, W. D. Snodgrass found himself the victim of backhanded—if not entirely disingenuous—praise for his masterpiece, *Heart's Needle*, written under his mentor's guidance. Lowell had already slighted Iowa in one of the most public ways imaginable, by calling it sterile in the dust jacket blurb of his own best student's book, which he was instrumental in creating. *Heart's Needle*, Lowell later acknowledged, inspired him to utilize "the keyboard as a mirror" in his intensely introspective *Life Studies*, the work that won the National Book Award in 1960.[6] Confessing that his pupil "did these things" with self-disclosure in lyric verse "before I did," decades later Lowell allowed for the possibility that "he may have influenced me though people suggested the opposite."[7]

The locus of Lowell's vacillating judgment of the Workshop extended from its surrounding rural Midwest culture to the program's preferred instructional method and the students' writing itself. Did Lowell find fault specifically in the Workshop model for creative writing, one that placed faculty and students in the role of the exacting editors questioning every detail of their diction and syntax? Or was he a turncoat by nature and temperament, chronically attacking those who loved him? Was his venom toward Iowa an expression of an older version of the bully he had been as a schoolboy, a terror who as a Harvard undergraduate physically assaulted his own father and later abused his first wife? Did his nickname "Cal," short for Caliban of Shakespeare's *The Tempest* and the Roman emperor Caligula, represent the impulsive base dark half of his personality? Or was he the genteel Boston Brahmin, carrying the most refined literary lineage in Workshop history, one tracing back to his great granduncle James Russell Lowell and cousin once removed Amy Lowell? Was this a brute or an elite man of letters?

A Virtue of Negation

For most of his life, Robert Lowell was planning on leaving. His dizzying array of thirty-nine addresses over the course of his lifetime attests to the no-madic existence he led, from the moment he first renounced his New England roots to flee for the South to his transatlantic crossings that led him to Iowa in early 1950. Lowell left his first two wives (the second after twenty-three years), vacillated wildly between university teaching posts, and swore off a fifty-cigarette-a-day addiction with steely resolve, only to return to it with new zeal. He staunchly resisted the United States government's role in World War II at a time when conscientious objection was almost unheard of and certainly lacked any of the cultural cachet of the Vietnam War protests he would fa-mously back with Norman Mailer in the late 1960s. His principled resistance earned him a federal prison sentence of a year and a day (reduced to five months for good behavior), much harder time than his New England forerun-ner Henry Thoreau, who endured a nominal night at the local Concord jail for his world-famous civil disobedience over the Mexican-American War. Lowell turned his back on his Protestant upbringing to join the Catholic Church, which he later abandoned. After faithfully backing the presidential bid of Sen-ator Eugene McCarthy, he recanted, withdrawing his support.

Lowell's three productive semesters at Iowa—which profoundly shaped his career by bringing him in closer contact with Randall Jarrell, John Berryman, and W. D. Snodgrass—somehow were not enough to sweeten his distaste for the place. "We're both sick of Iowa City," he reported on January 1, 1954, to Elizabeth Bishop, describing his and his wife Elizabeth Hardwick's attitude toward the Workshop's literary scene. But, he claimed, "I'm sick of explaining to Elizabeth why she shouldn't be" sick of Iowa City, amending what appeared to be his firm dismissal of the Workshop and its culture with a humorous negation of their consensual negative judgment of the place.[8]

Saying no was in Lowell's nature. He made precisely such "a virtue of nega-tion" when he received Paul Engle's first offer to join the faculty of the Iowa Writers' Workshop.[9] It came in 1947, close on the heels of his Pulitzer Prize for *Lord Weary's Castle*. Engle received a courteous yet definitive rejection. "I'm afraid I have decided to take the Library of Congress job," a consultant position with light duties. Further, "the pay is $5700 and the work is nomi-nal," an offer he could not refuse. "I feel sorry to do this after our pleasant correspondence, and all the trouble that you have taken in making these ar-rangements."[10] Engle was crestfallen that he could not cinch this rising star.

"It was inevitable that Lowell would bite that hand that fed him," a former student of Lowell's from Harvard noted.[11]

Engle, however, would not be denied the opportunity to enlist Lowell among the ranks of his faculty. Karl Shapiro, who had been attempting to teach at the Workshop while also holding down editorial duties in Chicago and commuting by train to Iowa City, 220 miles away, left the Workshop faculty in 1950 to take over as editor of *Poetry*. To replace him, Engle made a second try at hiring Lowell, and the deal this time struck Lowell as irresistible. "It's $2,000 for one course, supposedly for two hours a week; I want to get it lifted [to] $2,500 or $3,000 for two courses," he proudly announced to his mentor, Allen Tate.[12] Engle, intent on reeling in his prize this time, found the resources to accommodate his bid.

Through the assistance of Allen Tate, then acting in the role of his unofficial literary agent, Lowell secured his position at Iowa, set to begin spring semester 1950. Tate's negotiation on his behalf was among the greatest gifts he received from his mentor. "You are a wonderfully generous friend," Lowell wrote, overflowing with gratitude. He vowed that this gesture of kindness, especially given its professional ramifications, was one "I shall never forget."[13] Tate had backed him since the early days of his apprenticeship in the sultry Tennessee heat of 1937. The mentorship began when Lowell dropped out of Harvard after two years of undergraduate study to make the pilgrimage south to the poet's home in Benfolly, Tennessee, forty miles west of Nashville. He had expected a hero's welcome, but instead was told there was no room in the house, unless he would like to pitch a tent on the lawn. Taking the quip literally, Lowell promptly drove to Sears Roebuck to purchase an umbrella tent. He carefully unpacked and assembled the olive green shelter, where he spent the next three months experimenting with free verse and rhymed meter. The determined youth's resourcefulness had an endearing effect. Lowell would periodically burst in on Tate, clutching his ink-smeared drafts in breathless anticipation of his reaction. Tate chuckled to himself at the sight of his protégé preoccupied with his manuscript and totally oblivious to the herd of cows that had converged on the tent. The apprenticeship signaled his undying devotion to Tate, one of few commitments Lowell did not recant. When he was not working with Tate, Lowell attended classes taught by the poet John Crowe Ransom at nearby Vanderbilt University.[14] As the spring and summer of 1937 wore on, Tate increasingly took on the role of second father to Lowell, filling the void left by Lowell's violent break from his real father.

During his sophomore year at Harvard, a pivotal altercation forever changed Lowell's relationship with his father. Lowell senior had written to the father of his son's college sweetheart Anne Tuckerman Dick, asking "that you and Mrs. Dick not allow Ann [*sic*] to go to Bobby's rooms at college without proper chaperonage." After Anne showed him the letter, Lowell immediately sped home to demand an explanation and an apology. While Anne waited in the idling station wagon in the driveway, Lowell, uncontrollably furious, stormed in. His father rose from his chair to meet the oncoming assault, which began as a hail of shouts at close range. The row quickly escalated, as Lowell unleashed a flurry of blows that sent the old man sprawling helplessly to the floor of their family home.[15] The guilt and shame he carried with him from the incident had profound effects on both his creativity and his personal life. Lowell's later engagement to Anne eventually broke off under the strain of ongoing animosity between the families.

During the fifteen years before his arrival in Iowa, Lowell seemed to have lived a lifetime of harrowing experiences. His manic-depressive bouts drove him to violence during his first marriage, to the novelist Jean Stafford, a turbulent relationship that lasted from 1940 to 1948. Three years into their marriage, Lowell was sentenced to prison, on October 13, 1943, for his refusal to comply with the draft. The saturation bombing and other wartime tactics used by the Allies that resulted in massive civilian casualties were the main reasons he cited for his action.[16] The extra day tacked on to his one-year sentence made him a felon. After ten days in the West Street Jail in New York City, Lowell was transferred to Danbury, Connecticut, where he was incarcerated in federal prison for five months. Ironically, his time behind bars was perhaps the most tranquil of his tumultuous life. There, he "blissfully slept among eighty men, a foot apart, and grew congenial among other idealist felons" in an environment he found "gentler than [St. Mark's] boarding school or [Harvard] college." Ensconced in this "adult fraternity," Lowell "found life lulling. I corrected proofs . . . I queued for hours for cigarettes and chocolate bars . . . I read *Erewhon* and *The Way of All Flesh* . . . two thousand pages of Proust."[17] He was all of twenty-six years old at the time, a quintessential angry young man defiantly refusing to comply with his punishment's intent to make him suffer.

The fraught marriage that coincided with Lowell's prison sentence seemed doomed from the start. Even the courtship leading up to their wedding was marred with violence, the wreckage of which Stafford wore on her face in permanent scars. Lowell was behind the wheel in a horrendous car accident that shattered Stafford's face, causing extensive injuries that required major reconstructive surgery. Lowell himself walked away from the crash unscathed. According to David Laskin, Stafford not only "hid from him and told friends he was mad and murderous," but she bore "lifelong scars" from the "car accident he caused, perhaps deliberately."[18] Lowell's own father admonished him for tarnishing their exalted Boston name. To the shock of those who knew Stafford, she married him the next year, in yet another telling instance of his capacity to pivot on the fulcrum between destruction and love.[19]

Ruthlessly Serious

At thirty-five years old and surging at the height of his powers, Lowell made his highly anticipated entrance into Iowa City to assume his teaching position in the ice-hard chill of January 1950. His protégé Snodgrass recalled that his literary influence "had overwhelmed young readers, much as Swinburne's had an earlier generation in England," and as Emerson had the previous century in New England. Lowell radiated creative energy, transfixing the Workshop community with his irresistible allure.[20]

Integral to Lowell's powerful literary persona was the checkered past he carried with him to Iowa City. His reputation preceded him as "the one topic of conversation: the time he had done as a conscientious objector, his periods of madness, his past violence." Just nine months earlier, Lowell had been committed to a psychiatric hospital for a manic-depressive mental disturbance. Regarding his personal bearing, Snodgrass never forgot how "we were surprised to find" that although he was "tall and powerfully built, he seemed the gentlest of mortals, clumsily anxious to please."[21] His arrival "was marked by a sense among us that the ante had definitely been upped, that the workshop was moving onto a higher level," according to his student Robert Dana.[22] His patrician manner belied his raw sensibility. "In a central way, Robert Lowell was not quite civilized," Frank Bidart observed.[23] "However courtly or charming, casual or playful he was by turns, in his art and his personal relationships, Lowell was unfashionably—even, at times ruthlessly—serious." His signature rhetorical move in conversation and in his poetry was visible in how, "from his shaggy, renegade vantage point Lowell tended, sometimes in the most shocking way, to view our institutions in terms of one another, as though they were interchangeable. The West Street jail, for example, becomes a microcosm for American society" in much of his work.[24]

Just as Workshop members had built up Lowell into something of a messiah, he too had grandiose expectations of the institution and its students. Excited that he and his second wife, the writer Elizabeth Hardwick, would be taking on this new adventure, he readied himself for the challenge. He confided in Tate that he feared his Iowa students would be so "frightfully brilliant" that he committed himself to a rigorous regimen of preparation for his classes, "as if for one of those nightmare Ph.D. examinations."[25] Less than a year earlier he had unleashed one of the most bizarre manic displays exhibited by a literary figure of his stature. Iowa and the seriousness it entailed was for Lowell an opportunity to recommit himself to the profession, and reestablish his credentials as the nation's premier poet. In addition, he saw the Workshop position as an opportunity to establish his teaching credentials so he could return and teach there again. In this way, Engle's Workshop offered a secure and reliable source of income to fund a trip to Italy he had planned with Hardwick. He was also highly aware that the prestige of Iowa would counteract the damage his image had suffered from his recent manic-depressive episode.

The Iowa position was a country idyll for Lowell, a tonic for the utter bedlam of an incident that saw him brawling with police, straitjacketed and thrown into a padded cell. On a series of campus visits in the Midwest, Lowell rendezvoused with Tate at the University of Chicago, where his behavior became erratic. That evening at a restaurant, Lowell's wild antics created such a stir that management was forced to hustle him off the premises. He returned to his room, but his condition worsened into a fit of violent paranoia, prompting him to open his window on the busy Chicago street and shout obscenities at passersby, taunting and berating them. Four Chicago police officers needed more than ten minutes to subdue and handcuff a wildly ferocious Lowell. Psychiatrists at Billing Hospital diagnosed him with a "psychotic reaction, paranoid type," and placed him in custody. Tate talked authorities into allowing him to be placed on a train to Bloomington, the next stop on his journey.

Once in Bloomington, Lowell's mania erupted again, this time with twice the intensity. On campus at the Indiana University Faculty Club, Lowell "had run through the kitchen terrorizing the cooks and then run out into the streets." Once there, he meandered through traffic in a dazed stagger, as cars screeched and honked around him. He then darted into a movie theater, where he filched a giant roll of tickets. He stalked back out to the street with the ticket roll tucked under his arm, aimlessly knifing through downtown Bloomington, gathering speed with each step. His progress abruptly stopped when a group of police officers converged on him, forming a half circle. Trapped with his back to a plate glass storefront window, Lowell reflexively exploded with a torrent of blows at the officer who was in the process of handcuffing him. Taken by surprise, the badly beaten cop lay on the sidewalk, bloodied by the volatile cocktail of Lowell's strength, size, and alcohol-fueled rage. As more officers came to the scene, they returned the favor. A gang of Bloomington's finest surrounded the famous poet, roundly kicking and pummeling him into submission. Bypassing handcuffs, the police opted to place him immediately into a straitjacket for easier handling. Lowell later recalled of the incident that he was overwhelmed with "pathological enthusiasm" for the eradication of evil in Bloomington, "a place that stood for evil, unexorcised, aboriginal Indians." With messianic delusions, he believed he "could stop cars and paralyze their forces by merely standing in the middle of the highway with my arms outspread," a crucifix to behold in the banal broad daylight of downtown Bloomington in 1949, an otherwise staid and decorous midwestern college town.[26]

Workshop members inevitably mulled the question of whether Lowell would cause such a disturbance in Iowa City, commenting on his antics and arrests with as much enthusiasm and wonder as they probed the metaphysical fine tunings of his poetry. Hardwick stood by him firmly through the episode, and accompanied him to Iowa as his pillar of stability; her own causticity kept Lowell's native wildness under control. She was acutely familiar with the nature of his rages, aptly describing their effect in her poetry as a process by which "your old-fashioned tirade—/ loving, rapid, merciless—/ breaks like the Atlantic Ocean on my head."[27] "Lowell regularly hurt those around him," the critic Steven Axelrod explained. "As a boy he bullied classmates, and in his twenties he abused his first wife." His second, Hardwick, "understood and tolerated these episodes as a manifestation of illness," but others would be less sympathetic.[28] Certainly Workshop students were in an agitated state of suspense around Lowell, wondering if and when this efficacious powder keg would explode. The creative process was inseparable from his madness, as Snodgrass explained: "This incredible force and extension of Lowell's mind seemed to me frighteningly involved with his extreme personality changes, his manic-depressive episodes." Like Lowell's other students, Snodgrass monitored the famous poet for signs of outbursts, ever on the lookout for "violent episodes at Iowa."[29] Those close to him soon learned that "hidden under the sign of aristocrat and miscreant is a flawed, complex, brilliant, and productive human being, fully engaged with the currents of his time."[30]

Lowell at Iowa, 1950

On January 25, 1950, when the new celebrity poet and his famous author wife settled into their apartment at 728 Bowery Street, Hardwick wrote her mother-in-law with her first impressions of Iowa City. She found it "flat and ugly," a travesty of "snow mud and ice" utterly devoid of culture and history of the sort she was accustomed to in New England. Here, she said, anything over fifty years old is a landmark.[31] Lowell similarly found the landscape bleak, "gray-white, monotonous, friendly, spread-out, rather empty, rather reassuring," if not entirely devoid of culture. He delighted in the presence of "a theatre here that specializes in movie revivals—this afternoon we are going to *Ivan the Terrible*."[32] A strange mix, then, of "high brow movies, the new criticism," and sensational local news stories such as the Bednasek "tuxedo murder" trial shared the stage with constant reminders of the meaningless flux of rural life, as seen in how "every afternoon a pack of very harmless and sorry-looking stray dogs settles on our pathway." Oddly paired against its sophisticated intellectual culture, "this is one of the marks of Iowa City."[33]

Although he complained that "life in Iowa is a pretty dormant, day to day thing," Lowell knew it could restore his mental health by returning him to the original principles that had been so essential to his success. Thus his weekly visits to an Iowa City psychiatrist began a steady course of recovery. "I am well out of my extreme troubles," he reported to his mother in early 1950. Although he was candid about lingering effects of the breakdown, felt in "a stiffness, many old scars," and "the toil of building up new habit," he confirmed that "I definitely feel out of the old perverse dart maze."[34] The treatment he received, of isolation, electric shock, and drugs, brutal by today's standards, may have traumatized him more than it healed him. But after later departing Iowa to seek further help at Payne Whitney Psychiatric Clinic on Manhattan's Upper East Side, he was gradually returning to health despite the rebel in him, "a mean streak in me [that] somehow hates to admit it."[35] Tate identified the cause of the psychotic episode in Lowell's overly ambitious professional situation. "He had been pushed forward too rapidly as a poet and he had attempted a work [the *Kavanaughs*] beyond his present powers," Tate argued, according to his sense that an acute creative crisis was behind the episode. "He couldn't finish it," and thus commenced disaffiliating himself from the "three things that kept him together: the Church; he gave up Jean; and some months ago he virtually gave up poetry."[36] Like Icarus, Tate believed, Lowell had flown too close to the sun.

Unlike his first wife and the Catholic Church, both of which, "with a smile, he put off quietly," Lowell joined the Workshop faculty as a means of reentering the world of poetry and reestablishing his dominance in it.[37] Teaching at the Workshop failed to meet his lofty expectations. "My writing class is held in a *temporary*, modern, structure—plants and a large imitation Moore statue in

the window, student-art on the walls—all kinds," the antithesis of the permanent structures and authentic art of his days at Harvard. The workshop method
struck him as facile and sophomoric, a perfunctory procedure by which "we
arrange ourselves in a long empty, somehow dingy loop of chairs and hold
mimeographed copies of the 'poems of the week.' " The transience of the
place echoed his own sense of impermanence there, as a temporary visiting
faculty member with no investment in the future of the institution. Like the
roving pack of dogs that occasionally took up housekeeping in his yard, "All
during class, people drift in and out—looking for the sociology building,
warming themselves, killing time, holding whispered conferences." Needless
to say, "no one comes to look at the [student] art" adorning the walls, but its
cloying presence, a reminder of the lackluster creative skills of the student
body, means that "you never forget that it is attending you." The students'
writing itself would have demoralized him completely—"O, and the poems!
Everything from poetry society sonnets to the impenetrably dark"—were it not
for a few with genuine talent. He estimated that "about six of my students are
pretty good—at least, they do various things I can't and might become almost
anything or nothing."[38] Others showed early promise, but "then they all begin
to level off into Paul Engle," that is, into vapid mediocrity.[39]

To Lowell, writing was an intensely personal process, one that only a confidante or trusted editor could guide or nurture, as Tate had with his own work.
At the Workshop, literature provided models for students to emulate in their
own writing. Lowell had never developed his own creative writing repertoire
with a classroom of his peers dissecting his every word. Instead, Tate had fulfilled that role for him. The implicit acrimony and overt hostility during workshop sessions left him bewildered at the array of defensive postures students
produced, however understandably, given the savage arena in which they were
thrown. Those mimeographed "poems of the week" were the objects of fierce
contention, which they "defended with passion, shyness, references to Kant
and Empson mysticism." Their sophisticated array of survival tactics ranged
from theoretical smokescreens to poses of passive aggression.[40] He became
aware that more creative energy often went into defending their work than
composing it.

Lowell never pretended that his teaching, at either the Workshop at this
early stage or later at Harvard, nourished or sustained his writing. Although
not prohibitive to his creative process, "My kind of teaching," he said, "doesn't
intrude on my writing." He made clear that "it doesn't do me any particular
good." This was because teaching for Lowell was centered in the study of lit-

erature rather than creative writing. "You shouldn't think of writing while you teach; you should think of English and American classics, which is what I do."[41] Although Lowell was "a powerful, commanding man" at Iowa, "Students took his class because he was a great poet and a great man but few realized beforehand that Lowell was a great teacher of literature and an awful workshop teacher." Unlike others on the Workshop faculty, such as Donald Justice and R. V. Cassill, who greeted student work with their critical scalpels poised to dissect, "Lowell had very little help to offer in the form of direct, constructive criticism of line, structure, intent, execution of student drafts."[42] Rather than seeing his classroom role as a collaborator and coach of the sort Tate had been to him, he viewed teaching as a performance, according to his private school and Harvard education. He prepared accordingly, despite recognizing the futility in "boning up on what you can't use, then faking."[43] Much of teaching was theater, as he soon discovered ways of entertaining students with anecdotal stories of poets' private lives, or simply by reading poetry in a heavy accent, as he once did to their delight with a playful rendition of Burns in a swooping Scottish brogue. Levine recalled how Lowell read once "in what appeared to be an actor's notion of Hotspur's accent." Transforming the classroom into his stage, "his voice would rise in pitch with his growing excitement," his face would become animated by the words while "he tipped slightly forward as though about to lose his balance and conducted his performance with the forefinger of his right hand." These classes, decidedly disinterested in developing student writing, were performative "memorable meetings in which the class soon caught his excitement." Levine spoke for the student body when he described how "all of us sensed something significant was taking place." This fanfare obscured how, as a writing instructor, he was "visibly bored by his students and their poems," an attitude easily ignored in the wave of excitement generated by his willingness to play the part of Robert Lowell.[44]

Given his lofty credentials and celebrity status, no one at the Workshop—students, faculty, or administration—objected to the fact that he essentially was not teaching creative writing, but sharing instead his voluminous knowledge of literature. Lowell's own creative process was a matter he could scarcely articulate, much less teach, one that probed deeply within the recesses of his inner life. Students stood in awe of that inner life. Don Petersen, one of Lowell's pupils at the time, asked incredulously, "Can you imagine how hard it is to live as Robert Lowell, with that inner life?"[45] Students regarded him with a mix of reverence and jealousy.[46] Envying Lowell's creative power as so many

Workshop members had done likewise presented a similar ethical dilemma at the fulcrum of authorial greatness and insanity. Lowell's poetry had achieved such renown precisely because of the tumult of his inner life, the painful source of his greatest poetry. Lowell could achieve this kind of damaged grandeur as "a master of a powerful and fierce voice that all of us respected."[47] Poised, Lowell hewed close to reality from a revealing oblique angle expressed as brilliantly or more so than any living writer of his generation. Unhinged, he was an abomination, even to himself.[48] For Lowell to "get sick again" meant enduring "a gruesome, vulgar, blasting surge of 'enthusiasm,' " the doctors' word that could hardly express how "one becomes a kind of man-aping balloon in a parade—then you subside and eat bitter coffee-grounds of dullness, guilt, etc."[49] With such issues weighing so heavily, there is little wonder why no one objected to his failure to tend to the vagaries of his students' scansion, diction, and prosody in their pallid, ink-smeared, mimeographed "poems of the week."

The Tuxedo Murder

Lowell's twice-weekly performances before his adoring students usually began with a brief informal conversation about local events and news. Although the culture of midcentury Iowa City and its campus was not of particular interest to Lowell and Hardwick, the grisly "tuxedo murder" and the subsequent trial of a student, Robert Bednasek, fascinated Lowell, but not in the way it captured Hardwick's imagination. She became captivated, "moving heaven and earth to enter [the courtroom] as an accredited reporter," to gather material on the subject for a novel set in Iowa City. She found the trial a fascinating masquerade of pretension and bluff. It struck Lowell as "gruesome, blurred, silly, pitiful—sororities, fraternities, 'pinned,' 'chained,' 'they seemed happy' psychologists, Irish policemen—money, justice, and no good answer." While Lowell listened, Hardwick "talked a book" about the proceedings.[50]

The book Hardwick "talked," from 1950 to 1954, became her novel *The Simple Truth*. Hardwick and Lowell had first been exposed to the lurid details of the case through local media coverage. The *Iowa City Press-Citizen* reported steadily on the trial from March 17 to April 6, 1950. The campus paper, the *Daily Iowan*, described "a golden-haired senior coed" found dead following the winter formal held by the Sigma Phi Epsilon fraternity. Robert Bednasek was accused of strangling his girlfriend, Margaret Jackson, at his apartment just east of campus. There "was no evidence of any molestation of the beautiful

Kappa Alpha Theta coed," according to officials. Bednasek claimed she wanted to marry him, and that her death was an accident caused by his "impromptu demonstration of choking a person," which led to "one small bone being broken in her larynx." During questioning by police, Bednasek went berserk and lunged at one of the officers, "in an attempt to seize the .38 caliber revolver from his holster." Wrestling him to the ground, the officers managed to force the now hysterical suspect into handcuffs. They later testified that his "somewhat incoherent statements indicated that he intended to shoot himself."[51]

Hardwick used the occasion to satirize the intellectual culture of the campus from her privileged vantage point as Lowell's spouse and thus a Workshop insider. In her fictional narrative, a married male graduate student and the wife of a faculty member seek admittance to the trial. Their discussion of the courtroom circus quickly moves to ruminations on life in the small Iowa town and the state university where the killing took place. The student and his wife live in a one-bedroom apartment, a stand-in for the place Hardwick and Lowell rented in Iowa City. "Although only of moderate size this single room had so many recesses given over to some function of housekeeping usually placed alone that there was hardly anything, unless it might be the little spot in the center covered with a tiny, red tufted rug, that could properly be called the living room itself." The transient visiting writers in this university town "simply abhorred the place with a manic volubility. The aliens who had settled for good had more troubled minds, recalling sometimes with a sigh the lost hills and bays of San Francisco, horseback riding in Arizona, and most of all," especially from Hardwick and Lowell's New England perspective, "the great East from the Green at Concord." Among the menagerie of intellectuals also passing through the university "were many teachers from Europe . . . remarkable souls pacing the Iowa pavements." Those from overseas "were in America, no doubt about that, even if perhaps they had not bargained for so completely the real thing and wondered at their fate."[52] She astutely observes that "the citizens of Iowa shared the qualities of the weather: plain, open, their life was not luxurious, but not poor either, indeed prosperous." Among the tokens of civilization in "sedate and glamorous colleges, pictures in the galleries, and wine in the fowl pot," a flatness prevailed, so that "everything was indifferent to the eye." Her comments on the lack of diversity were telling. "In Iowa, a few Southerners even longed for a black face around Woolworth's on a Saturday night."[53]

In this climate, moreover, Hardwick depicts a distinct blindness to the simple truth that derives from a culture that is too intellectual for its own good.

When Bednasek was eventually acquitted, to her it was symptomatic of the rural intellectual enclave's liability to overanalysis, particularly from the vantage point of psychiatric evaluation, which was in its heyday and had played a central role in her husband's life. The jury's decision epitomized how psychoanalysis at the time could bury overwhelming evidence to the contrary by recasting the accused as *"perfectly* sane and normal, a good boy, more so than the average, one thinks." The reconstruction of the killer into an admirable figure, especially through the verbal pyrotechnics of psychiatry, struck her as appalling. With dripping irony, she has one character admire the accused's "sensitive face, but not what you would call *weakly* sensitive, either."[54]

Hardwick's "Iowa City murder novel," Lowell remarked after its completion in a private letter, " 'centers' about a student murder that happened in 1950 when we were first here. It's the best thing she's done," he estimated, which was high praise indeed considering her vast accomplishments in reputable literary journals up until that time. To him it captured the culture in ways he had not been able to articulate by being "very stern with a subdued satirical edge." He well knew how much was left off the page. "And everything she tactfully didn't say about the locale," he added, "is tearing through her."[55] The book was profoundly significant to Lowell. "Today we are holding our breaths and waiting for the reviews and publication of Elizabeth's *Simple Truth*," he told Engle. "Or rather, I am," he confessed, since "E. is typing a mile a minute, and launching off simultaneously into a book, an essay and a short story."[56]

"Solitude and Sweat"

The steady routine of the Workshop combined with the intriguing subject of the Tuxedo Murder—on which Lowell and Hardwick could sharpen their wits at a safe distance—to stabilize the pair by the end of the spring semester in 1950. After a brief teaching stint at Kenyon College, they indulged in the cultural richness of Europe, both of them hungry to take in its history, literature, and thriving intellectual culture. After an extended stay in the Netherlands, a place where "we like the people we have met better than literary people anywhere," they concluded, "one year is enough" in that nation.[57] Among their contacts there, Bill Burford, who had been "writing a long autobiographical poem," entertained them with his conversation, which was "a pure centerless flux. The three of us spent a long night. Burford managed to drink an entire quart of Dutch gin, so one had the contrast of unimaginable coherence and unimaginable incoherence." Lowell concurred with a friend who remarked that, with Burford, "You always felt he was about to make a point." Hardwick and Lowell grew closer on their European odyssey. Lowell happily reported to Bishop that, as his partner in crime, "Elizabeth has just said that the only advantage of marriage is that you can be as gross, slovenly, mean and brutally verbose as you want."[58] Next was Germany by way of Vienna, "then I will be teaching at Salzburg," he told Bishop, saving "the winter for Florence or Rome."[59]

Instead, they returned to Iowa, which once again beckoned as a retreat for Lowell in 1953, this time from three years of bohemian adventures with Hardwick in Europe, and to recoup his finances and stabilize himself on the solid ground of the Midwest. Iowa offered the "solitude and sweat" he desired.[60] "When I am not teaching," he told Engle, "I miss it and feel worthless."[61] The continent had been for him something like the island of the lotus-eaters in the *Odyssey*, a place of unimaginable sweetness almost impossible to leave. "It has been tempting to think of remaining in Europe almost forever, though I've never thought I would in earnest," he confided to Allen Tate.[62] To Engle, he wrote, "Europe for us is a little like Anteus and the earth: the more one has of it the more one's appetite for it grows. I could start a eulogy that would go on for pages."[63]

The New England Protestant work ethic he was raised with seemed to guide his decision to abandon his plans to remain in Rome until summer. "We're getting much too poor to be proud," he felt, "which is beyond the help of loans." Economic necessity beckoned, along with "a feeling of deracinated idleness" he compared to "lying in bed an extra two hours some half hungover morning, and delighting in the first hour and brooding greasily through the second and calling it pleasure or 'life.' "[64] He began to see through such self-deluding tricks that protracted indulgence into something more like sloth. Returning to Iowa promised not only a new adventure, but also a reconnection with the world's most reputable creative writing program. He made careful arrangements with Engle "to avoid . . . living in one room and a kitchen—especially without the Bednasek case to occupy my studious and volatile Elizabeth."[65]

Fawning over him from the start, sycophants scrambled for Lowell's affection during registration. They rushed to carry his bag and bring him coffee, "handing him half a dozen of the wrong kind of cigarettes, someone else lighting them."[66] His needs were already more than accommodated, as Engle had met his prior request, in addition to a salary that "will not be less than $5000," "to have some steady adult person like Bill Belvin as a part-time student assistant—particularly in the beginning to help with registration, selection etc." He was clearly receiving star treatment. Lowell's second teaching stint at Iowa continued to ride on the success of *Lord Weary's Castle*, the little volume of angry verse that burst him on to the literary scene in 1946. By 1953, students had an even deeper appreciation of its impact, which was a kind of twentieth-century recalibration of Emersonian antimaterialism. The book exposed capitalism as "the besetting evil" in which "the Egyptian and Babylonian exiles are combined with man's current self-imposed exile from God." Those capable of "achieving anagogic Truth" have been made fewer "by the materialism about them which minimizes their ability to contemplate." In the New England tradition of romantics rooted in Thoreau, and with a New York defiance traceable to Melville, *Lord Weary's Castle* expresses that "this materialism, in all of its aspects, gnaws most deeply at the man's soul and prevents him from achieving the mystical experience he needs for salvation," as Jerome Mazzaro explains.[67] The book gained an almost cultish following among Workshop students, whose well-thumbed and coffee-stained copies could be found in their apartments and dorms beside typewriters and left open on end tables throughout Iowa City. Unlike Mark Twain's definition of a classic, "a book which people praise and don't read," *Lord Weary's Castle* was at the heart of Iowa City's print culture in the early 1950s.[68] "By the time I left Iowa," Robert Dana recalled, "the cover of my copy was dog-eared and the dustjacket in tatters."[69]

In the spring of 1953, a precocious and exuberant freshman named Mary Jane Baker enrolled in Lowell's Five Poets in Translation course, and then in his Greek poetry workshop the following semester. Lowell's European escapade had primed him for a return to teaching at the Workshop, as the continental focus of these courses was designed to draw directly on his recent travels. He had saturated his desire to "take in" Europe, and now was focused on bringing what he learned in his two years on the continent into the classroom. Lowell did not come to Iowa with a political agenda so much as an aesthetic one rooted in modern languages.

Because instructor approval was required for registration in Five Poets in Translation, Lowell found himself inundated by Workshop students vying for a spot in his class. Baker was the only undergraduate seeking enrollment, and thus "was pretty well scared," especially given how the Workshop students "buzzed around him." The thirty-seven-year-old professor struck her as "shy and learned, with high hair and thickish glasses," the most celebrated and talked-about figure on campus. It was with considerable trepidation, then, that the young woman traversed the campus on a dark icy evening to Lowell's class, held in Union Temporary Building A, listed on her registration card as UTBA. Unlike her, the Workshop students were already quite familiar with "Utbas," as they called it, since it housed the office of the *Western Review* literary journal.

Operating out of his newly rented three-bedroom apartment, Lowell made feverish preparations for the course, "frantically" catching up on two years of books and periodicals he had missed while abroad. Five Poets in Translation, contrary to its title, focused on verse written in the original French, German, Italian, and Latin by such revolutionary romantics as Giacomo Leopardi. The course title, he admitted on the first day of class, was a bait-and-switch designed to increase enrollments. Baker recognized that the use of "tempting course names is a rather profitable advertising game they play at Iowa."[70] The content was thus much more demanding, since it covered "a subject" that challenged Lowell himself, one "in which I have to acquire and give out knowledge simultaneously."[71]

Despite such unrealistic and overly ambitious objectives for the course, Lowell's bearing in the classroom was cool and collected. Baker was taken by the sheer charisma of the author of *Lord Weary's Castle*, which John Berryman lauded for the way it "writhed, crunched, spat against Satan, war, modern Boston, the redcoats, Babel, Leviathan, Babylon, Sodom," leaving "a stormed impression of originality." She assumed Lowell would show some of the fire of that work, but she found "it strange that so much anger and contempt should be found in the poetry of a man who never raised his voice in the classroom," who instead "questioned more than he talked." His method was associative, expansive, and allusive; his frame of reference was steeped in Sartre, Baudelaire, and Valéry. Philip Levine saw this performance as well, but was not impressed, yet it transfixed Baker, who did not find fault in Lowell's lack of concern for student comprehension or opinion. Thrilled by the momentum of his unbridled mind, Baker did not begrudge his wanting to "push ahead with rapid talk." He never pretended to be Socratic, but poured himself into nuanced interpretations of poets like Rilke, which distilled time into "a miracle."

Baker later published her reflections on the experience in *Mademoiselle* in 1954, following a carefully worded "Editor's Note," designed as a release of liability distancing the publisher from Lowell's radicalism, particularly his conscientious objection to fighting in World War II. The note emphasized that Baker's piece in no way functioned "as a character portrait" endorsing Lowell's radical politics, but instead belonged to the genre of light-hearted memoir of the sort that "looks back on college days." Baker's admiration for Lowell, the editors assured, did not reflect the author's and, by extension, the magazine's politics. Their hope instead was that "the writer's enthusiasm" might simply be a token of a youthful ardor evocative of "their own excitement in the discovery of new knowledge with a good teacher." Despite their efforts to cast him as just another "good teacher," Lowell carried a criminal past to match his peerless literary status as America's premier poet. More than a "good teacher," he was a charismatic infidel to students like Baker. "Bored and confined by the fame and traditions a New England Lowell is heir to, he struck out from Harvard at the age of nineteen to study at Kenyon with John Crowe Ransom, Randall Jarrell, and Peter Taylor," she gushed, championing also "his pacifist convictions" that landed him "in federal prison."[72]

Baker earned what Lowell called "a freshman *A*" for the course, based on her enthusiasm for French poetry and her status as the only undergraduate in the class. Levine's bitterness over his B in Lowell's other course lasted for decades. It did not, however, prevent him from soliciting a recommendation from the powerful poet for a teaching position at the Workshop just two years after graduating. Lowell mustered four uninspired sentences on Levine, describing him as "a clear and steady writer . . . somewhere in the upper half of a very good class." The best he could report to Engle was, "I know no harm of him," in his tepid remarks.[73] Levine never joined the Workshop faculty. Baker, conversely, never saw Lowell as a means toward a professional end. Instead she found him an animated and entertaining presence, especially when he held forth with his hand aloft cradling a smoldering cigarette, "repeating a curve, as if he were stroking a ball. I cannot think of Lowell explaining something without that gesture of continuity," she fondly recollected.[74]

Unlike Five Poets in Translation, the other course at the Workshop Lowell taught in the spring of 1953 had a direct impact on his next work, *Life Studies.* In this poetry workshop, his twenty-three students submitted their "life works" to him two times per week. Although he reluctantly promised Engle to adhere to "the same business of mimeographs, discussion groups and interviews with poets," Lowell managed to circumvent his lack of interest in the students' writing by handing them his own.[75] He assured Engle that it would be effective "to put myself in the harness too and provide examples."[76] But given his celebrity status combined with his magnanimous bearing in the classroom, his disregard for the workshop method was not just tolerated, but embraced. Students were flattered, if not star struck, to receive the manuscript writings of an author of his caliber. It is hard to imagine that he expected anything but fawning and facile remarks from students who had been trained to direct their most critical feedback toward the writings of their own peers. When he solicited their advice for revision, Levine remembered nothing but gratuitous adulation. "Someone, certainly not Lowell, had typed up three and a half single-spaced pages of heroic couplet on ditto masters so that each of us could hold his or her own smeared purple copy of his masterpiece." Levine's working-class roots spiked his resentment toward what he took as a fatuous display of self-aggrandizement by a pompous patrician. He listened as Lowell read the poem in "a genteel southern accent," adopted by virtue of his closeness to Tate's Tennessee drawl and Hardwick's Kentucky dialect, which in Lowell's aloof New England air suggested that "the least display of emotion was déclassé." Levine's "horror swelled when several of my classmates leaped to praise every forced rhyme and obscure reference." Predictably, "no one suggested a single cut, not even when Lowell asked if the piece might be a trifle too extended, a bit soft in places." This was not an occasion for a workshop bloodletting so much as a coronation. "Perish the thought" of any revision at all; "it was a masterpiece!" was the consensus. Thus praise was heaped on the one person present who needed it the least, to Levine's mind—the same person "who certainly had the intelligence and insight to know it for what it was: bootlicking."[77]

But if Lowell was only looking for his pupils to worship him, he would not have drawn so much of their influence into the manuscript that was to become his magnum opus, *Life Studies*, which ended up winning the National Book Award. Interestingly, exposing his own work to students for their feedback, rarely seen among Workshop faculty, came during a turning point in his relationship with his protégé Snodgrass. It was in 1953 that Snodgrass was beginning to exert an influence on Lowell, who later confessed in a private letter that he began drawing more directly from his own personal experience, especially after the bare lyricism of *Heart's Needle*. The turnabout for Snodgrass "in one I had nearly worshiped and whose style had so dominated me" was jarring. Unsettled, he "became afraid" that Lowell "might be influenced by some of the destructive elements in my own life and behavior." His visits to Lowell were increasingly marred by his mentor's manic depression. Hardwick spurned Snodgrass's friendly overtures. He felt guilty—perhaps out of an irrational compassion—for the timing of his visits, which coincided either with actual attacks or "just before or shortly after." Lowell's deteriorating mental state was painfully human to Snodgrass, who felt "the changes were appalling."[78]

Lowell never maintained a fruitful or lasting relationship with Snodgrass, his most successful student at Iowa. But his movement toward his pupil's style registered a new sense of comfort on his second teaching stint at the Workshop. Although his students consisted of bright minds among "some very confused ones," as he wrote Tate, his mixed and often indifferent reaction to their collective writing belies his greater and increasing interest in Snodgrass and the confessional movement in poetry. This time at the Workshop, Lowell and Hardwick did not arrive as they had in 1950, as "the shy and lofty Eastern sea-board strangers," but instead were more integrated into the community of students and faculty.[79] Gerard Else, a classics scholar, teamed with him to teach the Greek poetry workshop in the fall of 1953, his last semester teaching at Iowa. As with the previous semester's offering, this course was unreasonably ambitious, particularly in its objective of teaching untranslated ancient Greek poetry to students with no training in the language. Despite this daunting challenge—Lowell called it "Greek in a Week," since it required immediate acquisition of the Greek language—Baker enrolled. To her surprise, Lowell's wife was in attendance among the sixteen students on the first day of class. Class began with the ritual of the couple's "borrowing each others' cigarettes" while they engaged the group in a casual discussion of current events. The first meeting "was a wonderful, open-window day and a breezy classroom" full of hope. The heat increased relentlessly with the demands of the syllabus. "Four of us took the final exam," a quarter of the original class.[80] Two of those four were Hardwick and Baker. One of the casualties was William Dickey, who remembered "sitting, naked because of the heat, in a cockroach-infested garret, a towel over my lap to catch sweat, a volume of Pindar in Greek in front of me, a Greek-Latin lexicon to my left, and a Latin dictionary to my right, trying to figure out what on earth was going on." When he shared these details with Else, chair of the classics department who was teaching the course with Lowell, the response was anything but sympathetic or helpful: "There, now you're finding out what scholarship is all about!" he roared with sadistic pleasure.[81]

That fall of 1953 was Lowell's last semester at Iowa. In late spring of 1957, Engle invited him back to teach, but Lowell demurred. He cited a desire to stay in Boston because "we're really located here," commenting, "it's really delightful, mossless creature that I am, to begin successive autumns in one place." Out of gratitude to Engle, he claimed to regret the decision, since "I do miss my friends and old superb Iowa students."[82]

Lowell's impact on Iowa City was permanent and profound. This was a time in the Workshop when poetry, rather than fiction, held prominence. He and Hardwick were the talk of the town, the scourge of frustrated talents like Dickey and Levine, and the inspiration for prodigies such as Snodgrass. Not his teaching, but his celebrity presence enriched the cultural cachet of the program while providing a stable point of departure and return for Lowell's boundless wanderlust and untethered journeys. His return confirmed Iowa City's prestige and reinforced the culture of poetry, visible on the men's room wall in Kenney's Fine Beers, the locus of literary discussion, where Dickey had "written the first line of *Beowulf* in Anglo-Saxon." Only in Iowa City in the early 1950s during the reign of Lowell would Dickey find "that a later visitor had amended my work by meticulously marking the scansion and the long vowels" there in the stall.[83]

Far from the Atlantic Ocean, Iowa provided Lowell with perspective on places like McLean's, the psychiatric hospital where he shared extensive time with "victorious figures of bravado ossified young." His fellow patients rocked in inner agony, staring blankly and hugging their sides. Others gallivanted about their floor, perhaps none with more panache than "Bobbie," who, "redolent and roly-poly as a sperm whale," occupies his own world as he "swashbuckles about in his birthday suit and horses at chairs."[84] Another, "flabby, lobotomized" and drifting in "a sheepish calm," offers no resistance to the brutal round of shock therapy he is about to encounter. "No agonizing reappraisal/ jarred his concentration on the electric chair—/ hanging like an oasis in his air/ of lost connections."[85] In 1950, Lowell arrived at the Workshop after a battery of treatments that left him "cured, I am frizzled stale, and small," eventually finding the self-possession to assemble a project like *Life Studies* and circulate drafts to both faculty and students.[86] As introspective as it was ambitious, the book came to fruition at Iowa, a place uniquely encouraging to such ruthless stares in the mirror to discover self and culture, as Lowell had in the famous line from this work: "These are the tranquilized Fifties/ and I am forty . . ."[87] If he could be true in his own self-assessment, he remained ever cagey when it came to his impression of the Workshop. Sterile, empty, and dormant were his leitmotifs when describing Iowa, yet when meeting his former student Robert Dana decades later, he remarked that the Workshop was "a great place." In the next breath, the reason for his plaudit unmistakably sounded as if it came directly from the promotional language Paul Engle had been trumpeting during the 1950s. "Most of my students have published books," he glowed, in a way that, on the surface, appeared to dispel "the general myth of his unhappiness at Iowa."[88]

7 • Mad Poets: Dylan Thomas and John Berryman

Coursing through the frozen prairie in 1950 aboard a night train from Chicago to Iowa City, where he was scheduled to deliver a highly anticipated reading hosted by the Iowa Writers' Workshop and attended by the wider campus community, the world-renowned Welsh poet Dylan Thomas did what came naturally—he imbibed with the locals. As famous as he was, Thomas was never more comfortable than at a bar cavorting with perfect strangers, swapping tales, and filling the room with his raucous wit and Welsh-English brogue. The fellow travelers he fell in with in this case were hard-drinking truck drivers, whose conviviality was not below this poet renowned for his BBC broadcasts and poetry volume *Deaths and Entrances*, published in 1946, that established him as a major literary figure. With Thomas in the mix, the otherwise drab dining car on this blindingly boring four-hour journey west across the Mississippi River valley was overflowing with high spirits. Thomas had boarded the train sober; but when Workshop faculty member Ray B. West, Jr., arrived to shuttle him to his speaking engagement, set to take place in the Senate Chamber of the Old Capitol just a few hours later, the poet was dead drunk. As West helped him from the train, Thomas bellowed in agony, "This is the night I don't go on!"[1]

Given the high stakes of Thomas's visit, a fast and furious remedy was necessary. Staff and administration had been long preparing for his arrival, rolling out the red carpet for this distinguished guest by situating his talk in the majestic gold-domed Old Capitol building, the architectural crown jewel at the heart of campus reserved for only the most auspicious occasions. Barely able to walk, Thomas was beside himself muttering an incoherent slur of profanity-laced epithets, disheveled and in no shape to face the university community's top brass. High-profile representatives from the publishing industry, including Seymour Lawrence, were also in attendance. This was a cast carefully arranged by Workshop director Paul Engle to be a glittering spectacle for potential investors in the program and to stimulate the professional development of his students. West knew the show must go on.

Thinking fast, West went where most Workshop faculty and students gravitated when facing an acute crisis, whether financial, personal, or creative—the Quonset hut main office situated a short distance down the hill from the Old Capitol building. Like Gabriel piloting the obliterated Freddy Malins across the dance floor and out of view for the sake of decency in James Joyce's "The Dead," West rushed Thomas into the office bathroom, which had an actual tub, dunked him in ice-cold water, helped him back into his clothes, and ushered him up the hill to the awaiting packed audience of literati and dignitaries in the stately confines of the Senate Chamber. Miraculously, as W. D. Snodgrass recalled, "he delivered one of his most beautiful readings," fully living up to the occasion Robert Lowell's introduction described in superlative terms. The purpose of the event, Lowell said, was "to hear an important poet, perhaps the most important of our time—a poet who had altered the modern trend, who seemed to have sprung from a different tradition than most poets today, who had revived what seemed to be a romantic sensibility at its best," as West later paraphrased it. His reading was mellifluous and powerful; "his syllables penetrated the far corners of the hall, each word distinct from the next, so that it seemed to hover a moment in the air like the flare of a rocket before giving way to the next one." The fireworks were delivered with a stately grace one could imagine of Lord Byron himself, his voice "sonorous and nearly Shakespearean" as he held the book with his arm theatrically extended. Between passages his arm lowered and his eyes glazed over. The public stage persona of the poetry reader, a consummate professional, transformed into the private romantic bohemian, a waggish buffoon whose "speech was slurred, shambling, obscene."[2] Then, beginning to read again, he raised his head, extended the book and shifted back into character, summoning back the oracular "strange compelling music of his native Welsh diction." Occasionally he would pause to pick up a glass of water, only to regard it with a look of horror and replace it quickly on the table, the chill of his jarring ice bath still deep in his bones. That "strange and wild" voice overwhelmed the room, leaving listeners marveling. "There is nothing like Dylan Thomas in poetry today. There is a wholeness, a harmony, a radiance about everything he has written which sets him apart," as Lawrence Ferlinghetti described his later performance in San Francisco in 1952.[3]

Thomas was the most notorious reckless romantic of his era, and his hostility to academic literary critics—he detested their "bloody nit picking"—paradoxically made him more attractive to university audiences.[4] Literary critics and creative writing teachers especially found appealing the authenticity of this performing poet, seemingly from another era, who lived for the music of verse.[5] From his early BBC days, oratorical performance was his strong suit; a Thomas poem was always better read in his own voice than silently on the printed page. In addition to influencing the faculty and students on the many college campuses where he read, "the tradition of oral poetry Thomas presented became a model as well for many of the younger poets who were to constitute the heart of the San Francisco Renaissance—the Beat Generation," as Beat historian Barry Silesky observes.[6]

Iowa was but one stop on his whirlwind tour of the United States that began in late February of 1950 and was intended to showcase that charismatic voice. Thomas's proclamation that this was the night he would not go on, which spurred the horrified West into action to ensure that he did, exposed his fear that his bacchanalian lifestyle might prevent him from meeting all the dates on the frantic schedule set by his agent, John Malcolm Brinnin. Starting at Yale and Harvard, he made stops for readings throughout New England and proceeded to the Midwest, which included the Universities of Chicago, Illinois, and Notre Dame before his journey by train to Iowa. The breakneck pace of the tour was daunting; he would keep more than thirty engagements over the span of three months. Almost all of his stops were at universities with jaunts into the broader literary and entertainment culture off campus. Across the bay from UC Berkeley he mixed with Beat poets in San Francisco, led by Lawrence Ferlinghetti at their haven in City Lights Books, and near UCLA, he fell in with Hollywood film icons Shelley Winters and Charlie Chaplin. Winters not only knew of Thomas but was familiar with his poetry. When he amorously took her enthusiasm the wrong way, she successfully rebuffed his advances. Chaplin hosted him at his home and treated his group to an impromptu comedy routine. When the star-struck poet said his friends in Wales would never believe he had been the guest of Chaplin, his host delighted him by instantly composing a cable and sending it off to his wife Caitlin in Laugharne.[7]

This was no perfunctory set of visits, but a carefully plotted tour arranged by his literary agent Brinnin to maximize Thomas's exposure and generate employment opportunities. What brought Thomas to Iowa was a combination of the sheer scale of Brinnin's colossal publicity network, fueling the literary equivalent of the Beatles' American invasion, and Engle's extraordinary capacity to attract the most significant writers of the era. Robert Lowell's presence on the faculty was the key to securing the date with Thomas, who had admired his poetry and sought a similar position to his at an American university as a means of continuing his career as a practicing poet. A key shift in Engle's responsibilities for the Workshop had led to his hiring of Lowell. When Ray West brought his journal the *Western Review* with him to Iowa, Engle's editorial duties ceased. West's *Review* lifted Engle's burden of running a new journal after *American Prefaces* had discontinued publication during the war years. This enabled Engle to concentrate his energy and time on expanding his network, which rapidly grew to include "every American and British writer of any accomplishment in the last sixty years," many of whom Engle brought to Iowa as faculty, both temporary and long-term, or students.[8] In a 1976 letter, West recalled that Engle was in New York soliciting funding for the program during Thomas's visit, noting that the "teachers of poetry during Paul's absence were Robert Lowell and John Berryman" and that the "Visitors who came to read and lecture included, most memorably, Dylan Thomas and Roy Campbell."[9]

Lowell, thinking like Engle, knew that Thomas's presence on campus would infuse the program with fresh energy. West had recently heard word that Thomas was nursing a horrific hangover after his Notre Dame engagement, when "the boys in Chicago had been feeding him boilermakers." Advised to restrict hard liquor and "keep him on beer," since "he loves beer and gets along well on it," West heard opposite advice from Lowell, who knew what kind of impact an unleashed Dylan Thomas could have on the campus community. With no limits to his behavior, Thomas might "be provoked into creating some scandalous fuss that would enliven the city," a comment revealing how little Lowell cared for the visitor's personal well-being in the process of exploiting his popularity for the Workshop's benefit. Thomas's stay with West extended to just under two weeks before he boarded a flight from Cedar Rapids to San Francisco to continue his tour.[10]

Since Thomas emulated Lowell and desired a position like his at Iowa, he knew that remaining as long as possible beyond the requisite night or two might pay dividends toward a future faculty job. In the wake of the tour, he entered negotiations for a position with the speech department at the University of California, Berkeley, despite his failure to comprehend the unit's purpose and self-definition. "I don't quite know what the function of this department is," he confessed, undeterred in his pursuit of an offer. "No date for my possible employment was mentioned, but I gather that it is under discussion now," he wrote a friend in hopeful tones.[11] During the planning of the tour, Thomas made his immediate short-term demands clear: "I don't want to work my head off, but, on the other hand, I do want to return to England with some dollars in my pocket." Aware of his own inability to handle money and perennial confusion about the location and time of his appointments, he gratefully handed over such matters to Brinnin: "I'll have to leave this to you. I hand the baby over, with bewildered gratitude."[12]

After returning from his trip, he wrote his wealthy patron Margaret Taylor about the position of poets in universities. On display in the letter is Thomas's capacity to play the mad poet persona on the page and not just in person. In it, he dramatizes his exhilarating and exhausting tour that kept him from his correspondence. "I was floored by my florid and stentorious spouting of verses to thousands of young pieces whose minds, at least, were virgin territory," he quipped with a clever double-entendre. Delighting in the sound of his rollicking recollection, he continued, "I was giddy agog from the slurred bibble babble, over cocktails bold enough to snap one's braces, of academic alcoholics anything but anonymous." In Iowa City, he was escorted in "powerful cars at seventy miles an hour," rocket-like speed for the time, "tearing from Joe's Place to Mick's Stakery, from party to party."[13] The letter then abruptly pivots as Thomas dons his poised and calculating alter ego, an identity acutely aware of the institutional parameters of making a living as a professional poet.

In sober exacting prose clashing with the madcap debauchery of the letter's opening two paragraphs, Thomas measures the landscape of professional positions for poets, paying close attention to the role of the Iowa Writers' Workshop. The shift suggests Thomas's use of the mad poet role was a gratuitous act for Taylor's amusement, a way of charming her before focusing on business. Now surveying his competition with deadly accuracy, he identifies the only well-known poets unattached to universities, "Wallace Stevens, Vice President of an Insurance company, and e. e. cummings, President, Treasurer, Secretary, & all the shareholders of E. E. Cummings Ltd, a company that exports large chunks of E. E. Cummings to a reluctant public," he observed with a jab at his rival. But Robert Lowell's career, he makes clear, is exemplary of the potential for a poet's professionalization in conjunction with American academic institutions in 1950. With great precision, he defines Lowell's position as "running a Poetry Workshop in Iowa State University [before it was renamed the University of Iowa], there to 'discuss the demands of the craft, to criticize the individual works of student members of the workshop, and to foster enthusiasm for poetry & the sense of criticism among them.' " He notes

Lowell's official title is "Poet in Residence" and that another writer runs a similar workshop only for prose. "Lowell is paid the same salary as an Assistant Professor: in his case, between 5 & 6,000 a year." The advantages to such a position are obvious compared with the dearth of such professional opportunities for poets in Great Britain. "The disparity in incomes, & in spending power, between America & here is so great," he noted, that one can only imagine "what money a similar post, if established here, would demand."[14]

Taylor had considered providing funds for the establishment of a program in creative writing like Iowa's at a British university, naming Thomas as faculty and perhaps director. The thoroughness and accuracy of his description of the various institutional arrangements for the employment of practicing poets at American universities suggest Thomas's serious desire for such a position. He specifically comments on programs for whom "the procedure is the same as in Iowa" in which "the Poet in Residence is engaged for one year only," comparing them to others. He described "other universities [where] the Poet is engaged for far longer periods, sometimes permanently." The variance of time frames also pointed to the possibilities "to arrange for other poets to come along occasionally as guests, & supervise the activities of the workshop (if it could be called that) for one session or more and/or to read or lecture."[15] Taylor demurred on that prospect, but maintained her support of Thomas by purchasing a basement flat for him and his wife Caitlin in London, under the assumption that it would place him in a more favorable position from which to search for employment. The couple moved in winter of 1951, but Thomas detested the accommodations, calling it his "London house of horror," and did not return after his second trip to the United States in 1952.[16]

Thomas's admiration of American university positions for poets was of course complicated by his disdain for criticism. The day after his reading in the Senate Chamber of the Old Capitol at Iowa, Lowell introduced Thomas to thirty-five MFA students in one of the Workshop's converted army barracks. Thomas, totally uncomfortable in the classroom environment, especially in the instructor's role if only as a guest speaker, was bewildered. He asked Lowell sheepishly after his lavish introduction what he was supposed to do. Lowell, barely concealing his frustration, "waved his arms in the air. 'Anything,' he said, 'just anything,' " West recalled. "Dylan explained that he was no critic, he didn't really know how to talk about poetry, the way critics did."[17] Instead, he asked Lowell for an anthology of British poetry, which he handed him. Thomas, suddenly comfortable and animated, leafed through the pages to the poems that he liked, read them with the same dramatic virtuoso flair of his performance the day earlier, and paused to explain why they appealed to him. He also made mention of poems he disliked and offered explanations for each. The critic in him emerged. Had he lived longer, he might have found his voice as a powerful instructor in an MFA poetry workshop like Iowa's.

Thomas's admiration of university poets helps explain why he was relatively well behaved on his trip to Iowa City. As his correspondence indicates, he was on a mission to establish a professional career in the manner of his friend Robert Lowell. The unusually long time he spent at the Workshop, and willingness to make a return visit, point to the value of Iowa in his estimation. He left a lasting impression and was long remembered mainly for the poetry, if not for a few slips triggered by whisky. On one occasion, he succumbed at Joe's Place in Iowa City, missing a dinner engagement and returning home to West's residence early the next morning. A woman had taken him to her apartment on the opposite bank of the Iowa River where she kept his glass full of Scotch all evening while reading from her own poetry. Thomas tolerated the abysmal poetry in exchange for Scotch, so he stayed, missing his dinner date and alarming the Wests, who did not hear him stagger onto their porch until long after sunrise. On another occasion, a discussion with a doctor's wife over martinis turned ugly. The conversation moved toward socialized health care, of which he was a staunch proponent, having benefited from it personally. "Why, you don't know what you're talking about!" she screamed at one point when she perceived one of his comments as an insult to her husband's profession. He shot back reflexively, "You bloody fuckin' bitch!" The phrase was a mere preface to what West described as "the most elegantly strung together sequence of obscenities she had ever heard uttered," profane poetry at its best, liquor-ridden misogyny at its worst.[18] If these were his most scandalous scrapes in Iowa City, he had behaved like an angel, especially compared with the ugly public battles—some devolving into embarrassing drunken tirades— with his wife Caitlin in San Francisco two years later.

Before he could make a concerted effort at securing a university position, Thomas died at the age of thirty-nine, on November 9, 1953, in a Catholic hospital in Manhattan just days after claiming, "I've had 18 straight whiskies. I think that's a record!"[19] Multiple complications—gout, upper respiratory infection, and several other untreated conditions—have been disputed since as the causes of death. Pathologists conducting the autopsy claimed that pneumonia, brain swelling, and a fatty liver were also contributing factors. He had complained of difficulty breathing and was rushed to the hospital, slipping into a coma for several days while doctors worked to revive him. Although

Thomas himself was unconscious, his wife Caitlin was the one "raging at the light" in accord with his most famous poem. She arrived at the hospital "stinking drunk," asking, "is the bloody man dead yet?" Complicating matters was the presence of Thomas's mistress, Liz Reitell, at the hospital. Deepening tensions further, Reitell was the assistant to John Malcolm Brinnin, Thomas's literary agent, who was also at his bedside.

Finding her husband in an oxygen tent attached to a respirator with a tangle of intravenous tubes protruding from both arms, Caitlin mournfully pressed her body against his. But in her drunkenness, she neglected to notice the effect of her weight on his lungs. His already labored breathing slowed dangerously, alarming his nurse, who intervened and banished her to an adjacent room. There she waited with Brinnin, whom she blamed for Thomas's suffering, since he had concocted the slate of professional engagements and projects that eventually overwhelmed the poet. Brinnin foolishly responded by attempting to calm her with whiskey. Becoming increasingly agitated, she flew into a rage and began smashing her head against a window, which would have shattered if it had not been reinforced with mesh wiring. Medical personnel descended on her, and Brinnin backed away. Turning her roiling emotions on them, she ripped a large decorative cross from the wall of the Catholic hospital and swung it fiercely, first at Brinnin and then at the orderly. Now completely unhinged, she wheeled with the crucifix gripped in her hands like a baseball bat, shattering a statue of the Virgin Mary before the orderly could wrestle her to the ground, blood filling her mouth and flowing from his hand where she had ground her teeth. Once Caitlin was safely removed from the scene in a straitjacket and rushed to a psychiatric unit, Thomas's mistress, Liz Reitell, whose presence Caitlin was unaware of, quietly crept back to his bedside where she resumed her vigil beside the wheezing patient.[20] Amazingly, Reitell had managed to avoid the entire frothing melee—a violent blasphemy in this otherwise somber Catholic setting—without a scratch.

Caitlin's attack on Brinnin was motivated by her contention that the agent was overzealous and that the promotional engine responsible for building Thomas up had instead torn him down. Interestingly, among all the promoters of literary talent at the time, no one was more acutely aware of Thomas's star power than Engle. The lasting effects of Thomas's visit on the Workshop were visible more than a decade after he tore through Iowa City like a cyclone. Workshop graduate Edmund Skellings, for example, was acutely aware that the oratorical brilliance of Thomas had elevated his celebrity status to rock star proportions. He thus launched his own tour of American universities as "the

American Dylan Thomas," according to the caption of a giant poster of the poet leaning earnestly into a microphone, striking the unmistakable pose of a charismatic lead singer of a band. Along with the poster, the standard packet of promotional materials advertising Skellings's "Electric Poetry" tour included copies of a descriptive pamphlet bearing Engle's blurb from the *Miami Herald* in bold letters at the top, heralding the act as "A new direction for poetry itself." Through Engle's marketing connections with the commercial advertising industry, and with Thomas as inspiration, Workshop talent was clearly being packaged and sold as show business. "Edmund Skellings calls his unique performance 'lyric theatre,' and one critic has called it 'spoken singing,' " according to the pamphlet. "But whatever one names it, this complex blend of rock and rhyme, humor, blues and psychedelics is a totally fresh exploration of how meaning happens in mind and mouth," it continued, leaving no movement in popular contemporary music unmentioned. Marketed as "acted poetry with original lyrics in the conventional beat patterns of popular song," Skellings's show was performed in scenes drawing from the tradition of live theater. A small vinyl 45-sized record under the label "Professional Associates Dania, Florida" is folded in with the poster and flyers with a playlist of his numbers, "Testing, The Lecture, Down in the Ghetto, Nowno."[21]

Thomas's impact on mass culture has not been replicated since, notwithstanding the efforts of Skellings, the self-described "American Dylan Thomas." Based on his *Collected Poems, 1934–1952*, Thomas was arguably the era's greatest living poet, perhaps best known for his lyrical masterpiece, "Do Not Go Gentle into That Good Night," a poem that eerily foreshadowed his own passing. "Rage, rage against the dying of the light" is directly addressed to his father but also functions as Thomas's vow to live out his final days in bold defiance. Indeed, "Wild men who caught and sang the sun in flight" is a prophetic self-description.[22] With the radio drama *Under Milk Wood*, which was later produced as a play, under way in New York City, Thomas died soaring at the height of his powers. By 1952, critics generally agreed with the proclamation by Philip Toynbee of the *Observer* declaring him "the greatest living poet in the English language."[23]

The Passing of the Torch

When it came to defending the memory of Dylan Thomas no one was more ferocious than poetry Workshop faculty member John Berryman. In fall of 1953, Lowell had been kind enough to allow several literati from Iowa City who were not enrolled students to attend his seminar. These impeccably dressed urbane amateurs regarded verse as an affectation or fine verbal ornament to life, vestiges of the rhymer clubs and literary cliques of the nineteenth century who typically churned out third-rate poetry to be read at their own group events with no ambition for publication or professionalization. Many were fans of Lowell's and were avid readers of Lord Weary's Castle. (Berryman's own accolades would mount in the coming years, reaching a zenith with a National Book Award in 1969 for His Toy, His Dream, His Rest.) Lowell had invited these dilettantes to class in part because they could always be counted on to praise his work and lend credibility to his status. So when they appeared in Berryman's class the following semester, in the winter of 1954, showing themselves as Lowell groupies by clutching their well-thumbed copies of Lord Weary's Castle to their chests, they faced less welcoming circumstances.

The poetry these affluent citizens wrote stayed within their own circle and thus uniformly received a self-congratulatory reception. Lowell only occasionally asked his non-enrolled followers to submit their work for the class's criticism, which was politely vapid, much like the poetry itself, as Philip Levine recalled. When Berryman demanded a poem from one of the group, the poet received a brutal initiation into the workshop method. Berryman began politely enough, reading the poem, which commemorated the late Dylan Thomas, and asking the class for feedback. When he heard nothing, he delivered his own, refusing to treat the poem with kid gloves. Incensed, he lit into the piece. "No, no," he said shaking his head violently, "it's not that it's not poetry. I wasn't expecting poetry," reflexively insulting the writer. A deeper moral principle had been violated, one that bore directly on the memory of the revered Thomas, whose manner of death might present the subject of a moving elegy in the right hands, but to Berryman was not to be treated with fictional flights of fancy. In this case, the poet had cast the doctors as the villains for losing Thomas, because they had subordinated his well-being to their own financial profit. Berryman, who had been extremely close to Thomas, raged at this conceit, charging, "it's not true, absolutely untrue, unobserved, the cheapest twaddle."[24]

Poets, of course, have artistic license just as fiction writers do, to recreate and recast events to evoke deeper truths otherwise hidden by strict adherence to the objective reportorial facts. Anne Sexton—who attended John Holmes's poetry workshop at the Boston Center for Adult Education with Robert Lowell (the two drove together and parked in the loading zone in honor of their ritual visit to the bars after each session)—was one of many poets adamant that the "confessional school" of poetry, which she had helped establish along with Snodgrass's aching portrayal of his separation from his daughter in *Heart's Needle*, had such latitude. "Unknown Girl in the Maternity Ward," she insisted, was not autobiographical; instead it featured a created dramatic identity as its voice and central figure. But Berryman, since the writing in this case was so far below qualifying as poetry, and since it so grossly solicited the memory of Thomas as an object of sentimentality, felt he was in the presence of an intolerable lie that threatened nothing less than the historical memory of Dylan and his generation of great poets.

He went on with his diatribe to set the record straight, emphasizing that the doctors who worked on Thomas "did not work for money." Although he did allow that the medical personnel "did not know who the man was, that he was a remarkable spirit," he insisted that their humanity drove them because "They knew only that he was too young to die, and so they worked to save him, and, failing, wept," as Levine observed.[25] Although Berryman did not name Thomas during his rant, Levine later confirmed him as the tragic figure of the poem who was too young to die. What drove Berryman into a tirade was the thought of Thomas being made a spectacle for the sake of saccharine third-rate poetry written by non-enrolled Lowell fans. Berryman, however, missed the poem's indictment of the American medical industry, operating according to a free market model in which doctors are rewarded financially for their work. The underlying assertion of the piece, hidden from Berryman's perspective, was that under the socialized medical care of Thomas's native Wales, with its presumably more compassionate doctors driven to serve humanity for its own sake, the poet might have survived. As seen by Thomas's own fierce defense of socialized medicine earlier with the doctor's wife, the topic was prominent in the culture, and he harbored passionate convictions about it. So it was a fashionable subject to superimpose on the circumstance of Thomas's death, but it became intolerably pretentious in the poem when overlaid with dripping sentimentality. Berryman's diatribe dispatched the guilty party, visibly shaken, from the room. Emotion pouring through him—the thought of such mistreatment of Thomas's memory in the popular mind struck him as profoundly toxic—Berryman was not able to continue, and thus dismissed the rest of the silent and stunned class.

The exclusivity of the program was never so bluntly applied as under Berryman's direction. This points to the changing climate at Iowa from its early days of communal cohesion, as recalled by Robert Penn Warren. The spring of 1941, the "most protracted" of his visits in Iowa City, was a time notable for

"the pervasive and communal literary sense . . . the interpenetration of interests among faculty (or a number of faculty) and students." He was struck by
"how people of basically different interests and trainings could find a common
ground, fruitful for all. I am sure most of those people never had found anything like that before or ever since," Warren remarked, politely qualifying his
praise in his next comment. "It is only natural that I should, over the years,
have wondered if this atmosphere could survive the great public success and
enormous size of the school."[26]

Frances Jackson, a disgruntled Workshop alumna, recalled a different culture in the next generation, which she believed suffered because "The workshop is just too big." Citing competition among students for valuable funding
and fellowships, and the unjust system of playing favorites, she complained:
"Those with financial aid are always in the limelight, are in 'The Hall' all day,
meet the faculty, become friends with them," a scenario that put them on the
inside track toward long- and short-term financial gain. "Then when it comes
time for teaching jobs, more fellowships, grants, awards, etc. they are naturally the ones who get them," she observed, her frustration with her own
stalled career apparent. "Iowa can do a whole lot for the chosen few. In fact,
because it is so large" (at the time, enrollment reached sixty), "I don't think it
can do as much for the average student." In this urbane and elite culture, "To
be a dominant figure at Iowa it would also help to be an articulate, intellectual,
verbal person from New York City. . . . No one would ever guess it was in the
Midwest by the tone that is set by New Yorkers. They are witty and verbally
flashy and others dim by comparison."[27]

Of course this clashes with Warren's utopic portrait of the program as a
rustic idyll. He loved the sense of community at the time of his visit, mainly
because he was already a full-blown literary celebrity when he arrived, and
thus had students and faculty fawning over him. In his view, the program was
intimate, but he also worried it had grown too large for its own good. Despite
such a liability, he alluded to how "the record of achievement stands to be
read" in the proliferation of student and faculty publications as testimony to
the program's success. Berryman and Lowell, essentially running the Workshop in Engle's absence on a fund-raising trip to the East Coast, represented a
key transition toward the cosmopolitan character of the program, and its status as a clearinghouse of dominant literary minds largely transplanted from
more diverse urban locations.

Thomas's visit to Iowa City and Berryman's subsequent defense of his
memory were watershed moments reflecting the increasing cosmopolitan

sophistication of the Workshop culture. Like Thomas, Berryman came to Iowa when his career was on the rise, but his personal life was in shambles. Thomas's death had raised demons for Berryman that he grappled with his entire life. They were perhaps never more visible than during his semester teaching at the Workshop, in the winter of 1954, just one year after Thomas's death. Berryman had been undergoing psychotherapy for six years before his arrival in Iowa City, a time of protracted anguish he was happy to escape through full immersion in the world of poetry on the remote Iowa prairie. He originally underwent the treatment, a battery of orthodox Freudian sessions of the "talking cure," to appease his wife after she discovered he was having an affair. The affair foreshadowed his second marriage, more than ten years later, to a woman twenty-five years his junior. These personal circumstances mitigated Berryman's professional life. Professionally, he was developing from a well-known to a world-class poet while tasting the personal liberation of psychological and geographical distance from his disastrous marriage.

Berryman's fierce stand on behalf of Thomas at the poetry Workshop was a testimonial to the life of arguably the greatest poet of the postwar generation, a fiery validation of the poet's memory bearing the standard of excellence and seriousness, which Lowell's followers pretentiously believed they could dabble in. Poets and poetry mattered more than mere diversion, and the project of producing professionals would be a demanding endeavor only for the fully committed. Further, Berryman's deep sense of identification with Thomas derived from the uncanny similarity of their dual personae, of the public professional poet and the private romantic wild man. Berryman carried the torch of the mad poet in Iowa City, as his life there pivoted between brilliant, uncompromising teaching and savage altercations with both faculty and students alike.

"Lowell left in January and Berryman came," as the future poet laureate Levine identified the spark that ignited his career. "Jesus, did the whole thing tone up. I was working well and hard, and he—though he was tough on me—was very encouraging."[28] Levine was not always comfortable with Berryman's methods, however. He remembered "Berryman being tough on one of my poems, a poem that showed I was growing, though not a very good poem." Then "Don Petersen came to my defense, making the point that the poem was evidence of real talent and lots of hard work and development, and that's what should have been said FIRST. Then rip it apart for what was wrong."[29] Berryman notoriously lacked such tact. A violent verbal altercation he had with Marguerite Young at a local bar ended with his arrest at his apartment, landing him in jail. Headlines in the papers the next day scandalized the university's administration, prompting his immediate removal from the Workshop.

The High Ones Do Not Go Gentle

Berryman's volatility at Iowa derived from the pain of losing "the high ones," the great poetic minds of his generation who "die, die. They die," as he wrote in *The Dream Songs*.[30] Homage and elegy were sacred and fiery forms to him at the time, informing his vitriolic rejection of the Lowell follower's poem on the death of Dylan Thomas. Thomas's reinvention of the elegy as a modern poetic form appealed to Berryman, who worked his entire career to master the art of homage in his own writing. Berryman reserved special admiration for Thomas's "A Refusal to Mourn the Death, by Fire, of a Child in London," proclaiming it "one of the profoundest elegies" written in English.[31] The year of Thomas's death, in 1953, Berryman had published his first major work, *Homage to Mistress Bradstreet*, which established him as a master of the elegiac lyric form. When asked in one interview why he wrote poetry, he said it was "For the dead whom thou didst love," trusting that they will read it, "for they return as posterity," citing a dialogue from Johann Georg Hamann quoted in Kierkegaard.[32] In Berryman's hand, elegy was an eclectic and jagged concoction of grief, anger, and humor deeply influenced by the strange and moving music of *Songs of Innocence and Experience* by William Blake. Berryman was also an expert in Shakespeare, regularly demanding his students revisit specific plays in order to eradicate the palaver from their style. With the gruff confidence of a physician prescribing the perfect medicine, he told Levine on one occasion to reread *Macbeth* as a model for honing the technique and tone of his verse.

Berryman's *The Dream Songs*, published in 1969, points to the concurrence of acute psychological turmoil and a surge of creative power that began to overwhelm him a decade earlier in Iowa. "Dream Song 36" is an elegy to William Faulkner, but derives from the mourning of Berryman's own father, whose passing haunted him his entire life, and clearly foreshadowed his own death. Like his father, who died of a self-inflicted gunshot wound on Clear Water Island in 1926, Berryman also took his own life, forty-six years later. Only twelve at the time of his father's suicide, Berryman turned the demons of this crushing tragedy into poetry. Unlike Anne Sexton, whose poetry enabled her to face her dark thoughts directly and exert some degree of emotional control over them, Berryman did not grapple with depression by aestheticizing the circumstances of his own death.

Berryman went in another direction with his darkness, focusing less on dialoging with the forces of suicide and instead on eulogizing the literary luminaries who were his contemporaries and, in several instances, close friends. Elegy in Berryman's hands ran counter to maudlin mourning and sentimentality, for a richer pragmatic sensibility that he certainly shared with Sexton. Berryman's poetic homage to Faulkner in "Dream Song 36" revealed the tragic self-immolation of the creative mind pervasive in a culture that believed "It's better to burn out/ Than to fade away," as expressed in the lyrics of Neil Young. Frost, Williams, and Eliot follow in "Dream Song 36," which takes the shape of a poetic memorial to the great minds of his generation. He mourns the passing of Sylvia Plath, Theodore Roethke, and Louis MacNeice, a list that finally gives way to his personal intimates, Delmore Schwartz and Randall Jarrell, the latter of whom achieved fame for imagining his own demise in a World War II bomber aircraft in "The Death of the Ball Turret Gunner." The gunner's metaphorical birth is figured as an awakening "to black flack and the nightmare flares" that destroy him and lead to the cold, perfunctory processing of his remains. "When I died, they washed me out of the turret with a hose," the voice reports from the afterlife with a knowing frankness about the hard coldness of the passage into death.

The poetic voice that speaks from the grave appears in the American tradition in Emily Dickinson's equally bleak image of the passage from life to death in "I heard a fly buzz when I died." Jarrell's remains are unceremoniously hosed out of a turret and Dickinson's senses abruptly shut down: "And then the windows failed—and then/ I could not see to see," after their last perception is a random fly rather than a grand vision of the gates of heaven.[33] A quiet rage— directed at the machine in Jarrell and at an indifferent deity in Dickinson— sounds a note of frustration and protest, at the cold inhumanity of the military-industrial complex in the former and the hollowness of conventional antebellum Congregational Christian dogma in the latter. Berryman similarly protests against the cosmic injustice of the disproportionately high numbers of brilliant poets that rank among the prematurely deceased.

During his darkest hours in Iowa, horrific visions of death menaced Berryman. Repeatedly awaking bolt upright in bed to a bombardment like Jarrell's black flack and nightmare flares, Berryman struggled to ward off the demons. In a letter to his mother dated April 9, 1954, he described how he had "been suffering lately from terrible waking-nightmares and fear of death." The bleak self-diagnosis pivoted on the fulcrum between a subconscious he could not control and the rational conscious life embodied by his identity as a

professional poet and intensely dedicated faculty member of the Iowa Writers'
Workshop. To shape the uncontrollable demons into art was the challenge, a
formidable one given the horror welling up from the trauma of his father's
suicide during his youth. The trauma was exacerbated in adulthood by watching his best friends and most admired poets pass before their times. Like William Blake, who turned his mad visions into the beautiful nightmares of his
lyrics and visual art, Berryman buoyed himself on the conviction that "life is,
all, transformation," a phrase that appears in his letter to his mother with the
resolve of a survivor.[34] At times in *The Dream Songs* he marveled at his own
capacity to endure: "I don't see how Henry, pried/ Open for all the world to
see survived," figuring himself as the voice of Henry, described in the pro-
logue as one who "has suffered an irreversible loss and talks about himself
sometimes in the first person, sometimes in the third." Asked once if he was
Henry, Berryman acknowledged that he was indeed, noting however that his
created poetic identity is free from the suffering of living: "Henry pays no income tax" and "Henry doesn't have any bats" like the ones "that come over
and stall in my hair."[35]

Berryman's dark humor, also notable in Blake, kept him afloat, even if it
still left him rudderless. During one class at the Workshop, Berryman recited
from memory Blake's "Mad Song," which skewers the condition of the romantic idealist. The poem reflects Berryman's core aesthetic and self-effacing
humor that enabled him to cope with life as mad poet. "I turn my back to the
east/ From whence comforts have increased," Blake writes, "For light doth
seize my brain,/ With frantic pain."[36] The dark humor in the lines satirizes the
singer's self-imposed incarceration within the parameters of time and space
and attempt to escape it by chasing after night. Berryman's best moments in
his own poetry similarly draw back from despair to mock it, not unlike Herman Melville, who routinely checked his own excesses through comic inversion, as when he skewers Ishmael's romantic idealization of life aboard
a whaler by placing him under the command of the mad Captain Ahab in
Moby-Dick.

As with Sexton, poetry kept Berryman alive. One can see him rescue himself from despair within the poems themselves, as in "Dream Song 36." Precisely when he is about to succumb to the dark notion of life as a curse to be
endured while all the brilliant literary minds have died, his tone shifts. He
adopts the vernacular and philosophy of a tough-minded and world-weary
survivor, and quiet assurance prevails: "Now there you exaggerate, Sah. We
hafta die./ That is our 'pointed task. Love & die." Without the capacity to rally

himself in the space of his poetry in this way, Berryman declined rapidly. In his last days, his depression and alcoholism finally interfered with his ability to write and perform at readings and lectures. Similarly, changes in Sexton's pharmaceutical therapy—particularly her shift to Thorazine—intended to treat her depression only sapped her energy and dulled her creative edge. Without poetry, or more precisely with poetry in a severely compromised fog, she and Berryman had little to live for.

Had he remained at Iowa, a different John Berryman, both poet and man, would have surely emerged. Despite his complaints to his mother about the alienating environment—"I detest Iowa City," he wrote—he qualified his otherwise damning impressions: "I don't *like* the people here much, but have nothing against them." The truth is that he was thriving at the Workshop in spite of himself: "Several of my students are good enough to be worth the trouble," especially Philip Levine and Anita Phillips. Behind the mask of the disagreeable curmudgeon was his admission that "everyone [is] very pleasant" and that his work in the classroom was both painstaking and satisfying, a labor of love he deeply valued. He had spent a great deal of time "setting up my courses, at which I've worked very hard and am teaching beautifully," an edifying yet exhausting enterprise that "has not left me much energy."[37]

Such creative burning Berryman identified with the brilliant flare that was Dylan Thomas's soaring Welsh-English voice, possessing a rhythm and wit of striking alacrity, tenderness, and verbal agility. The Workshop in Berryman's seminar hardly drummed the individualism out of students or formalized their writing. Thomas's meeting with students delighted in their diversity of voices and experiences; he would also be hard to imagine as a scold demanding regular meter. If Berryman had been harsh, it was only because "Even a class as remarkable as this one will produce terrible poems, and I am the one obliged to say so."[38] But what marked both mad poets was their openness and encouragement of young talent. As we saw, Lowell had discouraged Snodgrass on early drafts of *Heart's Needle*, demeaning what others considered courageous self-disclosure and emotional verve in treating the subject of his separation from his daughter. "Snodgrass," he groused, "you have a mind; you mustn't write this tear-jerking stuff."[39] Berryman gave opposite advice, never condemning early drafts as sentimental, and always pushing the metrical and formal limits of his syntactical expression. Levine received such guidance from Berryman, who inspired experimentation and unusual subjects, which the more formally inclined Lowell detested, tending instead "toward poetry written in formal meters, rhymed, and hopefully involved with the grief of great families, either current suburban ones or those out of the great store-house of America's or Europe's past," as Levine described. Levine's poetry would thrive under Berryman's eclectic, inclusive approach, inviting and vali-dating his poems on subjects from his working-class background in Detroit. But Berryman never neglected or ignored the use of formal meter as an object of experimentation itself. "He even had the boldness to suggest that contem-porary voices could achieve themselves in so unfashionable and dated a form as the Petrarchan sonnet," testifying to how "he was all over the place and seemed delighted with the variety we represented."[40]

Just as Dylan Thomas did "not go gentle into that good night," Berryman would himself be among "The high ones" who "die, die. They die." These mad poets burned through Iowa City, forever changing the place, upsetting the be-lief that literary professionalism necessitated the production of uniform work-shop verse. Instead of suppressing subjectivity and idiosyncratic individual perception, Berryman encouraged it in his classes, and Thomas embodied it in his madcap visit and virtuoso reading. Both undermined the common assumption that teachers like Lowell had standardized poetic form, when both Levine's and Snodgrass's training and publications suggest otherwise. Their work, like their mentor, did not fit the description of the Workshop's produc-tion of the disciplinary "quintessential *form* of literary professionalism" re-sponsible for generating "the academic poem of the 1950s and early 1960s," a species of writing "densely textured, tonally restrained, traditional in meter and form, replete with classical and mythological allusion and symbol."[41] In fact, Berryman's aesthetic liberated his students to draw from traditional met-rical forms and the rich symbolism of classical mythology—particularly according to the models of Shakespeare and Blake—to find a personal voice, like the ones Levine and Snodgrass discovered. His eclecticism indeed antici-pated the Language writing movement of the 1970s that rose in opposition to the academic poem advanced by such writers as Lowell. In this manner, Berryman shared more with the Beats, as did Thomas. That aesthetic also de-manded a full-bodied immersion in the creative process, one that left personal lives in ashes. Berryman and Thomas, whose madness was their poetry, em-bodied Jack Kerouac's "mad ones, the ones who are mad to live, mad to talk, mad to be saved, desirous of everything at the same time, the ones that never yawn or say a commonplace thing, but burn, burn, burn like the fabulous yellow roman candles exploding like spiders across the stars."[42]

Flannery O'Connor at Amana Colonies, with Robie Macauley (with camera) and Arthur Koestler, 1947 (Wikimedia Commons)

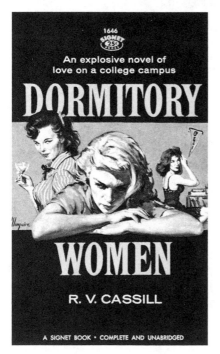

R. V. Cassill with a student at the Iowa
Writers' Workshop, 1960 (Courtesy of the
University of Iowa Library Archives)

Pulp fiction by R. V. Cassill, 1954: one of
many attempts to supplement his income
(Wikimedia Commons)

Paul Engle with Iowa Writers' Workshop students, circa 1950s
(Courtesy of the University of Iowa Library Archives)

Paul Engle (left), with Ralph Ellison, Mark Harris, Dwight Macdonald, Arnold
Gingrich (standing), and Norman Mailer, at the Writer in Mass Culture symposium
(sponsored by *Esquire*) at the University of Iowa, December 4, 1959
(Courtesy of the University of Iowa Library Archives)

Paul Engle (right), presenting *Midland: Twenty-Five Years of Fiction and Poetry, Selected from the Writing Workshops of the State University of Iowa* (1961) to President Virgil Hancher at the University of Iowa, May 11, 1961 (Courtesy of the University of Iowa Library Archives)

Paul Engle at a reception for the anthology *Midland*, Iowa Memorial Union, University of Iowa, 1961 (Courtesy of the University of Iowa Library Archives)

Peace March in protest of the Vietnam War, Clinton Street, Iowa City, 1960s
(Courtesy of the University of Iowa Library Archives)

Robert Lowell, above, January 1, 1965 (Photo by Elsa Dorfman; Wikimedia Commons)

Kurt Vonnegut, left, February 17, 1972 (Wikimedia Commons)

Margaret Walker, Poetry MFA 1942, the first African-American graduate of the Iowa Writers' Workshop, returned to Iowa to train as a fiction writer under R. V. Cassill. *Jubilee*, her doctoral thesis from 1966, was published by Houghton Mifflin. (Courtesy of the University of Iowa Library Archives)

Jane Smiley, October 31, 2009 (Wikimedia Commons)
T. C. Boyle, May 19, 2013 (Wikimedia Commons)

Marilynne Robinson, April 21, 2012 (Wikimedia Commons)

PART 2
THE WORKSHOP IN THE AGE OF AQUARIUS (1960s–1970s)

8 • Celebrity Faculty: Kurt Vonnegut and John Irving

In mid-1960s suburban Cape Cod, Kurt Vonnegut—whose ink sketches and signed monographs now command up to five thousand dollars each—was unknown and his books were out of print. "I was rescued by Paul Engle's Writers' Workshop in the mid 1960s," Vonnegut recalled, "and he didn't know me, and I don't think he had ever heard of me. He didn't read that kind of crap."[1] As an eleventh-hour replacement for Robert Lowell, who "decided not to appear" for his visiting teaching position arranged for the fall of 1965, Vonnegut leaped at the opportunity. "I needed the money. I needed the stimulation. I needed the change in scene," especially from an environment devoid of literary life. "My neighbors on Cape Cod didn't read me, didn't read anything, so I had felt like a pointless citizen there," he said.[2] The Workshop held promise to transform the forgotten paperback writer into a famous literary author. The exploit, however, was not without its hidden perils. "We are what we pretend to be," according to his ominous warning in *Mother Night*, "so we must be careful about what we pretend to be."[3]

In scrambling for a replacement for Lowell, Vance Bourjaily, one of Engle's trusted advisers, "assured [Engle] I was indeed a writer, but dead broke with a lot of kids," Vonnegut recalled. He had six children under his care, three of his own, and his sister's three boys he had adopted when she and her husband died within twenty-four hours of each other. This burden compounded the desperation attendant to being "completely out of print and scared to death."[4] The unlikely leap from freelance popular fiction writing to the world-renowned Iowa Writers' Workshop presented Vonnegut with precisely the opportunity to win the serious recognition he had longed for as well as the financial stability he desperately needed.

Suddenly immersed in a community of elite writers, Vonnegut embarked on a self-conscious effort to reinvent himself. With most of his training in science, "he had not read many of the great novels his colleagues had been fond of discussing." Like the young Richard Rodriguez taking it on himself to read the top one hundred canonical works of literature to build his literary success in the white community one book at a time, a syndrome he called "the scholarship boy," Vonnegut similarly began reading classics to socially assimilate.[5] His self-imposed "crash course in reading" was one of many signs of the self-consciousness he felt on his arrival in Iowa City for the fall semester of 1965. Reaching middle age "before I went crazy about Blake," he turned "forty before I read *Madame Bovary*, forty-five before I had even heard of Céline." Although he "grew up in a house crammed with books," he "never had to read a book for academic credit, never had to write a paper about it, never had to prove I'd understood it in a seminar." In literary criticism, he was out of his league. "I am a hopelessly clumsy discusser of books. My experience is nil," he confessed.[6] As the Vonnegut scholar Thomas F. Marvin points out, "For the first time in his life, he was expected to talk about writing, which forced him to think more deeply about his creative process."[7] He reached for anything he could find, including golf metaphors, to try to explain the proper form and rhythms of the game of creative writing. The challenge alone would have been formidable enough, had his arrival not been accompanied by whispers that he was a lowly purveyor of popular genre fiction, "a science-fiction hack" as one Workshop student alleged.[8] That particular slur would have gone unchallenged had it not been for Vonnegut's star student, John Irving, who rushed to his defense, precipitating a barroom brawl—a classic dramatic scene from 1960s Iowa City—over the aesthetic integrity of his beloved mentor.

Paperback Writer

In the years before his arrival in Iowa City, Vonnegut's enterprising journalistic bent had been visible in an early column he wrote for the *Cornell Daily Sun*, which led him to try his hand at popular magazine fiction as a way of sustaining his wife and children on Cape Cod. When he shared his work with Norman Mailer, however, he knew instantly that the stigma of the pulp market would make it difficult to enter the ranks of intellectual culture. "You are right in saying that what I write is slick," he replied to Mailer.[9] This realization did not prevent him from discovering that trade paperback publishers, with their generous advance contracts and signing bonuses, could provide an even richer source of revenue than magazines. Further, his magazine publishers began dropping out of business with alarming regularity.[10]

As the periodical press accommodating science fiction withered, the paperback market exploded. An outline and a first chapter, Vonnegut soon learned, could earn him an advance of three thousand dollars. He began to resemble the "Paperback Writer" of the Beatles' 1966 hit single about a man whose prolific outpouring of material is matched only by his shameless promotion of it: "If you really like it you can have the rights/ It could make a million for you overnight." On swivel racks in drug stores, bus depots, and train stations sat Vonnegut's first novels, *The Sirens of Titan* and *Mother Night*, along with his short story collection, *Canary in a Cat House*. "I was building a power base," he later admitted, "with sleazo paperbacks." With six children to raise, he knew his methods had to be ruthless. "This society is based on extortion, and you can have anything you want if you have a power base."[11] Although *Cat's Cradle* earned a favorable critical reception after its release in 1963, his work remained virtually invisible. "I wasn't even getting reviewed," he recalled. "*Esquire* published a list of the American literary world back then and it guaranteed that every living author of the slightest merit was on there somewhere. I wasn't on there . . . [and] it made me feel subhuman."[12] Any literary recognition of the hardcover editions of *Cat's Cradle* and *God Bless You, Mr. Rosewater* were rendered meaningless, as they too went out of print. The Faustian deal—prestige in exchange for the steady income of trade genre fiction—left him penniless.

Kilgore Trout, the writer whose works appear in a Manhattan porn shop in *Slaughterhouse-Five*, his breakthrough novel from 1969, expresses Vonnegut's regret for having catered to the lowest common denominator. The lament was perhaps never more acute than while working in Iowa City among literary elites on the manuscript for *Slaughterhouse-Five*, a novel he intended to write based on his experience as a survivor of the bombing of Dresden and a prisoner there during World War II. The novel's simple diction, staccato syntax, and truncated paragraphs bear the clear influence of the clipped reportorial language from his days on the Chicago City News Bureau in the late 1940s. "The Dresden book is about the size of *The Bobbsey Twins*," he feared, "and reads like a telegram."[13] In it, the protagonist Billy Pilgrim strolls through Times Square where, peering "into the window of a tawdry bookstore," he finds lowbrow kitsch, "hundreds of books about . . . buggery and murder, and a street guide to New York City, and a model of the Statue of Liberty with a thermometer on it." He sees "also in the window, speckled with soot and fly shit, four paperback novels by Billy's friend, Kilgore Trout."[14]

Billy enters the store and thumbs through a copy of one of Kilgore Trout's science fiction novels. He remembers reading it before, especially the scene describing how "the news ticker" reminded all the Earthlings "that the President of the United States had declared National Prayer Week, and that everybody should pray." In this science fiction dystopia, a self-reflexive parody of Vonnegut's own bleak visions, church and state are linked through capitalism. "The Earthlings had had a bad week on the market" and "lost a small fortune in olive oil futures." To their delight, after they "gave praying a whirl . . . Olive oil went up." Like the profaning of sacred prayer, the democratic function of the press, and the use of the White House for gains on the stock market in Kilgore Trout's novel, literature itself has been hijacked by the equivalent of pawnbrokers. The loss of the literary establishment to lowbrow culture is metaphorically expressed in how "The bookstore was run by seeming quintuplets, by five short, bald men chewing unlit cigars that were sopping wet." Vonnegut's unmistakable guilt for consorting with such media profiteers who "were making money running a paper-and-celluloid whorehouse" overwhelms his Times Square bookstore scene.[15]

But Vonnegut's guilt for allowing his work to circulate among such lowly media merchandise was only by association. The store's owner sees Billy reading a Kilgore Trout novel and tells him, "That ain't what you want, for Christ's sake. What you want's in *back*," where the true smut is kept. Vonnegut understood his work to be above what was in back, to have an entirely different set of concerns perhaps only perceptible, or even relevant, to cracked veterans such as Billy Pilgrim. Vonnegut was a veteran himself who had seen the horror of war up close, and longed for a deeper understanding of the afterlife and salvation. Representing Vonnegut's Constant Reader, Billy does not put down the book and go in *back*. Instead, he goes to the *back* of the Kilgore Trout time-travel dystopia to find the truth about salvation, very much motivated *for Christ's sake*. Could Jesus save us, he wonders? There he finds the novel's time traveler climbing on to the cross to detect signs of life in the Messiah as he hangs crucified before the Romans. To his dismay, he discovers, "There wasn't a sound inside the emaciated chest cavity. The Son of God was dead as a doornail."[16]

Vonnegut may have regarded the import of his work, like Kilgore Trout's, as clearly out of place among the trade paperbacks that crowded the shelves of the Times Square bookstore. But that is precisely how his writing was packaged in the mid-1950s, as seen in its appearance in the twenty-five-cent paperback *Tomorrow, the Stars* trumpeting "Thrilling Tales of a Time Beyond

Tomorrow!" on its cover, and his tale, "The Big Trip Up Yonder" under the imprint of Galaxy Publishing Corporation marketed by his agents, Littauer & Wilkinson.[17] Even these yarns distinguish themselves from the rest of the genre, especially through deeper concerns. Those concerns are for the sake of humanity in light of the nation's mechanization toward war and compromise of religion, press, and literature as it gravitates toward capitalistic greed. *Slaughterhouse-Five* in many ways represented his first self-conscious attempt at literary authorship, which he originally conceived as a narrative nonfictional account of his experience in Dresden. But he soon found that mode, and even realistic fiction, silenced his voice and stripped him of his creativity. He had indeed become what he had pretended to be as he prophesied in *Mother Night*—a science fiction writer. But the genre threatened to prevent him from his deeper aspiration to capture the countercultural ethos of his era in serious literature. Vonnegut did not need literature to save him from tawdry kitsch culture, a cesspool that swallows Kilgore Trout's profoundest insights. Instead he needed to import his science fiction aesthetic—an inescapably popular genre—into a novel of ideas. He produced that novel of ideas, *Slaughterhouse-Five*, which many regard as his greatest novel, in Iowa City.

As the first true trade genre writer to join the faculty of the Iowa Writers' Workshop, Vonnegut felt a sense of outsidership from his first introduction to Engle in 1965. Engle struck him as "a lean, gray-haired slightly crooked Supreme Court Justice dressed like Harry Belafonte," a curious mix of political cunning and flamboyant show business.[18] That year Engle had just been appointed to a six-year term on the National Council of the Arts, which also included John Steinbeck, Ralph Ellison, and Sidney Poitier. Engle distinguished himself on the committee by urging, "We need to spread the businessman's daring to the field of art."[19] But his definition of art did not include genre fiction. Totally unfamiliar with science fiction, Engle certainly had no agenda to usher writers of popular genre fiction into the program. His own interests were primarily in poetry, which for the Workshop had reached spectacular heights in the 1950s through visiting teaching by Lowell and Berryman, and an extended stay by the perpetually florid Dylan Thomas. The most popular fiction published by a Workshop faculty member before Vonnegut belonged to R. V. Cassill, whose steamy titles were part of the postwar art movement that shattered the divide between high and low art. "Pulp brought a second-hand modernism to mid-century America," according to Paula Rabinowitz's powerful study, a new sensibility that erased distinctions between a canonized figure such as Faulkner and smut.[20] Dell Publishing, which brought out

Slaughterhouse-Five in 1969, was known as the largest publisher of pulp and humor magazines, producing one of the most significant lines of comics in the industry. One might have expected Vonnegut to resist signing with such a publisher. Yet their "admixture of high and low was built into the industry," one that routinely hired "the bright boys from Yale and Princeton."[21]

That mix of high and low print culture has deep roots tracing back to the onset of World War II. As Rabinowitz explains, "The paperback as an object and a phenomenon was intimately tied to the war, as American paperback publishers scurried to fill voids opened when shipping books from England ceased after war was declared on Germany in 1939." Given this surge in paperbacks at the beginning of the war, the industry had been building momentum with exploding sales of original titles and newly "pulped" classics such as *Brave New World* and *The Great Gatsby*, now bearing sensationalistic covers inspired by the true-crime genre. During the postwar era, this movement opened the floodgates for "holocaust pulp" or "history pulp" immediately after the conflict ended.[22] Had *Slaughterhouse-Five* continued this dubious tradition two decades later?

Rather than allow others to raise this question at his expense, Vonnegut chose to preempt it, particularly through the delicate ethics of creating entertainment media out of human loss and tragedy. In conversations and interviews, he rehearsed his now famous line confessing his guilt for financially profiting from the tragedy. Jerome Klinkowitz, "one of the first academic fans" of Vonnegut's work, first heard it in a dinner conversation, and to him it seemed orchestrated at the time.[23] It then appeared in an interview in the *Paris Review* before it finally made its way into the introduction to a later edition of *Slaughterhouse-Five*. Vonnegut's first rehearsal of the line with Klinkowitz was specifically meant to weigh the impact of his complicity in the capitalist infrastructure of popular cultural production. Its successful reception in private signaled to him that it was ready for mass communication in the periodical and book presses. "The raid didn't end the war one day earlier, didn't save one life, not of an American soldier, Russian soldier or concentration camp inmate," he pointed out, reinforcing the pacifist theme of the novel. "Only one person benefitted from the bombing of Dresden," he said with a long pause. "Me." The darkness of the sentiment eclipses any potential humor in it. "I got three dollars for every man, woman, and child killed there."[24] By placing it bluntly in the context of the publishing industry and the larger capitalist pursuit of book sales, Vonnegut disclosed his darkest fear, that he had desecrated the memory of the dead and the authorial role.

The confession spoke to his roots in popular fiction, harkening back to his original construction of a power base through strategic communication, first for corporate America, and then as an entrepreneurial journalist and paperback writer. In this way, his work as a "Public Relations Man" for General Electric, from 1949 to 1951, as he listed it on his "Faculty Personnel Data Blank" for the University of Iowa, was crucially connected to his ambivalence about making a living from his fiction as a "Freelance writer" who was "Self-employed" from " '51 to present."[25] Commercial sales, most pointedly, had been a major source of income, as he had managed a Saab automobile dealership in West Barnstable, Massachusetts, after resigning from his position at General Electric.[26] The Saab dealership position, as one might expect, does not appear on Vonnegut's Iowa résumé.

Joining the Workshop without graduate academic training and lacking in literary credentials, Vonnegut was "always sensitive to how his material was being received, how his listeners were reacting." His lectures also were extremely attuned to audience reactions. Klinkowitz remembered how "time and again, I would marvel at how he'd work an audience, giving more of something when it seemed to be succeeding, dropping a topic the moment it threatened to go over like a lead balloon."[27] Evidence of this concern for reception, specifically into the category of literary author, as opposed to genre hack, surfaces in the attitudes of his most loyal students. His past as a Saab dealer and General Electric public relations man haunted him, as he struggled to decouple his public reputation from mass marketing.

Fighting Words

John Irving, Vonnegut's star student, fiercely defended his mentor's status as a literary author worthy of his faculty position at the Workshop. One night in an Iowa City poolroom, Vonnegut's commercial reputation came under scrutiny. The student responsible for what was taken as a galling slur had previously drawn the ire of Irving for claiming boxers could dominate wrestlers. Irving had been a serious wrestler, ranking his coaches with Vonnegut as "the father figures I latched onto in life." The offending student had been a follower of Nelson Algren, whose fiction Workshop Irving loathed. "I thought he was an asshole . . . a blowhard and a pontificator, but he had some students firmly in his thrall; he was a recruiter"—unlike Vonnegut, who to Irving did not engage in such shameless self-promotion to win the admiration of the graduate students. "Kurt just shuffled around; he didn't care if you took notice of him or not. He was both a mentor and a teacher. I loved the guy." Algren himself "used to try and bait me into a fight with him," Irving remembered of perhaps the most obnoxious participant in the Workshop rivalry between the wrestlers and the boxers. "A boxer can kick the shit out of a wrestler," Algren sneered at Irving on one occasion.[28]

So when Algren's student faced off with Irving, more was at stake than rival mentors. Workshop members were perennially obsessed with "publishing and 'the market' for books," Workshop graduate Eric Olsen remarked. "What was selling? What were the trends?" they wondered. "But then if you worried about trends, you were a commercial hack and shame on you."[29] This was precisely the allegation aimed at Vonnegut, and his most loyal student, Irving, by extension. The cumulative effects of flowing beer and trash talk over cracking billiard balls had all but obliterated social inhibitions. Hoping for an opportunity to prove his boxing skills, Algren's protégé hurled his most potent insult: "Vonnegut is a science fiction hack." Wounded deeply, Irving demanded to know if he had "read a single one of Kurt's books." "Only the covers," was the reply. Fighting words, to be sure, in mid-1960s Iowa City.[30]

Dropping his pool cue in disbelief, Irving shot back an epithet and riveted his eyes on the offender. He slowly approached, crouching in a wrestler's stance with his hands open in front of him. His opponent raised his fists and began bobbing rhythmically like a boxer. Tables overturned and people scattered, plates and glasses shattering in the tumult. Irving advanced, aware that "I just can't hit very hard," but preparing to deploy "the jab-hook combination as a means to get close enough to my opponent so that I can trip him." With lightning speed, the wiry Irving ducked a wild roundhouse right and with his downward momentum propped himself on one hand and swung out his legs in a flash, cutting down his opponent scythe-like at the ankles. Helpless, Algren's student crashed to the beer-soaked hardwood floor, his head cracking with a sickening thud. "A wrestling move," and with the desired result of "convincingly demonstrating—although never to Nelson Algren and not in his presence—that wrestling is superior to boxing."[31]

Although not physical, Vonnegut's own form of retaliation against Algren also deployed deceptive tactics. "I'm awed. You're one of the few important artists of our time," he inscribed like a cloying sycophant in a copy of *Mother Night*, "and the only one I know." A few weeks later Vonnegut reported to a friend that he had fleeced Algren to the tune of "several thousand bucks in a pot-limit poker game run by racketeers from the Graduate School." This was one of several instances of how "old Wobbly," as the frequently tipsy Algren was called, is "fucking up monumentally out here" in ways that included "bob-bing the Workshop in newspaper interviews."[32] The score may have been set-tled in the poolroom and at the poker table. But both triumphs did little to undo Vonnegut's reputation as a commercial hack. Algren's protégé's refusal to look beyond the pulpy covers of Vonnegut's books for the true nature of his work infuriated Irving precisely because it typified the superficial judgments used to marginalize otherwise worthy talent at the Workshop. In his view, Vonnegut's writing transcended the science fiction genre conventions repre-sented in its fanboy covers. But the paperback stigma persisted, with more than one student "put off by anything close to science fiction," according to Workshop alumnus Gary Iorio.[33] Irving was one of the few students who had actually read Vonnegut's novels, mainly because so few were still in print and accessible. "I'd read all his books, which were not easy to find then, and I be-lieved he was underrated—and unfairly categorized as a science fiction writer."[34]

Those straining for literary status derided such writing as so much show business and public relations, mass communication for profit rather than art. Besides Irving, John Casey, Gail Godwin, and others in the small cluster of talented students who called themselves the "Vonnegut people," few Work-shop students appreciated him in the early fall of 1965. "Many of my fellow Workshop students," Irving bitterly recollected, "dismissed him as unworthy of their precious time." Enrollments reflected his lack of popularity. "It wasn't hard to get into Kurt's fiction workshop."[35] Yet obscurity carried a unique ad-vantage, according to his colleague Marguerite Young. Vance Bourjaily, she attested, "would cut my throat if I went over big with students, so I am watch-ful."[36] Popularity came at the cost of the faculty's envy, advice that alerted Vonnegut once again to be careful who he pretended to be.

An Author of Distinction

Much of Vonnegut's efforts in his first year at the Workshop were directed toward establishing his credentials as a legitimate literary author. Toward the end of his second semester at Iowa, in April 1966, Vonnegut furnished the English department chair John Gerber with a copy of the galleys of a glowing review of *Player Piano* in *Harper's*. His rush to send the proofs ahead of publi-cation revealed the urgency of his desire to appear worthy of the prestige of his Workshop faculty position. He knew Gerber held sway as an arbiter of intel-lect on campus, and thus made a point of sharing his latest feat with an eye toward escaping the science fiction stigma that had followed him since his arrival.

This *Harper's* review in particular attested to Vonnegut's transcendence from the science fiction genre, a point he hoped would verify his credentials for Gerber against claims that Workshop faculty should hold doctorates. The reviewer, Richard Schickel, a renowned biographer of the glamorous Cotton Club jazz singer Lena Horne, articulated perhaps better than Vonnegut ever did himself precisely the dynamic by which to understand him as a serious writer, with a complex relation toward science fiction and humor. Schickel argued, much to Vonnegut's delight and Gerber's admiration, that he was not "simply a writer of science fiction, a distinctly *déclassé* popular genre which no important literary person takes seriously." Given the quality of his work, he continued, "it became obvious that science was only incidental to his fiction," and that "a new category" of black comedy now applies to him. This designation of dark humorist "placed him in somewhat more fashionable company, but it did not differentiate him from his peers any more clearly than he had been from his previous ones." The result, Schickel astutely observed, has given rise to a "Vonnegut cult," which overlapped with the "Vonnegut people," the small yet fiercely loyal band led by Irving. Despite such a following, "he has as yet to reach the wide literate audience that an unimitative and inimitable social satirist might reasonably expect to find these days."[37] He deserved a large, sophisticated readership, but it had eluded him thanks to the snap categorizations of science fiction and black comedy. More than this, he was a social satirist of monumental significance to our culture, its progress, and the moral conundrums that threaten it.

Gerber replied with an outpouring of praise and support that left Vonnegut feeling validated and vindicated. "We are thoroughly delighted that you are getting the notices that your work deserves. I'm joining your fan club, too," he gushed, "and am having a wonderful time going through your novels"— language that perhaps inadvertently disclosed his delight in the fiction as entertainment rather than appreciation of it as serious literature. Gerber went on to assuage Vonnegut's "fear that as time goes on, we'll be expecting Workshop lecturers as well as our more academic types to have Ph.D.'s." He assured him that such talk was directed more pointedly at Engle, whose highest degree was a creative writing M.A. and whose unilateral allocation of funds without English department consultation had been the object of scorn from Gerber and his unit. "I do think that the Director of the Workshop should probably have the degree," he affirmed as part of his larger campaign against Engle that effectively dismantled his reign by 1966. Without explaining how or why a Ph.D. should be necessary for directing the Workshop—no director has ever held the degree in the history of the program—Gerber and the English department had targeted Engle's lack as a weakness. "But beyond that what we need are men who are at once effective teachers and writers of distinction. You eminently qualify on both counts," he wrote, encouraging him "to stay here for at least an eon or two!"[38] Gerber's support of Vonnegut, he made clear, would not extend to Engle or the Workshop in general. That year, Engle was on his way out, and would soon be known, in Vonnegut's description, as "the former head . . . a hayseed clown, a foxy grandpa, a terrific promoter who, if you listen closely, talks like a man with a paper asshole."[39] Engle joined forces with Leslie (Hualing) Nieh at the time to establish the International Writing Program, and he fully dedicated himself to it by 1969.

Gerber's letter is even more bizarre in light of the fact that Vonnegut had no college degree whatsoever. "Nelson [Algren] and I have no futures in the field, since we have no degrees," Vonnegut wrote his wife. By comparison, "Bourjaily is loaded with them and is a university career man."[40] Vonnegut felt so acutely self-conscious about lacking a degree that he sought to complete his master's in anthropology from the University of Chicago, a program he had entered on the GI Bill despite lacking an undergraduate degree. He had dropped out of Cornell in his junior year, in January 1942, after being placed on academic probation the previous May for satirical columns in the *Cornell Daily Sun.* "I was flunking everything by the middle of my junior year. I was delighted to join the Army and go to war," he recalled.[41] Not surprisingly, those columns reflected a pacifist bent with a unique dark humor that would become the signature feature of his fiction, drawing attention from censors for the rest of his career. Chicago received the completed M.A. thesis he finished within the first ten days of his arrival, as a desperate measure to correct the glaring deficiency of any degree in higher education. That deficiency was all the more conspicuous since he had been charged with the task of educating and accrediting students in the most reputable creative writing graduate program in the world.[42]

At stake in earning an advanced degree was not only credibility among the Workshop faculty and students, but a much needed raise in salary, since he had entered with a contract of a mere $8,500, the lowest salary on the program's staff. The Chicago anthropology department, however, rejected his thesis comparing narrative rituals in primitive cultures to contemporary short story writing, on the grounds that "it was not valid to compare primitive and civilized societies."[43] Chicago eventually attempted to repair the wound, but only after Vonnegut had achieved worldwide fame following the publication of *Slaughterhouse-Five*. In 1971, long after he desperately needed a twenty-percent raise, which the master's degree would have earned him in his Workshop salary in 1965, Chicago awarded him the degree in anthropology based on his novel *Cat's Cradle*. The novel had been published in 1963, two years before his arrival in Iowa City. Vonnegut retaliated in his memoir, *Palm Sunday*, by howling, "the University of Chicago . . . can take a flying fuck at the moooooooooooooooon," his way of "telling a great university his true feelings."[44]

Chasing degrees was pointless, precisely because "the Workshop had always been staffed by professionals, so staffers have almost always been self-educated and worse-educated than you," according to the hilariously accurate advice he gave to author Dick Gehman, who had just accepted a teaching position in the program. "Forget your lack of credentials," he said. "The University is perfectly used to barbarians in the Workshop," and (except for Engle) the administration "thinks nothing of it," as shown by his correspondence with Gerber. Those lacking degrees were a near majority, he assured him; "Yates has no degree. Algren had one, but tried to hush it up (Journalism B.A., U. of Illinois)." The real credentials that make non-degree holding Workshop faculty "as glorious as any full professor" lie in their connections to the publishing industry, particularly the capacity to function on behalf of the budding writers as a literary agent. Rather than advanced degrees, one's faculty status would be secure as long as "you know REAL WRITERS and REAL EDITORS in BOSTON and NEW YORK." Since formal teaching was just a sidelight to this essential function, "classes don't matter much," and "the real business, head-to-head, is done during office hours in the afternoons" for the benefit of the students, which itself takes scant time and responsibility. This is because "Mornings are for writing—and so are most of the afternoons."[45] Although Vonnegut may have implored his students to avoid writing like mercenaries of the literary marketplace, hinging every aesthetic decision on its potential salability, he certainly understood the faculty role as informal publicist to ensure handsome profits from their work.[46]

The formulation that sophisticated audiences could expand beyond narrow niche followings provided an avenue for Vonnegut's ascendance. In a rare turn of events in publishing, after Scribner's edition of *Player Piano* went out of print, Holt, Rinehart and Winston reprinted the novel in 1966.[47] Even more striking is for a title to debut in paperback and later move to the literary prestige of hardcover, rather than the industry standard of the reverse. This was precisely the fate of *Mother Night*, which had disappeared from print after its initial paperback run only to rise again under the reputable imprint of Harper and Row. In a feat that Stephen King and other genre writers have attempted to no avail, Vonnegut had essentially crossed over into the literary establishment. The gatekeeper allowing Vonnegut entrance into such exclusive company in this case was *Harper's*, whose review prompted a reconsideration of his work. With all of his works now in print, his star was on the rise.

Even the trade press Dell reissued *The Sirens of Titan* in Vonnegut's magical year of 1966. Delacorte/Dell had distinguished itself by offering contracts for both hard- and soft-cover editions, which allowed the publisher to exceed the industry standard for advances and signing bonuses. The crossover model between trade and hardcover proved successful in the hands of Dell's Sam Lawrence, who signed Vonnegut to a three-book contract for the rights to both hardcover and paperback editions. Vonnegut scholar Dan Wakefield argues that Lawrence's "faith that writers he believed in who had not yet become big moneymakers would eventually earn back their advances and make his company a profit was borne out—most dramatically of all by Kurt Vonnegut."[48] Yet Lawrence's decision was not made on faith in the product alone. He also carefully took into account the rising stock of Vonnegut on the literary market, and seized him at the moment of his most precipitous ascent toward the apex of his powers. *Cat's Cradle* earned a contract with a New York producer for staging as a Broadway musical, and Peter Sellers of *Pink Panther* fame commenced filming *God Bless You, Mr. Rosewater*. Even Nelson Algren, whom Irving loathed as the antithesis of his beloved mentor, became a Vonnegut advocate. Unlike most Workshop novels produced as Hollywood films, a move typically frowned on in the program as execrable commercial pandering, *God Bless You, Mr. Rosewater* surprisingly won over the elitist Algren. "The novel happens to be excellent," he wrote. "It explores the problem of how to love people who are of no use with such fantastic humor that we at first do not realize that it is ominous" as resonant narrative art.[49] The paperback writer was now on the silver screen, Broadway, and most important, between hardcovers.

Not surprisingly, at the height of this Vonnegut renaissance, Gerber notified him that he would be receiving a pay raise, one calculated to entice him into remaining permanently at Iowa. His modest original "stipend of $8500 for the academic year 1965–1966" dramatically increased to $11,000 for the following year.[50] "In Iowa City I was central and spectacular," Vonnegut wrote, and "suddenly writing seemed important again."[51] Vance Bourjaily had lobbied for the salary increase in a letter to Gerber, writing, "It is Paul's and my feeling that he has done and continues to do an excellent job and deserves whatever increase in wages seems appropriate for a man of his high caliber."[52] The sea change in the critical reception of his work was profound, as a miraculous reversal of public reputation had taken place in just one year. Not everyone at Iowa universally accepted Vonnegut as a writer of distinction, and many critics seriously qualified their praise. Jerome Klinkowitz, the first academic to study Vonnegut's career, remarked how "Critics were confused by Kurt Vonnegut, Jr. He was weird. They hated to admit they dug Vonnegut," in part because doing so breached the divide between high and low art.[53]

Vonnegut tried to wipe away such critical confusion over the seriousness of his work by claiming that he was writing a historical novel, thereby positioning himself as a writer of more than just science fiction or comedy. "I have a novel about the Great Depression in progress," he promised, quite falsely, in a letter he wrote to Gerber when he accepted the position, "and will finish it there."[54] Instead, in his first two weeks at Iowa, he would "swim every couple of days, and do pushups and situps, and smoke worse than ever, and write not at all," except for work on the aforementioned "master's thesis in anthropology, which I've owed Chicago for 18 years."[55] Although he did not write about the Great Depression, his attention turned toward another historical event, the firebombing of Dresden in *Slaughterhouse-Five*, the seriousness of which he insisted on in the final words of its preface: "I've finished my war book now. The next one I write is going to be fun."[56]

The preface to the book also sought to preempt any potential bias against science fiction in the literary community, as well as Gerber and his readers, by describing the work as a painful and harrowing look back into the past. Yet the novel itself included such obvious genre conventions as time travel, interplanetary alien life, and futuristic dystopian settings. His own distaste for schlock fiction, on display in the Times Square bookstore scene, also belies a distinct drive for literary dollars, an instinct for capital reaching back to his days in public relations at General Electric. The capitalist in him seeking to control the power base appears in private letters and conversation throughout his two years at Iowa. Unlike such poets as Lowell and Berryman, Vonnegut never had the luxury of serial visiting faculty appointments under the protective patronage, income, and support of well-endowed universities. Before arriving at the Workshop, Vonnegut had been isolated, both professionally and financially, from the web of creative writing programs that had sheltered so many writers from the ravages of the free market. Financially unprotected, he resorted to selling cars to supplement his dwindling royalties. He had been a creature of entrepreneurial America, both in corporate culture and as his own authorial brand as a freelancer, an experience that tempered his outlook on the profession of literature. Thus, when Vonnegut announced to a cluster of students, in his typically humorous yet crushingly sad way, "how hopeless it was to be a young writer living in America—he vouched that advertising was the next big game."[57] They all had been laboring under a mistake, he claimed, since advertising was growing at a rate proportional to the decline of fiction writing.

Whereas such depressing prophecies of creative writing's demise as a viable means of making a living proved true for the aggregate population of aspiring authors in America, select Workshop students enjoyed the advantage of an inside track to success. "Capitalism will be kind to you one day," Vonnegut told Irving. His star student turned the statement over in his mind for years after, not sure of its intended meaning. Was he being sarcastic? Did this mean something about the salability of the fiction he was writing, or some future career outside of literature, in one of the lucrative fields he had been touting, like advertising? He finally confronted his mentor, asking, "Did you mean that you thought I was going to write a best seller and make a lot of money on my writing?" Vonnegut looked at him with a knowing smile. "Well, of course that's what I meant! What did you think I meant?" he shot back.[58] His prophecy came true.

Of Cult Heroes and Millionaires

At his parties, Vonnegut let his guard down, riding the euphoria of "belonging to a huge and extended family of artists," particularly his coterie of students, who impressed him as "so able and interesting . . . that I thought of them, almost from the first, as colleagues."[59] Untethered from his wife and children, whom he had left at home since "there are too many of them to move," Vonnegut quickly established his home as the epicenter for debauchery in Iowa City.[60] Scotch, his drink of choice, flowed like water. He reported with delight to a friend that it cost only "$4.90 a quart."[61] But he did not venture beyond whisky, meat and potatoes, and his conventional New England attire, keeping at bay the vegetarianism, exotic drugs, and tie-dye fashions sweeping through hippie culture in the 1960s. In 2005, he admitted to being "a coward about heroin and cocaine, LSD and so on, afraid they might put me over the edge," unlike the visiting professor Anthony Burgess, famous for A Clockwork Orange, and others who freely indulged during the era of psychedelic experimentation. "I did smoke a joint of marijuana once with Jerry Garcia and the Grateful Dead, just to be sociable," Vonnegut said, but since it had little effect on him, "I never did it again." His love affair with Scotch never backfired on him, since "by the grace of God, or whatever, I am not an alcoholic," which he surmised was "largely a matter of genes."[62] When consorting with figures notorious for drug-fueled mind-expanding experiences, such as Norman Mailer in 1960, he would offer conviviality and libations but typically little else: "we have no horse or Mary Jane, but plenty of gin, God knows."[63]

Favoritism among students ran rampant, won from professors in a variety of ways. One student ran drugs for the faculty member he most wanted to impress, while others offered sexual favors that in some cases led to long-standing affairs.[64] Vonnegut could provide Scotch for himself. But the other category proved more complex and difficult. In accepting a teaching position at Smith College long after his Workshop stint, he vowed, "I will not do there what I did when in exile in Iowa City in 1965, which was to interfere with a student's clothing." In a private letter, he prefaced his comments on the matter by insisting, "Not a word of this to anyone!" He then explained, "women have the power to renew the ambition and wit of men adrift, and have done that twice for me so far, once in Iowa City in 1965, and then Sagaponack," in the Hamptons on Long Island, New York, in 1991. Both encounters, he claimed, cured him of writer's block and primed his creativity. "Both times, after sleeping with these angels, I started writing and making pictures again." He pointed out that "Bellow and Mailer have renewed themselves in this fashion again and again, as though buying new cars," evoking the elation on the faces of middle-aged male customers he served at his Saab dealership in the 1950s.[65] The confluence of creative art and the advent of free love at the time converged in a perfect storm of social and cultural forces. Added to this, Vonnegut's naturally convivial spirit was in overdrive, in an attempt to entertain his way into the hearts of the Workshop members. If he lacked a degree, and if some had once looked down on his work as mere trade genre fiction, he might win their hearts—if not their money at the poker table—at his wild parties.

One encounter with a student, however, brought about the unintended consequence of a long and lasting love. In a particularly self-reflexive passage in a preface to *Slaughterhouse-Five*, he remarks, "I taught creative writing in the famous Writers Workshop at the University of Iowa for a couple of years," during which time "I got into some perfectly beautiful trouble, got out of it again."[66] Much of it was precipitated by a sense that marriage with his wife, Jane, had "become formal and strange, and not at all sexy," as if he were "the

Ambassador from New Zealand presenting credentials to the Foreign Minister of Uruguay." "I can't get it up for her anymore," he disclosed in a private
letter to his friend Knox Burger, but he could for "anybody else." Loree Wilson
Rackstraw, a "single mom, with two kids," was more than just "anybody
else."[67] Both agreed to her disclosure of their relationship in her book *Love as
Always, Kurt: Vonnegut as I Knew Him*. "Sustained mostly by the U.S. Postal
service" for decades after their first encounter in 1965, Vonnegut's affair with
Rackstraw initiated a far more substantial and mutually gratifying relationship than those typical of Workshop faculty and students, a part of the larger
system of privileges and entitlements pervading Workshop culture.[68]

W. D. Snodgrass attested to the sexual entitlement assumed by the male
faculty at the Workshop, such as John Berryman. Riding in the back of Snodgrass's car to a party, Berryman forced himself on an unsuspecting victim.
"Hearing her protests, I stopped the car," Snodgrass remembered. "John, this
is a proper lady who does not like to be mauled," he warned. Shocked, Berryman wondered what kind of woman did not yield freely to the advances of a
male professor. "What? You mean you don't fuck?" The car fell silent. Berryman then decided to back off, attempting to divert attention from his untoward behavior. "Oh! It's that word that bothers you: P-H-U-Q-Q. I promise
never to use it again," he said, as nervous laughter spread through the car. The
response condoned his pose of "little boy naughtiness." One of many un-
wanted acts of sexual aggression on Workshop students, such behavior "might
have seriously damaged a number of people, some of them innocent."[69] Although Vonnegut advised incoming faculty member Richard Gehman, "don't
ball undergraduates," it was only because "their parents are still watching."[70]
The comment implied that *graduate* students, whose parents were *not* watching, were fair game. Sandra Cisneros put it even more bluntly. "The teachers
were completely fucked up. They seemed to think that free booty was part of
their compensation package, and these young women, they look up to these
writers and think of them as being gods and don't realize that these are men
with no control over their lower [urges]." To her, Iowa was a "dysfunctional"
system where "we had the sick preying on the naïve."[71]

In addition to quid-pro-quo sexual exchanges, one of the other methods
students used to place themselves in the favor of a select faculty member was
drug running. The instructor might then invite the student to parties where
key publishers and agents, usually from New York, were present. "At Iowa,"
according to alumnus Don Wallace, "what they called 'financial aid,' was
really entrée, access, permission to write, a green light to the publishing

world." The system of preferment began with the selection of Teaching/Writing Fellows, TWFs, or "Twiffs" for short. When "agents came to visit, nonaid students never heard about it." Outsiders eventually learned of their fate, because "rumor clued us in," usually through "bitter drunken tales at parties of the shunned."[72]

The most notable of students who supplied faculty with drugs as a form of gratuity was Doug Unger, whose thesis adviser in the 1970s was John Irving. Unger, known for a variety of exploits, including being kicked out of the English-Philosophy Building by Workshop secretary Connie Brothers for sleeping on a couch in the program office over the span of three months, survived "with a shower and a locker to use over at the gym, and three squares at the Student Union."[73] Director Jack Leggett told Brothers, the program's ever watchful maternal figure of authority, "he's living in his office, get him out of there."[74] This was not an easy task, since he "hadn't paid rent for some time on the room [he] was supposed to be renting." He returned later in the day to discover that Brothers had disconnected the office phone, reasoning that he would seek proper accommodations if only to keep in touch with his contacts. She was right. He moved in with the actress Amy Burk Wright—the daughter of Raymond Carver, the National Book Award finalist and visiting assistant professor at the Workshop in 1973 for one whiskey-drenched year—and he later married her.[75]

In addition to his novel method of saving money on rent, Unger's exploits included trafficking drugs for faculty. He made a monumental investment of time and capital to provide Anthony Burgess with hashish, very much in the form of gratitude. He drove halfway to Chicago, "and fronted a whole month's pay" to "a guy I knew who had some really primo hash." Unger knew Burgess preferred it to marijuana, especially while writing music as a means of passing the night away to cope with his chronic insomnia. Unger would take "a discarded page of [his] manuscript and wrap the hash in it and tie it up with a green string like a little birthday gift and pass it to Burgess in his office." With the connection between the writing and the gift explicit through his imaginative selection of wrapping paper, Unger "made sure there was no charge to him because I admired his writing so much."[76]

Benefits accrued to those who could penetrate the private lives of teachers and win at the favoritism game. In response to Engle's directive to identify "any good students in your care," Vonnegut reported that he had introduced Ian MacMillan to his editor at Harper and Row, Roger Klein. The powerful editor "promised to do his best to get *Harper's Magazine* to publish something of Ian's." "I'm going to see if I can make money start coming out of [Ian's] ears within the next six months," he promised Engle, speaking directly to his supervisor's obsession with professionalizing—and indeed monetizing—the program's best talent. Even the "shallow and derivative" ones, Vonnegut suggested, with not a little veiled satirical irony, "could probably both make it in Hollywood," because at least they were "both funny and shrewd."[77] As his desire for literary prestige mounted, Vonnegut's private correspondence shows he never abandoned his instinct for capital. After hearing news of his friend Richard Gehman's generous advance for his novel, *Driven*, he cheered, "$5,267.49 to Gehman!" "Yummy!" he gushed, begging to know "How do these sons of bitches write thirteen books, or thirty-three, for Christ's sakes— or sell serials to the Post and then to the movies?" He found it "pretty damn demoralizing" that there were "twenty million copies of the Shell Scott books in print" among other signs of thriving competition in the literary market. Inspired to seize his own share of the market, the next month he solicited interest in his novel *The Sirens* from Macmillan of England, remarking of the agents, publicists, and promoters in the industry, "Boy—did I ever see some pretty whores!"[78]

When he was not using the Workshop as his own personal savings and loan—borrowing two thousand dollars at one financial low point during the late 1960s, eventually repaying it decades later in 1989—Vonnegut freely used the Workshop name to promote the careers of fellow writers outside the program.[79] He lobbied intensely for William Price Fox, another satirical novelist without academic credentials. The goal in bringing him aboard, he joked, would be to win "a clear majority in the Writers' Workshop of people with no fucking degrees whatsoever." He vowed that the Workshop would "make [Fox] a blooming culture hero and millionaire," just as it had begun to do for himself.[80] Working toward the same goal, he pressured his students on several occasions into commercial publication. He urged Gail Godwin to write about a love affair for a women's magazine in order "to make it as big as Muhammad Ali," asking in his best advertising voice, "don't [you] want to be that popular and wise in a magically simple way? I'd like to help." His advice on how to leverage the popular market amounted to a Faustian proposition daring her to cater to the masses as an avenue toward becoming a distinguished author: "Are you willing to pander to popular tastes in order to be published?" A story about a romantic tryst should not be anything to be ashamed of, nor should it be considered a compromise to one's artistic integrity, he insisted. Indeed, the cultural cachet of women's magazines had appreciated considerably since

Mademoiselle and *Harper's Bazaar* editor George Davis revolutionized their previously lightweight editorial content with the introduction of serious literature, a transformation that began as early as the 1940s. Writing for popular women's magazines "is how I supported myself for twelve years. I've taken jobs a damned sight worse than writing for Hallmark," he wrote, comparing his own commercial work to Engle's notorious sale of his own and his students' writing as greeting card verse and television screenplays for the middlebrow company. "I do not feel dishonored," he said. "What the hell. You'd be surprised by what you can say in a woman's magazine these days." Responding to the market not as a barbarian but as a principled artist, according to Vonnegut, should drive the production of "a good love story, and it will sell." Although such advice may seem anathema to the Workshop's elite code, all artists must face the exigencies of the publishing industry; "that's life," he wrote before signing off.[81]

Vonnegut himself sold a piece from *Slaughterhouse-Five* to the popular press—*Playboy* magazine—while at the Workshop in 1967, two years before it appeared in book form and catapulted him to fame. Robie Macauley, the Workshop alumnus and teacher from the 1940s who had been Flannery O'Connor's close friend, was instrumental in landing it in the men's magazine. Macauley had just assumed editorship of the magazine's fiction department, which he would enrich with the same vitality Davis brought to *Mademoiselle.* During his editorship, in 1965–1978, "*Playboy* was second only to the *New Yorker* in prestige as a place for serious writers to display their talents."[82] Such powerful names as Saul Bellow, Vladimir Nabokov, and Ursula K. Le Guin appeared there. The venue also served as a key stepping-stone in Irving's illustrious career. Popular crossover magazines featuring serious literature had yielded the desired results of profitability for Vonnegut. He thanked Macauley "for paying me so extraordinarily well" for the early draft of *Slaughterhouse-Five,* titled "Captured," and for prestigious placement among the best minds of his generation.[83]

Perhaps the most overlooked of Vonnegut's legacies to Workshop culture is his demystification of the writing process as a professional pursuit. One assignment from November 1965, written in the form of a personal letter addressing students as "Beloved," asked them to approach literature from the perspective of an editor in the publishing industry. They were not to play the role as if driven solely by profit, "a barbarian in the literary market," or as "an academic critic, nor a person drunk on art." They were to judge the fifteen stories in *Masters of the Modern Short Story* in order to learn the essentials of all great authors, according to Vonnegut: "Be yourself. Be unique. Be a good editor."[84] The latter category demanded judgment and sensitivity to audience and markets not typically associated with the Workshop curriculum. The assignment represents how his efforts at professionalizing his students' careers extended from behind-the-scenes connections to the publishing industry to encompass coursework with professional applications. The gesture worked against the grain of solipsistic introspection, on one hand, and mutual savaging in workshop critiques on the other. One of the beneficiaries of such assignments was Suzanne McConnell, who became the fiction editor of the *Bellevue Literary Review* and the author of numerous short stories, essays, and reviews in reputable literary magazines.

But of all Vonnegut's students who would become "popular and wise in a magically simple way," and make it as big as Muhammad Ali, John Irving stands out for the achievement of *The World According to Garp*. "I always knew John would make it big. He was always so preposterously *funny*." One of his most notorious exploits occurred at his twenty-fifth birthday party, where he treated guests to what he called the musical score for the future film version of his unfinished first novel. The audacious gesture self-reflexively cast humorous light on the inflated egos and pretentious expectations of celebrity status endemic in the Workshop culture. Beyond self-satire, an element of serious prophecy demonstrated to himself and the Workshop community that his work was destined for a mass audience and adaptation to film. "I often did that, picked the music for the film before I finished the book. Call it my mayhem confidence." Vonnegut found it irresistible. "Never lose your enthusiasm about your work," he advised Irving. "So many writers are *unenthusiastic*."[85]

Such Muhammad Ali–like bravado came back to haunt Irving when he later joined the Workshop as a faculty member, in 1972–1975. The disastrous reception of his novel *The 158-Pound Marriage* (1974) nearly ruined his career. Originally conceived in Iowa City, the book "was published to resounding silence," selling "fewer copies than either my first or my second novel," and the few reviews it received "were argumentative."[86] By 1975, he had committed himself with a renewed sense of humility to the project that would spring his career. His pupil Unger remarked on how powerful a learning experience it was to be "let in on his own creative process." He "let us read early drafts of his work, such as the false beginning to what later became *The World According to Garp*, that contained, toward the end, pages that he later wrote around a subject, followed its directions, then, after comprehending what he was truly doing in the book, how he discovered the real story."[87] Without the prestige of the Workshop behind him, the manuscript might have never been published, especially given the poor sales performance of his previous works. John McNally, author of the satirical novel *After the Workshop*, astutely observes that "the sales of John Irving's first three novels were terrible," and therefore "it's likely that *The World According to Garp*, his fourth novel, wouldn't have been published, at least not by a commercial press." In McNally's view, "this is where the publishing industry and, in turn, the chain bookstores that order the books and, in turn, dictate print-runs, shoot themselves in the foot."[88] But with the apparatus of the Workshop behind him, a lucrative advance contract was within reach.

In 1975, Irving was "a long way from finishing the novel, which was to be my fourth, and my first best seller" three years later.[89] Although he did not select the score for it, *Garp* became a major motion picture starring Robin Williams. The production earned $29.7 million on a $17 million budget. His success in film grew with *The Cider House Rules*, which won the Academy Award for best adapted screenplay in 1999. After Vonnegut and Irving achieved their colossal fame, they "were neighbors" in Sagaponack, in the Hamptons. "He used to ride his bicycle over to my house in the morning for a cup of coffee," Irving fondly recalled of the man whose creative vision he called "Irreverence for human beings and institutions. Kindness for individuals."[90] To Vonnegut, those individuals at the Workshop consisted of an "extended family . . . relatives of mine for life."[91]

He continued to promote the Workshop and his friends there long after he left. In a blurb for director Frank Conroy's *Body and Soul*, a novel considered one of the most powerful evocations of the experience of musical performance, Vonnegut sang the praises of his piano-playing prowess as an extension of his writing skill. Sent as a fax to the Workshop in 1990, precisely when Conroy was "telescope deep" into the writing of the novel that appeared three years later, Vonnegut's profile of Conroy's artistry functions as advance publicity for what would be the director's second—and best—novel after *Midair*, his 1985 debut in the genre, which received lukewarm reviews. With his signature wit and luster, Vonnegut crafted the piece to double as promotional material on behalf of the Workshop by attesting to the talent and sensibility of its director, whom he aptly characterized as "arch and dainty."[92]

In *Timequake*, published in 1996, Vonnegut's alter ego, the science fiction writer Kilgore Trout, dies at eighty-four, the author's own age at the time of his passing in 2007. The final stretch was not smooth sailing, as he would attempt to take his own life in 1985, and seek medical treatment through what he called "the latest chemical mood music, which is Prozac." In the past he typically weathered such bouts with grim determination, and would "take down the sail and batten the hatches."[93] Rough seas could be expected, as indicated in his illustration for *Slaughterhouse-Five* of a tombstone whose epitaph read, "Everything Was Beautiful, and Nothing Hurt," a vintage Vonnegut statement, as humorous as it is dark, in one pithy phrase.[94]

9 • Infidels: Sandra Cisneros and Joy Harjo

Sandra Cisneros, a twenty-two-year-old Latina from a Chicago barrio, sought refuge in the last row of her classroom in the English-Philosophy Building at the Iowa Writers' Workshop. She would have fled back to Chicago that fall semester of 1976 had it not been for her confidante, Joy Harjo. "We were just like Indians, sitting silently in the back of the room," Harjo recalled.[1] A Native American member of the Muscogee (Creek) nation with Cherokee ancestors, the twenty-five-year-old Harjo shared Cisneros's distinction, along with the African-American poet Rita Dove, as one of the first women of color accepted into the program. Hiding on the fringe of the classroom was one of their many compensatory gestures, which included Cisneros's suggestion that "maybe we should get a drink before class." But more than self-silencing and alcohol, what sustained them was the confidence that grew from the knowledge that, unlike so many of their classmates, "we are the ones who are publishing—Joy Harjo and I."[2]

A single mother of two children she had in her teens, Harjo bonded with Cisneros to form a safe haven from the program's prevailing white culture. Since the program's origin, the vast majority of the student body had consisted of ex-soldiers who valorized and sentimentalized their experience as combat veterans. By the mid-1970s a new wave of students, like the Harvard-educated Tracy Kidder, fresh from the battlefields of Vietnam and Korea, entered a program staffed by army veterans such as Marvin Bell. Workshop sessions spilled over into vigorous competition outside the classroom, in full-contact boxing and wrestling, as well as high-stakes poker. Anthony Bukoski, a classmate of Cisneros in 1976, contended that "all writers should know how to box." He proposed that "MFA students, the guys anyway, should be required to spar three rounds at least once a week." Notably, Bukoski was "a big Marine who had lost his front teeth in a fight with another Marine in Vietnam."[3] While the men were immersed in a culture conflating literary prowess with physical domination, Cisneros and Harjo had been the ones successfully landing their work—instead of punches directed at each other—with publishers.

In preparing her assignments, Cisneros searched for ways to circumvent the workshop method that transformed classrooms into intellectual theaters of combat. Paul Engle's founding principle was based on the belief that young writers overestimated their creative powers, a flaw that only astringent criticism could overcome. Such criticism was intended to prepare them for the presumably harsher publishing industry. The method inspired Cisneros and Harjo to conceive of their own alternative approach to creative writing. "You have to have balance, so you don't savage people," Cisneros discovered. "There wasn't balance at Iowa. There was no love," but instead narrow individualism, precluding "a sense of compassion there." In class, Cisneros faced either blank stares or a hail of destructive criticism. She responded to the competitive culture by asking herself each day, "*Okay, what can I write about now that no one can say I'm wrong.*"[4] Operating on that impulse, she created the majority of the material she later developed into *The House on Mango Street*, a series of vignettes in poetic prose based on her upbringing in inner-city Chicago.

Cisneros resolved to differentiate herself from her peers by defiantly deploying a "broken-glass and tin-can" inner-city idiom from her childhood to distinguish herself "from the pretty pastel syllables of my classmates."[5] During the late 1970s, the Workshop's "increasing prestige drew an increasingly mainstream student body often straight out of college." Those white, middle-class males directly out of college drew material for their writing from their privileged suburban worlds. They gravitated toward what Tom Grimes calls "the standard workshop product," several iterations of which Grimes confessed to having produced himself. These were narratives featuring "the sincere first-person narrator story about his dysfunctional family, capped by a maturation-inducing epiphany." Such adolescent fare was indicative of the conformist tendency to "write for workshop," calculated attempts at producing material "with the greatest chance of receiving the workshop's approbation." Such writing epitomized how students responded to the escalating pressure of the word's most prestigious program.[6]

Cisneros's counterreaction to the "politically unengaged, stylistically timid, contextually narrow, bourgeois subject matter" represented how "writing is fighting," as the African-American poet Ishmael Reed once said.[7] Like a

Brechtian placard interrupting the narrative flow of a scene to highlight economic inequality and social injustice, she found joy in orchestrating "rag-tag music" out of the "third-floor flats, and rears of rats, and drunk husbands sending rocks through windows, anything as far from the poetic as possible."[8] Not exactly Raymond Carver dirty realism, the exterior of the vignettes originally written as narrative poems reflected this deliberately simple quality, designed to subvert the dominant definition of poetry at the Workshop. One of the disturbing lessons she learned at Iowa "was that poetry belonged to the wealthier classes. It was an issue of privilege." Cisneros aired her disdain: "If I have to read any more of those dreadful boring obsessed-with-your-navel poems again I'm going to die. When I'm around poets of the working class," such as Joy Harjo, the woman at the back of the class with her, "I'm very much at home."[9]

Women's Activism at the Workshop

Despite Engle's official resignation from the Workshop in 1966, his presence was felt during Cisneros and Harjo's time at the Workshop in the late 1970s. Even though he had officially assumed the title of director of the International Writing Program, "Engle still had considerable power and influence over the program in 1980," according to English professor Brooks Landon's recollection.[10] It is telling that John Leggett would take over directing the Workshop after the interim leadership of the poet George Starbuck. Vance Bourjaily had originally been selected as Engle's heir apparent, but he was uninterested in carrying such a heavy administrative burden. Starbuck had no future in the position, since he fell out of favor with English department chair John Gerber almost instantly after assuming the directorship. Starbuck's liability was that "he was a typical poet; he was someplace else, doing his work, and trouble was always landing on Gerber's desk." To make matters worse, Starbuck had "fallen in love with his secretary and decided to take her back to New Hampshire, where he was from."[11]

The vacancy opened, and administration, starved for Engle's lucrative fund-raising powers, opted to draw the next director from the publishing industry itself, rather than from the ranks of creative writing or, even less desirable, academia. Then a senior editor at *Harper's*, Leggett represented the ideal candidate to institutionalize the Workshop's connection to the literary market and achieve Gerber's directive "to have a book editor on the faculty." Gerber favored Leggett because of his business acumen and administrative bearing; Workshop secretary Connie Brothers described him as a patrician, "a gentleman from an affluent background."[12] Leggett's successor, Frank Conroy, was a working-class New Yorker who came to Iowa in desperate financial straits. Unlike the bohemian Starbuck and the recklessly unpredictable John Berryman, Leggett struck Gerber and the deans as "more proper and dependable than the usual drunk visiting writers" that coursed through the Workshop.[13] Most important were Leggett's extensive connections to prestigious publishing houses.

Whereas Leggett's privileged position in the publishing industry may have aided faculty and students in securing lucrative advance contracts with powerful publishers such as *Harper's* and Random House, such advantages did not extend to Cisneros and Harjo. They received no inside track to publication of the sort Vonnegut provided for Ian MacMillan, for example, by introducing him to his agent and several influential editors at an Iowa City party the decade before. In sharp contrast to an elite Boston or New York publisher, the City of Chicago Transit Authority adopted Cisneros's work for its Poetry-on-the-Bus series, a project dedicated to displaying contemporary poems on billboards at city train and bus depots and on the interior of the trains and buses themselves. The first mass audience for her writing was not the literary Boston and New York readership Workshop graduates typically sought. Instead of print, her exposure was through public service readings and billboards, reaching the inner-city community where she was raised. She later served that community directly by sharing her gift of poetry and activist spirit through the establishment of the Latino Youth Alternative High School.[14] *Bad Boys* appeared in 1980 and developed into *The House on Mango Street*, which was relegated to the tiny and obscure Arte Publico Press, a niche house with limited reach. Harjo's first publication under the imprint of Puerto del Sol, a chapbook of such meager production quality it appears at first glance to be a slight pamphlet, exhorts the reader to pledge financial support to the single mother struggling to return home and raise her children. The dedication is to "my children who help me continue," and the back cover describes the author as "a native of Oklahoma," who "now lives in Albuquerque, New Mexico. If she ever gets enough money and the right work, she will go home."[15] The volume appeared the year before Harjo moved to the Workshop, which taught her to break down the art of poetry "into sterile exercises," as part of a broader "system that had separated itself from the community, from myth, from humanhood."[16]

Devoid of such community, myth, and humanhood was "the gray concrete" cell block of the married student housing complex Harjo moved into with her two children. "The rare appearance of the sun" seemed fitting for a financial situation that left her "with no assistance from the workshop."[17] Her aid instead came from a university program dedicated to assisting minority students. The Workshop denied funding or a graduate teaching position (a Teaching/ Writing Fellowship, or TWF), which would have waived tuition and paid her a stipend, leaving her to the mercy of other programs on campus that might aid her. Were it not for the fledgling American Studies unit on campus, which offered her courses to teach in American Indian culture and literature, Harjo would not have attended the Workshop. To be a woman "in that institution" presented a formidable obstacle. Selected along with Jayne Anne Phillips to perform for a group of possible funders of the program, Harjo was shocked to hear Workshop director Jack Leggett tell the audience "that the place was actually geared for male writers." Although she credited him for his transparency on the issue—his statement was "honest; it was true"—its import sickened her. "I remember looking at Jayne Anne Phillips," the only other female student on stage, "like, 'can you believe this? Then why were we sitting here?' "[18]

Strong women writers were not new to the Workshop by 1976. But few of them were comfortably situated or justly rewarded for their achievements. Flannery O'Connor, whose taciturn demeanor and nunlike bearing at the Workshop concealed a lion of creativity inside her, had to have a male classmate read for her in workshops. Phillips helped turn the tide in the next generation. She intimidated newcomers like Michael Brien in the fall of 1976, who "quickly realized my limitation for creative writing genius" when he "sat in class with writers of the caliber of Jayne Anne Phillips."[19] Such women introduced an entirely new dimension previously missing from the program that now threatened to realign its power structure.

Bejou Merry remarked that "the Workshop women were like accessories, and not germane." Socially, "the men organize the bar jumps: 'To Mama's,' and there is camaraderie among them." She recalled how women "shoppies" would often complain about their unfair treatment, but had failed to organize into a more powerful collective force. Cisneros and Harjo mainly clung to each other for emotional support while also mutually enriching each other's creative and professional growth at this pivotal moment in their careers. Beyond the defiant partnership of these women writers, the remainder of the Workshop women fended for themselves. "No organic group among women exists," the presence of whom was "unnecessary: decorative, not functional." Frustrated, Merry saw how "we are spineless because no organizational move toward insisting women writers appear exists," which she felt was a necessary measure to counter the fact that "not one outside speaker has been female." Silenced, "we complain of discrimination at the hands of our workshop instructors but we do not get together to do anything."[20]

Given this lack of organization, the most potent activism came through the radical literary experimentation of Cisneros and Harjo. Their alternative collaborative approach to writing tapped into externalized, horizontal planes of sociocultural context, rather than the narrow psychological introspection of confessional male poetry. Men, like David Romtvedt, also chafed against the program's tendency "to be competitive rather than cooperative, cruel rather than welcoming."[21] But even the more conscientious of the male Workshop students were at a loss for how to articulate their dissent in any productive or impactful way that might radically subvert the program's ethos at its core. The larger spirit of protest, moreover, seemed to have run its course. The Workshop's old Cold War conservatism had given way to the antiwar sentiment of the 1960s. During the late 1960s, students signed "their first anti-war petition on the steps outside the newly opened EPB," the English-Philosophy Building—constructed with riot-proof reinforced windows inspired by the University of California, Berkeley, student riots—that now housed the Workshop after decades in the Quonset huts under Engle's directorship. By the late 1970s, tales of quiet, unassuming graduate students like Fred McTaggert becoming an instant celebrity on campus in 1968, because he "got maced and billy-clubbed by the police for trying to stop the way," had become a thing of the past. Gone were the days when one "could walk down the street in Iowa City and hear 'Let it Be' floating out from every storefront."[22] By 1976, "drugs and politics had already passed out of fashion. Vietnam was over. Johnnie, the junkie, has already died in the bathroom of Hamburg Inn," a famous no-frills café east of campus. The most this generation could muster in the way of activism was "an occasional drunken pants-off streak across the Pentacrest."[23]

The energy of the nascent feminist movement at Iowa reached its most powerful and enduring articulation in the writings of Cisneros and Harjo. The first Women's Reading, held at Shambaugh auditorium in the late 1960s, "was packed with energy that would burst forth in the Seventies and Eighties," as Marcella Taylor idealistically recalled.[24] The reality was closer to Merry's assessment of sporadic expressions of resistance without the coherence to effect real change. That real change, however, came when Harjo, who "struggled with a chasm of loneliness" at Iowa, found a kindred spirit in Cisneros, who shared her sense that "the workshop culture was a foreign culture to me." As an "outsider," Harjo "perceived most of the students as from the East Coast with advanced degrees in literature." Cisneros had an undergraduate degree from Loyola University in Chicago; Harjo was a member of the University of New Mexico's first graduating class in creative writing. "There were a small circle of students" who appeared conspicuous to Harjo "in tight relationships with the faculty, who always had pat approval no matter what they wrote or said." The ethnic voice of her Native American roots clashed with the language of power wielded by these privileged students, who "knew the intimate language of the workshop" because they had "come up through the same literary worlds." The method of instruction did not treat language organically or spiritually. Instead she found herself in "a workshop climate bent on criticism and language surgery." Harjo "felt pressure to mimic the style."[25] (Not coincidentally, Rita Dove, the subject of the next chapter, also found herself conforming against her better judgment to the accepted standard of what she called "the Workshop poem.")[26] During her first semester, Harjo "locked [her] spirit away and wrote copy." With the inspiration and encouragement of Cisneros, "then I began to break free."[27]

Breaking Free

Discovering her artistic voice and vocational identity in opposition to received tradition was nothing new to Joy Harjo. Her future as a painter had been all but scripted for her, as her grandmother Naomi Harjo Foster and aunt Lois Harjo Ball were active artists whose pieces from their collections adorned her home. From the age of four, she "aspired to be like them." Then, years later as a college student, she announced to her graphic arts instructor, Nick Abdullah, her plans to withdraw from the studio art major to pursue creative writing. The decision came not out of spite for Abdullah or his methods, but out of a need to find the best medium through which to grapple with the demons of her familial past. Spousal violence traces back to Harjo's maternal grandmother, Leona May Baker (of equal parts Irish and Cherokee ancestry), whom she despised as a youth because of her insistence on telling painful stories of death and disaster from her own life.

The most traumatizing event Leona retold in excruciating detail centered on her tumultuous marriage to Desmond Baker. Desmond accepted employment with the railroad company, requiring him to move away for extended periods while Leona was left alone to raise their daughter and six sons. During his absence, she had an affair, which Harjo later deemed acceptable as a method of discovering "the lightness she needed to stay alive."[28] Harjo's view appears all the more defiant in light of the events that ensued when Desmond made an unannounced homecoming, whereupon he discovered Leona pregnant with another man's child. The beating he delivered was so severe that it sent Leona into premature labor. Bloodied from his attack, she summoned help, only to discover that it was too late—the baby arrived stillborn. Distraught, Desmond began ranting a suicidal litany of frustration, vowing to await his death on the railroad tracks, the site of his work that began their woes. Leona, refusing to be left alone to carry the burden of what would be a crushing double loss of her child and her husband, demanded to join him on the rails. With their children watching, the two clung to each other as the train approached, its hulking steel roaring toward them. But seconds before the train delivered its deadly blow, the couple jumped to safety. Suicide presented itself momentarily as a method of breaking free from a life of misery, "weighted down with seven children and no opportunities," as Harjo in adulthood compassionately described her grandmother's plight. Despite such harrowing circumstances, survival prevailed, as it had in Harjo's own life when she was forced to grapple with the trauma of near fatal domestic violence in her own immediate family. Discovering the language of poetry was integral to her own survival.

Harjo's father, a full-blooded Creek Indian, "drank off the sting" of his abusive treatment by his employers while working as a mechanic for United Airlines in the late 1960s. They taunted him with racial slurs and regularly called him "chief." He unleashed his anger on his wife in the presence of the five-year-old Joy. She recalled: "One of my earliest memories is my father hitting my mother, throwing her against the tiled walls in the bathroom. He's hitting, then choking her. I am pounding at the back of his jeans. I can only reach as far as the pockets."[29] After his death at the age of fifty-four, her mother married a man who "hated Indians and anything Indian," threatening to murder her children if she were to divorce him. On several occasions, "he forced Harjo's mother to play Russian roulette in front of the children."[30] The future world-famous poet—and a key figure in the Native American literary renaissance, recognized with writers like Leslie Marmon Silko—fell silent. Due to the cumulative trauma she witnessed at home, the young Harjo struggled to speak, a condition echoed years later in a line from her most famous poem: "She had horses who whispered in the dark, who were afraid to speak."[31] Her silence when called upon in the classroom angered her teachers, who issued threats and punishments in response.

Drawing and painting offered outlets for expression that words could not. But as she developed artistically, so did her desire to trust what her poetry workshop instructor David Johnson at UNM called "our instinctual mythic sense." Poetry taught her to speak again after being silenced as a child. "Poetry basically told me: You don't know how to listen, you need to learn how to speak, you need to learn grace, and you're coming with me."[32] She quickly learned that "the debris of historical and family trauma that can kill your spirit is actually raw material to make things with and to build a bridge . . . over that which would destroy you," as she beautifully articulated the process of healing through writing in her life.[33] From then on, she immersed herself in the art, which became integral to her refusal to surrender to suicide as her grand-mother had nearly done. In addition to this aesthetic imperative that prompted her calling as a poet, as a single mother of two young children, Harjo was forced out of economic necessity to specialize. The market for artists was nearly as barren as the market for musicians. She abandoned both out of a sense of responsibility to her children's future, and promptly applied to a handful of graduate creative writing programs, including the prestigious Iowa Writers' Workshop.

Those close to Harjo tried to dissuade her from applying. But "the word among serious creative writing students" designated the Workshop as "the place to apply." Feeling "no kinship with or draw to the middle of the country, to Iowa," she "struggled with the decision," especially since "place made a dif-ference." The curriculum and teaching method at Iowa stood as another for-midable obstacle, particularly because she had been raised according to "an approach oppositional to what was considered the Iowa writing workshop po-etry style." Words seemed to be mere abstract tools in their hands, in sharp contrast to Harjo's tradition, in which they "absolutely mattered and could change the weather or walk into the past or future, literally."[34] She had already developed an audience for her poetry after the publication of *The Last Song,* her chapbook in 1975 that brought her prominence among ethnic literary cir-cles in New Mexico, the home state of her first publisher, Puerto del Sol Press, and her undergraduate education.

Harjo's primary objective in applying to graduate school was to avoid tak-ing a job as a waitress, the only employment available to her, and set her sights on professional authorship. She reasoned that a two-year MFA could provide the mentorship she needed to expand her knowledge and skill in poetry and literature. At best, she hoped it might even bring her the greatest gift of all: a writing community she could identify with and proudly call her own. But telling signs of Iowa's alienating climate appeared. Unlike the University of Montana, New Mexico State, and the University of Arizona, which all offered her either scholarships or teaching assistantships to help defray the cost of tuition and housing, Iowa was the only program Harjo applied to that denied her request of financial assistance. When she wondered why she had even been admitted given such a paltry offer, insiders to the program laid bare to her the rampant corruption in the application process, in which "female students were picked on the basis of their photographs." After she arrived and witnessed firsthand "the predatory atmosphere in the workshop between many of the professors and female students" she could see precisely how the process functioned.[35] To her dismay, it became apparent that her appearance and not her poetry prompted her acceptance to the Workshop.

With the financial assistance of Leslie Marmon Silko, author of *Ceremony*, one of the most highly acclaimed Native American novels, Harjo purchased a pickup truck and drove with her children, Phil and Rainy Dawn, to Iowa from Indian country in New Mexico. She had little choice but to accept the offer to attend what she called "the Harvard of writing workshops."[36] Weathering the uninhabitable cultural climate there proved more difficult than she expected. But as she would write in her MFA thesis under Donald Justice, who also served as the first director of Cisneros's program of study before Marvin Bell replaced him in that role, "crows survive everywhere/ even in Iowa." There, along the banks of the Iowa River, Harjo took solace in nature, the infinitude of freedom that belonged to the "black sleek bodies" of birds born free and thriving "along the edge of the city river bed." The thrill of her realization that "they know they are the sun" enabled an undeniable connection with nature that was also hers, reinforcing her Native American belief "that there is/ an eternity of brilliant sky." Her own poetic voice sings just as the "feathered voices sing the blueness" of that sky. Crucially, they also "sing my blueness," in the poem's last line, alluding to both the azure heavens above and her melancholy they console.[37] The eternity in nature she witnesses along the river reaffirms her own capacity for endurance.

Without childcare assistance to alleviate the pressure of tending to Phil and Rainy Dawn, who were five and seven then, Harjo encountered some dark moments in Iowa City. Cisneros buoyed her with help babysitting, delighting in taking credit for the beauty of "her" little girl as they rode the bus, and leaving notes for Phil instructing him on the location of provisions, though he was barely old enough to read them.[38] With Cisneros's support, Harjo had the self-possession, precisely the sort that Adrienne Rich, another feminist poet of the era, admired in Emily Dickinson, to transform the sensation of "rocking off the edge" into powerful verse. "Out," another poem from her Iowa MFA thesis, offers insight into her struggle as a single mother in unfamiliar territory plagued by deadlines, hostile peers, and faculty. "Kids keep quiet," she writes, "I want to keep this madness/ to myself." Thoughts echoing her grandmother Leona's attempted suicide converge in the metaphor of the "Sun going down" and the overriding urge "to get this over with. To/ quicken the night/ with some simple violence,/ like it was/ before your fathers left." Each child had a different father, both of whom abandoned their responsibility for raising them. "Out" sets a telling tableau of the depth and complexity of the pain Harjo suffered in the steel gray concrete dormitories at Iowa, where she struggled to reconcile the demands of her creative writing career with the maternal commitment to her children. She faced the emotional desire to escape to a simpler time, or more drastically, seek the permanent exit signified by the stark title "Out" and the "Phone pulled out/ by the neck" in her dingy kitchen.[39]

At the Workshop, Harjo's ache for home, "what I am lonely for is the rhythm/ volcano cliffs/ dancing the hot Albuquerque nights," was eased by the realization that "We Are All Foreigners," according to the title of a poem in her MFA thesis. Although Harjo is a true native to North America, Iowa City's eclectic mix of itinerant intellectuals meant she too was a foreigner. One night out, "drunk" and "cold in Iowa City," she wrote, "we dance slowly back to the truck" in the parking lot of a local bar. A playful tone masks feminist resistance in the poem, as she calls out, " 'men ride in the back'/ I tell them/ 'it is the Indian way.' " Her friend Rosalyn shares a laugh with Harjo, as the women climb into the front in the cab, leaving the men to freeze in the pickup's open tailgate on the bone-chilling ride. The men reluctantly follow suit, unaware that "it is the opposite custom." In Iowa City, unlike Albuquerque, the "Indian way" is virtually unknown, especially among Workshop students whose disparate geographical origins make them "all foreigners here."[40]

Iowa City left Harjo without "a well-defined sense of place," an element she deemed essential to the works of "the strongest writers." Flannery O'Connor represented a model for how to evoke a local setting, but without a foothold in ecological or nature writing. Religious and psychological forces, according to Harjo's aesthetic, could animate a place. One of the challenges of being dislocated in a place like Iowa City was the overwhelming sense she and Cisneros felt of being "bound by strictness imposed by [the Workshop's] male-centeredness, its emphasis on nouns," and the prevailing urgency to capture and pin down meaning through concrete metaphor.[41] Poetic insights, she felt, were more connotative and discursive, butterflies to be set free rather than captured and anatomized. "Split the Lark," Emily Dickinson advised with brutal sarcasm, warning against the same obsessive drive toward the mastery of essences inherently rooted in nature. Then "you'll find the Music" and happily conclude your search for the essence of song. The result, however, is an eviscerated and silenced songbird from a bloody "Scarlet Experiment!" at the hands of a "Skeptic Thomas!"[42] It is no coincidence that both Harjo and Cisneros cite Dickinson as a foundational model they both emulated.[43] "There are no words," Harjo notes, citing an unidentified poet, "only sounds/ that lead us into the darkest nights."[44]

Iowa's Monkey Garden

A key scene in Cisneros's *The House on Mango Street* depicts a battle for control over a patch of small territory. In the empty lot that doubles as a playground, the boys tyrannize the girls by subjecting them to a game of their own devising. Tito is "one of the boys who invented the rules" in which Sally finds herself enmeshed. Esperanza, the narrator, who is an extension of Cisneros in her youth, rushes to Tito's apartment, races up three flights of concrete stairs, and breathlessly reports to his mother, "Your son and his friends stole Sally's keys and now they won't give them back unless she kisses them and right now they're making her kiss them."[45] Tito's mother looks up tiredly from her ironing and asks, "What do you want me to do . . . call the cops?" She rushes back to defend Sally herself, this time armed with a brick and a large stick. "They all looked at me," Esperanza says, "as if *I* was the one that was crazy and made me feel ashamed." Defeated, she retreats beneath a tree out of sight and tries to will her own death. "I wanted to be dead, to turn into the rain, my eyes melt into the ground like two black snails." The episode bears witness to the ritual of masculine power in this fallen Garden of Eden. The chapter ends with the boys firmly in control of the lot they call the "monkey garden." The significance is all too clear in the next chapter, "Red Clowns." In it, Sally's rape is rendered from her point of view, of "his dirty fingernails against my skin . . . his sour smell . . . The moon that watched." Language breaks up into the fragments of Sally's shattered consciousness, "The tilt-a-whirl. The red clowns laughing their thick-tongue laugh. Then the colors began to whirl. Sky tipped. Their high black gym shoes ran."[46]

Cisneros originally crafted early versions of these scenes of male-dominated space in Iowa City between 1976 and 1978. Also characterized by their own self-serving rules, Workshop sessions at Iowa echoed the monkey garden of her youth. Ironically, the program itself provided Cisneros with the theoretical tools for the deconstruction of its own patriarchal hegemony. In a Workshop class titled On Memory and the Imagination, she listened in silent disdain as her classmates and instructor ruminated on Gaston Bachelard's *Poetics of Space*.[47] What struck her was their unconscious class bias filtering their understanding of the broader concept of space through the privileged lens of suburban life. Cisneros could instantly see a gaping hole in Bachelard's construct, particularly as discussed by her white male classmates, of how human dwellings shape consciousness, memories, and dreams. Her sense of difference, she realized, emanated from the radically diverse community in which she was raised, an environment that was the antithesis of two-story houses in safe quiet neighborhoods with vast sparkling yards and white picket fences. Certain spaces in the Latino barrio, like the Workshop itself, represented contested territory that also sparked her retaliation on behalf of justice. That activism could be found in the poetic rendering of lives otherwise invisible.

Only years after graduating did Cisneros realize racism's subtle power. She "didn't have a name for it until after it happened. At Iowa I never thought of it as racism. I thought that I was the problem." But "that's the worst kind of racism, where you don't think you're good enough, don't deserve to be in that Workshop, don't deserve the MFA . . . you were admitted because they felt sorry for you."[48] Cisneros's sense of inadequacy in her "gender, ethnicity, and class" at Iowa prompted her to access the similar inadequacy she felt not growing up in a house like those of her classmates. *Coraje*, a volatile cocktail of rage and courage, enabled her to draw from this well of experience and emotion to craft what is now considered one the most significant works of American literature.

Writing in opposition to the Workshop's prevailing apolitical and classist poetics of space, Cisneros turned toward "the people I remembered" for her subjects. "In a sense I was being defensive and rebellious," defiantly wielding her deceptively simple diction and syntax in a world populated by whores, thieves, and drunks at workshop sessions. Those subjects and styles were her version of the sticks and bricks Esperanza brings to the monkey garden to mete out justice. "In this direction," she began "to move as far away from the style of my classmates," and in the process "found a voice that was uniquely mine." Her objective was not just to raise social consciousness, but to register shock—by showing, not telling, according to the creative writing mantra—in a dominant aesthetic blind to the realities of ethnic urban life. She aimed to present "young Latinos whose problems were so great" that they would make her "Iowa Writers' Workshop classmates faint." Her purpose grew from spiteful retaliation to the more constructive objective "to do something to change their lives, ours, mine." She would bring not only a startling revelation of the disadvantaged to the Workshop, but also insightful glimpses of the barrio's unsung heroes, its moments of beauty and kindness. She names her character Esperanza out of such hope, with the intention of showing how "their lives were extraordinary, that they were extraordinary for having survived." Their endeavors were worthy of the highest respect, despite their lack of credentialing through institutions of higher education, since "they held doctorates from the university of life."[49]

To the many readers who appreciate *The House on Mango Street* for its lyrical prose, it should come as no surprise that the novel began as a series of poems, rather than sketches and vignettes, written at Iowa in 1978. With the support of faculty such as Marvin Bell, Cisneros pursued narrative poetry with an emphasis on inner monologue. Despite being out of fashion at the time, E. A. Robinson's "Richard Cory" provided a useful model for probing community, economic inequality, and the inner lives of individuals within a specific social milieu. Through Robinson, Cisneros realized if she "could write monologues and do them in a voice that wasn't mine, it was a way of removing myself from writing about what I was living." In the process, her "poems became, sometimes, a kind of narrative, a fusion of prose and poetry." She was "heading toward *Mango Street*." However, she could not bring the project to fruition until she graduated from the Workshop, because she "felt so censored at Iowa in trying to write about myself as a young woman." Much of what blocked her had to do with shame. "I was ashamed at Iowa, so I wrote about an older shame," she explains. Imaginative distance from the Workshop setting and experimentation with "a younger voice, a girl's voice that went back ten years," proved ideal for the "vignettes of autobiographical fiction written in a loose and deliberately simple style, halfway between a prose poem and the awkwardness of semiliteracy," according to critic Penelope Mesic.[50] With that voice and vantage point she could find an imaginative space for creativity "someplace that was far from Iowa."[51]

By revisiting her childhood for the source of her creative work, Cisneros simultaneously accessed an outlet of escape from the threatening Workshop environment and a means by which to defy and challenge it. Through the retelling of Sally's first sexual encounter at the hands of her young rapists,

Cisneros could process her own initiation into the monkey garden of academia beginning with her undergraduate experience. Her undergraduate adviser at Loyola University in Chicago, the man who originally inspired her to be a poet, was an alumnus of the Workshop who had studied under Donald Justice. "He told me I just *had* to study with Donald Justice at Iowa." She applied, and in exchange for his support of her acceptance, her Loyola poetry professor initiated an intimate relationship. In retrospect, she is well aware of how naive she was to have assumed "my teacher was interested in me because he thought I was a good writer." Like Tito holding the keys from Sally, Cisneros's instructor "sort of helped himself, too. We had an affair," much to her regret later when she realized how badly he had deceived her. "I was very, very young, and I thought this is what writers do," that somehow it was built into a lifestyle where one is expected to "break rules and dance on tables and have affairs." Her application to Iowa came as part of the expected behavior her Loyola instructor demanded. At the time, "I did what I was told," she recalled of her efforts to conform to the lifestyle of professional authorship, only to discover its inherently sexist bias.[52]

Once at Iowa, Cisneros soon discovered that her affair with her Loyola professor had served as an initiation to Iowa's even more rampant and systematic sexual exploitation of female students. The trouble dwells in how "these young women" students "look up to these writers" who are in authority positions as their instructors, wielding undue power over their creative careers. Many of the female Workshop students, like Cisneros as an undergraduate, regard their faculty mentors as "gods and don't realize these are men with no control." Since graduating from the Workshop in 1978, Cisneros made a point of combating this culture of exploitation by making female students aware of their vulnerability to their own naive complicity with it. "I always talk to these young women," she explains, in creative writing MFA programs at Iowa and elsewhere, "and say be really, really careful here." She routinely warns them, "you're so naive and young and beautiful and you have no concept of your power, but the first person who pays attention to you, [and] you're completely blinded. And in my case it went beyond bad." She pointed out that "as instructors we have lots of opportunities to abuse our students because they look up to us." At the Workshop, "there was just a lack of respect and lack of honor there."[53] The program's sexual politics represented the literary monkey garden, a system of sexual exchange for career advancement, for keys to autonomy and power she already had, but that men in positions of power hijacked and held hostage.

Conceiving an Anti-Workshop

Soon after she arrived at Iowa in August of 1976, Cisneros was overcome with a desperate desire to leave. "Either I could have given up and left (my plan A), and *House* would have never been written, or I would have to get angry to overcome my sense of low self-esteem I felt there." Many writers of color during that period facing similar circumstances abandoned MFA programs. "If I hadn't had Joy there," she admits, "I would have left." With Harjo, she could channel her anger into enough creative energy to "light a city."[54] Harjo recalls that "the first worksheets were traumatic," especially because she and Cisneros "were the only two students whose poetry didn't appear on the worksheet for the first month." She too "wanted to quit the workshop," but remained because she "had invested too much time and money and decided to stay it out, at least a year."[55]

A pivotal incident occurred when Cisneros and Harjo resolved to confront their instructor for neglecting to include them in the weekly reading rotation. As the only students whose work did not appear, they grew increasingly uncomfortable with the galling exclusion. Hesitating outside the door of Donald Justice's office, they swallowed hard and exchanged a glance of mutual fear. Their gentle knock elicited a weary reply telling them to enter. "When he saw us," according to Harjo, "he started backing up, like we were going to pull out a switchblade or maybe scalp somebody." Few words were exchanged, but the solidarity of their protest made its presence felt. "We just looked at each other and walked away," Harjo recalled. "The next week our poems were on the Worksheet."[56]

Both met crushing silence when their work was circulated, as was the case when either of them made a comment. "When you said something in class," Cisneros attested, "there was this absolute silence in the room. 'Did I say something wrong?'" she wondered.[57] Something deeper than playground bullying was taking place. The resistance to diverse mythological impulses came in the form of "only those classical expressions pertinent to the dominant culture" qualifying for "recognition and kinship in the writing workshop," according to Harjo. She shared Cisneros's sense that "the workshops at Iowa were particularly brutal. Competition was rife and set us against each other." Harjo envisioned the alternative to the contentious workshop environment as an intimate and informal "kitchen-table community," united by trust in a shared bond of mutual support for maintaining high creative standards.[58]

Cisneros would adopt this inclusive encouraging model in her own teaching. Scholars of creative writing pedagogy have observed the ineffectiveness of its opposite in the "Bobby Knight school," named for the sadistic college basketball coach notorious for berating his players for their slightest misstep. As in the Workshop, "students learn to write in an economy of scarcity, where the only guidance centers on what *not* to do." This approach, Stephanie Vanderslice notes, "ultimately fails" writers in their early stages of development.[59] Cisneros's alternative method, applied with her underprivileged Chicago high school students in 1979, was ideally suited to her inclusive narrative voice. In *The House on Mango Street*, she intended to make the narrative "approachable for all people, whether they were educated or not, and whether they were children or adults. My ideal was to write in a way that would not make anyone feel intimidated, but welcome." Her populist vision of herself as a writer emerged when she was in fifth grade, when she imagined her name on an index card in the public library's card catalogue. "That card," according to her ideal, "would be wrinkled and dirty because so many people wanted to read her books."[60] To "say yes to everything" was a construct inspired in direct opposition to "the worst mistake a writer can make"—mistrusting one's instincts out of fear of a rigid audience waiting to pounce on flaws. Tolerance in this sense is more than aesthetic; it inheres as a politics of gender and shared power to "be open, be gentle, like a mother." In an environment without these vital elements, "which is what happened to me at Iowa, how can you grow?" she asks.[61]

While Harjo entered the Workshop in poetry and remained a poet throughout her career, Cisneros crossed over into prose, but without ever leaving verse behind entirely. Her sense of abandonment came when her adviser Don Justice told her in no uncertain terms that her poetry was third rate. Tracy Kidder, an Iowa MFA from 1974, told me he could explain Justice's decision, if not excuse it: "Justice was a neo-classicist" and simply "did not tolerate the sort of experimentation" Cisneros had done.[62] She poured herself into the hybridized poetic prose of the first three stories of *Mango Street* in one weekend at Iowa.[63] Glancing at drafts, Justice winced and pushed them aside. He first struggled to justify his distaste for them, then finally shook his head and concluded, "Well, you know, these really aren't poems." As prose, Justice refused to count them toward the MFA thesis because she was a poetry student not formally enrolled in the fiction Workshop. His authoritarian bearing reminded her "too much of my father."[64] She immediately sought the aid of Harjo, sharing the sketches with her confidante, "who was also having a hard time in the poetry workshop."[65] In retrospect, Cisneros wished she "had been a little older at Iowa," so she might have had the courage to assert herself as both a fiction writer and a poet, "trying to fuse the two" forms.

No one at the Workshop had ever completed a thesis in both areas, or received approval of it from a combination of poetry and fiction faculty. Marvin Bell, who took over the role of Cisneros's thesis adviser from Justice, had the most fluid and accommodating sense of poetry, allowing for, and even encouraging, a narrative emphasis. Bell's earthy eclecticism functioned as a viable solution for Cisneros, who otherwise had nowhere else to turn for aesthetic guidance among the poetry faculty to suit her desire for experimentation. She had been reading the "Latin American boom" writers and Nicanor Parra, whose "anti-poems, anti-upper class, anti-ivory tower, anti-pretty poems" captured her imagination. She thought, "*this is what I am*," in bold defiance of the poets she had been clustered with at the Workshop. Besides Harjo and Dennis Mathis from blue-collar Peoria, Workshop poets to her "seemed very pretentious and very upper class," quite the opposite of her community-centered orientation toward the craft. "Maybe Iowa was a family for some," she attested, "but it wasn't *my* family. I felt homeless."[66] *Mango Street*'s dedication, "To the Women," speaks to Cisneros's attempt to reclaim authorship for community and progressive gender politics. At the Workshop during the late 1970s, few showed concern over an author's contribution to society, or obligations to community. "And we *never* mentioned class," she recalled of a curriculum missing a sense of political efficacy. "I wish there had been some political direction," she lamented.[67]

That missing political component at the Workshop threatened to extinguish Cisneros and Harjo's ambition to develop a literary aesthetic responsive to issues of social class and economic inequality. The program also did not provide the career guidance they needed. During her literary career, Cisneros has struggled to reap the financial rewards of powerhouse presses, mainly because she lacked the necessary advising when she entered the profession. Mathis had lent his editorial skill, Harjo was instrumental in encouraging her to write, and Bell had been a loyal source of support on the poetry faculty. Sorely missing, however, was a figure to help her navigate the literary marketplace. Both Cisneros and Harjo had been excluded from the inner circle of students chosen for grooming and promotion in the publishing industry. It was not until 2004 that Cisneros landed her work with Vintage, a powerful publisher worthy of her caliber of work. This is mainly because "when I got out of Iowa, I learned the business side the wrong way, by signing on the dotted line." Only when she conscripted the aid of Susan Bergholz, who would become the most effective literary agent of her career, did she negotiate back the rights to all her major works she had signed away as a desperate young writer aching to launch her career.[68]

Harjo experienced similar trouble when small presses like Thunder's Mouth Press, despite publishing her signature volume *She Had Some Horses* through three editions beginning in 1984, initially failed to win her the wide audience she deserved. It was not until 2000 that a major house, in her case W. W. Norton, signed her to several new editions of her poetry. Like Cisneros, Harjo has won the attention of literary critics and enjoys a wide readership. *The House on Mango Street* has sold more than two million copies since its first publication. Its twenty-fifth anniversary edition sparked international media coverage and a massive book signing tour. Cisneros used the occasion to reaffirm her spite for the Iowa program; thirty years of experience as a professional author and activist only reinforced her sense of its flaws.

In a 2009 radio interview on the public broadcasting affiliate WNYC in New York, Cisneros asserted that the Workshop "wasn't so prestigious to me, it was rather horrible. I like to tell people that I am a writer *despite* the University of Iowa Writers' Workshop." In measured tones just above a whisper, Cisneros delivered her verdict on the Workshop. Since her graduation in 1978, she has neither recanted nor qualified her position. If any change is evident over the three decades of her commentary on the Workshop, it has become more resolute and firm over time. By 2009, she was a seasoned professional reflecting on the celebratory occasion of the release of the twenty-fifth anniversary edition of *The House on Mango Street* with dark yet candid testimony. She explained, the program "taught me what I didn't want to be as a writer and how I didn't want to teach."[69] A personal vendetta or bruised ego did not motivate her to challenge the widespread view of the Workshop as a prestigious and noble institution. Instead, larger political concerns for the silenced voices of minority and women writers have been behind her campaign, distinguishing her as the most acclaimed graduate of the program to blast it so consistently in public media for such a protracted span of time—now nearing four decades—all at the peril of her own reputation and career. Despite her awareness that "no one ever wants to hear from the malcontents," and despite the risk of alienating the powerful stakeholders at the Workshop who might hold influence over her status in literary circles, she has maintained her staunch opposition on virtually every media occasion when the topic of Iowa arises.[70] These include myriad live events, in print, television, and the public radio interview, which has drawn nearly 31,000 original visitors as a video on

YouTube. "We don't often hear from the dissonant voices of the people who are enrolled there, especially ethnic women and working class people." In response to the prompt from her interviewer, "It sounds like you absolutely hated it," she nodded vigorously, more than thirty years after graduating: "That's putting it mildly, yes."[71]

Featured on Garrison Keillor's *Literary Friendships* series for American Public Media, Cisneros and Harjo spoke of their struggle at the Workshop, a topic that surfaced within the first five minutes of the show. The two became instant friends in the fall of 1976 because they "felt odd" surrounded by "tall serious white men," according to Keillor. Never one to pass on exposing the humor in the hypocrisy of self-congratulatory mythmaking, Keillor quipped, "We tall serious white males feel responsible for the wonderful careers that they've had, for having given them the *shock*, the sense of resentment that may have triggered their creative careers."[72]

The Workshop, for all its sins, paradoxically inspired Cisneros's *Mango Street*, if only as a counterpoint written with a survivor's grit in opposition to the forces that threatened to destroy her creative spirit during peer critiques. She began *Mango Street* in Iowa "precisely because Iowa forced me," she explained, "to look inside myself as to what made me different from all those other classmates." With the outward support of Harjo, Cisneros made this intense inward turn. "Instead of quitting, which I felt like doing," she boldly defied those poised to tell her she was wrong. Harjo has repeatedly denied this motivation was also hers. Instead what drove her creativity was the prospect of "speaking the mysterious, the beautiful and unspoken" in such a way that a poem would become like a dwelling where "a spirit would want to live." Harjo acknowledged that the "care and attention" with which Cisneros "read and responded to her poems" prevented her from leaving the program. For Cisneros, Harjo represented a mature figure with the strength and survival to raise Rainy Dawn and Phil on her own in a place like Iowa. Together they emerged from this watershed moment in their careers with a renewed sense of vigor and faith in the aesthetic and cultural values that had sustained them through the program. Both committed themselves to what Harjo called "the real revolution—when we can see each other as human beings."[73]

10 • The Crossover: Rita Dove

Rita Dove stood transfixed by the volume of poetry in her hands, the cover of which read *Residue of Song*, by Marvin Bell. The twenty-one-year-old future United States poet laureate, who would become the first African-American woman to bear that title, looked up suddenly at the stranger breaking her concentration. "*That* book—I don't like it so much," the man curtly declared, furrowing his brow. The 1973 Bread Loaf Writers' Conference played host to many outspoken colorful characters, and this was one of them, Dove realized. After listening with a bemused look while she vigorously defended the book in her hand, the man inquired about the location of the conference bookstore. While leading him there, she continued to praise what she insisted was a powerful and searching work by an underappreciated poet. Several days later at the conference, she crossed paths with the opinionated stranger again. "She didn't know it was me," Bell later explained. Dove was "a bit baffled" by his ruse, realizing he had baited her into defending—with great enthusiasm—his own work.[1]

Four years later, in 1977, during her second year at the Iowa Writers' Workshop, Dove appeared in Bell's poetry class. Seated in the back row were two morose first-year students, Sandra Cisneros and Joy Harjo, who marveled at Dove's poise. When she was not holding forth with supreme confidence, Dove coolly "painted her fingernails in a rainbow of colors in class," to the consternation of her instructor and the silent approval of her classmate Jorie Graham. This display of unapologetic individualism presented a new challenge to the status quo of the Workshop. Decades later, when Dove was named poet laureate, Graham only half-jokingly invoked her in-class nail painting ritual as a force of institutional change: "I hope she does it in the poet laureate's office. It would be good for the office."[2]

Years after graduating, Cisneros told Dove she admired her for consistently contributing to discussion despite an environment Cisneros found so intimidating that she "gave up and didn't say anything." Although she knew her comments were likely to draw condescending stares and snide remarks, "she *forced* herself to say something in every class," which "took all her courage."[3] Dove's confidence derived from a sophisticated European frame of reference, gleaned from a Fulbright fellowship she held at the University of Tübingen the year before arriving at the Workshop in 1975. While there, she became fluent in German and spoke it confidently in mostly white intellectual social circles. Studying abroad in the picturesque college town offered her "a different perspective on Iowa. Had I not gone to Tübingen I might have been intimidated by Iowa," but the experience of going "to Europe first, where no one knew me, and where I had to get along in a different language," fortified her with "much more self-confidence than I had before."[4] Tübingen imbued her with cosmopolitanism beyond her years. She was all of twenty-two when she moved into her self-described "dive" apartment across the Iowa River from the Workshop.[5] Her Fulbright also encouraged new connections with foreign scholars at Iowa, including Fred Viebahn, who would play an instrumental role in her personal and aesthetic development. The social and cultural diversity missing from the regular Workshop she found not only in the intellectual and creative companionship of Viebahn—which turned romantic—but in an unlikely institutional nexus that was the invention of Paul Engle and Hualing Nieh in the late 1960s: the International Writing Program.

The "Workshop Poem"

Dove began her pivotal first year by devouring the works of the authors cited during workshop sessions. "I'd hear names" and take her cue, thinking, "I've never heard of these poets before, better read them." Even when "someone would *not* like a certain poet," Dove made a point of reading their work too. Despite her remarkable proficiency in German language and literature, she became acutely aware of "how naive" she was and how little she had read compared with her classmates.[6] Afternoon Workshop classes typically adjourned up the hill to the Airliner bar on Clinton Street where "the talk was poetry" in an atmosphere that seemed to intensify competitive jockeying for position initiated in class. "It was serious stuff" consisting of allusions to classical literature and mythology, with students rattling off lengthy passages from memory. This was a group in which most "people knew poems by heart."[7] Her "short-cut reading list" became a lifebuoy.[8]

As her exposure to literature expanded, Dove diligently strived to perfect her workshop assignments. But in the process, her writing fell into a trap, and she soon realized "what everybody says is true" about "an Iowa Writers' Workshop poem" being a stock literary product created with factory-like efficiency. To her horror, she discovered herself writing verse "that sounds like it came from Iowa," unconsciously "slipping into that [habit] easily." The high-stakes workshop sessions had bent her craft through "positive reinforcement," she explained. "If people in the workshop like your poem you try to do something like that the next time," until it becomes an unconscious reflex engrained in the creative process. She soon found herself "starting to write these kinds of safe poems that don't take risks, and as a consequence, after Iowa, for over a year I really didn't write any poems."[9] Dove's dedication to achieving the program's standard for success had inadvertently homogenized her craft and dampened her creative spark. The effects of poetry workshops are visible in her self-conscious use of "the strict forms of the sonnet and villanelle [that] are integral" to her earlier work, as critic Renee Shea points out. It was not until years after the Workshop that she expanded into "improvisation and individual expression" through the rhythms and sounds associated with music and dance.[10]

The transition was not without its challenges. Her diligent work ethic—writing daily from midnight to dawn until she drifted off, arising again before noon to resume her creative thrust—drove her repeatedly to attempt to resuscitate her poetry. But outside the context of writing for workshop, the flaw in her otherwise technically sound and fastidiously safe verse was that it lacked a voice with resonance. False starts abounded. She "didn't finish any poems" in the year following graduation because "whenever I tried to write one, it didn't sound like me." To her revulsion, "it sounded like a poem from some composite person," one unmistakably identifiable in the group identity of her poetry workshop classes.[11] That collective force was one to be reckoned with, as it actively discouraged experimentation while encouraging conformity through a Skinnerian system of punishment and reward. She "felt pretty paralyzed after the Workshop," sensing at every turn "the Workshop looking over my shoulder." By deliberately crossing over into fiction, she undid her Workshop training to regain her poetic voice. Although she vowed to keep that prose fiction in a drawer, to "let it rest in peace," she later published it as her first short story collection, *Fifth Sunday*, in 1990, and a novel, *Through the Ivory Gate*, two years later.[12]

In light of Dove's creative paralysis after graduation from the Workshop, her MFA thesis bears the unmistakable imprint of the Workshop pedagogy and curriculum. Her schooling interfered with her education, as Mark Twain would have it, through training "in sensation and the manipulation of representation in The Image," according to Robert McDowell. "The standard lesson plan, devised to reflect the ascendancy of Wallace Stevens and a corrupt revision of T. S. Eliot's objective correlative, instructed young writers to renounce realistic depiction and offer it up to the province of prose." The result was a narrowing of poetry into "subjectivity and imagination-as-image; it has strangled a generation of poems." Dove's peers became pretending play-actors, or "dissemblers," in this manner, a tendency she simultaneously resisted and replicated.[13]

Between flashes of brilliance, her MFA thesis is a derivative youthful imitation of the styles and subjects of H.D. and Dove's thesis supervisor, Louise Glück. Her riddle poems, for example, are the products of a Workshop exercise in writing poetry without naming the subject. "Riddle" demonstrates her mastery of the assignment. "When I see you, my intestines/ squirm," it begins, followed by a series of clever images ending with her subject's violent end: "Rain drives your family to the sidewalks,/ where their split pink tongues accuse each pedestrian of murder." The poem remains straitjacketed both by the parameters of the assignment and Dove's response to it with this gratuitous teacher-pleasing confection, a graduate version of her earlier acculturation into the role of high school honor student. Much of her thesis amounts to such well-executed classroom exercises as "Riddle: The Vase." In it, Dove strains for the classical imagery of John Keats's "Ode on a Grecian Urn." "It is the graven image of a poem/ whose clay feet are natural,/ who stands on a waxed table," the pun on anthropomorphic and poetic feet all too conspicuous as she rounds out the portrait in "its dirt belly stuffed with tulips/ or peacock feathers."[14] Such striving yet constrained work possessed enough nascent creative power to meet her instructor's expectations and withstand the scrutiny of her peers. But soon after graduation, it became clear to her that such success was hollow. Catering too obediently to institutional demands, she realized, threatened to domesticate her expansive international vision, which eventually revolutionized the world of poetry.

The German Connection

By her second year in the program, Dove grew increasingly discontented with the Workshop's American literary focus, which proved too narrow for her worldly purview. Crossing over to the eclectic and diverse culture of the International Writing Program, if only informally as a charter member of sorts, infused her with new vigor. American perspectives on race had tried her patience. She recalled standing out for all the wrong reasons: "I was the only Black person in the Iowa workshop at the time," which burdened her with "other people's guilt." Even without that burden, "being a student in a creative writing workshop is a very naked experience," leaving young idealistic minds vulnerable to damaging criticism. Add to this the predicament of being "the only person representing any other culture, and you're setting yourself up doubly," she explains. Guilt can play havoc with critical standards. She noticed that her peers lowered their aesthetic standards when her poetry was up for review. With her race in mind, "they started making allowances" for her identity "as a hyphenated poet—as an African-American-woman-poet, or a Latin-American-gay-poet, or whatever." When the burden of guilt mounts, suddenly "the rigor drops; it's this condescension which is so insulting, because as a serious writer one approaches the art with all the rigor of non-hyphenated poets." At workshop sessions, she could see the pattern repeatedly in her fellow students, who would not "talk about the poem in terms of techniques or its aesthetic," but only "the subject matter." Thus "poems dealing specifically with my heritage," she attested, "always got the worst," as in the least helpful, "comments, because people could not find a way around the guilt."[15]

The third floor of the English-Philosophy Building was home to the International Writing Program (IWP), where Dove found welcome relief from such condescension. Fred Viebahn, a young German poet, epitomized the prevailing attitude toward her poetry among scholars visiting from abroad through the IWP, a non-degree-granting program that offered housing and office space for up to five months at a time. Viebahn was among the IWP fellows, an eclectic blend of twenty-five visitors per year who occupied an entire floor of the Mayflower dormitory north of campus by City Park on Dubuque Street. They came from all over the world, representing more than twenty different nations at any given time. Paul Engle, along with Hualing Nieh, raised over $3 million from 1967 through the early 1990s, which allowed more than seven hundred writers to immerse themselves in the literary culture of Iowa City.[16] Viebahn was a beneficiary of this sinecure, which afforded him an extended period unburdened by teaching requirements to pursue his creative endeavors, conduct research and translation projects, and explore the region. The primary purpose was to offer writers a creative space and an opportunity to share their nation's literature and their latest projects at a two-hour non-credit seminar held once a week on a rotating basis. Dove attended these seminars, drawing stimulation from the rich array of literatures and authors on display. In this environment, she could circulate with scholars who were not American and thus bore none of the guilt of the U.S. slave-holding past when interacting with her. IWP scholars not only treated her on equal footing, they also took active interest in her German proficiency as a valuable skill otherwise overlooked in the Workshop's limited curriculum and culture.

Dove noticed at Iowa "that everything ran by clique. The fiction writers stuck together, the poets stuck together," and even "the wrestlers had a bar" and "the visual artists had a bar." The social subdivisions were impermeable, a caste system that seemed "crazy" to her. The urge to explore other groups was sacrilege, an unpardonable sin that was actively denied. "I remember trying to get a couple of the graduate students in the Writers' Workshop to come to some of the seminars" for the IWP, she recalled. To her shock, "they shied away," seeming "not to want to see and hear from writers other than a few select Americans." She "was rather disgusted by that," knowing that xenophobia deterred some, while others "wanted to believe that they were the only writers in the world." This was exactly "the kind of arrogance" she despised most. The cliques within the Workshop itself also seemed to raise insurmountable barriers dividing young scholars from fruitful exchanges. Not only was there a "reluctance to meet foreign writers": an equally powerful pressure to "stick to your group" of narrow subcultures designated by genre delimited literary and creative expansion.[17] After being awarded a Teaching/Writing Fellowship, Dove was offered office space in the English-Philosophy Building, but was told that she might find her office mate unacceptable. She shot back a look of disbelief to the inquiring secretary, Connie Brothers, asking, "Is there something wrong with him?" Brothers replied, "No, we just wanted to check" since he was in fiction and not poetry. Expecting a refusal or some sort of compromise, Brothers was stunned that she was open to meeting another student outside of her specialization. "Sure, that would be wonderful," Dove said without hesitation. Reflecting years later on the entrenched segregation of Workshop students according to genre, she commented that "the notion of prose writing and poetry writing as separate entities has been artificially created, partly as a result of fitting writing into the academic curriculum where it is easiest to teach them separately." In her own work after graduation, poetry and fiction indeed became "part of the same process" because "it's all writing; there are just different ways of going about it." Looking back on her days at Iowa, she frankly revealed, "one of the things I deplored when I was in graduate school was just how separate the two were kept; the fiction writers and the poetry writers didn't even go to the same parties."[18]

The social dynamic at Iowa for Dove, as for Harjo and Cisneros, embodied the intellectual climate. Harjo and Cisneros faced a different challenge, because, unlike Dove, they did not venture beyond the exclusive Workshop circles. Dove instead discovered in the IWP a vast and thriving network of scholars eager to exchange ideas and launch projects. She removed herself from the "high-powered" gatherings that consisted of "more political shuffling" than "students getting together and caring for one another." She "simply withdrew from that" because she "just didn't like it, and so the second year I don't think very many people saw me." She "said bye after class and went to my apartment" but more often to the IWP offices or to the Mayflower dormitory that housed the international writers. She knew "the first year might have slowed me down in terms of poetry," but she was determined to cross campus and reach out to this community of scholars from across the globe to prevent it from occurring again during the second.[19]

Just as Dove's original decision as a youth in Akron, Ohio, to study German was an act of rebellion against the institutional conformity of her junior high school that favored French, she reached out—against all social cues and cultural precedence—to the international students. "Always a maverick," as she later described herself.[20] Unlike her self-conscious Workshop classmates struggling to define themselves in the process of their professional development, the IWP's authors "had paid their dues" and "had been working at it a long time."[21] These foreign writers appealed to Dove the same way Ralph Waldo Emerson had gravitated toward the "finished men" in his circle of protégés a century earlier in the creative writing enclave of Concord, Massachusetts. They had outgrown the strident and often histrionic self-expression of early development and now bore a firm confidence in their aesthetic and professional visions. Dove similarly relished the opportunity to escape the pressure-filled cliques dividing the hypercompetitive young writers of the Workshop for a group of accomplished professionals who had advanced beyond the angst of the self-conscious developmental phase. They were eager to take her into the fold, rather than compete with her.

By the end of the spring semester of 1976 at the Workshop, Dove's extended time away from Germany had begun to take its toll on her fluency. Her mastery of the German language held special value, since it brought her both social autonomy and access to her own untapped aesthetic power through an undiscovered rich literary tradition. To sharpen her edge, she volunteered as a translator for what the IWP established later that year as the Translation Workshop. Transgressing into the IWP offices from the Workshop as none of her classmates had, Dove inquired about the availability of such work. "If there's a German writer," she offered, "I'd be willing to help translate" for the fall semester of 1976.[22] Enter the bespectacled, bright-eyed Fred Viebahn, a wellspring of energy with a quick smile and flowing locks cascading over his shoulders, a creature like none she had encountered in the Workshop.

Viebahn breezed into Iowa City a literary prodigy, a wunderkind from Cologne with six book-length publications including a novella, volumes of poetry and short stories, two novels, and a play to his credit at the age of twenty-nine. His first book, *Die Schwarzen Tauben*—which prophetically translates as *The Black Doves*—was named the German Book of the Month in 1969. In 1973 he won the literary prize for young writers of the City of Cologne, and his first play, *Blutschwestern*, debuted on stage in 1976 at Torturmtheater Sommerhausen. Unlike Dove's Workshop classmates, Viebahn was a seasoned and accomplished author. Soon after the wheels of his plane skidded onto the tarmac of Chicago's O'Hare Airport marking his first day in the country, IWP fellow Peter Nazareth greeted him and drove him to Paul Engle's house in Iowa City. Once there, he was introduced to a bright young Workshop student; "she was beautiful," he recalled, immediately attracted to "her colorful fingernails and fluent German."[23] To his delight, she had introduced herself in his native language, this time playing the role of accommodating host rather than the culture-shocked Auslander she had been in Tübingen. The circumstances for their falling in love at that instant could not have been better orchestrated. Viebahn's overwhelming sense of presentiment on his first day in America met with Dove's joy in reawakening her slumbering verbal prowess in the German language.

The longhaired and leather-jacketed German intellectual seemed heaven sent in his woody 1970 station wagon and John Lennon glasses. A photograph of the striking couple—confident, carefree and on the brink of literary greatness—posing next to the vehicle captures them basking in the sun at the beginning of their lifelong emotional and intellectual journey together. Known for its agriculture and conventional midwestern homogeneity, the state of Iowa in the mid-1970s seems an improbable place for the meeting of this transnational interracial intellectual couple. Dove never would have expected it herself based on her first impression of Iowa. When she turned on the TV several days before her Workshop courses commenced in late August 1976, only to discover "the pig reports" and little else, she wondered, "What am I doing here?" Spending her twenty-third birthday inexorably alone in this barren farmland left her "completely depressed." Two years later, however, she would learn that Iowa, particularly through programs such as the IWP, was a relative bastion of progressive racial politics compared with institutions such as Florida State University in Tallahassee. A job offer at FSU presented a tempting opportunity, but the couple demurred because they "felt uneasy taking an interracial relationship to upstate Florida."[24]

Connie Brothers, the Workshop secretary in 1975, remembered the couple as a perfectly suited pair whose long-term future together seemed as if it had been aligned in the stars. "She married him" four years later, in 1979, Brothers said, noting that everyone familiar with them was not surprised. "Rita was and still is outgoing," Brothers recalled, noting that she began her efflorescence when the stranger from Cologne entered the scene. That fall of 1976, Dove was awarded "a teaching/writing fellowship [that is the Workshop's] very best category of financial aid." She proved to be "fabulous" as an instructor that semester, "since she had such a wonderful personality" and sophisticated background in literature and culture. Brothers described how Viebahn and Dove frequently "met on the same floor of EPB [the English-Philosophy Building]," and at other gatherings arranged by Engle. She explained how "in those days, Paul Engle wanted students from the Workshop to get to know the people in the IWP, so he had a number of social events that allowed that to happen."[25] Whereas Engle had encouraged collaboration with the Workshop in order to build on the momentum established by the program, the Workshop director John Leggett had little incentive to reach out to the IWP. The IWP's purpose and scope existed entirely outside required courses, faculty, and degree granting for which the Workshop was responsible.

Although Engle actively encouraged Viebahn and Dove's collaboration, she "stopped translating his work" if for no better reason than she had fallen in love with him. Their intimacy heightened expectations for translation beyond what either of them could realistically reach. She could hardly conceal her anger, calling to his attention the flaws, "you *know* there's this, you missed that." Likewise, he would find fault in her translations of his German poems, because she "couldn't get something into English."[26] Ironically, the work that united them precipitated the first major conflict of their relationship. Putting an end to translating each other's work opened up new channels for collaboration. Indeed, Dove credits Viebahn for many of her daring crossovers into other genres and subjects, including her first novel, *Through the Ivory Gate*. In the acknowledgments, she writes, "My heartfelt gratitude goes to my husband, Fred Viebahn, who literally 'made me do it.' "[27]

Viebahn's translations of Dove's poetry into German proved especially difficult because they were written according to the Imagist aesthetic inspired by the poetry of H.D. (Hilda Doolittle). Successfully translating these works was nearly impossible for him, given the surreal disconnected images of her verse, which eluded his own mastery of English. To Dove's good fortune, Louise Glück, whose approach is heavily influenced by the Imagists, arrived at the Workshop for the fall semester of 1976 for a one-year appointment as visiting lecturer. Although her classroom teaching was not effective in Dove's estimation, "Glück was extremely good one-on-one; she was uncanny."[28] Integral to the aesthetic of H.D.'s *Hermetic Definition*, which Glück introduced to Dove, is the exploration of unconscious urges of guilt, sex, and love.

The writings of H.D. were perhaps even more influential on Dove than the tutelage offered by Glück. Both the prose and poetry of H.D. had been nothing short of a revelation for her at the Workshop, as she was transfixed by its "strange and wonderful" powers that were "so very musical in its own insistent phrasing." Indeed, the distilled intensity of H.D. meant that she could only "take her in very small doses," a mind so brilliant she feared she would "start sounding like her." She admired H.D.'s capacity "to take the outrageous circumstances of her life" and craft something "which was absolutely beautiful" and "not be self-indulgent" or "confessional in any sense."[29]

Crossing the Color Line at Iowa

The Yellow House on the Corner, Dove's first book, published in 1980, reflects what was then called the New Black Aesthetic, which signaled the end of the Black Arts Movement in several important ways. The poems in the volume resonate with the New Black Aesthetic's defining features of "borrowing across race and class lines, a parodic relationship to the Black Arts Movement, a new and unflinching look at black culture, [and] a belief in finding the universal in oneself and one's experiences."[30] Her early experimentation with the universal in her own experience, particularly her adolescence, appears in her Iowa MFA thesis in poems such as "Adolescence II." Highly prestigious journals including *Antaeus* and the *Paris Review* featured this and other poems from her thesis. "Adolescence II" and "Nigger Song" earned space in two high-profile anthologies at the time, *The American Poetry Anthology* and *Eating the Menu*. Both poems simultaneously departed from the Black Arts Movement and challenged the expectations of her Workshop classmates.

Dove's Workshop classmates expected her writing to represent the Black Arts Movement primarily because they knew so little about the emergent New Black Aesthetic. "I was the only Black person in the Iowa workshop at the time, and I think many Black writers who have been in workshops will have had the same experience: you're always the only one. There falls the burden," not only of white guilt, but of advancing an aesthetic palatable to a white audience. Indeed, the chief complaint against her work was that her treatment of subjects was too abrasive and vitriolic. Such a situation arose when her poem "Kentucky, 1833" was spotlighted for discussion. It depicts a Sunday on a plantation, which is the "day of roughhousing," music, and boxing that draws "Massa and his gentlemen friends" who "come to bet on the boys." These celebrations quelled and redirected any underlying rebellious impulses so that slaves returned on Monday to their labor with new vigor. Dove captures the essence of this insidious design in how the young slave "Jason is bucking and prancing about" like an aroused animal, feeling his oats, spurred by "Massa" who "said his name reminded him of some sailor, a hero who crossed an ocean, looking for a golden cotton field." The prose-poem's final image is of Jason, the boxing match "winner," "sprawled out under a tree and the sun," looking at the sky as if it "were an omen we could not understand, the book that, if we could read, would change our lives."[31] In these last phrases the perspective poignantly shifts to the collective pronoun, extending Jason's experience to the slave population as a whole.

The moving "Kentucky, 1833" stands as one of few exceptions to how Dove's Workshop training, "which although helpful, had a stultifying effect on her poetry," according to Malin Pereira, author of *Rita Dove's Cosmopolitanism*.[32] Peer criticism of this ambitious piece tellingly reflected the Workshop culture's inability to appreciate the poem's powerful expression of the New Black Aesthetic. Complaints centered around one comment, "Well, I feel like someone told me that in order to be healthy, I had to take a spoonful of medicine a day, but I'd rather take an apple a day," which established the class consensus, Dove recalled. The point drove home how "for some people the horror of events and the political aspect of a poem make it impossible for them to see any aesthetic merits." This accounts for "one reason poetry with political or sociological content often gets short shrift" and why it is "very hard for people to be able to discuss that material in a technical sense." The opposition gave her valuable insight into her own potential: "At the same time, that comment was the first indication I had that I was onto something good." She thus resolved to pursue what they told her to avoid.[33]

The criticism of "Kentucky, 1833" found fault not in its edifying glimpse at the injustice of a particularly pernicious aspect of slavery—the ideological import of its faux "celebrations" and system of rewards—so much as its method of doing so. Indeed, calling for "an apple a day" rather than the bitter "spoonful of medicine" she was offering spoke of the white readership's demand for black experience rooted in the triumphalist narrative of the Black Arts Movement.[34] The New Black Aesthetic, as her poem demonstrates, takes a fearless look at black experience not to create an essentialist view of it, but to broaden it across racial and historical boundaries. Labor exploitation, literacy, and capitalism resonate beyond the historically specific subject while revealing a painful glimpse at a day in the life of a Sunday on the plantation.

The most pivotal year of Dove's early career occurred in 1976, which marked the official end of the Black Arts Movement as well as her introduction to Viebahn and the IWP. Signs of the Black Arts Movement's long decline surfaced as early as 1959, in Lorraine Hansberry's play *A Raisin in the Sun*. A key scene in it depicts the young, idealistic Beneatha Younger's indoctrination into Afrocentrism by her new boyfriend, who plays a recording of tribal music for her. Beneatha's drunken brother Walter Younger unexpectedly stumbles in from the local bar, jumps on the coffee table, and launches into a mock oration as if he were a warrior chief. The scene calls attention to the Black Arts Movement's ignorance of pressing contemporary urban problems in the African-American community such as alcoholism and unemployment. This was one of many critiques exposing how the movement unraveled in the 1960s and 1970s. In addition to such criticism, "the black revolutionary journals also lost their constituency." By the early 1970s the most significant of them, *Black Dialogue* (1964–1970), *Liberator* (1961–1973), and *Journal of Black Poetry* (1966–1973), all ceased publication. By the time Dove arrived at Iowa in 1975, they were all defunct, except for the Black Arts Movement's flagship journal, *Black World*, which finally ceased in February 1976, during her second year. By the time of her graduation from the Workshop in 1977, the culture "experienced a marked impetus toward more consciously literary and theoretically based analyses of African-American texts."[35] That year the Modern Language Association and the National Endowment for the Humanities endorsed a new study aimed at liberating critical discourse from "fundamentally ideological or sociological methodologies that tended toward the naively reductive."[36] It was precisely that naively reductive critical discourse that frustrated Dove's attempts to write poetry like "Kentucky, 1833" at the Workshop.

Dove refused the role of spokesperson of her race. "Given my middle-class background, there were many kinds of experiences that I had which could not *only* have been experienced by Blacks." "Adolescence II," for example, depicts a surreal scene of searching sexual awakening whose poignant vulnerability explodes the sanctioned racial valor of the Black Arts Movement. This and other poems about adolescence that appeared in *The Yellow House on the Corner* engaged "topics, which were for everyone." Therefore she "submitted them to magazines with that in mind. The slave narratives came a bit later," with the notable exceptions of "Kentucky, 1833," and "The Transport of Slaves from Maryland to Mississippi," both of which encountered resistance in workshop discussions.[37] The latter is a stirring pastiche of historical prose and poetry describing a slave mutiny on a wagon train ironically sabotaged by "a slave woman" who "helped the Negro driver mount his horse and ride for help."[38] It offers an early glimpse of Dove's powerful experimentation with nonfiction sources, which reached full fruition in the Pulitzer Prize–winning *Thomas and Beulah* (1986), her narrative verse rendering of her grandparents' history. Such transgression across genres began for her in Stanley Plumly's Forms of Poetry course, which she found "absolutely liberating: we read prose—not just fiction, but imaginative nonfiction memoire, travelogues." The environment, unlike her other Workshop courses, appealed to her because of its crossover dynamic that resulted in "a class of poets discussing the strategies of prose."[39]

Dove's difficult decision not to send her manuscripts to "Black magazines" speaks to the depth of her disaffiliation from the Black Arts Movement. Pressure mounted at Iowa to adopt more palatable modes of expressing political subjects and to localize her subjects instead of crossing cultural boundaries. She actively "resisted being typecast," which posed a particularly difficult challenge, since Toni Morrison and Alice Walker had not yet made it "possible for people to imagine that a black writer doesn't have to write about ghettos." The Workshop, rather than the more eclectic and culturally diverse IWP, had not shown signs of "a readiness for people to accept" individuality "on both sides, Black and white." The program's racial politics in 1978 still reflected the attitude of the 1960s, when authors of color were expected only to "write what they know" and mainly represent their race. The strident first wave of "necessary overkill" was essential for placing race on the literary and political agenda in the 1960s, because "in order to develop Black consciousness it was important to stress Blackness, to make sure the poems talked about being Black, because it had never really been talked about."[40]

The Workshop's habitual assessment of authors of "minority groups" according to "whether they adhere to a genre" presented a barrier to creativity for Dove. She looked to Zora Neale Hurston as a model for how an African-American woman writer could avoid this trap, in which "the genre is making them, instead of them making literature." Dove knew that writers of color who define themselves as cosmopolitan could often be accused of "being too loud," on one hand, or absurdly, "playing up to whites" on the other.[41] This crossing of boundaries played a major role in her first book after the Workshop. *The Yellow House on the Corner* is deliberately "very domestic," yet with the intention of reaching beyond parochial boundaries. The life she depicts there, like the house itself, "is on the corner," she reminds us, "on the edge of domesticity," poised to evoke "a sense of something beyond that—outside of that boundary, there is something else."[42] Whereas Cisneros embraced her role as representative of inner-city working-class Latino Americans, Dove refused to play a similar role on behalf of African Americans. Although Dove was "incredibly excited about some aspects of the Black Arts Movement" in the late 1960s, she increasingly saw it as an industry that compromised the complexity of the notion of "black art." "The concept is not pure," she argued, because "the insistence on black art is just a device, a way of establishing territory or generating publicity."[43]

Dove knew she could not accurately speak for a ghettoized black American adolescence, given the middle-class privilege of her upbringing in Akron, Ohio. Her childhood home was filled with her father's German books from his war years—he insisted on learning the language of the enemy—as well as scientific journals and texts that were tokens of his status as the first African-American chemist at the Goodyear Tire and Rubber Company.[44] Surrounded by more material than she could read, she was stimulated by "all these different cultures that swirled around" her. "I experienced the world as a kind of feast, a banquet," she recalled.[45] She was named a Presidential Scholar, one of the nation's top one hundred high-school seniors, and graduated summa cum laude in 1973 at Miami of Ohio. These were "rather sheltered college years at Miami University, in the rural setting of southwestern Ohio" where she "filled the role of the striving, gifted Black student." In Germany, and later in Iowa, she "was on display" in these strange environments "where some people pointed fingers at me and others pitied me as a symbol of centuries of brutality and injustice against Blacks." Whereas she felt alienated while living abroad, "both from my home country and from the place I was in," she also recognized how "serious travel can heighten the awareness of a writer to see many sides of a story."[46] Occupying that liminal space in Germany had an illuminating effect on her powers of observation. At Iowa, her development came under threat from the retrograde racial politics of the Workshop, but the IWP provided an outlet for the development of her newly acquired skills in German language and literature.

Dove dared to cross more than just color lines at Iowa. Her core principle, "I just don't believe in boundaries," is embodied in her willingness to venture into unfamiliar cultural terrain.[47] Occupying both African-American and international literary worlds, she "refuses and ironizes clichéd political discourse and aesthetic dilettantism," as critic Terry Steffen points out.[48] Her Imagistic personal lyric mode, for example, is on display in works such as "Adolescence II." "Can you feel it yet?" ask the surreal "seal-men with eyes as round as dinner plates" to the speaker of the poem, who is on the verge of her sexual awakening. They wait for a reply but she does not know what to say. "They chuckle" and vanish, with a knowing "Well, maybe next time."[49] "Adolescence II" stands with "Nigger Song: An Odyssey" among her greatest Iowa achievements, the latter of which staunchly refuses conventional racial discourse.

The ironic political discourse of Dove's poetry was inspired in part by contemporary East German authors. Since "overtly political opinions other than party line were not allowed," they encoded their writings with political significance. No matter how abstract or highly subjective East German poetry may appear on the surface, "there is always something in between the lines talking about oppression," Dove explains. But for many East Germans exiled to West Germany, that political edge embedded in richly metaphorical language became dull. Sara Kirsch epitomized how the "latest poems seem very lax" after the transition to the West. Dove suspected that indifferent audiences in Western capitalist culture "took the wind out of the sails" of such Eastern dissent writers.[50]

Dove's engagement with the German language at Iowa through Viebahn and the IWP encouraged exploration into what was then considered forbidden territory for an African-American woman writer. "Agosta the Winged Man" and "Rasha the Black Dove" explicitly deal with German subjects, and thus risked stirring controversy, particularly among advocates of the Black Arts Movement. She imagined their objections: "Why are you writing about a white—German!—artist?" To avert such a hostile reception, she deliberately avoided exposure. "I didn't think I was strong enough to withstand the political fallout," she confessed. Thus she opted to "keep out of the political fray" by withholding such volatile material from publication. She "waited" and "stepped out as a writer later, when things became more tolerant."[51]

Dove's thesis supervisor, Louise Glück, played a strong role in encouraging her work with German subjects, as in "The Bird Frau."[52] As a New Yorker born of Hungarian immigrants, Glück lent a vital internationalist perspective to Dove. In her thirties, with only a single volume of poetry to her credit, *First-born* (1968), Glück advised Dove at Iowa from 1975 to 1977. Unlike other faculty members who attracted graduate student advisees through their literary awards and star-studded publication records, Glück appealed to Dove amid the narrowly Americanist Workshop faculty. It was not until decades later that Glück's star rose when she won the Pulitzer Prize in 1993 and the National Book Award for *Faithful and Virtuous Night* in 2014. Glück, like Viebahn, provided a vital bridge to foreign subjects. Her influence testifies to how Dove believed "one of the greatest tragedies of the Black Arts Movement was its insistence upon Afrocentric arts to the exclusion of others." Such an exclusive purview was tantamount to insisting that "all the world's resources were traitorous somehow," she contended.[53]

The expectation that African-American writers must be limited to functioning as "the medium for proposing activist solutions to racial problems or for explicit black proselytizing" struck Dove as profoundly incongruous to her creative development.[54] She also denied other doctrinaire uses of literature, particularly the Workshop's nationalistic rhetoric handed down from the Cold War. At Iowa, the IWP occupied a liminal space in the bureaucratic infrastructure of the university. Its balanced representation of authors from Chile, Ceylon, Taiwan, and Romania formed a kind of literary United Nations. Since IWP writers did not come to Iowa to pursue a degree, and since Iowa did not subsidize them through grants, the IWP's funding structure demanded almost twice as much capital as the Workshop. But with Engle's massive industrial and federal network financially backing Iowa's literary mission, the IWP flourished. The bulk of the capital necessary to run the IWP came from a rich wellspring outside of Iowa, just as it had for the Workshop. Indeed, of the $200,000 Engle raised for the Workshop in 1966, less that $10,000 in revenue was drawn from Iowa sources.[55]

Thus with little local funding to support the international travel and monthly stipend for scholars like Viebahn, Engle had to look to other sources. These invariably included U.S. embassies and cultural affairs bureaus, which began to send "the best talent from their assigned countries." Viebahn ranked at the top of Germany's list, and thus received federal support for his visit, funded in part by the U.S. Information Agency. Engle's explicit aim was to win favor abroad for the U.S. capitalist system and its attendant political democracy, a Cold War objective embedded in the Workshop and its aesthetics that Workshop alumnus Eric Bennett and critic Mark McGurl have discussed.[56] Engle boasted, "the first books that show America in a positive light in Hungarian, Rumanian, and Polish were written by writers in our program." In addition to providing a stimulating outlet for seasoned worldly young authors like Dove, Engle's concern was ideological. This is evidenced by how he touted Xiao Qian in 1979 as "the first prose writer from the People's Republic of China to visit America since 1949." After his IWP visit, Engle reported with pride that Qian's piece in the *People's Daily* "was the first article praising our competitive system ever to appear" in that journal, "which is read by 500 million people." To avoid the appearance of producing apologists on behalf of free market capitalism, Engle pointed out that the Chinese novelist Ding Ling, who served two prison terms in her country for her political activism, came to the IWP to spread the message of human rights in the free world.[57] Indeed, as Bennett points out, "Engle's vision for institutionalized creative writing was both shaped and motivated by the Cold War" in an attempt to use "culture (and government help) to fight communism."[58] Bennett dates the Cold War at Iowa from 1945 to 1965, but evidence suggests the vestiges of its rhetoric persisted well into the 1970s in certain instances.

Despite the persistence of Cold War rhetoric into the 1970s in Iowa's writing programs, the Vietnam War and developments abroad complicated the ideological climate and infused it with activism, protest, and defiance of authority. Viebahn was no apologist for the free market; Dove, as mentioned earlier, believed better poetry came from East German writers, and that the capitalist system of West Germany actually functioned as a deterrent to powerful literature. West Germans were bombarded by consumer culture and thus looked upon poetry and the arts indifferently, or as an irrelevant pastime incapable of competing with commercial media.

Dove's resistance to being recruited as a soldier for ideological warfare resonates through an early poem she began at Iowa titled "Upon Meeting Don L. Lee, in a Dream." Using her signature surreal Imagism, she situates herself in the audience of a Black Arts Movement rally. As the intensity from the podium escalates, the speaker's hair begins falling out, "suggesting the decay of the ideology that Don Lee embodies."[59] Dove's dissent toward doctrinaire aesthetics not only criticizes his "exclusive celebration of blackness," it "is a comic feminist putdown of masculine posturing" prone to the sort of "homophobic and racist polemics that Lee preached," as the critic Pat Righelato aptly explains.[60] Dove said of her motivation to dismantle Lee, "I was kind of terrified of being suffocated before I began" a career as a professional author, and thus penned her own poetic declaration of independence.[61]

Defying Alice Walker

The young woman with the flashy fingernails whom Marvin Bell approached at the Bread Loaf conference for writers may have played the naive and eager young apprentice to his tweedy wizened author figure at the beginning of the 1970s. But by the middle of the decade, she had become a force to be reckoned with in the world of American letters, as no less a figure than Alice Walker would soon discover. While Dove was still enrolled at Iowa in 1975, editor Daniel Halpern selected "Adolescence II" along with "Nigger Song: An Odyssey" and "This Life" for *The American Poetry Anthology*. As an occasion for celebration heralding an auspicious professional debut for the twenty-three-year-old author, the volume's publication brought the unanticipated result of inciting outrage from one of the most prominent figures in African-American literature. When Dove's phone rang, she never expected Walker, the author of the famous short story "Everyday Use," to be on the line. At the time, Walker's career was on a steady ascent, building momentum toward its zenith. In less than a decade, she would receive both the National Book Award and the Pulitzer Prize for *The Color Purple*, achieving both worldwide fame and a permanent place in the canon of twentieth-century American literature. Walker, who had served on the editorial board for the newly published volume, informed Dove in no uncertain terms that she "refused to read at the book launch in San Francisco because a 'racist poem' had been published in the anthology." To Dove's horror, Walker went on to identify the poem in question as Dove's very own Iowa product, "Nigger Song: An Odyssey." Incredulous, Dove pleaded for an explanation, whereupon she learned that "Alice objected to the use of the word 'nigger,' even by a black writer."[62]

With her heart in her throat, Dove hung up the phone, wheeled around and marched toward her typewriter in the cramped apartment on 24 Van Buren Street in Iowa City. Gathering her poise, she typed out "a letter explaining my philosophy about the word." She defended her intent "to redeem the word, to reimagine it as a black concept," a deft political move anticipating LGBTQ activists' later reclamation of the term "queer" from derisive usage. Days later, a letter appeared with a return address reading "Alice Walker." Her fingers trembling, Dove tore open the letter. Although the tone was stately, it was insistent in its refusal to compromise. The "polite, dignified letter" recognized

Dove's "right to use whatever words I choose but argued that we should not use such words in the company of white people." Reaching this part of the letter, Dove raised her eyes and quietly made a vow to herself: "No one's going to put me in that kind of cage—not whites, not blacks, not even myself." Her dedication to total creative autonomy at that moment was complete. She vowed to write without limitation, to use any language, cross any cultural boundaries, and invoke any subject on her creative journeys. As for the poem Walker denounced for its use of one of the world's most offensive and politically charged words, she knew her art would rule the day and "defy whatever nefarious purposes people may want to use it for."[63]

Such aesthetic freedom echoed the lifestyle Dove led after she graduated from Iowa in 1977. Two years of intensive poetry training at the Workshop took its toll. She grew weary of the "Workshop poems" she had become so adept at writing. She became impatient and disenchanted with the cadences and sounds of her own poetic voice. The bureaucratic university system—with its rules and competition for Teaching/Writing Fellowships—also contributed to her fatigue. It is not surprising, therefore, that Dove embraced fiction to refresh her creative spirit. She also rejected an opportunity to return to academic life by turning down the most significant job opportunity of her career. The choice between the tenure-track assistant professor position at Florida State University and the prospect of joining Viebahn at Oberlin College in her birth state of Ohio was difficult. While in Ohio, he taught classes in German literature and directed plays; she enrolled in art classes and launched a collection of short stories that later appeared as *Fifth Sunday*. After two years at Oberlin, they spent two more years abroad in Israel and Berlin, a time she refers to as their "salad days." The untethered, bohemian freelance life brought them the autonomy and freedom they desired. Her second book, *Museum*, came to fruition at this stage. After two years overseas she grew concerned that she had lost her poetic edge in English, "the precise tone of a phrase." Prose offered a more forgiving genre where "the damage was more manageable" than poetry. In 1981, she returned to poetry and the academy, this time as a faculty member in the creative writing program at Arizona State University.[64] Although she has moved appointments throughout the remainder of her career, she has maintained academic employment ever since.

On Iowa Avenue just east of the Pentacrest, Dove's words appear beneath pedestrians' feet in a commemorative plaque: "Sometimes/ a word is found so right it trembles/ at the slightest explanation." The quote is one of a series of immortal lines from famous Workshop faculty and graduates that include Flannery O'Connor and Kurt Vonnegut, embossed on the walkway along the avenue leading toward the majestic golden-domed Old Capitol building. What makes it stand out from these luminaries is precisely what distinguished her formative years at the Workshop—literary art's liberation from explanation by critics and ideologues intent on binding it to social duty, which, for Dove, defies neat categorization. Like a perfectly chosen word in a poem, Dove's career at Iowa was as unique as it was irreplaceable. Perhaps most telling of her legacy is the line that follows: "You start out with one thing," as in her first year at the Workshop before meeting Viebahn and discovering the IWP, "end/ up with another, and nothing's/ like it used to be, not even the future."[65] She propelled herself toward that future, inspired by the East German poets who delicately, but aggressively, challenged authority and crossed boundaries in their writing: their tacit credo was to expand imaginative horizons beyond the limits of "the larger community censorship of the individual imagination."[66]

11 • The Genius: Jane Smiley

When Jane Smiley first arrived at the University of Iowa in 1970, she was a newlywed and self-described "graduate student wife" with no particular professional ambition. The phrase "trailing spouse" had yet to be coined, as few dual-career couples existed at that time. Her mind was hardly idle, however, after she and her husband, John B. Whiston, whom she had met as a sophomore at Yale, moved into an idyllic farmhouse outside Iowa City near the rural town of Wellman. Rent was $25 per month, which Whiston's stipend from the University of Iowa's graduate program in medieval history helped defray, along with Smiley's job "making teddy bears in a factory" for a paltry $1.65 per hour. As with her Workshop classmate W. P. Kinsella, who transformed the vast fields of Iowa into the setting for his novel *Shoeless Joe* (later adapted into the film *Field of Dreams*), the magic of "the era of the back-to-the-land-movement" where they could "live a pastoral, idyllic life" had captured her imagination. Organic farming was in its ascendency, preceding the farm-to-table movement by roughly forty years. Prominently displayed on the coffee table was Barry Commoner's *The Closing Circle: Nature, Man, and Technology* (1971), while the domestic farm drama *The Waltons*, her "favorite show," played on the television.[1] Amid the pleasures of self-reliant days filled with gardening, canning, and drawing energy from solar and wind power came the deep satisfaction of finding wholesome alternatives to technologized commercial agriculture and its mounting environmental degradation. Although the prospect of professional authorship had yet to enter her mind as a viable future, Smiley had already sown the seeds of the creative process. Two decades later she would draw on her memory of this domestic idyll for *A Thousand Acres*, her tour de force recasting of *King Lear* in Iowa, which won the Pulitzer Prize and the National Book Critics Circle Award in 1992.

The unexamined life of a trailing spouse in rural Iowa was not worth leading. From her early days standing in line for registration at Yale (on exchange during her sophomore year at Vassar) with a budding young actress named Meryl Streep, Smiley thrived at the epicenter of intellectual and creative culture. Her omnivorous mind is apparent in her publications, which include thirteen novels and biographies of Charles Dickens and John Vincent Atanasoff, the inventor of the computer. Among her nonfiction is a potent 591-page tome, *Thirteen Ways of Looking at the Novel*, which features commentary on no fewer than one hundred classic novels. Her original intent in auditing graduate courses in English at the University of Iowa was to pursue a Ph.D. in Norse literature and culture. Upon her acceptance to the doctoral program in English at Iowa in 1972, she immersed herself in academic research and dabbled in fiction writing as a diversion. But the pastime soon became serious after she shared her stories with some friends from the Workshop, Rush Rankin and Stuart Dybek. Both were spellbound by her natural talent. On their recommendation, she applied to the program and was admitted in the fall semester of 1974.[2]

At the Workshop, Smiley soon collided with a culture of literary production less intent on intellectual exploration and more on fierce competition. "In that period," she recalled, "the teachers tended to be men of a certain age, with the idea that competition was somehow the key—the Norman Mailer period." The culture of creative writing at Iowa, she learned, patterned itself after Mailer's notorious conflicts with dissenting critics, disputes that often boiled over into fisticuffs. "If you disagreed with Norman, or gave him a bad review, he'd punch you in the nose," she said of the norm adopted by the pugnacious Workshop culture. In this group, male students and teachers engaged in boxing—regularly bloodying and knocking each other senseless—not merely as their preferred leisure activity and form of exercise. Instead, boxing served as a ritual integral to a particularly pugnacious strain of the Hemingwayesque ideal of hypermasculine authorial identity. To them, literature was not a body of knowledge to be researched or a craft to be mastered, but a means through which to assert dominance. According to behavioral expectations modeled after Mailer, authors "were supposed to get in fights in restaurants."[3]

The woman who loved horses, grew up reading Nancy Drew, *The Dana Girls*, and *The Black Stallion*, and now watched *The Waltons* while canning her own vegetables thus found herself in a curious dilemma. Hers was not the Raymond Carver hard-drinking school of dirty realism that resonated so well with Vietnam veterans, boxing aficionados, and hardened drug addicts like T. Coraghessan Boyle. Survival for her demanded a firm commitment to "all those years of guarding my stuff—no drinking, no drugs, personal modesty and charm, [and] a public life of agreeability and professionalism."[4] Maintaining this level of professionalism was particularly challenging amid the beery and combative culture of her male colleagues. Instrumental in meeting that challenge was Barbara Grossman, her diminutive confidante with astute business savvy, who eventually obtained a position in the publishing industry powerful enough to launch Smiley's career toward world fame.

The Hemingway Defense

As one of the few women in the program at the time, Smiley remembers the literary men of Iowa City during the early 1970s with a mixture of queasy disdain and comic distance: "The seventies were the years of swaggering male writers, editors, and F. Scott Fitzgerald (the 'sensitive' alternative to Norman Mailer—both drunks and as such entirely familiar to me and of no interest)."[5] These male icons defined the authorial role at the Workshop, in the process alienating writers like Smiley, whose tactful demeanor and intellectual prowess stood out even among the Ph.D. students in the English department. Sensitive male students who modeled their writing and lifestyles after Fitzgerald meshed with visiting professors such as John Cheever, a bow-tied gentleman inseparable from the flask discreetly tucked beneath his lapel, which kept him inebriated all hours of the day. Cheever embodied the urbane authorial alternative to the "would-be Hemingways and the macho followers of faculty member Vance Bourjaily, who hunted and fished."[6]

Director John Leggett cut a gentlemanly figure, with whom East Coast sophisticates could identify. The Leggett-Bourjaily divide "was perhaps best exemplified by the two Ray Carvers," according to Eric Olsen. One resembled Hemingway's own Nick Adams and published in journals like *Kayak*, "and the [other] Ray Carver was edited by Gordon Lish and published in *Esquire* and the *New Yorker*." Among the male Workshop students, "it was not enough to admire them both," or vacillate from one to the other: "you had to pick a side."[7] Without a model to emulate, female students were left searching.

Smiley did not identify with many who regarded the writing life at Iowa City in the early 1970s as an opportunity to "get drunk and stoned and laid—or try to—at the Workshop, because it seemed, that's what writers did."[8] Dylan Thomas's madcap antics, along with other charismatic visiting writers who stormed through town like rock stars, reinforced and justified this authorial image that many young men at the Workshop pantomimed. From the perspective of a trade author struggling to enter the ranks of literary fiction, Stephen King describes the 1970s as a time in which writers self-medicated with drugs and alcohol as a token of their need to take the edge off their heightened powers of perception and acute sensitivity. According to the "Hemingway Defense," which King says has "never been clearly articulated because it would not be manly to do so," the justification for alcoholism among male authors "goes something like this: as a writer, I am a very sensitive fellow, but I am also a man, and real men don't give in to their sensitivities." He explains that "Only sissy-men do that. Therefore I drink," reasoning, "How else can I face the existential horror of it all and continue to work?" Any self-destructive pain associated with hard drinking is met with the justification that "I can handle it. A real man always can."[9] Any literary history of Iowa City in the 1970s inevitably courses through the Airliner, the Mill, Mickey's, and Joe's Place, watering holes that nurtured these Hemingwayesque fantasies.

The drinking habits of Smiley's male classmates at the Workshop fueled the masculinist logic of "the Hemingway defense" during this "Norman Mailer period" when competition prevailed over collaboration. Mailer, boxing, and booze all were essential to the locker-room ethos at the Workshop behind its one-upmanship and ongoing challenges, taunts, and self-aggrandizement.[10] Displays of drunken bravado carried over into the workshop classroom. Smiley describes her instructor Vance Bourjaily and others as "writers, not teachers." Like T. C. Boyle, Smiley could plainly see that "they knew a lot about writing, but hadn't given a lot of thought to how to communicate what they knew." She admitted that her disdain was partially a "reaction to those hypermasculine guys because they did not praise and criticize" but they "did alienate the students." Further, "they didn't analyze" student writing sufficiently. She laments how "we weren't given the tools to know what was wrong." Boyle mentioned that instructors like Cheever and Bourjaily could only encourage him to carry on in the most general terms. "We had our instincts, but not tools," Smiley attested.[11]

The few students chosen as favorites received close attention. Boyle spent many evenings conversing with John Irving, his thesis adviser, and Cheever over drinks at the Mill, which was the watering hole of choice for Workshop members in the mid-1970s. Female students were instead subjected to harsh scrutiny designed to test their will, a process rationalized as a pedagogical rite of passage. Smiley recalled that when "one of the instructors had taken a particular shine to the work of one of our fellow students, he expressed his admiration for her potential by devoting himself to trashing her work." The trial extended throughout the entire semester, and included private workshop sessions. "He would have her into his office, and then subject her to brutal line-by-line criticism, making her defend every word, every phrase." The instructor claimed his harsh course of action came about because he "held her to a very high standard" and was dedicated to challenging her.[12] Smiley knew she was fortunate to have avoided such abuse.[13] "Thank God, that I was not this teacher's pet" and "that I was seen to have much smaller potential." She thus realized the benefit of being misjudged by male faculty who found her "work was of so little interest that it could be safely ignored by the powers that be (or were)."[14]

Smiley recognized those inquisitions as displays of dominance designed to intimidate at the symbolic nexus of bureaucratic authority—the faculty office. In sharp contrast to the office as a site for the reinforcement of teacher-pupil and master-apprentice roles, the collegial exchange of trade secrets took place off campus. Perched at the hill on Burlington Street near campus, the Mill functioned as a site free from institutional authority, hierarchy, and rank. There faculty shed the role of teacher, falling back on their identity as practicing writers; students played the part of apprentices to the literary trade. Recent pedagogical research by Mary Ann Cain describes such settings as constituting "a space of radical openness" characterized by informal exchange and mutual trust.[15] Top women students instead were systematically disempowered of the impetus "for representation, not simply as individuals but also in various forms of collective action." According to Cain, such collective action "demands and creates space for the kinds of courses and curricula that would disrupt their relationship to the academy, specifically the binary social relationships (teacher-student, expert-novice) that structure institutional hierarchies."[16]

At stake in this pedagogy in which Smiley dreaded becoming the teacher's pet was a gender power dynamic rooted in an uneven and highly contested politics of space. Along with Smiley, Workshop women such as Sandra Cisneros and Joy Harjo were all too aware of such confrontational meetings female students endured in the offices of male faculty members. Heightening that awareness was Gaston Bachelard's *Poetics of Space*, which had been taught in the program during the mid-1970s. Bachelard prompted Cisneros to politicize this otherwise apolitical aesthetic. Bachelard observed how violence functioned as a significant dimension of creative space in which "the imagination acts not only on geometrical dimensions, but the elements of power and speed." Space, he observed, could take on both sublime and monstrous qualities forming "an aggression," like the intensified spaces for learning at the

Workshop, in which "there is a sign of violence in all these figures [of creativity] in which an over-excited creature emerges from a lifeless shell."[17] The paradoxical presence of violence and aggression in creative scenarios, however, could not convince Smiley that their place in the Workshop's social dynamic was somehow natural. She was acutely aware of this social construct, just as Cisneros was in her rejection of Bachelard's class-biased view that houses were somehow universally tranquil spaces, a point eliding the turbulent one of her own underprivileged upbringing.[18]

Although her instructors were largely indifferent to Smiley's extraordinary talent—which enabled her own escape from their control—her classmates clearly recognized it. Doug Unger noted "that a few fellow writers were going to have huge success and were on their way: T. Coraghessan Boyle, Allan Gurganus, Jane Smiley, Richard Bausch."[19] Although she typically held herself aloof in class much as Flannery O'Connor had the generation before, she would defend fellow students on occasion who were treated particularly unfairly. John Leggett, the Workshop director who also taught a graduate seminar, prefaced one class with an especially cruel barb at a story about a bizarre body builder by the young Glen Schaeffer, who felt the piece represented his best work. "I guess there's a fashion in contemporary literature for the incomprehensible and preposterous and we have a booming example of that today—anybody want to visit the scene of this crime?" Leggett announced. Eager to rile the class, the class wit George Lewis shouted, "Light the torches! Get the monster!" Schaeffer's heart sank as he slid down in his chair, wishing to disappear. To his surprise, a measured and professional voice emerged from the back row. The individual "who spoke up for me in class" was "Jane Smiley," Schaeffer recalled. His rescuer "sitting in the back of the room" had earned the respect of the student body because "she'd been posted on a Fulbright to Greenland" as part of her doctoral research. To his astonishment, she articulated the work's strengths better than he could have at the time, praising its capacity for "invention."[20]

Smiley deliberately positioned herself at the back of the class to downplay her obvious strengths to the instructor, in this case Leggett, for fear of becoming his pet. Preferred students distinguished themselves to their instructors through an imaginative array of methods, including dressing fashionably to project an image of a precocious young author. Ensembles did not need to be "up-to-the-minute, expensive, or straight out of *Vogue*." Instead, attire was "distinct and chosen with an eye toward standing out from the crowd," according to Smiley. One preferred student in particular had taken to wearing "an elaborate brocade dressing gown when he was alone at home." Smiley instead wore unpretentious, average-looking ensembles specifically intended to blend into the background, "whether that was jeans and sweaters or peasant dresses (remember, this was the seventies) and Birkenstocks." By contrast, pets "dressed as if every day was a special occasion," costuming themselves for distinction, and conducting themselves in a manner calculated to impress teachers and visiting editors.[21]

Smiley explains that "the pets were able to distinguish themselves in an attractive way," and were "knowing" in that they reciprocated "the use to which the teachers and editors thought of putting them." They "didn't wait until the day the teachers and the editors introduced themselves to bone up on the work of that person." The pets however were not the only knowing students in the Workshop. Others "sensed what was at stake, but couldn't act on their knowledge." These "mavens or nerds," as she calls them, "were not petted—this was where the style and the manner came in." For her part, Smiley "did not feel like a pet," nor did she "feel like a nerd," since she did receive an occasional "passing pat on the head." On the margins, she "felt free and happy and more or less out to lunch." She pressed on with her work and "cared hardly a thing for most of the teachers or the editors," but instead "adored" her "fellow students." Boyle, on the other hand, went to considerable lengths to insinuate himself into conversations with Carver and Cheever at the Mill, whom he regarded with awe even decades later when he wondered "why the local historical society hasn't affixed little brass markers to the stools they perched themselves on" while "draining glasses and lighting cigarettes" as paragons of the Hemingway defense.[22]

Communal Living

At the time of her entrance into the Workshop in the fall of 1974, Smiley had a reputation among her peers as a Vassar graduate who, during the summer of 1970, had lived near New Haven in a leftist commune with radical student activists from Yale. She was also known for completing two years of study toward a Ph.D. in English specializing in Norse literature.[23] If Smiley had deliberately made herself obscure in the eyes of her instructors, she actively embraced her fellow students. They admired her intellectual accomplishments, distinguished by an impressive body of research that she later used to construct *The Greenlanders*, originally drafted as an 1,100-page manuscript and later culled to a spry 558 pages. But as a creative writer, her confidantes knew she was vulnerable. Stretching out her lanky six-foot frame on the floor of her close friend Barbara Grossman's teaching/writing fellow office, she "lamented that I wasn't a genius, would never be a genius, the years of genius were long past (I was twenty-seven)." Grossman, who was twenty-four at the time, listened to Smiley's litany of self-doubt while perusing the workshop stories for the day. "She knew I would get over it," Smiley recalled.[24]

Smiley not only possessed the intellectual prowess to succeed upon her entrance to the Workshop; she also had been no stranger to living in close-knit communities of intellectuals. After her admission to the doctoral program in December 1972, the following spring she and Whiston ventured abroad to Europe, where they hitchhiked throughout the continent, eventually landing at the L'Abri Fellowship outside Lausanne, Switzerland. This strict Calvinist commune, founded eighteen years earlier, had transformed in 1973 into "an intellectual fundamentalist sect," according to Smiley. Its right-wing leanings, furthermore, had become commercialized in a way that inadvertently influenced the ideological formation of evangelical American political conservatism. This rigid cultish community, furthermore, fervently defended the aristocracy and social hierarchy against the populist adoption of secular humanism. Although Smiley found them "more or less harmless," the experience galvanized Whiston's Marxist leanings in opposition to the elitist core principles of the remote Swiss commune.[25]

Soon after the L'Abri Fellowship interlude, Whiston parted ways with Smiley to do political activist work on behalf of rural laborers. He fell out of love with her when he discovered "his true love was for Marxism." In leaving Iowa, he abandoned not only his marriage, but also his academic career. "He didn't think grad school was political enough so he went to Montana to organize workers," Smiley explained. Rather than follow him to the remote northern Rockies, she "stayed in Iowa City and got involved with a guy who tended bar at the Mill." Hers was a "typical Iowa City story: come with one person, leave with another."[26] In the middle of her study for the MFA at the Workshop, her divorce became official in 1975. By 1978, she married the historian William Silag, whom she had met at Iowa City. The divorce from Whiston had the effect of releasing Smiley from domestic commitments to enable her full immersion in the social matrix of the Workshop's literary community.

With its hypermasculine hegemony, the Workshop represented another sort of intellectual fundamentalist sect. But Smiley discovered a circle of friends who affirmed its function as a "community to meet like-minded people" for socialization essential to authorship, especially as a channel toward

professionalization into the publishing industry. The myth of the isolated author appears largely fabricated in light of how "nearly everyone who succeeded
was part of some sort of literary group. There is hardly anyone who thrives on
being solitary," she observed, situating the Workshop among literary collec-
tives such as "Virginia Woolf and her circle," "Thackeray and his friends," and
the New York City coteries from Washington Irving's Knickerbockers to today's Greenwich Village. Creative writing thrives in such cohesive enclaves,
according to Smiley, for whom "the idea that you would somehow not thrive
in a more communal environment is absurd."[27]

The literary circles Smiley mentions as the historical forerunners to the
Workshop, however, were all deinstitutionalized, informal social networks.
Although many may have called themselves clubs, such as James Fenimore
Cooper's Bread and Cheese Club of the early nineteenth century, none were
affiliated with higher education and accredited programs in large state-funded
universities forwarding a broader academic mission. With institutionalization
comes the threat of sterilizing the creative process, a dilemma Smiley circum-
vented by learning "to ignore her teachers." She instead tended to her classmates' ideas "and didn't care too much about what my teachers thought." In a
talk she gave in Iowa City in 2015, she backed the importance of "paying attention to what your fellow students say, because they're going to be your readers,
and because your professors are going to die."[28]

Despite these efforts to minimize her instructors' impact on her creative
development, Smiley was acutely aware of the beneficial ways they could influence her writing. She thus selected her instructors with great care. Those
who might thwart creativity were faculty who reminded her of her parents—
understandably enough—who represented a generation out of touch with the
new sensibility of the Age of Aquarius. With that new outlook came the need
for an instructor whose methods were amenable to developing female authors.
The patrician John Ward "Jack" Leggett, a graduate of Phillips Academy and
Yale, had served as editor and publicity director at Houghton Mifflin in Boston
from 1950 to 1960 and as editor of Harper and Row in New York until 1967
before he came to Iowa. He had been recruited for the Workshop faculty to
provide a sense of gentility and propriety to a faculty that English chairman
John Gerber and President Virgil Hancher had deemed too bohemian and
habitually unaccountable. The epitome of bland, Leggett struck Smiley
"as someone who would have shown up at a party given by my parents—
preposterous, well mannered and educated, always kind, frequently ironic and
even rueful, but not vivid enough to capture my attention." Worse still was

Vance Bourjaily, who "seemed even paler" from her perspective. For her, "there could not be," with one notable exception, "an interesting person" among the faculty "from University City."[29]

Only Jane Howard, a young, free-spirited staff writer for *Life* magazine, stood out as potentially interesting, even though she was primarily a journalist with no experience writing fiction. "Having never published a paragraph of fiction or taught anyone anything, could I be qualified?" she asked Leggett. "Don't worry," he insisted, "come anyway." She arrived when it was "so humid that envelopes sealed themselves shut, on the same day Gerald R. Ford pardoned Richard Nixon, on the same day Evel Knievel tried in vain to catapult himself across the Grand Canyon."[30] Howard was hired to teach for one semester, which happened to coincide with Smiley's arrival in the fall of 1974. Howard's mix of anthropological and sociological theory with immersive journalistic reportage appeared in her 1978 book *Families*. In it is what Smiley calls "a chapter about us" as part of a larger study of rituals and gatherings that reveal how families are not dying, but evolving in new ways. Under the pseudonym "Philippa," Smiley appears as a cohesive figure of their group in Iowa City. Howard excerpts a personal letter from Philippa describing the formation of their circle. "The Workshop afforded us an official relationship to one another—random, as in families, and somewhat ritualized," Smiley told Howard. She explained that "every group on the verge of becoming a clan needs someone who does the drawing together, who is conscious of the group's potential a little sooner than the others are," identifying their own vital roles in the process since "you and I are both avid drawers-together." She had originally been responsible for drawing Howard into her circle with Grossman and Gurganus. "If you will remember," she reminded her, "I bearded you in your den and virtually pressed friendship on you."[31]

Howard was grateful for Smiley's forward invitation to join their circle of friends, a gesture that broke social norms of interaction. No one asked instructors fifteen years their senior to dinner with the bald overture, "I want to make friends with you," effectively leveling the teacher-pupil hierarchical space between them.[32] Howard's portrait paid tribute to their bond that inspired creativity despite being in a place ham radio operators referred to as "zeroland" and whose divorce rate, as Howard put it, was "four out of three," and was "not modern enough to support chapters of Al-Anon, Weight Watchers, and advanced classes in Transcendental Meditation."[33] Their group thrived despite Philip Roth's bromide in which he had warned visitors to "take plenty of synthetic fabrics, otherwise you'll never get the smell of hamburgers and French fries out of your woolens." Citizens of Iowa, Roth pointed out, "stand up and salute decorum and restraint," yet "what is new is hideous: the new girls' dormitory, like watered-down Reno, the new police station, like cut out cardboard, the tract houses, like more cardboard."[34] Despite such cultural deficiencies, Howard's final proclamation was as endearing as it was validating: "The Iowa Writers' Workshop, whose students and teachers spend four regular and uncounted spontaneous hours together every week, has probably spawned as many healthy clans as any institution in America."[35] Ironically, Smiley felt the piece had signaled Howard's permanent departure from her and the program, in effect "officially putting us in the past tense."[36] The heartfelt tribute to Iowa, Smiley realized, was Howard's way of atoning for breaking ties to the Workshop where she taught for only one semester.

In Howard's class, Smiley felt instantly at home. "She was a character," unlike the bland Bourjaily and uninteresting Leggett, "and we became friends instantly." She was particularly drawn to her New York City sensibility and the way "she would say anything and then laugh." But more than her personal characteristics, Howard's affiliation with the Upper West Side's collective of female authors particularly appealed to Smiley. Her apartment at the hub of writers' haunts such as Zabar's, H&H Bagel, and the New Yorker movie theater combined with her status as *Life* magazine writer to make her "an emissary not from the New York male literary scene but from the New York female social scene." This attribute, along with her infectious laugh, friendly disposition, and classroom demeanor that was pure fun, struck Smiley as a welcome relief from the high-stakes pressure of Bourjaily's and Leggett's seminars. "It was clear, though, and a relief, that she neither knew what she was talking about, fictionwise, nor had any plans to lever us into fancy literary journals." Fourteen years her senior, Howard was much less like a parent than "that sister who had broken away, gotten herself a wilder, happier life, and was now returning to tell us about it."[37] That New York City life reaffirmed for Smiley the importance of understanding authorship as an intrinsically social enterprise. Howard gloried in her stories of the Upper West Side literary scene, regaling her students with details about the pleasures of writing in a community characterized by mutual support and lively exchange. The myriad friends whom she frequently housed had alarmed Smiley when she later stayed at Howard's apartment, because each possessed their own duplicate keys, trafficking in and out at will. The apartment functioned more like a collective than a private residence, making for a dynamic social network that captured Smiley's imagination. She immortalized the scene in her novel *Duplicate Keys*, which dramatizes this culture and the vibrant characters who surfaced unexpectedly at the apartment.

Howard testified on behalf of a writing life amenable to women. She stood witness to a liberated, decidedly nonviolent, creative space that might be construed as the 1970s version of *A Room of One's Own*. The life of a professional woman author, Howard's example revealed, had its benefits given the right social environment, material comforts, and creative autonomy. In *Families*, Howard describes her New York writing life as nothing short of utopian. "I'd be a fool not to like eleven windows overlooking the river, plenty of jade plants, bright colors, more books than I'll ever find time to read, records that I'll never really listen to, recipes that I'll never cook." Access to stimulating conversation with practicing professional women authors was within an effortless "short walk or bus ride away." Others "tend to fetch up as houseguests, which is fine as long as they let me carve four solitary hours out of each day." Although some solitude is necessary for authorship, she asserted, "A place too long unpeopled can get to smelling tomblike."[38] This inherently social model of writing characterized by creative autonomy and horizontal relations was irresistible to Smiley.

Compared with the rest of the Workshop faculty, Howard's teaching methods stood out as the most transparent, spontaneous, and disarming. Unlike her male colleagues, she carried her intellectual prowess with a journalist's wit and populist aplomb. By comparison, Smiley had visiting faculty such as Gordon Lish, Ted Solotaroff, and Stanley Elkin to choose from, all of whom were martinets in the classroom, old-order pedants who did not hesitate to crack the whip. Lish "was hard on you," Smiley remembered, Solotaroff "was into that too," and Elkin "used that 'who do you think you are?' teaching method." These abrasive tactics were as repellent as they were ineffective, according to Smiley, who deeply opposed such attempts "to arouse your pride and challenge you to greatness" to the exclusion of the "more cooperative . . . teaching style [she] preferred."[39]

Barbara, Believe Me

Jane Howard did not initially take Jane Smiley under her wing. She "took to Barbara" Grossman, Smiley's friend, instead, "and then took me in." Grossman was essential to Smiley's success in navigating through the Scylla and Charybdis of faculty members like Elkin and Lish. Since she had been vying for Gurganus's attention and approval, Smiley was miffed when he paused to ask "a short person to join us" on a walk from campus into town. At the time, Grossman seemed to represent an obstacle between Smiley and the charismatic Gurganus with his Gatsbyesque smile—"simultaneously merry, welcoming, rueful, and irreverent"—and a personal style that was "archaic, elegant, and pale." Along with this charm, his experience as a second-year student in the program distinguished him as a potentially valuable guide to the foreign territory of the Workshop. He had become something of a local legend when his instructor John Cheever sold his story "Minor Heroism" to the *New Yorker* without telling him beforehand.[40] Walking up the hill, the two women flanked Gurganus—the six-foot Smiley on one side and the five-foot Grossman on the other—talking only to him and not each other. The diminutive Grossman was all but invisible to Smiley who was straining to find something to "come up with to impress His Elegance." Suddenly, Grossman popped out in front of them, squared her shoulders before Smiley and said, "Want to be friends?" as if she were Tom Sawyer proposing an irresistible business venture to Huck Finn.[41]

With her bold and authentic self-introduction, Grossman set the keynote for a lasting friendship that would form the foundation of their literary circle. Smiley's connection to Grossman was a milestone event with profound implications for her social life and professional career. In the two years before joining the Workshop, Smiley did not identify with campus culture at Iowa, which "was still reverberating from the late sixties—the plate glass windows of the university bookstore had been broken so many times in antiwar riots that they had been replaced by cubbyholes." She felt disconnected from the activist fervor on campus in the early 1970s. Whereas no lasting political effect remained from the Vietnam War protest era, certainly the social impact was visible in how "students lived together in loose, commune-like groups." In those groups, drugs circulated freely, since everyone seemed to have "a roommate who devoted himself to smoking and/or growing marijuana," while sexual promiscuity was viewed as "a token of solidarity."[42] Whereas none of these radical commune-like groups had appealed to Smiley, Grossman's circle suited her temperament ideally. In particular, the class taught by Jane Howard had a revitalizing influence that profoundly shaped her creative development.

Howard's class with Grossman set the blueprint for Smiley's literary success. In it she learned more about the craft from her classmates than her instructor. Her own writing for the class amounted to "enigmatic seventies stories, vaguely threatening and fragmentary," tales that had elicited responses she was ill-equipped to understand or retain. Her classmates' stories, however, including Grossman's tale of a teenage girl who resorts to eating the body of her boyfriend on a canoe trip gone awry, were alive with intrigue. Smiley's vivid memory of their best tales testifies to the depth and intensity with which she originally read them. Unlike Tracy Kidder, who rarely put his stories up for workshop sessions and instead attacked his classmates' work with cutting criticism, Smiley found the imaginative power of her peers inspirational.[43] In addition to Grossman's grisly tale, she admired Bob Chibka's capitalization of all nouns and Joanne Meschery's depiction of a vindictive mother who sends her daughter a nightgown sewn shut at the bottom as a sign that she should stop having children. A story by Tom Boyle later published in *Descent of Man* as "Bloodfall" transfixed Smiley with its depiction of seven members of a commune who dress in white and sleep through cataclysmic plagues culminating in a downpour of bloody rain that drenches and reddens their crisp white uniforms.[44]

Such powerful writing among her peers inspired Smiley's own work the following spring semester of 1975. Howard had returned to New York City, where she would resume writing for *Life* and begin *Families*. Gurganus was preparing to graduate with other second-year students who were dear to her. The social terrain of the Workshop had shifted under her feet, leaving her without a trusted faculty mentor. Grossman led Smiley to consider taking a course from visiting writer Henry Bromell, an Amherst College graduate and author of *The Slightest Distance* (1974), published by Houghton Mifflin. Bromell offered Smiley the technical expertise in fiction Howard had lacked. His lofty credentials, however, were not intimidating; a befuddled presence decentered his authority as their instructor. Smiley recalled that although he was their teacher, Bromell "was just the same age as every boyfriend I had ever had." Playing the role of veterans, Smiley and Grossman considered him the novice finding his bearings in his new life of teaching and writing in the Midwest. "We showed him around." In this way, Bromell "expanded our group instead of floating above it."[45]

If Howard had offered Smiley a glimpse into the ideal lifestyle for a woman author during the 1970s, then Bromell demystified the process of literary production for the most powerful presses of the publishing industry. Whereas other male professors had badgered her into publishing in "fancy journals" in class, the understated Bromell inspired by example in informal settings. She read his book, for example, and discussed it over dinner with him in a watershed moment that "shortened the distance between the impulse that brought us to Iowa City and the potential realization of that impulse." Production, in the end, prevailed over the mystified concept of genius to Smiley. Bromell enabled her to see through the facade of the self-appointed sages of the program who bestowed their wisdom from above. Unlike other instructors, "he had nothing to bestow upon us except the tangible evidence that what you really had to do was write that book and that was way more valuable than genius."[46]

Something in Smiley opened up, giving way to a surge of creativity she initially rode for the sheer thrill of it. What began as a kind of "daring joke" to her amazement sustained itself through an entire narrative. "Jeffrey, Believe Me" was Smiley's breakthrough story, written in Bromell's class. He had inspired her without trying to inspire her; he had shown her the way to success without telling her in any prescriptive way. Production, she realized, could be stymied by excessive self-consciousness and a halting overemphasis on perfection. Smiley had established a relationship with Grossman and others in Bromell's class she described as "congenial" and "very forgiving of one another." This was contrary to the Elkin and Lish "who do you think you are?" approach to creative writing pedagogy, "designed to 'toughen' students so that they could withstand inevitable adversity and criticism as artists." Smiley thus found an outlet from this approach tailored to war veterans "for whom the humiliations of boot camp and the paint of the basketball court were easily internalized metaphors."[47] Writing in a state of constant fear stymied production for Smiley. "You can't be a novelist by being a perfectionist because if you are never satisfied, you won't get the book written." The key, she realized in Bromell's class, and in the writing of "Jeffrey, Believe Me," "was production, not perfection."[48]

"Jeffrey, Believe Me" stands out among Smiley's Workshop writing for the unique character that emerges through the narrative voice of the story, a cracked figure of suave elegance. That persona grew out of Smiley's lavish yet intimate dinner parties for which she would dim the lights, play Sinatra, and don a "lace-covered vintage satin nightgown from the twenties or thirties," a slinky number ideally suited to the candlelit formal ambiance. The meal itself she prepared from *Gourmet Cookbook* and served on fine china. What if I were to seduce my gay friend on such a night, she mused? The scenario she drew out clearly had such fine feasts and Gurganus in mind, a Navy veteran who went on to win the Lambda Literary Award in 2001 for fiction that celebrates or explores LGBTQ themes. Of his days in the Navy, he says, "imagine 4,000 men, ages 18 to 23, floating around in the South China Seas for 35 days" to fathom "the mischief and the energy and the volatility and the testosterone

and the erotic swill."[49] Smiley is careful to point out that her story "was all fiction," but not without a serious and deep connection to the dinner party persona that she donned for guests as a kind of entertainment piece. As an
imaginative extension of herself at these parties, the narrator seduces the
character of Jeffrey, whose preference for men and occupation as a builder of
model boats parallels Gurganus's own gender preference and work as a meticulous assembler of fictional worlds. The key to the story's success was how
Smiley had "gotten inside the mind of a woman who had done something I
would never have done." The protagonist draws the unsuspecting guest into
her web with fine food, conversation, prodigious amounts of alcohol, and
marijuana-laced brownies. "You must have felt hungry, because you had another," the narrator says of her dessert generously "lathered with icing" and
baked with "dope ground into marijuana flour . . . disguised by a double dose
of double Dutch." When he reaches for a third, she "wanted to ask, 'And why
do you prefer men, Jeffrey?' but I merely said, 'You smell good,' and got up to
clear the table."[50]

The loving description of Jeffrey echoes her own admiration of the dashing
Gurganus as a New Yorker–published prodigy and pet of the program. "Really,
you have done handsomely," she says in apostrophe. Gurganus originally
trained to be a painter; his fictional counterpart, Jeffrey, plays three instru-
ments. Like Gurganus, "everyone agrees you are a raconteur, and yet a tem-
perate man" with a "graceful and generous mind." He is effortlessly successful
with an endless list of minor virtues: "you leave proper tips, you hang up your
clothes, you are not too proud to take buses." As the narrator builds the profile,
she stops herself short, "not wishing to embarrass you." She shows restraint
by dropping "the subject, adding only that we both know what a remarkable
child you were and that you have been steadily successful."[51]

This was not the first time Smiley had creatively woven her friends into her
stories at her own peril. "Long Distance" is the fictionalization of "a story told
to me by a drunken date" about an extramarital affair he had with a Japanese
woman while he was abroad teaching in Osaka. "He gave me permission,"
Smiley recalls, "but when I later showed him the story, he never spoke to me
again." The depiction of the affair and its painful aftermath in which Smiley's
friend rejects the woman's plan to live with him in America—"she had all
sorts of expectations that I couldn't have fulfilled"—caused the woman to
break down completely, crushing "every single one of her strengths, everything she had equipped herself with to live in a Japanese way." After the story
was published, another of Smiley's friends who appears as a character in it

was approached without warning by his pastor who asked if he knew the author. "It took six months for the brouhaha to die down."[52] Smiley's penchant for inciting scandals through her fiction appears in her article titled "Can Writers Have Friends?" "Jeffrey, Believe Me," unlike these other stories, is in a curious way nothing Gurganus would ever be ashamed of, as it embodies Smiley's conviction that creative writing, at its best, is "not an object or a possession. It is an act of love."[53]

If not for Barbara Grossman, this story that began as a "daring joke" might have remained unpublished. Indeed, Smiley composed it originally to circulate privately among her intimates as an extension of the self-consciously camp theater of their formal dinner parties. She kept it private "for a few days," she explains, but soon realized, "I liked it. The woman's voice was consistent from beginning to end; the dinner seemed detailed and plausible." Greater aspirations for the story mounted. She slipped it to Grossman during a workshop session to abate the tedium of listening to "an older male" read at the head of the classroom. Barbara "placed it quietly on her desk and began to read it, surreptitiously removing each page when she was done with it." As the instructor at the head of the class droned on, Barbara suddenly burst out in laughter, "a disruptive and wholly inappropriate bark," drawing the stares of everyone in class, to which she "smiled deflectively." The outburst was the sincerest endorsement Smiley could have imagined, one that indicated the story was ready for publication. Feeling like she had "just received the best compliment ever," she knew from that moment on, "I was on my way."[54]

Grossman's reflexive validation of "Jeffrey, Believe Me" represented more than her recognition of the story as an inside joke drawing on their mutual familiarity with Gurganus. The prophetic moment anticipated Grossman's role as Smiley's future editor who would later acquire her first novel, *Barn Blind*, for publication at Harper and Row. Prior to its publication, Grossman had encouraged Smiley to submit "Jeffrey, Believe Me" to *Triquarterly*, where it appeared in the fall of 1977. This was precisely the sort of elite journal her male instructors had used to intimidate her. Now, entrance into it seemed as smooth as the 1930s satin nightgown—and seductive narrative persona—she effortlessly slipped into. Grossman both inspired Smiley's breakthrough story and provided the key industry connection behind the publication of her debut novel that followed.

The story functions in some senses as evidence of Smiley's response to the combative, male-dominated nature of the Workshop, representing her way of reclaiming the patriarchy's seduction narrative from a female point of view.

"Jeffrey, Believe Me" was remembered by Connie Brothers as one of Smiley's breakthrough stories that defied her image as an author of domestic farm dramas, the wholesome fan of *The Waltons* raised on *Black Beauty* and Nancy Drew books. In the story, homosexuality is treated as a curiosity to be explored and even conquered, forbidden terrain like feminism in T. C. Boyle's "A Women's Restaurant." Although the ethics of the story seem dubious, one should note that she conceived it in a pre-Stonewall cultural context.[55] "Jeffrey, Believe Me," according to Brothers, marked a milestone when the Norse and medieval literary scholar ventured into the sort of perversity and antic absurdity typically associated with Boyle's fiction. The story affirmed the range of this "tall and confident" writer capable of "pushing the boundaries like Tom Boyle," as Brothers recalled.[56] Just as Boyle had ventured into *Penthouse* with "A Women's Restaurant" while he was at Iowa, Smiley published a story titled "Good Intentions" in *Playgirl* in 1979, two years after the appearance of "Jeffrey, Believe Me" in *Triquarterly*.[57] Squarely operating in the genre of female erotic fantasy fiction, her *Playgirl* publication offers further evidence of Smiley's willingness to appropriate the opposition's method in the gender war.

The reception of *The Age of Grief*, in which "Jeffrey, Believe Me" appeared, was instrumental in establishing Smiley's reputation in the world of letters. The *Washington Post* claimed in 1989 that although she had written four novels, including *The Greenlanders*, a fourteenth-century epic saga, her "reputation is based primarily upon The Age of Grief."[58] The *San Francisco Chronicle* described the seduction tale in the volume as "a woman's narrative explanation of how and why she tried to seduce her gorgeous male friend, who prefers men." The reviewer credited her for engaging serious themes but leavening them "with humor and short sentences and many precisely described moments that give the reader a rush of authenticity."[59] The *New York Times*, however, held her Workshop training against her, alleging that some of the volume suffers "from a certain constriction, as though dialogue and events were being crammed into a neat and preconceived package." But "Jeffrey, Believe Me" was not a "Workshop story" in the sense of standardized uniformity, the prose equivalent of the "Workshop poem" Rita Dove inadvertently found herself writing in the wake of her training. Smiley conceived the story specifically as a project to be enjoyed outside the parameters of coursework and workshop sessions. The reviewer nonetheless appreciated its unique contribution to the volume as a "silly mannered monologue about a woman attempting to seduce a gay male friend."[60]

Having broken into such fresh creative territory, Smiley began to dread the onerous task of completing her dissertation. She accosted her Ph.D. adviser, declaring that she "wasn't looking forward to writing [her] dissertation." "Good," he replied, "Because I'm not looking forward to reading it."[61] Not content to walk away from years of research empty-handed, she persuaded Leggett to accept a creative thesis for her Ph.D. Given her trajectory toward creative writing, he was happy to accommodate her request. She soon leveraged the degree into a tenure-track faculty position in the English department of Iowa State University in Ames, some two hours west of Iowa City.

Where was genius for Jane Smiley? As her instructor Henry Bromell demonstrated, it was in productivity. As her friends Barbara Grossman and Allan Gurganus showed her, it came from love and wit. Together, these elements ignited the creative imagination. Perhaps Smiley's final word on the notion of genius in literature as part of her ongoing efforts to deconstruct and demystify its widely abused and sexist applications to male canonical writers appears in her book *Thirteen Ways of Looking at the Novel*. In it, she puts Herman Melville's *Moby-Dick* to the test. Although she insists in the chapter "Reading a Hundred Novels" that her "list was never intended to be a 'Hundred Greatest,' " she still assesses each with particular attention to how those works "illuminate the whole concept of the novel." Melville's mighty book, which many tout as the great American novel, presented a trial she had not anticipated, demanding two separate entries to the single one- to two-page commentary the others on her list receive. She distilled Melville's technique of maintaining reader interest into a two-pronged strategy focused on "the inherent strangeness of whaling, and the author's quest (expressed in his varieties of style) to exhaust the spiritual meanings of obsession (or 'monomania,' as it was called then)." The length of the novel, she argues convincingly, is due to the time it takes to (re)train his audience. His novel "must be long," she explains, because "it takes a while for the author to impart to the reader enough information to enable the reader to make sense of everything the author wishes to communicate," much like Bach retraining his "listener's ear and listener's mind to his musical ideas." She urges that the novel is worth the time and effort to relish "the double strangeness of Melville's vision—the exotic locale and visionary ideas—above every other joy that novels can afford." But in a "Note added later," Smiley recants. She claims that despite its status according to many as "the greatest American novel . . . it clearly didn't make enough of an impression on me" because she had "internal arguments with the author all the way through." She wondered why she felt a duty to appreciate *Moby-Dick* despite not enjoying it, asking whether this was "because the concerns of the novel are extremely masculine and I really don't care about them." Revisiting the novel in an attempt to grasp it at a deeper level seemed out of the question. Such a rereading would be "like going out on another date with someone who was okay but not compelling the first time."[62]

As with "Jeffrey, Believe Me," Smiley's creative self-discovery even later in life through revisiting classic novels inevitably involved the realization that she had caught herself in a posture of reverence under the spell of the patriarchy. In addition to her disavowal of Melville for the alienating effects of his hypermasculine sensibility, Smiley has also boldly dismantled another monument of the American male literary canon: *The Adventures of Huckleberry Finn* by Mark Twain. To associate it "with 'greatness,' " she argued, "is to underwrite a very simplistic and evasive theory of what racism is and to promulgate it," because "no matter how often the critics place in context Huck's use of the word 'nigger,' they can never fully excuse or fully hide the deeper racism of the novel."[63] Her point, made in a *Harper's* article in 1996, appeared during the height of the culture wars on academic campuses led by such critics as Jane Tompkins, who deconstructs the gender ideology of the institutional mechanisms of canonization in *Sensational Designs: The Cultural Work of American Fiction, 1790–1860*. While on the English faculty at Iowa State University, from 1981 to 1996, Smiley had joined the ranks of feminist critics advocating for a reassessment of the male-dominated literary canon to include such works as Harriet Beecher Stowe's *Uncle Tom's Cabin* and Fanny Fern's *Ruth Hall*.[64] Her argument led the way for a restructuring of critical understandings of our literary heritage, unearthing a forgotten feminist tradition from a politicized perspective akin to the work of activist historian Howard Zinn in *A People's History of the United States* on behalf of oppressed and forgotten lives otherwise rendered invisible in traditional histories of the United States.

Genius, Smiley soon discovered, was hardly natural and innate in certain individuals. Instead, she found it a social and—particularly from her experience at the Workshop—institutional construct. Her two methods of breaking through the facade of sexism and privilege driving both literary canon formation and the selection of teacher's pets at the Workshop were an emphasis on production in her own creative work, and a painstaking and meticulous dedication to historical truth in her understanding of American literature. Twain's suggestion that befriending a black person was a panacea for racism, she realized, provided no real solution to the deeper institutional inequities embedded in the structure of society. Barbara Grossman and Jane Howard would prove instrumental in enlightening her to alternative models of literary production, in the process enabling her to transcend the limitations of gender and explore uncharted, and even forbidden, creative territory. Finding humor and satire in Iowa subjects only began with "Jeffrey, Believe Me," and extended to her novel *Moo*, which targets "academic writing programs, literary fellowships, and visiting teaching posts" in a way that calls into question the politics of educational bureaucracy, precisely the institutional nexus against which she discovered her voice as a novelist in the Iowa Writers' Workshop.[65]

12 • Red High-Tops for Life: T. C. Boyle

Shortly after his admission to the Iowa Writers' Workshop, T. C. (Tom to his friends) Boyle—eventually the winner of six O. Henry Awards and known for his Pynchon/Márquez-inspired madcap fiction leavened with serious moral import and visceral detail—was feeling exceptionally confident. During the first weeks of fall 1972 as an instructor on his Teaching/Writing Fellowship, his writing reached new heights as he began his simultaneous pursuit of both a Ph.D. in Victorian literature and an MFA in creative writing. Having achieved a rare distinction as a top student in both programs, which did not overburden so much as reinforce his creative development, he felt nearly invulnerable. The workshop method fit his temperament perfectly; its Darwinian scramble for survival resonated with him as both an effective pedagogical tool and an aesthetic concept that he would parlay into his first stories in *Descent of Man* (1978), a title inspired by Darwin himself. So when a nonregistered "friend" of a student requested to "sit in" on his class, he instantly agreed.[1] It was 1972 and Boyle's roots in the free-spirited culture of Peekskill, New York—one of the most liberal communities in North America at the time—dictated a universal openness to the creative process. As the instructor of record, he was more than willing to flout the layers of bureaucratic approval and highly regulated formalities endemic to large, state-funded educational institutions. An open-door policy seemed apt.

The "guy who had his story up who asked if he could bring his buddy" sat silently as the class began dissecting his work. Uninitiated into the ritual of workshop sessions that called for pointed commentary on the core weaknesses of the story under scrutiny, the visitor immediately registered signs of discomfort, his face reddening and fists clenching. One venomous comment led to another, cascading into an inexorable torrent. Now squirming and flushed with rage, the student's friend seemed ready to explode. "You know, the symbolism is so obvious," one student sniffed with an air of pompous dismissal that positively unhinged the author's guest. Just then, "the guy's buddy slams his fist down on the table and shouts, 'Fuck symbolism!' " and erupts into a thundering tirade.[2] As the class degenerated into a verbal melee, Boyle ushered the young man out, vowing never to allow guests to attend and cursing himself for his naive openness. From that day forward, he disallowed authors to speak while their work was being discussed. The incident held up an unbecoming mirror to the program's culture of creative production. The shocked outsider's Ludovico-like perspective on the classroom dynamic also exposed Boyle's own conditioning to the program's sophisticated brutality, a system he had thrived on as a student and now perpetuated as an instructor.

Boyle's acculturation to adversity and emotional trauma traces back to his upbringing in working-class Peekskill. Raised by alcoholic parents who drank themselves to death, he was all of twenty-four when his father succumbed to a fatal combination of alcohol-related diseases at the age of fifty-four. Eight years later, when Boyle was thirty-two, his mother passed away at fifty-seven. Profoundly "disturbed in some way about life," his father drank severely and with the morose resolve of "a sort of suicide" committed "consciously and deliberately." Boyle witnessed the torturous decline during his formative years and responded with spite, acting "very rebellious and disdainful of them" throughout his adolescence.[3] To atone for not reconciling with his father while he was still alive, Boyle dedicated his novel *World's End*, winner of the PEN/ Faulkner Award in 1988, "in the memory of my own lost father."[4] Since he "never really had a chance to come to . . . rapprochement with him" because "he was dead before anything like that could happen," Boyle crafted the novel as "a search for a father, not in an autobiographical sense, but in a metaphorical sense."[5] Fiction offered a space to repair the trauma. In the rancorous household of his youth, the pursuit of higher education toward a professional career, much less literary fame, seemed unthinkable, especially to this son of an orphan with an eighth-grade education and a mother who never attended college.

The elite learned community of the Workshop—his classmate Joy Harjo called it "the Harvard of creative writing programs"—seemed worlds away from his humble origins.[6] Before arriving at Iowa, Boyle taught public high school for four years after earning a bachelor's degree in English and history in 1968 from the State University of New York (SUNY) at Potsdam. Unlike many of the privileged Workshop students of the 1970s such as Rita Dove, who had been groomed for success in a home and school environment suffused with intellectual culture, Boyle's house contained no reading material except for the daily newspaper. His one and only undergraduate application went to SUNY Potsdam because its low standards all but guaranteed his admission despite his poor grades. His deplorable high school record ruled out any hope for attending a competitive undergraduate program. In the fall of his freshman year, his original intention to major in music to break into the jazz recording industry derailed when his saxophone audition went awry.[7] Literary study thus presented itself as an alternative to dropping out, much less an avenue toward literary renown, wealth, and fame.

In the absence of sound guidance from his parents, the rudderless Boyle chose a double major in history and English because he believed it was the easiest alternative to music. The degree afforded him few employment options other than high school teaching, so he grudgingly applied at his alma mater Lakeland High School, a humiliating and regressive return to the very building in which he had refused to obey his own teachers in his adolescence.[8] Prior to Iowa, education and employment for Boyle were predicated on accessibility rather than quality. Before applying to the Workshop, he had settled for the schools and jobs that were available, much less competed for them. Iowa presented him with an entirely new challenge, mainly because competition, especially career building and self-promotion in the competitive free market, were anathema to the communal freewheeling lifestyle his parents, relatives, and friends had encouraged. Complicating matters further, Boyle "had never been west of New Jersey" and "didn't know Iowa from Ohio—or Idaho, for that matter," as he later admitted. Undeterred, "My girlfriend and my dog climbed into the car, we marked out the route on the map, and headed out on I-80."[9] The heaviest thing they carried was the gargantuan monkey on Boyle's back—a tenacious heroin and Quaalude addiction that had been steadily seizing his will for the better part of a decade.

Adrift in the Counterculture

Like Jay Gatsby attempting to elude his working-class roots, Thomas John Boyle changed his middle name at the age of seventeen to Coraghessan in a stroke of self-invention built upon sensational designs for the future. Bent on performing and entertaining his way to success, Boyle had no intention of pursuing a conventional vocation to earn his living. "Job? Who needs a Job?

Fuck a job, I'm going to be an artist," he brazenly proclaimed, his frizzy shoulder-length hair parted down the middle framing mirror shades he "wore at breakfast and dinner, in the shower, in closets and caves," as he says of his largely autobiographical narrator in "Greasy Lake."[10] As a child of the counterculture, Boyle never encountered any objections to this sort of ambition. The stereotype of rock and roll, red high-tops, drugs, and the New York hippie scene—complete with draft-dodging, free love, and flower power—was the lived reality that influenced Boyle's defiantly liberal attitude toward his future occupation. Corporate America of the sort Paul Engle cajoled into supporting the Workshop was anathema to this setting. Drug trafficking vied with macramé and artisanal crafts as the preferred sources of revenue in his neighborhood in Kitchawank Colony of Westchester County, New York. Boyle described it as "one of the most liberal communities, certainly, in America," a place with "many Russian Jews who founded an anarchist colony which later became a Communist colony."[11]

The prospect of teaching high school would have been unthinkable to Boyle before he graduated from SUNY. But in assessing his meager options, it became evident that a teaching position offered, despite its laughably low salary, a ready escape from the Selective Service's massive draft for the Vietnam War. Boyle never questioned whether, but only how, he might dodge the draft.[12] Returning to Lakeland High as a teacher kept him rooted in Peekskill, "where whole blocks were burnt out and boarded up in the wake of the Martin Luther King riots." Remaining in this community brought with it the liability of exposure to its drug culture that drew him increasingly deeper into its clutches. "I was twenty-one, and I was unreflective and dope-addled, washed along in the hippie current like the spawn of a barnacle."[13] He soon fell in with the hardened junkies and dealers whom he had previously only seen on the street, but never consorted with. From 1969 to 1970, heroin was his cruel mistress. Like the figures Allen Ginsberg envisioned in "Howl" a decade earlier, Boyle epitomized the best minds of his generation, searching "for an angry fix" at dawn "burning for the ancient heavenly connection to the starry dynamo in the machinery of the night."[14]

Just as Ginsberg found literary inspiration from the loss of Carl Solomon to madness, Boyle saw a friend step off the precipice into the abyss. The event "scared the holy sweet *literature* out of me," he remembered, a cold blast of arctic wind that alerted him to his own mortality.[15] Boyle renounced heroin forever, if only to replace it with the less visible yet powerfully habit-forming magic of Quaaludes. The ride on that train lasted another two years, until

1972, when it gave way to yet another addiction: fiction at the Iowa Writers' Workshop.

That journey through the phantasmagoric nightmare of a double-addiction covering four solid years had the unintended effect of focusing Boyle's powers of observation like never before. The sheer terror of addiction unearthed a channel to creativity through a glimpse at the dark underside of the counterculture. This deadly serious world challenged the mainstream culture's tendency to trivialize the hippie lifestyle as the frivolous cavorting of so many feckless tie-dyed clowns in the mud and driving rain of Woodstock. The Vietnam veterans populating Boyle's first Workshop class had not taken the counterculture seriously until they were exposed to Boyle's work that extended from "The OD and Hepatitis Railroad or Bust," published in the *North American Review.* The story sounded this dark note from a young talent on the rise who had been there himself, a piece rife with the dirty realism he would come to nearly worship at Iowa in the work of Raymond Carver. The tale resonated with Neil Young's haunting ode to "the needle and the damage done," especially its final melancholy image of how "every junkie's/ like a setting sun."

The twelve Vietnam veterans of his fifteen classmates in Vance Bourjaily's class uniformly repurposed their combat experience for creative material. So when Boyle's story went up for discussion during the first week, the class was disappointed that "it wasn't about Vietnam" but "about being a hippie in a certain hippie milieu, one who shot dope."[16] Much of the narrative was confessional, expanding on his admission that "I was the hippie's hippie, and immoral to boot, and never gave a thought about putting a needle in my arm."[17] Since the cool Bourjaily's classroom presence provided a stabilizing effect— he would routinely stop class to roll a cigarette while his students silently watched—the story did not explode into controversy as it might have in a more contentious class like Frank Conroy's. His classmates thus approved of the story with reservations. Their opinion had little bearing on the young Boyle anyway, who was far more interested in what his instructors thought of his work. He found himself jonesing for the praise and support of the Buddha-like Bourjaily, and consummate professionals like John Cheever and John Irving, affirmation and encouragement constituting precisely "what a young writer needs to feed his addiction." With time, the chemical substances yielded to writing as the new source of euphoria and inner power, especially evident in a series of stories that the best heroin highs could never match. They were "mad, absurd, hyperbolic, but mine, all mine"—stories that made him feel "strong, superior, invincible," armed with an "arrogance" that functioned like a "preemptive strike against his own weakness."[18]

It was then that the new literary addiction took hold according to his formulation that "writing is an obsessive-compulsive disorder."[19] Boyle never quailed at putting up stories early and often in workshop among the older Vietnam veterans, most of whom knew he was a draft-dodger. He established himself as a veteran of another kind of war, this one an inner war of addiction that brought him exhilaration and ecstasy, but at the expense of his body and mind. Although he avoided "the hepatitis train" that claimed his friend, Thorazine treatments became necessary to subdue the vivid nightmares that plagued him. His very sanity hung in the balance in this Faustian deal. If Boyle, more than any other writer of the Age of Aquarius, grew to love the Workshop, it was because, as he said, "I felt a power. I wrote." The "beauty of this addiction" was that it simultaneously drove out the old chemical dependencies that threatened his longevity and transformed him into a blue-veined zombie, an emaciated victim of a ravenous parasite. Instead, writing grew vitality, extending rather than truncating his life; it assured his survival with sustenance instead of jolting him with temporary euphoria at the cost of physical and mental decadence. As the short stories churned out, he held each one up and admired it as "Something new. Something of value." He moved on to novels, writing his first, *Water Music* (1981), in a white heat in 1976. "The addiction was full blown finally and surely terminal now," blasting out a streak of frenzied wakeful dreaming that eventuated in 104 breathing chapters. Careening with unstoppable momentum, he "began writing in the mornings, seven days a week," and has "been working on that schedule ever since."[20] The project burgeoned from "having done a Ph.D. in nineteenth-century British literature and reading maybe a hundred three-volume novels" from that era. Thus "going to graduate school at Iowa—first for the MFA and then the Ph.D.—was transformative for me," especially "as a way of expanding my very limited worldview and improving my writing."[21]

Whereas the Workshop for many inflicted wounds that left permanent scars, this literary boot camp functioned as a method of chemical detoxification for Boyle. If his friend's overdose in Peekskill had scared the literature out of him, then the Workshop continued that process through an academic challenge of a caliber he had never faced. In his first creative writing workshop in high school he discovered a sense of triumph in winning over a potentially hostile audience. He presented a short play for discussion titled "The Foot," precisely the admixture of mad, absurd, and hyperbolic elements that would become his signature aesthetic. As at the Workshop, his classmates were "unanimous in their contempt for one another and by extension one another's work." The story nonetheless drew laughs from his otherwise hostile peers and teacher, who could not resist the bizarre dark humor of his drama depicting a Florida boy devoured completely by an alligator except for his fully intact foot—shod in a neatly tied sneaker—that his grieving parents keep as a memento prominently displayed on their living room coffee table. His cinematic eye for distortion and inversion anticipating the bizarre humor of the Coen brothers and echoing the magical realism of Gabriel García Márquez had set the blueprint. "Instant audience" approval meant positive reinforcement, a combination that made the workshop system ideally suited to Boyle's aesthetic development.[22]

Boyle's belief in workshops began with "The Foot" and extended to Iowa's premise of subjecting young writers to unrelenting discipline under the hard glare of criticism. He thrived on the challenge, lived for the fight, and reveled in the way victory left him "flushed with the sort of exhilaration that only comes from driving the ball over the net and directly into your opponent's face." His domination of the Vietnam veterans at Iowa workshop sessions was particularly satisfying, since he had spent the war teaching high school as a means of avoiding combat.[23] They had every reason to loathe this hippie runt with scraggly long hair, but his voice and fearless eyes gave no quarter. Alighting with sinister charm, he could disarm them in an instant, his long sloping nose a cross between Charles Dickens, Charles Manson, and a court jester.

In the 1970s, behind the dissenting view of the Workshop as an escape from parental authority, the responsibilities of marriage, jobs, and the rigors of the literary marketplace, lurked the specter of Vietnam. What were these pseudo-aesthetes doing in Iowa, other than shirking their duty? Nelson Algren asked in The Last Carousel, his 1972 collection of nonfiction pieces that included a particularly venomous vivisection of the Workshop. "The longer I hang on here the longer I stay out of Vietnam," he heard one student say while he taught there with Kurt Vonnegut in the late 1960s. "It's a respectable way of dropping out," another admitted. Certainly Boyle had used his high school teaching job the same way—"after college I was teaching to avoid the draft," he admitted—and had successfully brokered his prestigious North American Review publication of "The OD and Hepatitis Railroad or Bust" for admission to the Workshop. While on the faculty at Lakeland High School, he began writing without any preparation, "went into it cold and did a lot of drugs, and being a crazy young hippie, I began to send them out." Since all his literary heroes had some connection to the Workshop as instructors or students, he decided to apply there, sending "OD" and another story, "Drowning," which later appeared in *Descent of Man*. On the strength of both, he was admitted. His literary circle in which these stories were produced would appear to reinforce playwright Ed Bullins's contention, to which Algren attached his ringing endorsement in 1972, the year Boyle entered the Workshop: "It would be healthier for a writer to socialize with drug addicts than with a clique of hacks," according to the premise that "writers in groups are with few exceptions the most impotent and pernicious of tribes to infest the planet."[24] Boyle indeed thrived creatively, if not physically and mentally, when he socialized with drug addicts—and became one himself—while writing the two pieces that earned him admission to the most prestigious writing program in the world. But where his example deviates from Algren's maxim is precisely in his efflorescence within the Workshop environment.

It was there that he discovered the thrill of becoming a professional author. When the *South Dakota Review* paid him twenty-five dollars for "Drowning," he was ecstatic at monetizing his creative talent in this first step toward professionalization: "$25 for the product of your brain? You could buy a lot of beer in Iowa City back then for that," he quipped.[25] As with Robert Lowell during the 1950s, Boyle used Iowa as a place to reclaim a sense of stability and seriousness toward the craft. During the particularly turbulent interludes in Lowell's life in which he had served in federal prison, gone berserk in public on several occasions, and destroyed relationships with those close to him, he made steps to return to Iowa to recalibrate his sensibility and achieve the poise necessary to regain his top form as a creative writer. But Boyle's life was far less erratic and changeable than Lowell's, instead progressing along a surprisingly linear trajectory launched precisely upon his publication of "OD" and admission to the Workshop. Lowell had thirty-nine different addresses and myriad faculty appointments throughout his life. Boyle, by contrast, had only one job offer, from the University of Southern California, which commenced in 1978, the year after he graduated from Iowa. He has remained on the faculty ever since and continues into his late sixties at the rank of full professor. Unlike such capricious figures as Lowell, Boyle has been exceptionally loyal in his personal and professional lives, remaining with his first and only wife, whom he married in the late 1970s. He made a similar lasting and seemingly unbreakable vow to his publisher Viking Penguin, which has brought out, with one exception, all of his twenty-five titles since he signed with them in 1984. The Workshop indeed had the same sobering effect of reining in an

otherwise untamable creative vision and lifestyle to match. Those seeking cultural stimulation in the Workshop environment would be deeply disappointed
in the boxy buildings and blank-faced agrarians of the larger setting. Conversely, they would find cosmopolitanism in the eclectic and elite faculty and
students if not in other programs on campus such as the International Writing Program, as Rita Dove had done.

Boyle imprinted on Iowa, which provided the setting for him to rid himself
of his addictions and discover his craft. In the process, he launched one of the
most prolific and successful publication streaks with a major press in the history of the program. Iowa indeed changed his life and sowed the seeds of his
success. He recently returned for a reading, and later mentioned how he appreciated the audience's presence, regardless of "whether they're nice people
or not, or whether they're idiots, who cares? There they are, they're living and
breathing."[26] Refusing to judge Iowa in this manner should not be confused
with a sense of distance or alienation from the program, which his own daughter Kerrie attended and graduated from at his behest. Her picture at graduation, beaming arm in arm with her father in the bright May sunshine, adorns
the Dey House office of long-standing Workshop secretary Connie Brothers.
The framed photo hovers just over her shoulder as she sits at her desk, a cherished memento in an office cluttered with decades of memories and artifacts
of the program's writers; she glows when asked about it. She recalled how
Boyle had appreciated taking John Irving's class, because "John never read
from a book; he always read from whatever he was working on that was in
progress."[27] Brothers was something of a surrogate mother to Boyle at Iowa, as
she held a deep appreciation of his unique voice and creative talent. By contrast, Boyle's own mother barely read or understood his fiction. While listening
to him read "Heart of a Champion," his parody of the *Lassie* television series
he called "one of the funniest stories I've ever written," "she never cracked a
smile." When he finished, she solemnly declared, "that was moving."[28]

Boyle recalls his days at Iowa as "the time when I became serious about
writing—as [about] my life." His intensity toward the craft was not simply a
means of making a living as a professional author so much as it was a process
of finding an alternative to the self-destructive life he had been leading. He
describes himself before Iowa as "a degenerate, writing sporadically, and listening to a lot of bad habits" that mired him in a spiral of addiction. When
writing became steady rather than sporadic, he found success, first in the immediate feedback at Workshop from his peers and instructors, and then from
his flawless grades. He is "very proud" that he maintained "a perfect 4.0 in all

of my graduate work," and that he was perceived as one the program's best students. In the process he found himself maturing emotionally and professionally, realizing that this was what he "wanted to do" and thus "pursued it vigorously." Undergraduate school, by contrast, was "like punishment." In this way, "Iowa bailed me out." The program "started a whole new phase in my life," Boyle recalled.[29]

The jeremiad of his life follows a recovering addict's master narrative, complete with abject self-loathing. "I was stupid, just a defiant, dope-shooting, heroin-shooting, car-driving maniac, and I just thought that that was the way to be." He lived like "some sort of existential hero," such as Raskolnikov in Dostoyevsky's *Crime and Punishment*, the protagonist of Camus's *The Stranger*, or little Alex the violent teenage hooligan in *A Clockwork Orange*. He flatly proclaims, "Now I'm rejecting that attitude. I've seen another face of life," and found something sacred—his own creativity—at the Workshop. His addiction, however, did not abruptly cease once he arrived at the Workshop. Instead he sought psychiatric treatment from a variety of "shrinks" who "thought I was a very disturbed youth." The Thorazine they prescribed was brutal, even to a hardened heroin addict, "a pretty heavy drug" that had contributed to the suicide of the poet Anne Sexton the decade before. He explains how he rejected it "finally and everything else" in an effort "to make something else" out of his life "which is more traditional and more satisfying for me." The solution was in his own creative talent: "I became dedicated to my art," and in the process "grew up at about the age of twenty-five or so. I went to Iowa to escape New York" and its "very bad drug scene."[30]

Instant Audience

With the wretched New York drug scene safely behind him, Boyle turned his sights with the zeal of a recovered addict on literary achievement in the Workshop. An early photograph of him at his typewriter captures the moment. Disheveled, and not a little annoyed by the photographer's request to have him turn away from his work for an instant to face the camera, he looks out with monomaniacal piercing eyes, mischievous and hot on the trail of an invisible narrative yarn, rechanneling the chemically driven absurd, mad, and hyperbolic hallucinations into literary art. He looks the part of the hippie, but one riveted to his cause, unwilling to yield to any distractions in his way, "betraying friends and ex-lovers and dreaming like a zombie over the page" until his vision comes to life.[31]

The system of rigorous peer and instructor feedback in class meant that his work would receive what he called an "instant audience."[32] This informal means of publication in workshop sessions provided immediate results in a controlled, experimental environment for a sense of the work's potential reception in the literary market. The savage individualism and petty sniping did not deter him from capitalizing on precisely the workshop method's function as envisioned by Engle decades earlier. Boyle found value in Engle's original vision of the workshop method as a manner of publication simulating the pointed criticism one could expect from editors of presses like Little, Brown or Viking and reviewers of the *New Yorker* or the *New York Times*. Boyle's conception of authorship derived directly from his narrative persona of wise-guy performer and entertainer, brimming with the sort of fearless pluck and panache that made him an instant star of workshop sessions.

For Boyle, authorship was predicated on Dickensian performance, the literary equivalent of crowd surfing into the hands of the audience, giving oneself body and soul in a transparent act of complete surrender. To him, Charles Dickens epitomizes this dedication to authorship as performance art. "You have to envy him his famous readings," Boyle has said, because "he was [the] Mick Jagger of his day, the movie, the stage show, and all the rest, all rolled into one." He envies that power Dickens possessed, which "we poor pathetic scribblers can only dream of in these techno-obsessed days."[33] Boyle's website, launched in the late 1990s, typifies his conception of authorship as a process of self-disclosure and immediacy with his readers. He regularly posts commentary with photographs from his private domestic life, one even featuring him curled up in bed in a beany. In 1995, his outrageous live appearances captured the attention of the *New Yorker*, which portrayed him as "a skinny man in his late 40s, with bushy hair and a goatee who dressed like he was 25 and had a dead-black morbid outlook on life and twisted everything into a kind of joke that made you squirm."[34] His public image embodies the wise-guy narrators that his readers adore. Boyle's loyalty to his readers is evident everywhere on the site, especially in his prompt, authentic, and thorough replies to their queries. Among literary authors, he was an early adopter of Twitter to leverage his popularity on social media to expand his reach. This brand of authorship synthesizes the elements he always admired in Dickens, "a quintessential artist who was a very popular author, and who also wrote brilliantly and well and originally."[35]

On writing as performance, Boyle casts the authorial role as profoundly social, contrary to the widely accepted sense of the occupation as detached solitary endeavor. Instead, he thrives on "getting up onstage and doing every-thing I can to engage and entertain an audience." Charges that he is nothing more than a standup comic, a kind of literary court jester, rankle him. He la-ments that he has "been misunderstood and even reviled in some quarters, as if literature is some sort of priesthood and by making people laugh and writhe I'm somehow an apostate." He argues that "literature is alive, a living, vital art form that needs to appeal to its audience—not pander to it, but appeal to it in the highest and lowest way." Bringing literature to the audience as he does rescues it from becoming "exclusively the province of the academy, of intel-lectuals," whereby "the average person's experience of [it] is in the odious form of a classroom assignment." This formulation of authorship poses a di-lemma for Boyle in the digital age, for "Who can achieve the conscious-unconscious state of the reader when everything is stimulation, everything is movement and information?" The worst nightmare for authors is to allow the culture to relegate them to a role "like Kafka's Hunger Artist, performing as-tonishing feats for a nonexistent audience far more interested in life and vital-ity." Digital culture's promise of instant gratification stands as formidable competition to "our antiquated and self-indulgent arts" such as literature.[36]

The antiquated self-indulgence of authorship, former Workshop instructor Nelson Algren alleged in the early 1970s, was cause for scandal. Algren esti-mates that "Of the eighty-odd students whose work I read at Iowa at least thirty were too disturbed, emotionally, to write coherently in any language," he complained. "Only two used English lucidly; and neither of these was native-born."[37] Much of the problem, he insisted, came from the lack of powerful and successful models among the faculty whom students might emulate. Faculty writing was lax, he claimed, because professors could depend on a steady sal-ary unlike the youthful Hemingway in Paris under Gertrude Stein, for whom "Hunger was good discipline. You could always go into the Luxembourg mu-seum and all the paintings were heightened and clearer and more beautiful if you were belly-empty, hollow hungry."[38]

Without such vulnerability in the free market, Algren argued, a pernicious complacency sets in whereby the steady university salary decouples creativity from the financial consequence of critical reception. Such salaried positions eliminate the entrepreneurial scramble of authorship, and thus the prospect of critical failure as a threat carrying real economic consequences. Algren points out the influx of authors in unusually high concentrations at creative writing programs like Iowa's, where they lack a financial incentive to produce quality work to reach a paying audience. The *New York Times* made a similar point about the financial dividends that accrue to the teaching-writer at the expense of literary quality: "Iowa City is the place where a poet can relax in the knowledge that a regular paycheck will come in no matter how badly the book goes." Algren adds, "That it can go badly enough to embarrass readers, without stopping a paycheck, is demonstrated by the founder-poet's odes to fried rice," a swipe at Paul Engle's less-than-stellar corpus that includes such nuggets as *Corn: A Book of Poems*, from 1939.[39]

As the antithesis of complacent faculty members indifferent to the reception of their writing in the literary market, students like Boyle competed intensely to establish themselves in the publishing industry by landing stories in respectable journals and earning a debut contract with a prestigious press. Many had been groomed for success in this environment, including students such as Rita Dove, a summa cum laude graduate at Miami of Ohio, who carried prestigious awards, publications, and honors upon entrance into the program. Instead, Boyle was closer to the "bone hungry" young Hemingway whose heightened powers of perception were driven by a ravenous ambition. With the same steely resolve Boyle used to overcome his demons—"I used to have a lot of nightmares as an adult and I willed myself not to have them"—he dedicated himself to his craft.[40]

Boyle knew his success depended on his knowledge of the publishing nexus. He learned very little about the craft of creative writing outside of workshop sessions, which he mainly used as a litmus test for whether to continue nurturing a story to fruition. Noticing that his instructors would congregate at Iowa City bars to discuss the business of literature, including which journals and presses were on the rise and which had faltered given changes in editorial personnel, he made a point of mastering the market. He was streetwise enough to know that great writing would amount to little without an aggressive promotional apparatus behind it, and thus began a relentless marketing campaign on behalf of his own writing that continues to reach its tentacles across transmedia outlets, from his website to social media.

Boyle's tutelage in the finer points of literary marketing took place at a bar in Iowa City called the Mill on Burlington Street, a short walk up the hill from the Workshop's location at the time in EPB. Raymond Carver was a fixture there, a larger-than-life figure among Workshop faculty whom students worshipped as "the best short story writer of his time," and who "amazed and inspired" the young Boyle. His conversations with Carver were never concerned with the structure and method of fiction writing, so much as the challenge of finding remuneration for it. "We didn't talk much about craft," he recalled, but focused on "selling stories to little magazines—selling them, that is, once they'd been brought up out of nothing and given shape." The creative process "was just a given," an individual "path you took because you were a writer able to assimilate all the stories there ever were and make something wholly different out of them."[41] If the method of creative writing did not bear mention in these off-campus conversations, it was only because attention focused on placing material rather than producing it. John Cheever, also a towering presence among the Workshop faculty at the time, was "very drunk all the time," and provided no "structural analysis" or details on how to improve, Boyle remembered. "You're right on track kid, keep it up," was all he could offer, but to Boyle, it came as encouragement to carry on. To this day, Boyle remains mystified as to how he managed to build his writing without any substantial aesthetic guidance, noting that "somehow, and I don't know how, my work seemed to come together." Although his instructors were "very gracious [and] very generous," he "never got much advice from anyone" in the art of fictional narrative.[42]

Beyond what he could glean from Carver about placing his stories in the little magazines, Boyle's mastery of publishing industry networks was attributable to his own relentless investigations. "When I was scrambling to publish," he explains, "I knew every magazine and every editor, and everything that was going on and all the gossip." Thoroughly enmeshed in the social matrix of literary publishing, Boyle sought out through informal conversation information essential to his success, including "how to get on with an agent," and "how to send out a manuscript." What he was not told, he "found out just by trial and error."[43] To his great advantage in navigating the literary market was his position as assistant fiction editor of the *Iowa Review*. His supervisor was fiction editor Robert Coover, who was in London at the time, but through extended correspondence became a loyal advocate and mentor to Boyle. They would share thoughts on the ten manuscripts Boyle had screened for him from the bulk of submissions, from which Coover selected three or four to be published in the next issue. Coover indeed was instrumental in springing Boyle's success, particularly the year after he graduated in 1977, when he "did the whole Eurail thing as a rag-tag hippie trotting around Europe with my wife."[44] When the two arrived in London, they were treated to a warm reception from Coover, who threw a party in their honor to introduce Boyle to several publishing literary insiders. At the London party, Boyle met his agent who landed him his first two book contracts with the reputable publisher Little, Brown, and who later proved instrumental in engineering his Viking deal that cemented his career, making him one of its most lucrative and long-standing house authors.

Intermediaries played a crucial role in Boyle's rise to fame. He nonetheless has claimed to loathe the use of literary circles to his professional advantage, insisting he has "never cultivated anyone in a position to advance me" and has stayed "strictly away from literary and film circles, choosing rather to speak directly to my audience."[45] He repeatedly casts himself as a lone wolf learning both the craft of writing and its promotion in the publishing industry on his own through trial and error. This is only partially true, but sounds a note that harmonizes with his authorial image as a radical individualist on the fringe, always skeptical of authority and institutions. Yet his deep and abiding dedication to the Workshop represents surrender to institutional authority rather than defiance of it. He claims not to talk to other authors or teachers of creative writing. "I don't know the other teachers in my own department" at USC "and what they do," just as he is oblivious to the craft of other practicing authors, confessing, "I don't hang out with other writers and don't talk to other writers."[46]

His current justification for remaining outside literary circles is calculated to make him appear immersed in the alternative social milieu of his readership. "Have I missed out? Maybe so. But I have been pleased and honored to have a wide readership for my books and it is to that readership that I owe my loyalty." But gaining that readership to begin with required several crucial relationships with key figures in the publishing industry to spring his career. He acknowledges his benefactors from "grad school rocks like Vance Bourjaily, John Irving and John Cheever, to editors like George Plimpton and Lewis Lapham, and my agent, Georges Borchardt," whom Coover had introduced him to in London. "They saw me. Plucked me up. Held me. Guided me."[47] Fellow Workshop students had less influence, with the notable exception of one female colleague. When it came to assembling what would be his most controversial story written at Iowa—a scandal that became a local legend and topic of gossip throughout both campus and town—he relied on her intermediary efforts to infiltrate the domain of his subject, which was off-limits to men. The story that followed, and its controversial place of publication, unleashed a lion.

The Grace and Rubies Affair

If Boyle had been so well positioned in the literary market through his fashionable editorship at the *Iowa Review*, why would his final publication as an Iowa student coinciding with his graduation in May 1977 appear, of all places, in the tawdry pages of *Penthouse* magazine? The momentous timing of the story, "A Women's Restaurant," occasioned something far more respectable since it sounded the final note of his impressive and prolific record at Iowa, one that would leave a lasting impression of Boyle's impact on the program and literary history. Hardly a paragon of literary renown, *Penthouse* blights his five years of stellar publications at Iowa that began with his auspicious debut in the *North American Review*. Boyle's curriculum vitae, however, was the least of his concerns when he sought a publisher for "A Women's Restaurant," a short story version of a roman à clef entrenched in local controversy. As the only Iowa City subject of all of his Workshop writings, the story functions as Boyle's parting shot at the town's culture and politics.

"A Women's Restaurant" demanded research into Grace and Rubies, a local feminist eatery (originally named without an apostrophe), library, and gathering place that banned men from the premises. But the source of his information was mainly the news media, despite rumors that he infiltrated the establishment in drag. As with his imaginative reconstruction of Battle Creek, Michigan, in *The Road to Wellville*, Boyle did not spend much time on research for "A Women's Restaurant." He admits to having no patience for embedded journalistic investigation. "I am no James Michener, living in Texas for twelve years so he could write about the geology, history, and cattle raising."[48] It was commonly known that the restaurant's owners recorded the names of its all-female clientele over the age of ten. A life membership, required upon the first visit, entailed signing its bylaws and paying a one-time fee of fifty cents. Such minimal requirements for membership were a thinly veiled means of acquiring legal status as a private club to legitimate the exclusion of men. The nominal fee signaled the political rather than commercial priority of the establishment, in sharp contrast to the exorbitant dues charged at elite men's clubs such as Augusta Golf Club or Bohemian Grove. Located on 209 North Linn Street in Iowa City, near the famous Hamburg Inn No. 2 that has hosted presidential candidates since the advent of the Iowa caucus in the 1970s, Grace and Rubies opened in 1976 and closed two years later under legal pressure and ongoing resistance fueled in part by Boyle's story.

By placing the piece in *Penthouse*, Boyle deviated from his literary pattern of publication in order to make a political counterpoint against the restaurant's exclusion of men. His satire of the women-only establishment would bite more ferociously in this more uncouth and therefore offensive venue than its relatively sophisticated counterpart, *Playboy*. Grace and Rubies had raised local opposition based on allegations that it charged too little to be designated a private club bearing the right to exclude certain patrons; editorialists maligned it in the local press as a haven for man-hating feminists. In November 1976, several months after it opened, assistant city attorney Angela Ryan deemed Grace and Rubies "not private," and turned the matter over to the city's Human Relations Commission for investigation. Mayor Mary Neuhauser argued that "the 50-cent membership fee" did not "qualify the establishment as a bona fide club."[49] The Achilles heel of the club was that "its membership-selection process had no screening, no interview, no limit to the number of social members, no possibility of rejection, no criteria other than being a woman."[50] That the figures leading the legal assault were women presented a paradox, which appears less ironic in light of their defense against civil rights discrimination. " 'I'm just afraid we'll see several more of these places springing up, and they'll bar blacks or minorities or other groups,' " the mayor argued.[51]

Cut from the cloth of Poe's madmen, the obsessive narrator of Boyle's tale leads the reader through his thought processes as he plots to perpetuate outrageous acts. This protagonist is no murderer and intends no harm, but is obsessed in a way suggestive of Poe's psychopaths whose elaborate exploits are lovingly told with pinpoint precision. The subtlety, however, was lost on the real proprietors, a lesbian couple named Grace and Rubie, whom he lampoons into an unflattering Dickensian caricature by accentuating their obtuse clash of large/small, dominant/submissive, aggressive/passive, "butch/fem" characteristics. Boyle renders Rubie as a spindly woman with a close-cropped "brushcut" shorn at the behest of her domineering counterpart, "the towering Grace" with "angry eyes." Rubie "looked like a Cub Scout. An Oliver Twist," one of Boyle's several nods to Dickens.[52] The protagonist is bent on discovering their inner world, since all he knows he can decipher from the refuse in the trash bins outside the building. He imagines an inner paradise made all the more desirable because he is excluded for his gender, a crime that runs "afoul of antidiscrimination laws," a phrase suggesting Boyle's more than casual familiarity with local news coverage of the city attorney's and mayor's investigations. His narrator is obsessed with ascertaining "what goes on there, precisely," which "no man knows." Since he is a man, he is "burning to find out."[53]

After several unsuccessful attempts at entering the feminist enclave, first by simply trying to walk in, then by attempting to sneak in through the back, the narrator of "A Women's Restaurant" finally resorts to drag. While seducing a lesbian biker girl, the narrator excuses himself to use the restroom. In his drunkenness, he forgets to sit down while relieving himself to conceal his identity. "A head suspended over the door to the stall"—it is Grace, whose "face was the face of an Aztec executioner."[54] He blasts out of the stall sending her into the sink opposite, and scurries out of the restroom, his wig askew. In a madcap scene, he bursts past the patrons, overturning plates and chairs, cutting through the kitchen as Grace screams, "STOP HIM! STOP HIM!" in a full-throated howl of the dreaded male pronoun. But blocking the exit is the "pixie Rubie," who lowers her right shoulder "like a linebacker" and sends the narrator pinwheeling head over heels, landing with his "face in coffee grounds and eggshells." In the coda he reflects on his exploit, muses on the pleasures of drag, and considers seriously seeking the assistance of a surgeon so his next entrance could be made with "no dissimulation."[55]

Like the reformers of Boyle's later novel *The Inner Circle* (2004), the narrator of "A Women's Restaurant" obsessively and irrationally pursues his quest in a humorous, outlandish plot. The parody of the social scene bears the imprint of his fellow Workshop graduate Flannery O'Connor, who similarly delighted in sending up cultural progressives in "A Good Man Is Hard to Find," Boyle's favorite short story. The satiric and "jaundiced eye" O'Connor turns on society informs the method of "A Women's Restaurant." In an unmistakable reference to the protagonist of "Good Country People," Boyle features a girl with a plastic prosthetic leg in his tale.[56] The story's literary import is considerable, but is nonetheless secondary to his political intentions. Although it may well bear the dubious distinction of the most literary work ever published in *Penthouse*, its agenda was hardly docile or neutral, despite Boyle's claims to the contrary decades later.[57]

The placement of the story in *Penthouse*, Boyle insisted, was prompted by the meager income of five thousand dollars that he and his wife, also a graduate student, earned at the time. He therefore "was happy to publish the story where I could and to receive actual money for it." The starving-student alibi, however, did not satisfy those associated with Grace and Rubies, whose attorney charged that the business "has been singled out among all the private clubs in this city for harassment."[58] Boyle recalled that "the patrons of Grace and Ruby's [sic] read the story in print . . . and felt I was attacking them or feminism or their right to privacy."[59] After cataloguing the odd menagerie of patrons, "washerwomen, schoolmarms, gymnasts, waitresses, Avon ladies, scout leaders, meter maids, grandmothers, great-grandmothers, spinsters, widows, dikes, gay divorcees, the fat, the lean, the wrinkled, the bald," including the O'Connoresque "girl with a plastic leg," the narrator "finds something disturbing about this gathering of women, this classless convocation, this gynecomorphous melting pot."[60] Many alleged the story was a mean-spirited swipe at the women's movement, to which Boyle retorted, "It is not a malicious story."[61] He explained, "it does not seek to devastate feminism (tweak it maybe, I'll admit to that), but in a twisted sort of way, to celebrate it." He "had a confederate do my snooping for me: a bona fide member of the opposite sex," whose identity he has refused to disclose but is likely to have been his wife. The concept for the story originated from his Workshop instructor John Irving, who suggested crafting a tale based on "the idea of men in drag vis-à-vis the feminist movement."[62]

Grace and Rubies was ripe for satire as a feminist hub in the heart of Iowa City, especially given its division of the sexes. But the joke is also on the infiltrator who insinuates himself into the all-women's restaurant.[63] Although Grace and Rubies restaurant closed down after only two years in operation, it has been immortalized in an entry on the feminist blog *Lost Womyn's Space*. The piece pays homage to the restaurant and takes Boyle to task for appropriating it for "a pornography-obsessed male audience—even in lightly fictionalized form." The commentator accuses him of "exposing, redefining, and highlighting" not only the club but "all women's space to this [*Penthouse*] audience as pornographic girl-on-girl fantasy for the male gaze."[64] Grace and Rubies may have risked liability for discrimination against male patrons, according to journalism student Lynne Cherry, writing in the *Daily Iowan* in 1977. But activists defended the establishment as a symbol of the women's movement and its struggles to achieve progress. The drafty dining room is "made to feel cozy by the feeling of comradeship among the members and the cheerful wisecracks issuing from the kitchen." Boyle's story never mentioned its function as a headquarters for women's cultural events. Posted on its walls were "handwritten notices for such things as a club meeting, a costume party, intramural flag football, and a women's clinic." Women's literature, news, and politics overflowed from the library "that consisted of donated books, mostly by and-or about women, and some feminist newspapers."[65] Grace and Rubies drew attention in a 1977 article in *Dyke: A Quarterly* published a year before the establishment closed. One contributor could see that the restaurant's days were numbered, but quipped with a note of optimism that "if it takes the commission as long to investigate Grace & Rubie's [sic] as it does to investigate sex discrimination in employment claims, the restaurant will be around for a number of years, no matter what the outcome."[66]

Teaching at the Workshop and editing the *Iowa Review* placed Boyle in a position of gatekeeper for the first time in his life. In that role, he would deal with pitched histrionics of one particularly irate classroom visitor and screen hundreds of manuscripts for the Workshop's most influential journal. The disarming humor of his fiction, and the sheer mastery of its artistry, speak to his capacity to keep the wolves off his scent in the controversies that have arisen during his career, especially the one precipitated by his story about Grace and Rubies.

Boyle's legacy to the Workshop is his loyalty to the program and the craft— one job, at USC, one publisher, Viking—throughout a long and fruitful career characterized by an unusually open relationship with his readers, as his online presence shows. His willingness to leverage digital media, especially as an aging baby boomer, to expand the scope of his audience speaks to the versatility and vigor with which he has built his impressive career. Unlike Workshop veterans such as Kurt Vonnegut who have enjoyed massive audiences only to face charges of hack writing in predictable mass market genre fiction forms, Boyle has effortlessly pulled off a stunt worthy of Dickens himself by writing literary narrative with an exceptionally broad appeal. "There is a very fine distinction between these things, literature and genre fiction," he mentions, "for language and for what's going on under the surface." The best writers "take you some place you've never been before." At Iowa, he meshed that wide-open spirit of exploration beyond genre conventions with discipline, rigor, and craft, initiated by his own drive to escape his addictions and replace them with a creative one fueling his vitality. The velocity of his record is all the more remarkable in light of the playfulness he maintains, as seen in how "he still wears red Converse high-tops."[67]

PART 3
THE FRANK CONROY ERA AND
BEYOND (1980S–PRESENT)

13 • The Mystic: Marilynne Robinson

On a sultry opening day of the fall 2012 semester, students poured into Marilynne Robinson's seminar on Problems in Modern Fiction. Room 224 of North Hall—perched on the east bank of the Iowa River near the Workshop's Dey House—had never seen so many occupants. With every seat filled, students vied for standing room at the back wall and sat in the aisles. Although such seminars in creative writing at the University of Iowa typically attract no more than twenty students, skyrocketing demand for the course more than tripled that number in the wake of the Pulitzer Prize–winning publication in 2004 of *Gilead*, Robinson's second novel since her cult classic *Housekeeping* appeared twenty-four years earlier. Even with the enrollment limit raised to forty students, twice the usual number for such courses, Robinson accepted eighteen more, for a total of fifty-eight on the final roster. The runaway popularity of the course—it filled at a record seventy students by spring 2013—was just one of the many local signs that the instructor's career was undergoing a full-blown renaissance.[1]

Not only Iowa's student body had discovered Robinson. Her publication of *Home*, the prequel to *Gilead*, in 2008 won the Orange Prize for Fiction in the United Kingdom, cementing her status as a world-class author "considered as essential as Nabokov and Conrad." That year, the *Times* of London proclaimed Robinson "The World's Best Writer of Prose."[2] Among her most devoted readers was Barack Obama, who, in an unprecedented gesture by an American president, assumed the role of journalist and conducted an interview with Robinson that appeared in two installments in the *New York Review of Books*, in the autumn of 2015. Moments after he had placed the National Humanities Medal around her neck in July the previous year, the president confided, "Your writings have fundamentally changed me, I think for the better, Marilynne—I believe that."[3]

The most powerful writers among the Workshop student body have chosen to work with Robinson. When I asked her about her mentorship of Ayana Mathis and Paul Harding, whose stellar critical and popular success has raised the standard even among Workshop graduates, she was modest about her role in their ascent. Insisting instead on crediting the faculty at large, as well as the extraordinary talent of the incoming students at the Workshop, she initially refused to pinpoint any specific influence she may have had on their work except to note, "as it happens, Paul and Ayana chose to work closely with me." However, she had "no doubt that they also profited from the advice of my colleagues." Lowering her guard, she disclosed that although they were particularly strong, both needed "an attentive reader" along with "the kind of advice about the special psychological and emotional demands of writing that I could give them from my own experience with this very difficult art." This demanding process of creative development for them was not the painless organic one Marguerite Young had fostered in the previous generation. "The essential point" for Robinson in her tutelage of these future powerhouses was "to encourage confidence in the project the writer is strongly drawn to," no matter how incongruent with market demands or literary trends. Her focus was to help each of them "find the writer he or she should become. My teaching method comes down to attempting to be a sensitive reader and critic." Again portraying modesty, she quipped, "I am happy to take credit for what Paul and Ayana have done and will do, but the credit really belongs to them."

Emerson similarly dismissed any suggestion or implication that he was behind the success of any of his protégés, including Henry David Thoreau and Margaret Fuller. But for them, as with Harding and Mathis, the literary mentor they selected changed their lives. Robinson allowed that her two best students' decision "to work closely with me" proved to be the most pivotal of their literary careers not only for the aesthetic guidance she provided, but also for crucial connections to the New York publishing industry that included Ellen Levine's powerful literary agency.[4]

Like other Workshop instructors, Robinson's ascendance to world-class notoriety has relied on the power of commercial media—despite her principled renunciation of it—to expand her audience. Among former and present Workshop members, however, she is the last to embrace digital communication as a means of promoting her professional career, lacking the sort of aggressive online marketing and leveraging of social media of T. C. Boyle and Ayana

Mathis, for example. Yet through the status of her Workshop affiliation, she has landed her most potent media events, particularly the Obama interview and her appearance on *The Daily Show with Jon Stewart* in 2010 to promote her book *Absence of Mind.* Stewart's producers sought her out as a provocative contrarian voice challenging the assumption that science and religion share nothing in common. The interview ended with Stewart asking, "Who's right?" in the debate between science and religion, to which she dryly replied, "I am."[5]

Other notable media entities have sought out Robinson. Bob Silvers, the former editor of the *New York Review of Books,* first reached out to her on behalf of President Obama, who called the move an "experiment." Prompted by his desire to use his final days in office to "have a conversation with somebody who I enjoy and am interested in," he tapped Robinson because she was "first in the queue."[6] Suddenly she found herself an accidental media celebrity, an unusual role for the self-described "unfashionable" defender of mainline Protestantism and ardent critic of materialism and the new atheism.[7] Robinson composes deeply interior novels about dying rural preachers, in longhand with ballpoint pens and legal pads, and is a fierce opponent of popular media culture, so it comes as a shock to see her celebrated by *Vogue* and featured in the digital magazine *Vice* in an interview with a former student. Her appearance with Obama went viral as an offbeat rhythm in the digital news cycle, as "precious few are the moments when brilliant, cult-y fiction writers ascend to the all-important status of Trending Topic."[8]

Levine's Trident Media Group, which represents Robinson, has provided Workshop members with much of the publishing-industry support that Paul Engle had provided earlier. Without the prestigious Workshop affiliation that gained her privileged access to Trident, the tepid reception of her first novel *Housekeeping* in 1980 might have meant there was little hope for the resurrection of her career as a novelist nearly a quarter century later. Further, her time away from fiction was not a case of losing the creative impulse or knack for the craft. Nor did she suffer from intense media attention before 2004 of the sort that robbed Ralph Ellison of the solitude necessary to write another novel after the colossal achievement of his *Invisible Man,* a National Book Award winner that one critic called "the most important novel since World War II."[9] *Housekeeping* posed no such dilemma, because the book initially had attracted so little attention. The project began as a series "of extended metaphors" of the sort she had been analyzing in her doctoral dissertation on Shakespeare at the University of Washington. "I just kept writing these little things and putting them in a drawer." After several months, she pulled "out this stack of things and they cohered." She could see "what these things implied" and "where the voice was."[10] Once she assembled it into a coherent narrative, she assumed it was "too private a novel" to ever be published, much less reach a wide audience. But she persisted in finding a publisher, Farrar, Straus and Giroux, only to be warned that it might not be reviewed.[11] It was indeed reviewed, but only narrowly. *Housekeeping* barely survived after clearing its first print run of thirty-five hundred copies, after which "it finally straggled into paperback. There was one bidder. It could have expired."[12]

During her hiatus from the novel from 1980 until 2004, Robinson did not face the fruitless struggle of Ellison, whose career as a novelist sank under the gargantuan weight of his unpublishable two-thousand-page manuscript. Nor was she devising a project, like Michael Chabon's *Wonder Boys*, specifically to overcome creative paralysis in the wake of her first novel's success. She had initially received no outpouring of praise for *Housekeeping* from overzealous critics like those who heralded Chabon as the next F. Scott Fitzgerald—and in the process froze him in his tracks—after his debut title, *The Mysteries of Pittsburgh*. Robinson's creative will was impervious to such external forces. Instead, she deliberately embarked on a series of nonfiction projects in theology, cultural criticism, and environmental activism. Dissatisfied with her doctoral training, she sought more. When she joined the faculty of the Iowa Writers' Workshop as a visitor in 1989 knowing little about the state, and with no intention of remaining longer than a few semesters, she instead found precisely the environment for such research. The trilogy of novels, *Gilead* (2004), *Home* (2008), and *Lila* (2014), which together form the crowning achievement of her career, would not have been possible without her immersion in theology and ethics throughout the 1990s. "I stayed" to become a permanent member of the Workshop faculty in 1991 "because I learned to love the place," she said, describing the decades as "very fruitful years for me because the customs and culture of the Workshop support the kind of life writing requires."[13] Free from distraction in this rural setting, she could pursue a contemplative life, yet one bent on combating fear in its most repugnant cultural and political manifestations, in the process valorizing and reclaiming mainline Protestantism for the socially liberal left.

Banned in Britain

After the publication of *Housekeeping*, Robinson spent the next two and a half decades writing mostly nonfiction, much of which she admitted consisted of unfashionable theological inquiries into John Calvin and political polemics.

Her defense of culturally and politically unfashionable positions carries an unapologetic boldness, as seen in *Mother Country: Britain, the Welfare State, and Nuclear Pollution*, published in 1989, just two years after *Housekeeping*'s motion picture release.[14] A more calculating author, such as T. C. Boyle, might have sought to capitalize on the film by producing another novel. Besides the small word-of-mouth cult following for *Housekeeping*, the only audience Robinson captivated in the wake of the film consisted of litigious detractors of *Mother Country*. The incendiary invective incited a lawsuit from Greenpeace and drove Britain to threaten an embargo. Her assault on Greenpeace stunned environmentalists who deem the organization unassailable. Yet she has launched similar critiques of the Nature Conservancy and the Sierra Club, alleging that "the most important issues are not in the conversation," which instead fixates on how consumers should "stop using spray or other ridiculous minor things that won't add twenty minutes to the world's life while" other "horrible depredations" go unchecked. Her relentless focus on larger issues exposes the flaws of seemingly benign conservation organizations, highlighting for example the naive proposition of "saving the whale without saving the sea." She has concluded that "there is no environmental group whose methods or priorities I consider useful. Zero."[15] Such courage infused her major works to follow. In the wake of the libel suit, Robinson refused to redact passages in *Mother Country* in which she condemned the British government and Greenpeace for toxic waste in Britain.[16] The British government retaliated by banning the book in the United Kingdom.[17]

The lawsuit absorbed considerable time and energy. Robinson's unwillingness to compromise to reach a broader readership speaks to her commitment to crusading for justice over promoting herself to elite British literary circles and their attendant critical communities. Henry David Thoreau, whom Robinson cites along with Emerson, Dickinson, and Melville as having the greatest impact on her work, shared this professional ethic that placed social reform before self-promotion. The jail time Thoreau served for his refusal to fund the Mexican-American War, for example, subordinated his reputation in the literary marketplace for the higher principle of civil disobedience. Further, his assault on the industrial intrusions into what he considered the pristine sanctuary of Walden Pond—with the shrieking steam engine violating the quiet woods and railroad track lacerating the land—parallels Robinson's staunch defense of the natural environment in the latter-day muckraking of her *Harper's* exposé journalism that fueled *Mother Country*. Her investigative reportage revealed that the British nuclear reprocessing plant of Sellafield had systematically covered up its practice of pumping radioactive waste into the Irish Sea.[18] Still worse, Greenpeace was fully aware of the practice yet abetted it by distributing "false information about its role in chartering legislation to stop the disposal of toxic waste at sea." Despite the accolades she has received from her literary novels, "she still calls" the journalistic *Mother Country* "the most important thing she has ever written."[19] She stated, "if I could have written only one book, that would have to be the book."[20]

The 1989 lawsuit against Robinson's British publisher for *Mother Country* could not have come at a worse time. That year she had separated from her husband and was undergoing plans for divorce while independently raising their two boys. The book had received mixed reviews, with some critics denouncing it for being excessively strident and one-sided. Its supporters, however, generated a groundswell of support strong enough to land it on the list of finalists for the National Book Award in 1989. Much of the support for the book derived from the radically liberal community around Skidmore College, where she taught for the New York State Writers Institute. By spring of 1991, the Workshop's director Frank Conroy extended her an offer to join the permanent faculty. Among Robinson's supporters was the highly acclaimed author Susan Sontag, who addressed Conroy regarding her hiring. Since Sontag had been in self-exile overseas without her mail forwarded in order to finish her novel *The Volcano Lover*, she had missed the news. She also regretted missing "the chance to recommend Marilynne Robinson for a permanent post at Iowa," adding that "Iowa would be very lucky to get the author of *Housekeeping!*"[21] Conroy replied, "She got it. With tenure. We're all very happy, needless to say." Not missing the opportunity to book her for a speaking engagement, he asked, "Is there any way I can lure you out here for a visit/reading next fall?"[22]

With the new position at Iowa and her divorce and libel suit settled, Robinson welcomed the opportunity to settle west, if not precisely in the region of her upbringing in Idaho, certainly in a rural community situated near the leafy Mississippi River valley. There she could be ensconced in nature as Thoreau was at Walden Pond and contemplate what Emerson called the infinitude of private man. At least one critic has found Robinson's pattern of literary production "sporadic" and "willfully eccentric," especially given her predilection for retrieving mainline Protestantism in an era of cultural materialism that has called into question conventional religion.[23] She has assumed the less than popular stance of defending Christianity from such imposing figures as Richard Dawkins, who delivered a slashing criticism of the damage incurred by organized religion, measured in human lives beginning with the Holy Wars, in *The God Delusion* of 2008. Before Dawkins, Jack Miles's *God: A Biography* in 1995 led the attack on the Bible's status as ultimate moral authority and evidence of a benevolent deity by casting it as a carefully crafted work of literature whose main character is God himself.

Much more than her affinity for long sentences and challenging vocabulary inspired by Herman Melville—she identified Ishmael, the narrator of *Moby-Dick*, as her single favorite character in all of literature—this decidedly unfashionable quality of Robinson's extends deeper, to her predilection for the writings of John Calvin. She defends Calvin for "the power of the metaphysics and the visionary quality of his theology," particularly his "admiration of what the human mind does." She objects to "positivism that rejects anything—the self, the soul, or God—that cannot be explained empirically" in her essay collection *The Givenness of Things*.[24] Her predilection for nineteenth-century homiletics and Emersonian modes of rhetorical expression stem from an epiphany she experienced while teaching *Moby-Dick* at the Workshop at the age of forty-five. Melville's vision of Calvinism inspired her reading of *The Institutes*, the text that initiated her exploration of Reformed theology.[25]

By the late 1990s, Robinson was completely immersed in theology and nature. Her collection of essays *The Death of Adam* is written in a manner and tone unmistakably reminiscent of Emerson's own lectures and essays. Her lyrical prose combined with her polemical edge to make her work extremely provocative to academic readers. *The Death of Adam* essays intensified interest in *Housekeeping*, especially among those who analyzed it in more than seventy scholarly articles, essays in edited volumes, doctoral dissertations, master's theses, and over fifteen interviews.[26] Her writing from 1998 to 2003 was done while on leave from the Workshop after winning the Mildred and Harold Strauss Living award, a prize giving $250,000 over five years with the express purpose to "free writers from the obligation to earn a living other than through their writing."[27] She waited until the eleventh hour before finally returning to the novel in the fellowship's final year.

Each of Robinson's novels, including *Gilead*, which broke her long silence in the genre, took roughly eighteen months to write. Despite appearances to the contrary given the decades separating *Housekeeping* and *Gilead*, the process was quite smooth and organic.[28] *Gilead* sounded her return to the literary scene in thunder. The novel's glowing review in the Sunday *New York Times Book Review* was heralded by director Frank Conroy as a "a very big deal." He told reporters, "people have been waiting for this book for a very long time," an achievement marking "a big moment for contemporary literature" and affirming her status as "one of the best writers of our time."[29]

Gilead, like *Housekeeping*, does not strain for esoteric or postmodern modes of expression, but wields ordinary vocabulary and mythic structures drawn primarily from the Bible. A telling moment occurred when Robinson was asked in an interview in 2009 if she could find any words to describe God or the meaning of life, a question intended to elicit lengthy and subtle rumination about the strengths and limitations of language to convey spiritual meaning. She instantly replied that she "would not hesitate" to "use the basic Biblical vocabulary."[30] To her, these are not only the best linguistic and mythopoetic tools for describing God, but the most effective for writing fiction, particularly an epistolary novel like *Gilead*, written in apostrophe by a dying Protestant minister. Writing longhand on lined paper, she runs through each sentence several times mentally before committing it to the page, so that her first drafts contain almost no crossed out or inserted material. The holograph manuscript of *Housekeeping* is a fascinating document that reflects the longhand composition process she continues to use in the digital age.[31] The relative ease with which she has written each of her novels is due in part to the fact that she is "not terribly interested in clever writing" and has never questioned her intuition of *when* she should write: "Something comes to mind and I can sense a certain heft to it—that it has the weight of a novel." She never comes to the page without a clear sense of the narrative voice, setting, and plot mechanisms she wishes to play out. "I go into a certain self-induced trance and write it until it's done."[32]

True to Emerson's precepts in "Self-Reliance," Robinson never despaired of being an author of more than one novel in the decades between *Housekeeping* and *Gilead*. Her courage and self-possession shine through her conviction during those years that "my greatest fear was that I would write a fraudulent book simply to escape the embarrassment of having written only one novel." Her absorption in *Mother Country* and *The Death of Adam* testify to the seriousness with which she took to nonfiction as a pursuit worthy of her best thinking, rather than a method by which to somehow retrieve her voice as a novelist. Indeed, nonfiction writing functioned as Robinson's real work during these intervening years, as the ardent activism of *Mother Country* and its ensuing international legal battle attest. This was a period during which she had "nothing fictional" on her mind, and thus "wrote a fair amount of nonfiction during those years" when she "was absorbed by that work." Hardly a means to an end, her nonfiction represents a body of work whose quality rivals that of her novels. Many novelists unaware of this activity have imbued *Gilead* with mythic status as evidence of its author's miraculous rebirth, "as if she had risen from the dead."[33] *Mother Country* stands as the greatest achievement of Robinson's career, in her estimation. "Writing nonfiction," she explains, "has been my most serious education, and for all those years kept me from even glancing in the direction of despair."[34] Her war with British industrialists for blighting the environment ranks among the boldest of Robinson's activist writing.

Courage Teacher

The ethic of courage, which set her at odds with the British government in *Mother Country* as well as atheist intellectuals in *The Death of Adam*, has been the linchpin of Robinson's success as both an author and a creative writing instructor. Appealing to her students as well as prominent readers such as Barack Obama, that principle of courage is rooted in combating the cultural predilection toward fear in all its manifestations, from xenophobia and homophobia to anti-gun control. Robinson's essay "Fear" examines the false equation between Christianity and patriotism made in headlines such as "Is Barack Obama a Christian?" She has staunchly opposed the tendency for Christianity to "become entangled with exactly the strain of nationalism that is militaristic, ready to spend away the lives of our young, and that can only understand dissent from its views as a threat or a defection, a heresy in the most alienating and stigmatizing sense of the word."[35] Like Emerson in his Harvard Divinity School address, she diagnosed the culture's malaise within the ideological locus of fear, a force that has not only inhibited self-expression of "unfashionable" ideas, but has created a tyranny of conformity to accepted topics and modes of articulation. Indeed, her editor laughed when she shared her plan to follow *Housekeeping*, a book she initially thought was too private to publish, with one "about a minister dying in Iowa in 1956," which was yet another story that "seems borderline incommunicable."[36] Although such subtle psychological drama is as introspective as it is devoid of external physical action, it still commands an impressive readership.[37]

Like Emerson, for Robinson the educational imperative is driven by dissent toward "the prohibitions of an unarticulated kind," ones "culturally felt that prevent people from saying what they actually think." The distance of the secular humanist environment has unleashed a deluge of interest on campus in Robinson's work. Students from faith-based backgrounds seek her out because of the inhibitions—indeed fear—they otherwise feel on campus in discussing the sacred in their studies and lives. Robinson finds her students are reticent to engage in larger questions of their place in the universe and, when they do, often avoid the difficult questions by leaning on superficial clichés. She notes that "Jewish or Catholic" students "can make all the jokes about their mother or the nun, but in terms of saying on one's deathbed, 'What will it mean that this is how I described myself, how does the cosmos feel as it nestles in my breast?' they are completely inarticulate about that."[38]

Robinson herself has never feared thinking on this cosmological scale, which is a key reason why her classes leaped in enrollment threefold since 2005. Her appeal to students derives not from a charismatic physical presence—her demeanor and temperament are instead those of a soft-spoken prophet—but from the quiet force of her conviction and expansive range of vision. Books she has taught typically function on an epic scale; *Moby-Dick* and the Bible have never been so popular among students as in the context of her courses. She is not a proselytizer for her own Congregationalist faith so much as a "courage-teacher," as Allen Ginsberg called Walt Whitman, actively pursuing her unique brand of mysticism.[39] Religion "helps you concentrate" by shielding out distractions, she asserts through the narrator of *Gilead*.[40] To her, those distractions are never more toxic than in popular media, particularly television. From her earliest days, she knew how to concentrate, carrying around a copy of *Moby-Dick* with her at the age of nine.[41] The contemplative life for her is a literary pursuit that, although solitary, brings companionship by accessing those people and entities not physically present, a process in which "writing felt like praying," as the protagonist in *Gilead* declares.[42]

Her pedagogical leanings parallel her own reading, which focuses on theology and science rather than contemporary literary fiction. Emerson was no different; he read very few novels by his contemporaries, but embraced the astronomy of Alexander von Humboldt.[43] Emerson viewed the stars as an extension of natural science much in the way Robinson does, particularly with an eye toward "the almost arbitrary given-ness of experience, the fact that nothing can be taken for granted." Herein lies the miraculous in which "everything is intrinsically mysterious as a physical object, or as a phenomenon of culture, or as an artifact of the history that lies behind it."[44]

This sort of mysticism that draws from the ontological world should not be confused with that which "diminishes what we know by every means that gives us access to it." Unmediated divine power, she urges, is always before us in "the simple spectacle—one actually quite complex—of what we are and where we are." She locates the miraculous in the everyday present, the beauty at the end of a splashing oar, and the vaulting ecstasy of Emerson's transparent eyeball fully suffused in nature. "One of the important things that happened to me" was her discovery as a child of "the wilderness around me" that "never felt like emptiness" but "always felt like presence." This early discovery of the sacred in nature never left her and has, as she says, "probably done as much to form my mind as anything." The key to such ecstatic moments of gnostic mysticism is an appetite and intensity that resolves to "never have the experience of banality," but to approach life "as if there was something extraordinary around me."[45]

The fear of identifying the good, Robinson has proposed, is a symptom of a collective skepticism raised as a deflective shield against commercial culture. "It's as if when you describe something good, you are being deceived or being deceptive," she points out, a condition of fearfulness that has removed us from the ecstatic mysteries around us.[46] Constantly armed with skepticism, we are unable to reach those euphoric moments, such as the one John Ames experiences at the conclusion of *Gilead*. "I love the prairie!" he exults, ecstatic in nature's power to reveal its divine energies. "So often I have seen the dawn come and the light flood over the land and everything turn radiant at once, that word 'good' so profoundly affirmed in my soul that I am amazed I should be allowed to witness such a thing." The ecstasy calls to mind Emerson overwhelmed by the beauty and power of nature, reveling in "almost a perfect exhilaration. Almost I fear to think how glad I am."[47] Like Emerson, Robinson voices through the character of Ames the insistence that the miraculous is not isolated to miracles chronicled by the prophets in the Bible, but vibrantly exists in the present moment. Orthodox Unitarians led by Norton Andrews deemed Emerson a heretic in the 1830s for claiming miracles to be omnipresent, especially in nature, rather than limited and isolated to those in the Bible described by Christ's prophets and disciples.[48] Ames saw a similar truth to the one Emerson observed, confessing that despite his training about the limitation of miracles to those witnessed by the prophets, and "for all I know to the contrary," the morning stars "still do sing and shout" as miracles in the living present.[49]

Robinson maintains that overexposure to popular culture breeds a disbelieving skepticism endemic to materialistic consumerism. At Iowa, she found the ideal location, "here on the prairie," as she says through Ames, where "there is nothing to distract attention from the evening and the morning," not unlike Thoreau at Walden Pond in his quiet sanctuary isolated from the distractions of "this restless, nervous, bustling trivial Nineteenth Century."[50] According to Robinson, situating oneself spiritually demands that there must be a "prevenient courage that allows us to be brave—that is, to acknowledge that there is more beauty than our eyes can bear, that precious things have been put into our hands and to do nothing to honor them is to do great harm."[51]

Robinson has gravitated toward popular science because it puts her in touch with the largest dimensions of thought and existence accessible to humanity. She has said that scientific writings, specifically of the cosmos, place her in the presence of thinking on such a grand scale. It takes bravery, she argues through the exalted final words of John Ames, to think on this scale. Iowa gave her that scale, a place to correspond her own life's purpose that "seems Christlike to be as unadorned as this place is, as little regarded." Her sentiments toward her own contemplative existence in Iowa are unmistakably apparent in Ames when he professes his love not only of the prairie, but for the tiny rural community where he has made a living. "I love this town," he proclaims, believing his own death will signify the commitment of his life to it, his final gift of "going into the ground here as a last wild gesture of love."[52]

In this sense, writing is not a cleverly aesthetic craft, but instead "testimony," a process of bearing witness with the courage to speak out on behalf of what one loves. Her Bible in this sense is a liberating force that unleashes inner individual power. As such, it can circulate as radical contraband for social justice not unlike its former function on the Underground Railroad. She reminds us of another historical period when the "Wycliffe Bibles and Tyndale Bibles, which you could be killed for owning" during the Protestant Reformation, "were circulated widely" as "very subversive" documents. Wycliffe was at the center of "an amazing attempt to spread literacy and scriptural understanding into the common world." Her eyes light up as she envisions "little Oxford students creeping out at night to take a page of Matthew to a hovel somewhere and tell someone what it actually said."[53] The role of the writer is to assume such courage to testify to one's devotion, as in her bold affront to the British government in *Mother Country*, the functional equivalent of a Wycliffe Bible.

Proudly Unfashionable

Robinson has assailed corporate media for hijacking the notion of popular culture from its original association with grassroots folk culture. To her, what used to be an organic expression of the populace is now "an industrial product that is sold by the means that any industrial product is sold by, and the selling is very intense because the people making the product are also in a position to sell the product—the media." She laments that too many writers are inclined "to push some extreme . . . to be more violent, be more sort of disrespectful of human life."[54] She blames larger industrial pressures for the more conspicuous literary figures engaged in this process, who might include Chuck Palahniuk (of "Guts," which appeared in *Playboy* in 2004), Bret Easton Ellis (of *American Psycho*), or T. C. Boyle (of "Drowning" in *Descent of Man*), contestants in a race, her point suggests, for the mantle of the most shocking. Yet harrowing scenes in her own novels offer shocking situations and characters, such as Doll's brutal upbringing of the title character in *Lila*, as well as the arresting blaze that culminates *Housekeeping*.

If "people are making culture for themselves," rather than producing literature for a market, they would be "sitting on the back porch singing a song that they maybe thought up the words for, and 200 years later people will be singing the same song." To engage in the type of production necessary to create works that "are truly popular" demands a unique discipline to shield out—to the extent that one can—the more virulent forces of media. This media condition is what Richard Lanham has called "the attention economy," in which "modern materialism turns out to be an intellectualized, spiritualized affair." Misplaced spiritual investment in mainstream media products is a result of what Marshall McLuhan predicted in 1959 would be the "chief business of the age."[55] Robinson points out that scandal on television is constantly vying for our attention, which advertisers value in the billions of dollars. "If something is supposed to be enormously scandalous, people will turn it on" to see if it really is, then "talk to each other" and gnaw on it "like chewing gum." In this sense popular culture to Robinson is a severe and "continuous distraction that carries people from day to day in no significant way," occupying valuable time and space that could instead be used "more imaginatively, more humanely."[56] Her critique, however, risks dismissing the totality of commercial media rhetoric, which she has directly benefited from through her own television appearances—in addition to those of her protégée Ayana Mathis on Oprah's cross-platform media empire—that operate at the intersection of entertainment and edification.

Her artisanal novels depicting pre-digital lives untouched by urban centers lend them an anti-materialistic quality that is not without its commercial appeal. In his interview with Robinson, Barack Obama commented that her writings appeal precisely because they exist outside the Twitter-driven sensationalist news cycle. He regretted how "my poor press team [is] tweeting every two minutes because something new has happened, which then puts a premium on the sensational and the most outrageous or a conflict as a way of breaking through the noise—which then creates . . . a pessimism from all those sturdy, quiet voices." In this sense, he takes solace in Robinson's novels for honoring the quiet voices that do not succumb to pessimism "in some quiet place" but who strive to "do something sensible and figure out how to get along." The resurgence of book clubs, Robinson points out, represents a way for readers to recover the literary life from the headline-driven circus of internet distractions. Gatherings to discuss "unfashionable" books like *Gilead* have created a critical mass—especially in the case of Robinson, who now trends on *Vogue* and *Vice*—that qualifies as popular. She has said that although "no book can sell in the way *Gone with the Wind* sold," the "literature at present is full to bursting . . . with an incredible variety of contemporary voices," including her own distinctly unfashionable one.[57]

Robinson's resistance to the tide of popular culture extends to her defense of humanities-based education against pressure to train the future American workforce for competition in the global economy. On a frosty December evening in 2015 at the Englert Theatre in Iowa City, she delivered a lecture titled "The American Scholar Now," which was billed as an appraisal of the current state of higher education in the spirit of Emerson's scathing jeremiad from 1837, "The American Scholar." Her aim, like Emerson's, was to "raise radical questions about the nature of education, culture and consciousness, and about their interactions" in order to diagnose how "there is a splendor inherent in human beings that is thwarted and hidden by a deprivation of the means to express it, even to realize it in oneself." An "unconscious surrender" to widespread conformity, especially to prevailing materialistic standards of traditional occupational aspiration, formed her main concern.[58]

Firmly in the role of Emerson, Robinson took direct aim at one of the guests of honor, Bruce Harreld, who was seated in the front row. Harreld had just been hired as the new president of the University of Iowa amid a firestorm of controversy. His appointment was unilaterally imposed by the regents despite the faculty's nearly unanimous opposition to it and ardent support of other viable candidates for the position. With no experience in university administration, Harreld, whose accomplishments exclusively lie in the business world as a corporate CEO and IBM executive, received vocal resistance from the university community. The faculty officially censured him and Workshop students joined the graduate employee union in a public statement claiming, "the hiring process was hijacked by the Board of Regents," which "underscores their view of the university as a business rather than an educational institution," a broader pattern Robinson's lecture later emphasized.[59]

In the lecture, published the following March in *Harper's* as "Save Our Public Universities," distinct echoes emerge of Robinson's admiration for midwestern universities' historic role as a counter to the slave economy. "If it seems to be failing now," the university system still maintains these seeds of hope in its original principles. The failure, she urged, was due to how administrators "have forgotten what the university is for, why the libraries are built like cathedrals and surrounded by flowers." Instead of "the stripping down of our society" and universities "for the purposes of our supposed economic struggle with the world" according to capitalist measures of prosperity, we need to see their future "as a tribute and an invitation to the young, who can and should make the world new, out of the unmapped and unbounded resource of the mind." The funneling of higher education into business imperatives appears in "the many fields that are influenced by economics, for example psychologies that subject all actions and interactions to cost-benefit analysis, to—the phrase should make us laugh—rational choice." This trend directly threatens creative writing, which "is utterly, hopelessly anomalous by these lights," prompting its practitioners "to run for cover to critical theory."[60]

A similar argument appears in "Humanism," her essay from 2015 in *The Givenness of Things*. In it, she more stridently laments how "we are less interested in equipping and refining thought, more interested in creating and mastering technologies that will yield measurable enhancements of material well-being—for those who create and master them at least." She deplores how "we are less interested in the exploration of the glorious mind, more engrossed in the drama of staying ahead of whatever it is we think is pursuing us," sentiments echoing Emerson's warning regarding the effects of capitalism's encroachment into intellectual culture.[61]

On a biographical level, Robinson's Emerson-inspired address lamented the imposition of the business world's economic standard on humanitarian intellectual culture as a way of offering her own appeal on behalf of the rural contemplative life. The measure of a university's "success in vaulting graduates into upper tiers of wealth and status" dangerously elides how "many of its best and brightest prefer a modest life in Maine or South Dakota, or in Iowa."[62] Education, she reminds us, thrives in such locations without the materialistic trappings and capitalist mentality of major urban centers. Her own career embodies how a thriving literary life is possible on the prairie she extols through the spiritually vital John Ames in the final pages of *Gilead*.

The closing appeal in Robinson's lecture echoed Emerson's emphasis in "The American Scholar" on the importance of higher education as a process of "exercising the highest functions of human nature."[63] The challenge she posed was "to find in oneself the grandeur that could make the world new" despite the current funneling of intellectual pursuits into economic models that too frequently results in an "unconscious surrender or failure to aspire."[64] Her transcendental measure of success directly challenges the financial one President Harreld represents. In 1837, one decade before the University of Iowa's founding, Emerson similarly exhorted his listeners to break from pressure to conform to conventional vocational aspiration inclined toward "a vulgar prosperity that retrogrades ever to barbarism" visible in the acquisitive pursuit of "display and immediate fame."[65] Robinson's opposition to the transformation of higher education into training for the future labor force resonates with Emerson's warning against the increasingly narrow specialization of the occupations. He sees this process in the reification of humanity into its tools of labor, whereby "the priest becomes a form; the attorney a statute-book; the mechanic, a machine; the sailor, a rope of a ship." Under these industrial circumstances, the American scholar becomes "a mere thinker" without action, "or still, worse, the parrot of other men's thinking."[66] For both Robinson and Emerson, the intrusion of the methods and objectives of business culture into the context of humanitarian education can stymie creative powers. This view counters Paul Engle's vision of acculturating Workshop students to the "delicate aggression" of the literary marketplace. Creativity might falter in an industrial setting, Emerson argued, due to "disgust for the principles on which business is managed," a condition liable to turn the most spirited minds "of the fairest promise" into "drudges" or make them "die of disgust."[67]

Discipline

The example of Robinson's own creative process—a rigorous isolated discipline galvanized against the distractions of popular culture—sets an imposing if not unreachable standard for her students, especially for those not sharing her solitary temperament. Many envy her almost monastic dedication to the literary life, one that harkens back to Flannery O'Connor's devotion to the craft. "I have this sense of urgency about what I want to get done," Robinson explains, "and I discipline myself by keeping to myself."[68] When faculty or students invite her to dinner or a social gathering, she typically demurs. "Lots of people go out to dinner after workshop," she said in 2004, with fifteen years' experience as a faculty member. "I have no small talk, none," she confessed, wincing at the thought of attending a social engagement with her colleagues.[69] Maggie Conroy, Frank Conroy's wife, provided much of her companionship over the years. Robinson spent an hour every evening on the phone with her mother until she passed away. Her social distance appears a factor of her intensely contemplative life.

The rigor of Robinson's instruction could be quite daunting to young writers. Reza Aslan, currently one of the world's foremost experts on Islam and Christianity, "went to the Workshop primarily to work with Marilynne Robinson, and I think of her as a genius." But once in her classroom, he became "very, very disappointed in her as a teacher," because "she doesn't have too much patience for those who deviate from what she has to say" and "doesn't appreciate experimentation in fiction at all." He speculated that her lack of encouragement derived from her own aesthetic, as seen in her "prose that's so polished and clean you could eat off it." He found her rigidity unbearable, pronouncing her "very closed off and very much living in the wrong century."[70] Robinson has explained her approach: "Through the discipline of introspection ... the mind—this deeper mind—makes selections on other terms than one's front-office mind," noting that the key to creative writing is "finding access to your life more deeply than you would otherwise."[71]

When pressed to describe precisely how students can develop their writing, Robinson stressed—in her uniquely Emersonian way—nonconformity to "the same dialect that is being spoken around them" according to the culture's prevailing literary conventions in both contemporary and classical fiction. Literary rebellion for its own sake she equates to "breaking China," a form of "being creative, when in fact it's as subservient to prevailing norms as ... obedience to them would be."[72] In "Diminished Creatures," an essay from 1999, Robinson laments the stultifying effects of the concept of genius represented in a pantheon of canonical literature. As in Emerson's "Representative Men," she objects "to the habit of treating such works as categorically different from anything we ourselves can aspire to." We "feel the thinking of Whitman and Dickinson," she argues, and in turn "they help us feel our own."[73]

The worst of student vices is "underachievement," according to Robinson, in the sense that one "has a good thing to give, but denies it." Students can find this expectation severely intimidating, especially when compounded by pressure to develop an uncanny "peripheral vision of the world" while not just revering classical literature, but regarding it as an attainable model for their own writing. Her bearing in class Micah Stack has described as "a beatific presence"; her vocabulary, according to Lan Samantha Chang, the current Workshop director and a former student of Robinson's, was arresting. Chang has "vivid memories of sitting in the classroom making lists of words that she used that were not typical," and "watching," awestruck, "her sentences fly through the air."[74]

Although Robinson purports to "do no harm," her student Thessaly Le Force explained while interviewing her professor: "There are times in workshop when you point out a fundamental problem with a story," administering a deft and fatal blow, whereby "the story can just lose its head." This was not just her own private impression, but one shared by the class in general: "We call it the guillotine." Le Force testified, "Intellectually, it's as if you pull the bottom out of a story and the whole thing falls away." Hearing this for the first time, Robinson took it as "a learning experience."[75] A similar sentiment overwhelmed Thoreau when his mentor Emerson directed him to feed the manuscript pages of his poetry into the fire, signaling the end of his poetic apprenticeship under the Concord sage.[76] While on one hand fulfilling the hardline Iowa tradition established by Paul Engle of caustic criticism toward student writing, Robinson has moved progressively in the classroom to dismantle the credos of "show don't tell," "write what you know," and "good characters are never interesting." Her against-the-grain approach to the literary marketplace un-teaches the presumption that successful student writing "must project forward the dominant styles and trends of the decade" if it is "to be published and acknowledged."[77]

Robinson stands out among Workshop faculty of the Frank Conroy era as the first to bring the Bible, God, and the writings of John Calvin, Herman Melville, and Ralph Waldo Emerson into the classroom. "These days people read the Old Testament, or the Hebrew Scriptures, to condemn them, if they read them at all," she notes.[78] Calvin enters her teaching the way he influences her writing, primarily as "a misunderstood humanist" with "secularizing tendencies," akin to the "celebrations of the human one finds in Emerson and Whitman."[79] Contemporary and ancient astronomy dramatize her conviction that "the place of humankind in such a universe is exalted."[80] For her, literatures of antiquity, Copernicus, Ptolemy, and Galileo showcase the universe, "the constant at work in it all." She is perhaps more blissfully out of touch with the latest trends in contemporary fiction and critical theory than any Workshop faculty member. Despite being one of the world's most renowned novelists, she confesses, her "favorite genre is not fiction."[81] By transforming fact and knowledge into faith and feeling, Robinson situates her work in relation to atmospheric science: "to take into account what is simply true, that the reality science describes, whether macrocosm or microcosm, is elegant, exuberant, fantastical, virtuosic."[82] She is curiously antique yet distinctly relevant to our modern culture in ways no literary agent would ever imagine possible, operating on a cosmic scale of existential significance worthy of Emerson himself.

14 • The Warrior: Anthony Swofford

There is a dark scene in *Jarhead*—Anthony Swofford's 2003 chronicle of the 1991 Gulf War later made into the blockbuster film that brought him acclaim—in which Swofford describes how he nearly committed suicide. The tableau depicts the Marine sniper "standing in the middle of my own barracks room, placing the muzzle of my M16 in my mouth and tasting the cold rifle metal and the smoky residue of gunpowder." He had just endured "a torturous thirteen weeks of bootcamp" during which he read his mother's letters, pondered the infidelity of his girlfriend back home, and sunk into despair. This "move toward my sister," whose serial suicide attempts and institutionalization for depression affected his formative years between the ages of twelve and fourteen, seemed inevitable. Justifications came with alarming ease. They included the broad "history of my family and of the species" along with more immediate "rumors of the enemy's superior fighting skills." Each was a mere tool of the suicide, which had taken on a life of its own. "The suicide's job," he realizes, is not "to *know*, only to *do*," a sentiment echoed by the poet Anne Sexton, who wrote that suicides are "Like carpenters," because "they want to know *which tools.*/ They never ask *why build.*"[1]

The legendary "pink mist" U.S. Marine Corps Surveillance and Target Acquisition Scout Snipers revere as the token of "a proper head shot" now threatens to become Swofford's own. Locked and loaded, his weapon is on "burst," which means it will send not one but three rounds through his head, leaving little chance for a botched effort. Just as he is about to obey the command of the suicide's will, his platoon mate Troy bursts through the door. Survival, in this case, is a matter of running, which Swofford does at the behest of his fellow Marine. Troy yanks the weapon away. "I need to go for a run," he says.

"You coming?"[2] The two venture out into the desert night, circling the base at its outer fringe, their boots slapping the sand rhythmically and their lungs filling with hot Saudi air.

Running with Troy is a ritual of survival, but one tinted with the dark realization that he could never outrun depression and suicidal impulses. Tellingly, the men do not run a linear route, but in circles, an apt metaphor for the cyclical nature of his disease. "We run in silence . . . and the hours pass, and even though we're going in circles," he begins to recover, feeling like he is "running away from whatever I left back in the barracks." But he soon realizes he is "swirling around the thing until it becomes part of the swirl, and the swirl becomes a part of me, and I'm still a part of that small sickness . . . but it no longer has me bent over at the waist, chewing the muzzle of my rifle." His bouts with the disease are not over. He fears "maybe someday in the future I will revisit the sickness, but for now I'm done with it."[3] In his 2012 memoir, he recounts another moment when he "sat on the couch for eight hours thinking about killing myself." He "had the rope and the sturdy beam, and any one of thousands of trees to choose from. But," in a more protracted and isolated trial than the kinetic aerobic ritual of survival he shared on his all-night run with Troy, he "chose to live."[4] At Iowa, he would learn to cast the experience as something wider than himself. His training had effectively prepared him to become the author of the definitive narrative of the Gulf War, the next volume in the annals of classic war literature after Tim O'Brien's *The Things They Carried.*

Carrying New Weight

It had been nearly a decade since Swofford had seen combat in Kuwait in the Gulf War when he unearthed his ruck, a case containing his belongings that accompanied him during the deployment. "After six or seven moves, and eight and a half years after [his] discharge," he dusted it off to inspect its contents. The things he carried during war he carried through community college in Sacramento, then to undergraduate school at UC Davis, and now to Iowa City and the famed Writers' Workshop. He did not have to carry these things with him, as many Marine veterans happily sold their rucks to any army/navy store for an easy profit of three hundred dollars cash, which to him at the time was "the equivalent of an outrageous bar tab." The economy of scale for an outrageous bar tab, however, would change dramatically soon after his graduation from the Workshop. The financial windfall occurred when *Jarhead* was published by Scribner and produced by Universal Pictures under the direction of Sam Mendes, whose *American Beauty* in 1999 won five Oscars. Swofford's skyrocketing fame and fortune in the wake of the critically acclaimed book and wildly popular film escalated his definition of an astronomical nightclub bill to five thousand dollars, the tab for one particularly raucous evening at a famous strip club in Las Vegas, as he confessed to his appalled father.[5] The escapade was one of many alcohol- and drug-fueled spending sprees that squandered a significant portion of his *Jarhead* earnings, as he described it later in *Hotels, Hospitals, and Jails: A Memoir*.

The thing Swofford carried to Iowa City in his ruck with the most potential value to him as a Workshop student was his war journal, a resource he knew would be invaluable in the development of his writing, one that might distinguish him from his talented and credentialed peers. Prior to the journal, Swofford's only other creative writing consisted of "bad poetry" that at this stage was worthless to him.[6] Pulling the journal from the bottom of the ruck beneath his gear, he was crushed to discover that its entries were "sort of scant."[7] Looking back in 1999 in earnest on a war that ended in 1991 would prove challenging indeed, especially with the intention of mining his memories for literary gold.

More than just his journal was slim. His former self was a lean twenty-year-old whose uniform he unearthed in Iowa. His camouflage issues seemed oddly foreign, like the clothes of another man entirely. They bore the marks of his experience in the desert, "ratty and bleached by sand and sun and blemished with the petroleum rain that fell from the oil-well fires in Kuwait." Standing in the basement of his rental house in Iowa City, he shed his civilian clothes to don the uniform once again, hoping to conjure the spirit of his military bearing. Stepping into the familiar pants that traveled the world with him, he realized that due to his sizable girth, "the waist stops at my thighs." The physical demands of his deployment that had him exercising thirty hours per week yielded a body that stood in sharp contrast to his current sedentary frame—"since I've been out, I've exercised about thirty hours a year"—turning the process into a comic struggle. "The blouse buttons, but barely." If he was to transform his time in Kuwait into literary art, neither his "journal with its sparse entries" nor his too-small cammies offered themselves as access points to his past. Both were too narrow. The process of retrieving his prior jarhead identity would prove more difficult than perusing a diary and donning the uniform he wore when he scribbled his elliptical entries in it. "I am after something. Memory, yes. A reel. More than just time."[8]

His chronicle had been years in the making: "I've been working toward this—I've opened my ruck and now I must open myself."[9] Swofford told me, "I started writing *Jarhead* the day after I graduated from the Workshop," after focusing exclusively on fiction for two years. "But I'd written two hundred thousand words under the tutelage of" Frank Conroy, Chris Offutt, and Joy Williams at the Workshop. "Under them," he explained, "I had learned the art of prose storytelling." From writings completed for the Iowa MFA, "I pulled one eight-page chunk of autobiographical USMC boot camp stuff from my thesis and dropped it into the *Jarhead* manuscript."[10]

Searching elsewhere in the ruck, Swofford began to piece together the documents and artifacts, particularly the letters that might spark his memory. In the 1960s, Kurt Vonnegut had no ruck to rummage through when he began assembling materials in Iowa City for *Slaughterhouse-Five*, his book about military service and surviving the Dresden bombings during World War II. But as with Swofford, the resource Vonnegut expected to be most valuable—in his case interviews with friends and war buddies in Europe and the U.S. who had survived the ordeal—profoundly disappointed him, leaving him to his experience and memory, the only resources he could trust. When Vonnegut consulted with a Hollywood producer about the prospects of his idea becoming a bestselling novel and subsequent film, he was admonished for his attempts to write an "anti-war book." "Why don't you write an *anti-glacier* book instead?" the producer quipped.[11]

For Swofford, the industry for war literature and film in the twenty-first century had advanced beyond Vonnegut's mid-twentieth-century norm of uniformly heroic pro-war narratives. Vonnegut was taking a radically unique perspective on World War II from the point of view of those on the ground beneath an Allied air raid, revealing that the Axis powers were not the only ones capable of raining hellfire on civilians in lyrical towns of storybook beauty like Dresden. Swofford also disrupts expectations for traditional war narrative. As the critic Jon Robert Adams astutely observes, *Jarhead* "presents the soldier's experience of war as *not* matching civilian expectations of what makes a man," particularly by requiring "them to see those they would call heroes as deeply troubled by their war experiences; as soldiers wounded in the heart; as whiners justified in complaining."[12] Swofford attests that service can leave veterans with "cheap, squandered lives" and little hope for eternal peace, for "more bombs are coming."[13] Just after the appearance of *Jarhead*, Swofford made his pacifist stance even more explicit. He characterized Operation Iraqi Freedom as "America's ill-advised and corrupt war," confessing that he fully regretted enlisting in Operation Desert Shield. Long before the internet and Wikileaks, when Swofford first joined the Marines in 1988 just two years before the launch of Desert Shield, he had little access to data detailing the violence, corruption, and atrocity of war. With such information, he "might have gone to college at eighteen rather than having signed the [Marine Corps] contract." His signature embroiled him in a political quagmire reminiscent of Vietnam, only this time fought in the name of large multinational corporate oil interests, an imbroglio he calls the "South*west* Asia" conflicts that would later include Operation Desert Storm.[14]

For the literary Swofford to don the subjectivity of his unlettered warrior self was a daunting challenge, especially since his ambition was to achieve nothing less than the definitive chronicle of the Gulf War. *Jarhead* therefore deploys an astonishing range of voices and perspectives, from political analysis, introspective psychology, and anthropological profiling to profane colloquialism. The text functions at once as personal memoir revealing his deepest vulnerabilities, from incontinence to attempted suicide, while also forwarding a forceful argument on behalf of enlisted soldiers subjugated to political conflicts directed by government officials who will never see action. Like the soldier Kropp in Erich Maria Remarque's *All Quiet on the Western Front*, who envisions an alternative to war whereby the leaders of nations battle one another in giant stadiums to settle their disputes, Swofford similarly voices his dissent toward the military-industrial complex that has thrown him into this predicament in the first place. Kropp, like Swofford, is a "thinker" who proposes that a declaration of war should require "the ministers and generals of the two countries, dressed in bathing drawers and armed with clubs [to] have it out among themselves. Whoever survives, his country wins," he suggests, reasoning, "this would be much simpler and more just than this arrangement where the wrong people do the fighting."[15]

By contrast, the lean young Swofford was gung-ho, primed by the inadvertently pro-war Vietnam films *The Deer Hunter* and *Apocalypse Now*, which the troops watch together in a beer-drenched frenzy. As he told the *Daily Iowan* just after the publication of *Jarhead*, "I wanted to run around and see the world and learn how to kill people."[16] Operation Desert Shield was ostensibly billed as a mission "to protect, to shield Saudi Arabia and her flowing oil fields" from encroaching Iraqi forces. Their commander charges the troops to "shield enough oil to drive hundreds of millions of cars for hundreds of millions of miles, at a relatively minor cost to the American consumer." The troops "joke about having transferred from the Marine Corp to the Oil Corp, or the Petrol

Battalion." But Swofford observes a deeper psychological function behind their drollery, particularly how "we laugh to obscure the comedy of combat and being deployed to protect oil reserves and the rights and profits of certain American companies, many of which have direct ties to the White House." Behind this is a web of "oblique financial entanglements with the secretary of defense, Dick Cheney, and the commander in chief, George Bush, and the commander's progeny." To the troops on the ground "who will fight and die," the "outcome of the conflict is less important" than it is "for the old white" billionaires who have tremendous amounts of capital "to gain or lose in the oil fields, the deep, rich, flowing oil fields of the Kingdom of Saud."[17]

Such incisive analysis reflects how the literary Swofford of Iowa City in 2001 carried considerably more ideological weight than his former warrior self. His cynicism at the age of twenty was a stripped-down version of this powerful combination of bitterness and disillusionment that crystallized over time on the political motives behind Operation Desert Shield. Writing in *Slate* after the film release of *Jarhead* in 2005, Nathaniel Fick affirmed the veracity of the cinematic depiction of the grunts' perception of the political strategizing by the "bureaucrats [who] have a lot of jawboning to do" safe behind lines. "When discussion in the movie turns to whether war is just a bid for oil," Fick writes, "one Marine turns to his buddies and says, 'F— politics. We're here. All the rest is bullsh—.' " To Fick, who served in Kuwait in 2003, "this rings true," because "Marines don't pick their battles." This sense of futility in being captive to the will of government officials renders troops' discussion and activity on the battlefield apolitical. Since any sort of activism or protest—aside from the rash option of outright mutiny—is pointless for modern soldiers deployed in the Middle East, their lives become a waiting game of psychological preparation for conflict. The endless hours are filled not with earnest political debate, but with "silly formations, reckless football games, and endless conversations about girls left behind."[18] Any inclination toward critically analyzing their predicament is neutralized or disengaged altogether by the immediate threat of facing the enemy in combat.

If the lean Tony on the front lines had no time for politics in the social milieu of his fellow Marines, the ample one brought the full weight of his sizable literary training and sophisticated frame of reference to bear on the subject. As a Workshop student writing fiction in 1999, Swofford explored the outer dimensions of the military experience considered taboo or off-limits at the turn of the twenty-first century. He freighted his memory with the weight of literary allusion, as seen in the epigraph from Arthur Rimbaud's "A

Season in Hell" for his 2001 MFA thesis: "I called to my executioners to let me bite the ends of their guns, as I died. I called to all plagues to stifle me with sand and blood."[19] Rimbaud sounds the keynote for his rebellion against the military-industrial complex in this collection of short stories. The stories dramatize the broad spectrum of tortured inner lives represented in the Marine Corps, from a homosexual recruit to an aging veteran who hungers to return to action.

The critical dimension of Swofford's writing during this period appears to have been lost on *Jarhead* screenwriter William Broyles, Jr., who showed little interest in conveying Swofford's bitter invective. "Our story" as depicted in the film "is apolitical," according to Broyles. "It's about young men who join the Marine Corps to find a place for themselves in life."[20] Swofford's story is instead a complex revelation of the struggle for status among the troops based on killing a hostile enemy, a quest whose intensity is inversely proportionate to their concern for the larger political purpose of the war. The "wreck in your head" in the aftermath of war is the willingness "to go back in time, back to the Desert for the chance to kill. You consider yourself less a Marine and even less of a man for not having killed while at combat." This distinction, more than any other form of service by way of saving comrades, surviving a severe wound, or executing a winning strategy or tactical maneuver on the battlefield, "means everything."[21] Swofford's revelation is that he was a killing machine who did not kill. A commanding officer had opted to call in air strikes rather than allow him his chance at validation as a true Marine. This meant the war for him, as for so many other Marines, was akin to playing the role of the hobos in Samuel Beckett's play *Waiting for Godot:* all preparation, anticipation, and no action. The final words before the curtain, "Yes, let's Go." The stage direction: *They do not move.*[22]

Privileged Observer

Among the outpouring of critical acclaim for *Jarhead* that flooded the press after its publication in 2003, one of the most precise insights came from Martin Amis, the writer and son of the world-renowned English novelist and critic Kingsley Amis. Perched atop the world of contemporary literature as one of its most trusted arbiters, Amis steered away from the sort of praise for the book that typically situated it among the classics of war literature, from Homer's *Iliad* to *The Things They Carried.* Instead, he situated the book as a "work of reportage from a 'privileged' observer"—his scare quotes indicating an irony that resonates with Swofford's deeply critical stance toward the Marines. In that nonfiction genre, Swofford displays "genuine talent," according to Amis.[23] Immersive journalism has been a mainstay of Swofford's writing, a strong suit that has served him far better than his forays into fiction.

Jarhead "deserves its acclaim," as one reviewer wrote, especially for its capacity to connect personal experience to the broader industrial context, such as troop deployments and the price of oil: "By late September, the American troop count in Saudi reached 150,000 and the price of crude oil has nearly doubled."[24] Such claims combined with detailed testimony about dysfunctional equipment, abuse from commanding officers, and inhumane treatment to prompt the U.S. Marine Corps to issue an official statement, proclaiming, "the movie's script is an inaccurate portrayal of Marines in general and does not provide a reasonable interpretation of military life."[25] If *Jarhead*'s politics are any indication, such condemnation from the Marine Corps Office of Public Affairs was a badge of honor to Swofford, whose work was admired for its journalistic cunning.

Exit A, Swofford's first and only novel that followed *Jarhead* in 2007, on the other hand, "deserves no acclaim" according to William T. Vollmann, reviewing the book for the *New York Times*, because "it doesn't convey life vividly or believably," and most damningly, it lacks the journalistic yet deeply connected criticism of *Jarhead* that transcends conventional memoir. Critics registered shock at Swofford's hollow and clichéd writing in *Exit A*. Where was the privileged observer, reviewers wondered, and his anthropological angle of vision that could capture and define an entire military culture and the fine gradations of each of its subcultures? As Vollmann diagnosed the problem: "It analyzes nothing. Whatever distinctions and connections it makes remain superficial at best." Its prose, he argued, "befits a Harlequin romance novel," rather than functioning, according to its publicity announcements, as "confirmation of Swofford as a major literary talent."[26]

Exit A is an attempt to extend and amplify a touching scene in *Jarhead* depicting Swofford's tryst with an Okinawa restaurant owner's daughter named Yumiko. This is Swofford writing relationships and erotica at his best. In the sleepy seaside town of Naha, where the lovers conduct an affair despite her having a local boyfriend, we hear of them snorkeling in "the ocean blue like a welder's flame" and making love in "her father's three-cylinder Suzuki van" to aromas of "burnt engine oil and seaweed" and "the slow slap of the ocean on dark volcanic rocks." On his last night on the island before permanently shipping off the base, Yumiko sneaks into his private barracks. The scene is as painful as it is beautiful, a lyrical aubade lamenting the arrival of dawn. "As the sun broke into the barracks, we wept, and she kissed my chest softly."[27]

The unexpected strength of romance writing in the range of skills displayed in *Jarhead*, however, was lost on some readers. In particular, Elisabeth Piedmont-Marton's "Gulf War Memoir Syndrome" alleged that *Jarhead* was falsely canonized. Piedmont-Marton narrowed her sights specifically on the sniper's Gulf War memoir. Among her most damning comments were that his writing struck her as "MFA-ish and sometimes gratuitously swaggering and crude" with its "derivative and self-involved" narrative voice. This was in direct opposition to critics like Michiko Kakutani of the *New York Times* and literary gatekeepers like Mark Bowden, the author of *Black Hawk Down*. Piedmont-Marton considered their overblown praise "to participate more in a discourse of desire" for the book's success "than a discourse of critique."[28] That discourse of desire, academic Jon Robert Adams argues, is tantamount to a larger cultural desire for closure to the Vietnam syndrome, which is known as the malaise of engaging in a series of unwinnable conflicts with no measurable progress. Adams points out that the desire to find literariness where it does not exist in *Jarhead* places the text "in a literary lineage of great war literature—literature that's ostensibly written only about great wars."[29] According to this argument, to canonize Swofford is to transform the Persian Gulf War of 1991 into a great war, and therefore one that American culture can understand as a resolution to a worthwhile conflict. But neither the text of *Jarhead* nor its political impact on the Marine Corps, as evidenced in its public condemnation of the film, bears this out.

The ideological and cultural purposes of Swofford's canonization notwithstanding, there remains a serious question of the unanimous praise that seems to have created a feeding frenzy based on the endorsement of several key gatekeepers to war classics. In particular, Bowden, in a review conspicuously titled "The Things They Carried," heralded the book as "some kind of classic . . . that will go down with the best books ever written about military life." The essay's title, of course, implies that Swofford is the heir to Tim O'Brien while also appropriating Vietnam paradigms for his canonization.[30] Kakutani was even more explicit in ranking *Jarhead* among the greatest war narratives of all time, describing it as "a book that combines the black humor of *Catch-22* with the savagery of *Full Metal Jacket* and the visceral detail of *The Things They Carried*."[31]

What much of this critical discourse in the initial reception of *Jarhead* reveals is a neglect of the category of privileged observer within the genre of literary journalism. Piedmont-Marton's accusation of MFA-ish writing breaks down under close scrutiny, especially in light of the unique trio of instructors, Frank Conroy, Chris Offutt, and Joy Williams, who trained Swofford at Iowa. Her objection to his "crude gratuitous swagger," further, reveals a blindness to its function as a crucial element of *Jarhead*'s narrative persona, one that reveals Marine attitudes and mores. This almost anthropological level of insight into the culture of military life is potent precisely because of its capability to demonstrate that swaggering bravado—and the vulnerabilities beneath it.

Swofford's tutelage under Conroy was pivotal in the development of his understanding of the memoir's generic affinity with literary journalism from the vantage point of the privileged observer and ethnographer. Conroy, who was director of the Workshop when Swofford attended as a student, had also ascended to fame in his early thirties with a debut memoir that placed him at the forefront of the genre. Conroy's *Stop-Time*, like *Jarhead*, received enough "fame and credibility [that] stemmed from the 1967 memoir" to last his entire career.[32] Swofford would spend years just as Conroy did struggling to regain his literary voice. But what he learned from Conroy at the Workshop was a respect for *Stop-Time*'s accomplishments, particularly its unflinching depiction of an absentee alcoholic father and painful upbringing by an itinerant mother who fell in with a drifter. As an instructor, "Frank's decorous spine controlled the modes and moods of the room," Swofford told me. His course had such a profound impact on his creative development that, he confessed, "I still have the yellow pad that I took notes on for his workshop. I reread it a few times a year" to revisit to the core principles of "the art of storytelling" as he learned them from this "master teacher."[33]

With Conroy on his MFA thesis committee, Swofford's supervisor of the project was Chris Offutt. Offutt's disarming and affable bearing in the classroom was the opposite of Conroy's intimidating tactics and Joy Williams's exacting, intensely professional workshops. Williams was notorious for running "her workshops as though she were a NY editor who'd never met the writer who had tossed a manuscript through the transom," Swofford recalled in an interview with me. Although "a few egos were battered" in her workshop, he was convinced it was worth having "that mind working on one's writing." Offutt's class was a collaborative and upbeat exchange, by comparison, with the instructor providing "a bottomless well of enthusiasm for the truly crazy attempt we were all making at becoming working writers." Reflecting back, he realized Offutt had "played a pedagogical trick on us by letting us think we were his peers, and thus raising the bar to heights we might not otherwise have reached." Swofford benefited from "his attention to story, world, and word discipline" in ways he had not anticipated.[34]

Offutt's mentorship of Swofford at Iowa from 1999 to 2001 is thus a curious pairing. Where precisely would a Kentucky-raised graduate of Morehouse State with no military experience overlap in Swofford? At first glance, Offutt's work bears little relevance to Swofford's interest in transmuting his Gulf War experience into literary narrative. When Swofford first met him in Iowa City, Offutt had published the regional short story collections *Kentucky Straight* (1992) and *Out of the Woods* (1999) and the memoir *The Same River Twice* (1993). His next memoir, *No Heroes*, was in progress when he was mentoring Swofford at the Workshop. Beside his collegial approach to teaching, how could Offutt's nostalgic naturalism in his celebrations of his Kentucky home— "When I feel lonely, I go to the woods . . . that's shagbark hickory my favorite tree . . . I got a little bit of owl in me"—have been the guiding force behind Swofford's magnum opus?[35]

Offutt himself was a privileged observer of his own father's career as a mass market writer of pornographic novels. Swofford's MFA thesis, "Escape and Evasion," is rife with raw sexuality that challenged the program's relatively liberal standards. The Workshop historically had been open to erotic detail in student writing, with some instructors even teaching its proper technique, as in R. V. Cassill's own interest in literary erotica. Offutt's *New York Times* feature, "My Dad, the Pornographer," is a frank disclosure of his publication of licentious literature bearing such titles as "Bondage Babes" and "Sex Toys" with Greenleaf and Orpheus in the 1960s and Grove Press in the 1970s and 1980s. Totaling more than four hundred novels, his work even included an erotic comic titled *Valkyria*. Offutt's father wrote "pirate porn, ghost porn, science fiction porn, vampire porn, historical porn, time-travel porn, secret agent porn, thriller porn, zombie porn, and Atlantis porn."[36] It seemed that there was nothing Offutt had not seen from an insider's vantage point in the world of forbidden fiction by the time he began mentoring Swofford.

Director's Cut

Sexuality abounds in the fiction Swofford wrote for his MFA thesis. It is a violent weapon in the hands of a predatory homosexual named PFC Brockner in the title story "Escape and Evasion." The story of the fictional Ether Bandit serial rapes that take place on a Marine base is told from two alternating perspectives split between Brockner's psychopathic sadistic rendition and Sergeant Savine's narrative. Savine is ostensibly the voice of heterosexual normativity, a leader of a sniper unit like Swofford's USMC Surveillance and Target Acquisition/Scout Sniper platoon. As an extension of Swofford himself, he is written sympathetically in blunt contrast to Brockner, who is a savage preying on a series of young Marines he systematically stalks, etherizes, and violates. Gritty and nearly unbearable scenes of bloody rapes fill the story, which begins with the cracked Brockner fantasizing about forcing himself on his recruiting officer after being asked the requisite questions for new enlistees at the time: "Do you now or have you ever had homosexual tendencies? Are you now or have you ever been engaged in a homosexual relationship?" His unspoken response is that he "will gladly take you back to the head, the head as you call it, and show you" that homosexual sex "is not necessarily a relationship and absolutely more than a tendency."[37] Such screening for homosexuality, according to Swofford's narrative logic, is entirely justified to prevent the entrance of such toxic individuals into the military. After Savine and his men follow the trail of the brutal attacks on innocent young recruits, they retaliate by accosting Brockner and allowing his victims to exact their gruesome revenge with a flashlight that leaves him "a mess, blood and muscle tissue exploding from his insides out." Brockner is depicted as taking perverse pleasure in the attack. Savine prevents him from hemorrhaging to death by applying "a pressure bandage to his wound and injecting him in the hip with two morphine syrettes." The twist ending depicts Brockner recovering in the infirmary and finding his name on "the Division crime blotter as another victim of the Ether Bandit."[38] The counter-assault therefore backfires, as the real Ether Bandit, who epitomizes the view of homosexuality as a toxic threat in the military, thus lives on safely disguised as a victim in the unit.

Offutt, having grown up in an environment of radical tolerance and no-holds-barred experimentation in literary sexuality, was perhaps the most likely of any Workshop faculty member to condone Swofford's overtly homophobic story, which formed the culminating project of his Workshop training. Swofford's MFA thesis reads like the director's cut of *Jarhead*, venturing into territory Hollywood never would have. Indeed, it is telling that the title story in his MFA thesis, "Escape and Evasion," appeared in *Sex for America: Politically Inspired Erotica* (edited by Stephen Elliot) in 2008, just one year after Swofford's foray into romantic genre fiction in *Exit A*. Viewing the film *Jarhead* in 2015 in Iowa City, Swofford remarked, "the thing that shocked me about watching the film just now, having not seen it in a decade, was just how sexist and homophobic the world was." On the one occasion where Swofford has differentiated his book from the film, which he otherwise typically praises for its fidelity, he insisted, "I'm pretty sure my book isn't that sexist and homophobic." It is ironic that he would find "there's something about seeing the rendering of it on film that felt . . . dangerous and unsavory," especially since those words apply equally to the politics and aesthetics of his own MFA thesis.[39]

Swofford returned to the Workshop as an instructor in 2007 after two years as a celebrity in the media spotlight. In the wake of the film, he received more critical acclaim and toured the television talk show circuit, including an appearance on *The Daily Show with Jon Stewart* in April 2003. In April 2016, he told me that when he "taught at the Workshop in 2007 shortly after Sam [Lan Samantha Chang] took over the directorship," he was afforded a unique "perspective on the generational and cultural shift" that took place between his cohort at the end of the Frank Conroy era and the new one under Chang. He characterized the change in leadership as progressive, and "important if one is to consider the history of the Workshop and the idea of it moving forward."[40] Workshop secretary Connie Brothers, who had been in the main office for several years before Conroy arrived, confirmed the sentiment, noting that many minority and women writers in the program had distinct disadvantages during the Conroy era. She remembered Swofford as a "wonderful addition" to the Workshop since he had "just come back from fighting in the Gulf War," and was "working on a nonfiction book."

Swofford may have been working on a nonfiction memoir, but his MFA thesis consisted of short stories, ones nonetheless containing eight pages that went directly into *Jarhead*. In the mid-1990s, the second major nonfiction writer, John D'Agata, was admitted by Jorie Graham into the poetry Workshop, where he took courses while enrolled in Iowa's nonfiction writing program. Conroy's own masterpiece *Stop-Time*, it should be remembered, is nonfiction but "reads like a novel," as Brothers observed.[41] Stephen Bloom, an Iowa journalism professor and Conroy's friend who shared a booth with him most afternoons at the Chesapeake Bagel Company in downtown Iowa City, said, "the book was the best kind of fiction because it was numbingly true."[42] Conroy, one learns in *Stop-Time*, was an abused child who endured bizarre and brutal treatment at the hands of his deranged father.

When Conroy arrived at the Workshop in 1977–1978, he hardly took the program by storm. "He had never taught before and was feeling insecure about it," Brothers recalled. It was not until years later, after he returned in 1987 to take over as director, that he allegedly drove one student to tears and made another faint with his vitriolic criticism during two particularly spirited workshop sessions. But Brothers qualifies the legend by pointing out that the student who collapsed had been to the dentist earlier in the day, and was "still feeling a little woozy" from the medication. "When her story [for workshop] came out, he probably said something quite harsh, and she did faint," Brothers confirmed. Conroy was chosen over several candidates for the directorship mainly on the strength of his work as an administrator with the National Endowment for the Humanities literature division. He remained as director for the next eighteen years, until his death in 2005. "What's important about the Workshop is who is admitted, and who you get to teach," Brothers observed. "Frank was excellent at choosing who to admit, and was amazing at selecting faculty. Strong students and teachers create success that reproduces itself." A major strength was his connection to the publishing industry. Conroy's "strong opinions" during workshop sessions meant that if a story came up "and he hated it, and he said it, the result definitely damaged some people, because they thought they were tougher than they were." She went on to explain, "if you write something from your soul, and somebody tells you it isn't good enough, it can't help but hurt you. Some people thrived on that atmosphere and some people didn't."[43] Swofford, who had survived boot camp, was one of the students who thrived in this environment.

Swofford in fact appreciated the discipline Conroy emphasized, noting how he "always ran professional and polite workshops that had only one concern: the quality of the writing."[44] According to the old Paul Engle approach to creative writing pedagogy, Conroy was convinced only strict and severe discipline could lead to that quality. Swofford recalled Conroy saying "on the first day that writing was about character and that character was wrapped in discipline." He explained, "For Frank, character was sitting at the computer or with that yellow pad until you were totally exhausted," a view of the creative process as necessarily laborious and painstaking.[45] This approach to literary production as a torturous trial of self-sacrifice only increased students' psychological and emotional investment in their writing, correspondingly heightening the damage suffered and losses incurred by the barbs they received during workshops.

Attending the Workshop with Swofford and writing under Conroy's supervision in the late 1990s was Reza Aslan, currently a professor of creative writing at UC Riverside. Speaking at the famous Prairie Lights Bookstore in Iowa City on April 7, 2005, one day after Conroy had passed away, Aslan told of how he was actively recruited, or perhaps poached, by the director. "This is exciting work, young man," Conroy said in a low growl, his voice rough from

decades of cigarettes and Scotch. Aslan's fiction had exceeded his expectations. When Aslan enrolled and attended his first workshop with Conroy, he
thus volunteered to be the first to put up his work, submitting the exact same
piece that Conroy had found so brilliant. Terribly underestimating his new
mentor, Aslan assumed the piece would be praised since "he had already
given it his blessing," leading him to believe "I was the pet." "So I turned it in
with all confidence." What he received was "two and a half hours of abuse, I
mean the *worst* kind of abuse." Aslan explained, "he absolutely *destroyed* this
text, at one point—and I'm not making this up—he actually started reading
passages in a funny voice to emphasize how *bad* my writing was." He joked
that unlike one infamous student, he "managed not to faint," but still felt
"tricked" and "bamboozled." Conroy later asked him "how I liked my first
workshop experience," a kind of baptism by fire. Aslan, trying to put on a
brave face, "lied and said 'oh, it was great, I learned a lot!' " Conroy said, "I've
been doing this for twenty years. I know who's got it and who doesn't. You've
got it, but the problem is you don't know how to write." Aslan said, "he was
right. And in the next thirteen weeks he taught me absolutely *everything* I
know about writing."[46]

Conroy's salty classroom demeanor should not overshadow how consistently he fought for and defended his students. Pinckney Benedict, for example, earned the James Michener Award for 1988–1989, an esteemed distinction
that granted $7,000 paid out in monthly installments for one year beginning
in September 1989. The stipulation, Conroy made clear, was that he must re-
side in Iowa City and "not take other employment, and teaching in particular
is out, while you hold the fellowship."[47] Benedict did precisely that when he
realized that the grant's monthly payments of a paltry $583 could barely sus-
tain him. Once Michener himself discovered that Benedict had taken a teaching job at the Hill School, a private boarding academy for ninth through
twelfth grade, he became livid. "Laboring through the third version" of his
current manuscript, Michener found it particularly irksome to "compare my
very hard work with his teaching in a school for the sons of millionaires,"
something that "struck me as so out of proportion that I had to protest to Nelson, our money watchdog."[48] Conroy promptly replied with a gracious mea
culpa, apologizing that such an egregious indiscretion "happened on my
watch," and offering to return the grant. With tact and diplomacy, he assured
Michener's watchdog Nelson that his student Benedict "feels bad about the
situation, and would, I'm sure, return the Michener-Copernicus money over
time if so directed, although it might take quite a while."[49] Based on such a

compelling appeal and forthright confession, Michener took his cue from Conroy to assume the role of the gentleman patron and assured him that "certainly Benedict should not even think of returning the money," instead suggesting he should pass along the proceeds "when he's hit a big novel" to benefit "those about to make the same effort."[50]

Life After *Jarhead*

The progressive cultural shift marked by Lan Samantha Chang's directorship in the wake of the Conroy era seemed ahead of Swofford's gender politics, at least as portrayed in the pages of *Exit A*. The *Daily Iowan* criticized those politics in the novel's hypermasculine protagonist Severin Boxx, "the son of a colonel, resident of Yokota military base, and star linebacker of his high school football team." These details prompted the reviewer to ask sarcastically, "masculinity anyone?" In addition, the novel played into the romance genre for women readers so stereotypically that it appeared the author "forgot to make his characters human," in what reads like "a recycled romance movie," a point also made in Vollmann's *Times* review. The *Daily Iowan* review appeared on the day of his scheduled reading and signing for *Exit A* at the Prairie Lights Bookstore. "If you happen to attend" the reading, the reviewer snidely suggested, "patiently wait through the sections of *Exit A*. Then raise your hand and politely ask him to read something from *Jarhead*."[51]

As of recently, Swofford was in the process of relocating to the West Coast after several years raising his new family in New York.[52] His career hangs in the balance, but promises new ventures given the vibrant multimedia landscape. Television and film projects are in the offing, and his marriage to Christa Parravani has yielded several opportunities for professional collaboration. He contributed to Parravani's reading event, for example, for her powerful memoir titled *Her* about the loss of her identical twin sister.[53] His legacy with the Workshop remains that of a warrior-author at the turn of the twenty-first century, a product as much of Frank Conroy's embattled classrooms as the battlefields of Kuwait. Swofford's epigraph in *Hotels* most poignantly captures the heaving tumult of a reception that canonized him in the early 2000s and crucified him by the end of the decade and into the next. Thomas Bernhard's words epitomize his career: "War is the poetry of men, by which they seek to gain attention and relief throughout their lives."[54] War, poetry, and attention continue to be the heaviest things he carries on his path—in literature and life—toward the relief of ever elusive peace.

15 • The Voice: Ayana Mathis and Mass Culture

Harpo, the multiplatform billion-dollar entertainment production company, is a palindrome for Oprah. Although the company may not appear to bear the name of Oprah Winfrey—the most significant force behind the migration of literature into popular culture—its ethos and brand values mirror the identity of the former daytime talk show host who runs its operations. With each recommendation for her book club accounting for more than one million additional copies sold, "The Oprah Effect" (also known as the "Oprah bump") creates instant bestsellers.[1] In 2007, *Business Week* reported that, for driving book sales, "no one comes close to Oprah's clout: Publishers estimate that her power to sell a book is anywhere from 20 to 100 times that of any other media personality."[2] Her sway over a massive audience has given her a profound literary influence, as Ayana Mathis discovered one brilliant autumn afternoon in Paris in early October 2012, when her mobile phone rang.

It was a request for an interview, and it initially struck Mathis as an onerous task, especially on the first clear day of her vacation after a solid week of rain. Her agent, Ellen Levine, advised her to prepare for a call at two in the afternoon. Although the thirty-nine-year-old Iowa Writers' Workshop graduate from 2011 knew that an interview with *O, The Oprah Magazine* might expose her new novel, *The Twelve Tribes of Hattie*, to a large number of readers, she asked if it could wait, especially if the editor only "needed a quote" that might take "fifteen minutes."[3] She had not considered that the popular magazine was the most successful startup ever in the industry, turning a $140 million profit in just the first two years of its existence.[4] Her attention, instead, was fixed on sightseeing with her partner under the bright Parisian sky. But the magazine's editor insisted. By two o'clock, Mathis had hurried back inside, but "the phone didn't ring." She opened her laptop and glanced at the time. At 2:12, the phone rang. "Can I speak to Ayana Mathis?" the voice inquired. "Yeah," she blurted out, unable to mask her impatience. Then, in a calm measured tone, the voice replied, "This is Oprah Winfrey."[5]

Mathis immediately took it as a ruse, flatly replying, "No, it isn't." The voice insisted, "No, no it is, it's Oprah Winfrey."[6] The request for a short interview with an editor for O, The Oprah Magazine had been a setup to enable Winfrey to break the life-changing news herself. The Twelve Tribes of Hattie had been selected for Oprah's Book Club 2.0, Winfrey's revamped multimedia reading group that launched in 2012, following the cancellation of The Oprah Winfrey Show along with its associated book discussion club after a fifteen-year run from 1996 to 2011. Oprah's Book Club 2.0, which adopted as its first title Cheryl Strayed's Wild: From Lost to Found on the Pacific Crest Trail, operates as a joint venture of the Oprah Winfrey Network (OWN) and O, The Oprah Magazine, leveraging social media platforms and producing special e-reader editions of its adopted texts. Through early 2013, Mathis was treated to a book launch unmatched by any faculty or graduate of the Iowa Writers' Workshop, one propelled by the twenty-first century's most powerful amplifier of literary talent. But what remained to be seen was whether the packaging and branding of Mathis for mass consumption—which she found at times "overwhelming and destabilizing and bizarre"—would distort or somehow compromise the voice she had developed at the Workshop in 2009–2011.[7] Also at issue was whether Winfrey's endorsement would undermine the loyalty of Marilynne Robinson, her mentor, who was a notoriously sharp critic of commercial media.

Winfrey informed Mathis that she could not utter a word of her selection for two months, until December, at which time the press release and publicity strategy would be in place. Until then, Winfrey said, celebrate. That she did. She and her partner "decided to be splashy and absurd," Mathis fondly remembered of the night she toasted the birth of her new career over champagne—"a bottle I couldn't afford"—and oysters. They "stumbled home," delirious in the moment, when the chaos of fame and fortune still stood at a safe distance in the future. Oprah had said she "could tell my nearest and dearest," which included her mother, her partner, and her best friend and fellow MFA from the Workshop, Justin Torres.[8]

Voice Lessons

When Mathis's close friend Torres first visited Iowa City in 2008, he had underestimated the xenophobia of the rural Midwest. A gay New Yorker of Puerto Rican descent who applied to the Iowa Writers' Workshop in his late twenties, Torres was not prepared for the lack of diversity in the program. The majority of the programs he applied to had accepted him. But Iowa, through the work of Director Lan Samantha Chang, pursued him most aggressively. On his campus visit, he experienced immediate culture shock. In particular, when he visited classes, he was stunned by what Matthew Salesses calls "the loss of voices of color to the white straight male default of the writing workshops."[9] These were still very much Paul Engle's workshops, where competition and criticism prevailed over cooperation and collaboration. When minority students tried to defend their writing, Torres observed, these often turned into defenses of themselves and their own ethnic identities. During his visit, Torres's "reservations and hesitations were mainly about the diversity of the program and the diversity of the town." He explained, "I was coming from Brooklyn as a queer Puerto Rican, and I was nervous about what it would be like to come to Iowa City." Much of his concern centered on the energy he would have to pour into surviving in this campus culture. "Sometimes it's just exhausting going into a class of middle-class, straight, white people," he confessed, an environment in which he felt "just automatically that 'other.' "[10] His discomfort was acute enough that he resolved to attend only under the condition that his best friend, Ayana Mathis, attend the program with him. In the absence of any support system he could find at Iowa, he would bring his own with him from New York.

Mathis—who had been dabbling in poetry, freelance journalism, copy editing, fact checking, public relations, and translation projects—found the opportunity irresistible. During her itinerant childhood, she moved frequently with her mother. Raised in the Germantown section of Philadelphia, Mathis lived in New Jersey and other locations following the estrangement of her mother from her father and the rest of the extended family. Unlike Torres, Mathis did not fear the prospect of living in an alien culture, especially one where she stood out as an ethnic other. Indeed, she had lived in Florence for two and a half years before moving south toward Siena to Barbarino Val d'Elsa, a small, picturesque, medieval walled city with a thousand residents in the hills of Tuscany. While in Southern Italy contemplating a magazine career as a travel writer, Mathis continued to write poetry and struggled to learn the language to maintain her position as a server at a cocktail bar. But after bringing the wrong drinks to exasperated patrons too many times—especially those not interested in translating their orders for a server whose Italian was "nonexistent"—she abandoned "this tragic waitressing job" and returned to the United States. She had attended NYU, Temple, and the New School but dropped out without a degree; freelance writing and fact checking for magazines, she had hoped, might lead to a more secure position as an editor.[11]

Once Mathis returned from Europe to New York, she began writing nonfiction, mainly autobiographical creative vignettes, representing her first real foray into prose, which laid the foundation for her fiction. She began crafting the narratives with the notion that she "would shape them into something like a memoir."[12] That memoir took shape at a New York friend's art studio in West Chelsea where Jackson Taylor, author of *The Blue Orchard* and associate director of the New School's Graduate Writing Program, led an informal class. Arranged by word of mouth, this group consisted of Taylor insiders looking to develop their writing independent of a formalized program. Taylor found much in Mathis's memoir to admire, and imbued her with the courage to persist in fulfilling its promise. The sessions were held in the studio of a woman named Ultra Violet, a former member of Andy Warhol's Factory. Mickey Mouse figurines, artifacts, and dolls occupied every square inch of wall and counter space, making for a surreal environment. The ubiquity of reproduced pop culture in these surroundings paradoxically put the writers at a critical distance to mainstream consumerism and entertainment media. Mickey Mouse in so many forms was no longer Mickey Mouse, but an abstraction functioning like Warhol's famous repetition of the Campbell's Soup label and Marilyn Monroe's image, all casting a critical eye on mass production and consumer culture.

Before the Workshop, Ultra Violet's studio was Mathis's workshop. Taylor, "an amazing teacher," fostered eclecticism, tolerance, and diversity in an open environment that encouraged risk taking and creative experimentation. Mathis recalled "people working in different genres," with a wide spectrum of verse, creative nonfiction, and fiction. The writers themselves, who included Torres, seemed an embodiment of "one of those 'dreams of New York,' " a vibrant array of diverse tastes "with just *completely* different backgrounds— racially different, economically different, different professions—engaging in impassioned and interesting conversations about writing." Free from the polarizing constraints of formal education in traditional MFA programs that pitted students in competition with one another for fellowships, grades, and even publications, the group thrived creatively in the "funny and bizarre, but kind of wonderful" setting of Ultra Violet's Mickey Mouse–bedecked latter-day Warhol art studio.[13]

The "language-reliant poetry/prose hybrids" Mathis developed in Jackson's studio constituted the writing sample she submitted for admission to the Iowa Writers' Workshop.[14] Buoyed by Taylor's and Torres's encouragement, she resolved to fictionalize her memoir and send it with her application. Unlike the complete novels and short story collections—many published—among the samples of the more than one thousand applicants she was competing against for admission, her fictionalized memoir was a meager thirty-two pages, just two over the minimum requirement. Yet the admissions committee heard the voice of a young writer with a powerful future in the world of letters. The piece proved instrumental in her acceptance to the Workshop, along with Torres's persistence in urging Chang to accept her.

From copy editing English translations of publicity materials for small businesses and wineries in Tuscany, Mathis found herself accepted to the most competitive creative writing program in the world. Admission to the Workshop has become widely recognized in popular culture as a life-changing event. The concluding episode of the third season of the HBO television series *Girls*, in March 2014, dramatized the euphoric experience of being accepted to Iowa Writers' Workshop. The scene depicting the character Hannah Horvath clutching her acceptance letter could not overemphasize the triumph of the moment. A form rejection letter from the Workshop dated February 27, 2015, which went viral on the internet because of a verb tense error in the first sentence, illustrates the extraordinarily remote chances of being accepted; signed by Director Lan Samantha Chang, it informed the recipient, Julie Mannell, that "this year, one-thousand and twenty-six people applied for twenty-five spaces."[15] This staggering ratio distinguishes the Workshop as the world's second most selective graduate program in any field, far more difficult to enter than the schools of law or medicine at Harvard and Stanford, and behind only the teaching arm of the Mayo Medical Clinic.[16] Mathis's promising writing samples, along with the strong endorsement of Taylor and Torres, combined to earn her admission to this elite program.

Once enrolled at the Workshop, Mathis and Torres both encountered tension. They had been working on their memoirs, which put them in the perplexing situation of offering themselves as subjects for the scrutiny of their straight, white, mostly male peers. Although the Chang era brought a sharp increase in opportunities for people of color like Mathis and Torres, the climate was not yet entirely accommodating. The exhaustion of attending classes as "other" set in for both of them. Mathis described one particular incident involving a workshop session for a story that later became part of *The Twelve Tribes of Hattie*. "One of the characters" in the story "is referred to as having something like almond skin, something that would identify the character as black," she explained. As her peers bore down on that detail, "there was a person in the workshop who said they had been reading happily up to that point, but then felt they were reading a story about race—which somehow invalidated what they'd been reading up to that point." The author, the student argued, was gratuitously foregrounding race to cover for a lack of aesthetic merit. When Mathis pointed out that "things like that certainly happened," Torres reported that such moments "make you want to pull your hair out."[17]

The Twelve Tribes of Hattie, which Mathis wrote entirely at Iowa against such untoward resistance, centers on Hattie Shepherd, a beautiful "high yellow" woman who moves from Georgia to Philadelphia in the early 1900s after her father was murdered by a group of white men. Hattie marries August, a dockworker who turns out to be a drinker, gambler, and womanizer. They have eleven children, nine of whom survive. Over time, Hattie's once vibrant and hopeful spirit becomes embittered and worn down from the burden of losing two babies, raising nine more, and dealing with an undependable husband. At one point she takes her youngest daughter and runs away with a young lover, but then realizes he too is unfaithful, so she returns to her husband.

This narrative did not come without a struggle. Mathis divulged how she was crushed by her mentor Marilynne Robinson's critique of her first attempt at writing a fictionalized memoir. Robinson chided her for creating characters that "aren't sufficiently in the situations in which she placed them," urging her to abandon the project and start over. Although she felt her fictionalized autobiographical vignettes expressed a deep part of her experience, she succumbed to the overwhelming pressure from both peers and mentor to adopt an altogether new narrative voice and locus of subjectivity through "the primacy of invented character." She began to internalize the insistence that the voice of her fictionalized memoir "was stilted, and wrong, and ridiculous," hurtful allegations that Robinson reinforced. The pressure to conform to the conventional standard of the workshop short story was squarely upon her, a predicament Sandra Cisneros had experienced during the Jack Leggett era of the 1970s. "Of course," Mathis recalled of this baptism by fire, "I was completely devastated."[18]

The final judgment on the narrative voice of Mathis's autobiographical memoir carried disturbing racial implications. The logic of the class's consensus on her work in effect condemned and rejected her racial identity, particularly as the voice of her well-traveled life. She remembered returning for Thanksgiving break in the fall of 2009 to her partner's apartment feeling emotionally violated. She headed for the shower, weeping profusely. Submitting herself to such abuse for another month seemed impossible to endure. The crying lasted for a full day, leaving her partner helpless to find a way of consoling her. If the thirty-two-page fictionalized memoir was strong enough to gain her admission to the program, she thought, surely it could pass muster at a workshop session. By this point, Hattie Shepherd had yet to arrive in the story, and there was no clear sign "that she would, at all." Stunned by how savagely and swiftly her writing was "beaten up" by her peers, she sunk into "a crisis." Friends consoled her by attempting to normalize her experience as one shared by most new Workshop students. This expected hazing ritual, they assured her, was common. The crisis that followed, the rationalization went, "happens to a lot of people in their first semester at Iowa, especially after you get a little beaten up." Thoughts of self-doubt plagued her: "What am I doing here? I am not really a writer! Oh my God!" The desperation was almost indescribable. "I am making it sound really light, but at the time" it was a weight she could not bear, a "*huge* crisis of faith."[19]

After "twenty-four hours in tears," Mathis poured a drink and pulled herself together. She remembered thinking, "Well, what are you going to do? You're here. You have to do something. You can't just spend the next two years weeping" and assuming the MFA would magically appear. The prevailing culture of the program drove her away from her creative instincts. "I do not consider myself a short story writer," she said. But pressure to specialize in short story writing was overwhelming; mastering it was the only option for survival. "I'll try to write some stories anyway," she resolved. Before leaving the program, "I'd try."[20]

Her first foray into the short story involved a teenage mother whose infant died, precisely the scenario with which *The Twelve Tribes of Hattie* begins. That story "was a kind of strange hybrid of the first and last chapters" of the novel. Each of her subsequent stories built on the one before, so that they "became a prism through which" Hattie, the matriarch at the heart of the novel, "could be refracted." Although each of her characters could be construed as a window into the Great Migration, her intent was not to write a historical novel. The title's reference to the Twelve Tribes of Israel became "a metaphor of nation building and leaving a situation of bondage and coming to a situation of freedom," which is finally disillusioning, a place that "is not what folks thought it would be."[21] Mathis's turn to the short story drew on her Pentecostal background for biblical themes of mass exodus. The novel's organizing theme depicts African Americans fleeing oppression in the South only to encounter different kinds of racism in the North. It draws on the Bible's rendition of the Israelites' emergence from the wilderness of Egypt only to encounter the Babylonians, theological patterns actively encouraged by Robinson.

New Inflections

The fingerprints of Marilynne Robinson are readily apparent on Mathis's Iowa MFA thesis from 2011. Robinson made a career of fashioning narratives out of the complex interiority of preachers' lives that form the subjects of her world-famous trilogy of novels, *Gilead, Home,* and *Lila.* The first of three stories Mathis submitted as her thesis explores the inner world of Six, a teenage preacher who heard his calling after a terrible accident left him physically and emotionally scarred for life. As depicted in her published novel, the accident occurred when his sisters, Cassie and Bell, were rolling their hair in curlers in their home in early 1940s Philadelphia. Ordering their brother about, they asked for more bobby pins, sending him to "tell mother we need the hot comb in twenty minutes." He played along, assuming the role of their butler. Bell lit the hot water heater and opened the faucet valve. Water rushed "into the tub in a torrent," billowing steam "hot enough to cook an egg." When they requested a clean towel, he was "just about to stand for an exaggerated pretend bow when he lost his balance and fell into the tub." His sisters screamed and pulled him from the tub, horrified as "he convulsed on the tile." "Feeling as though his flesh was sliding off of his bones, he blacked out" the moment his mother Hattie entered the room."[22]

After such Morrisonesque interludes from Six's past, we return to the present setting of a revival tent in Alabama where the young preacher is about to deliver a sermon. Two years earlier he heard his calling, which "came over him like a fit; it hijacked him suddenly." The story echoes the anxiety Mathis suffered during her own "crisis of faith" when she dreaded returning to the Workshop after the Thanksgiving holiday in 2009. Six's crisis fittingly occurs in a public forum in which he is under pressure to produce inspiring wisdom for a congregation of judgmental listeners. He approaches the pulpit with absolutely nothing prepared, looking out at a sea of unsympathetic eyes. He hears mumbling, "He ain't no bigger than a minute," and his eyes flood with tears.[23] But soon he finds his voice. Midway through the sermon a shout of "Amen!" rises from the crowd, unleashing a floodtide of spirit in the congregation. Suddenly "his anxiety was replaced with an ecstasy that spun like a ball of fire."[24]

Mathis self-reflexively inscribes her triumph over her own traumatic experiences as a first-year Workshop student into the self-conscious and terribly blocked adolescent preacher Six, who eventually finds his voice and uplifts the congregation. Her method shares a long literary history of self-reflexive fiction dating back to Cervantes's *Don Quixote* and Laurence Sterne's *Tristram Shandy*.[25] She came to the short story by way of memoir writing with Jackson Taylor. Now in the realm of fiction, she deftly debunks the notion of romantic inspiration as a reliable resource for creative inspiration, especially for generating moving lyricism on cue before a judgmental audience. Although Six had been "hijacked" by the Holy Spirit when he first heard his calling, he certainly has no means by which to consistently recreate that inspiration. He instead more pragmatically considers his audience's expectations and selects his material for the sermon accordingly. Mathis would learn to summon her most powerful prose in precisely this manner, particularly under the guidance of Robinson.

In a "webisode" video interview on Oprah's Book Club 2.0, Mathis dutifully recites the "three lessons" she learned from Robinson, all of which actively discourage self-reflexivity. The autobiographical impulse did not derive from Robinson, but was Mathis's own, traceable to her earlier memoir writing, as well as her identification with James Baldwin. In him, she saw "a writer who looked like me" and seemed as though he "understood the singularities of my experience." When she encountered his deeply autobiographical novel *Go Tell It On the Mountain*, "it was as though the two of us were huddled on the couch, just he and I, whispering our lives to one another."[26] But Robinson advised her to resist the autobiographical impulse by delving into her characters' inner lives. "Primacy of character" was of the utmost importance to Robinson, followed closely by "truth telling," described as being as "truthful as you can be in your writing at all moments." Particularly challenging was Robinson's insistence on being able to articulate, on demand, "five reasons for any character doing anything." When asked in workshop sessions why a particular character stumbled and fell down a flight of stairs, Mathis confessed, "the most I could ever come up with was three."[27] The lesson remained unchallenged because of the authority figure at the head of the class. "It's an impossible standard, one which I'm sure Marilynne meets but the rest of us mortals cannot," Mathis told Winfrey, who smiled and turned to the camera with an earnest word of encouragement to the viewer: "Keep reading, see you soon, stay in touch online."[28]

Mathis's comment corroborates the sentiment of Thessaly Le Force and other students who have struggled to attain Robinson's standards that govern her own practice. In the acknowledgments of *The Twelve Tribes of Hattie*, Mathis praises Robinson for pushing her beyond her comfort zone, and for "the rigor of her standards, which urges me forward, even when I have reached my limit."[29] Mathis regards the hardship suffered under Robinson as necessary to her success, sounding a note Mark McGurl has observed in the masochistic strain of Workshop culture dating from Flannery O'Connor.[30] For Mathis, subordinating her life to writing was a series of compromising trials that made adversity and hardship integral to the learning process. Learning with Robinson and her other Workshop instructors, she recalled, "made me want to be better, to do better, even when it was hard. . . . Especially when it was hard."[31] The creative writing instructor as martinet is now a pedagogical prototype that has spread well beyond Iowa. Many are convinced that badgering students is the only way to inspire growth. Some instructors such as Dan Barden in other programs have gone so far as to proclaim, "one of the things that makes me a good teacher, I'm convinced, is that I'm a bastard."[32] Creative writing professor Margaret Mullan has credited the harsh conditions of the sexist learning environment of her MFA training as a key factor in her success. Although "it was very much a guys' program," she insisted, "I kind of needed that. I needed to be kicked around a little bit."[33]

The Iowa experience for Mathis reflects a clear pattern in which she faced "impossible" standards only Robinson could meet, felt pushed beyond her limits, and was pressured to defend her creative choices. Mathis grew as a memoirist under entirely different, and indeed opposite, nonviolent circumstances among the cadre of literary artists in the Mickey Mouse–themed studio under the informal and supportive tutelage of Jackson Taylor. Indeed, she was poised in that setting to become a memoirist of the caliber of her friend Justin Torres.[34] His *We the Animals* was published by the prestigious Houghton Mifflin Harcourt and received an Indies Choice Book Award under the category of Adult Debut along with nominations for several others. Torres never faced pressure to shift genres the way Mathis did when she adapted to short fiction against her natural understanding of herself as anything but a short story writer. Taylor's scene—diverse, eclectic, and mutually supportive—was in her past by the time she arrived at Iowa. As Lan Samantha Chang has acknowledged, "there are huge cultural differences between Iowa City and New York a large number of students face when they arrive here."[35] Just as Sandra Cisneros in the previous generation adapted her poetry to conform to the short stories her Workshop instructors insisted she write, Mathis bent the natural shape of her creative spirit to fit the Workshop mold, particularly as dictated by Robinson. Her mentor drove her to write stories that she eventually turned into the novel, a process that left her in a state of "creative and physical exhaustion when I sent it off."[36] The prestige and professional rewards for enduring that process, however, were extraordinary.

The Whiteness of Workshop

Behind the trying pedagogy Mathis endured at Iowa after leaving the accepting one in New York, the shibboleth of narrative voice—and the specter of Toni Morrison—loomed large. According to Mark McGurl, author of *The Program Era: Postwar Fiction and the Rise of Creative Writing*, the writing program cliché of "find your own voice" arose in the post-1960s culture that valued creativity as exhibited in the works of the acclaimed African-American novelist Toni Morrison. Earlier eras alternately centered on "write what you know," emphasizing experience as displayed by Tom Wolfe, and "show, don't tell," which fixated on craft as embodied by Flannery O'Connor. McGurl's schema here is helpful in defining the social and pedagogical context of Mathis's graduate education, one characterized by a culture of uniformity that depended on these mantras as rallying points.[37] The novelist and critic Anis Shivani identifies "find your own voice" as currently the most conspicuous among the commonly believed and repeated sayings in MFA creative writing programs. Often it is used to tyrannize students into conforming to prevailing modes of expression. Such standardization conditions the social matrix of creative writing programs, he argues, so that they risk becoming havens for "talentless people afraid to independently carve out a broad career in letters as used to be the case."[38]

Unlike Torres, whose minimalist memoir was the result of repeated workshop sessions that negated much of his original drafts, Mathis was escorted out of the genre altogether. *We the Animals* epitomizes the minimalism McGurl defines as a distinguishing characteristic of Workshop writing in "an aestheticization of shame, a mode of self-retraction," one that paradoxically functions as a "form of attention-getting."[39] But once in the realm of fiction, her training steered her away from an aggregate voice, one that might don the pluralistic identity of the speaker of Langston Hughes's "The Negro Speaks of Rivers," for example. The Workshop's formula was that " 'voice' equals strictly private voice, not a universal voice."[40] Mathis appeased her workshop audience by withdrawing her voice from the narrative and placing it in her characters. McGurl describes this process whereby "the properly impersonal narrator must try, however quixotically, to relinquish her speaking role, distributing as much of it as possible to characters in the story and retreating to the back of the imaginary theater of fiction to pare her fingernails."[41]

As an African-American woman writer, Mathis faced pressure to find her creative writing voice at a distance from her ethnicity, while also somehow replicating the achievement of Toni Morrison. Winfrey affirmed what Workshop members expected of Mathis from the moment she entered the program. "I can't remember when I read anything that moved me in quite this way, besides the work of Toni Morrison," Winfrey effused. This of course pleased Mathis, but it also set extremely high expectations. "It's a great deal of pressure," she admitted, careful to align herself with Morrison only insofar as she shares "coming out of a similar tradition of post-Civil Rights literature with black women as subject."[42] Comparisons to Morrison, she insists, should not reach beyond these shared categories of period, subject matter, gender, and race. In an op-ed she wrote for the *New York Times* after taking her position as a Workshop faculty member, Mathis was even more candid about the role of MFA programs in "inspiring inflated expectations—after all, the formalized study of writing isn't an alchemical formula by which every student becomes Tolstoy, or even publishes a book." She went further, observing the damaging effect of being held to such standards in the context of "the MFA's workshop model" and "its intense scrutiny of new work [that] can be crippling for some writers."[43] Much of that scrutiny, she found, centers on voice.

Shivani points out similar abuses of the concept of voice as a superficial "subterfuge, allowing one to judge individual effort without making any real attempt to penetrate the infinite densities of style." It becomes a vapory attribute of writing that requires little justification on the part of the arbiter, something "anyone can critique. How does one critique voice anyway? What does one say, except utter inanities? Your voice is too sarcastic. Your voice is too hallucinatory. Your voice is too boozy." But such distinctions are moot, as Shivani points out, since voice is "something beyond critique," because "you either have it or you don't." At the Workshop, voice often masquerades as code for another style of writing that the instructor and workshop peers expect to see. "I don't think you've found your voice yet" is the message to young

authors like Mathis, rather than those who, like T. C. Boyle, ostensibly con-
form to the white male "reigning voice, the Michael Chabon [and] Jonathan
Lethem off-kilter irony." There is pressure to "get with the program, the
Manhattan-Brooklyn affectedness or else."[44]

Creative writing programs have been known to stifle the voices of ethnic
writers and steer them toward conventional forms of expression. Junot Díaz
reports an incident in which a young Latino writer was told by his workshop
peers that the diction of his story was too elevated, that people in the barrio did
not sound nearly so intelligent. To Díaz's disbelief, the "fellow writer (white)
went through his story and erased all the 'big' words because, said the peer,
that's not the way 'Spanish' people talk. This white peer, of course, had never
lived in Latin America or Spain or in any US Latino community—he just
knew." Worse yet, the instructor "never corrected or even questioned" the peer
for making these racially insensitive suggestions.[45] Siddhartha Deb reinforces
Díaz's position by observing how "the lack of diversity in MFA programs . . .
seems to translate into the astonishingly narrow range of contemporary
writing."[46]

Lan Samantha Chang bitterly recalled Frank Conroy advising her in no
uncertain terms that if she did not want to be typecast, she should avoid writing stories with Chinese characters.[47] Anthony Swofford described the Workshop as "a very white place" when he attended from 1999 to 2001. "I'm sure
that changed year-to-year, but my two years felt super Caucasian." In addition,
"there weren't many economically disadvantaged students in 2001," he told
me.[48] This is precisely the institutionalization of conformity that Chang herself rebelled against by aggressively recruiting both Mathis and Torres. Mathis
is careful to factor in class, gender, and sexual orientation in calling for "MFA
programs to take special care to admit and nurture . . . writers of color, L.G.B.T.
writers, working-class and poor writers," so that diversity is a "mandate" and
"not empty policy-speak."[49] As the pedagogical equivalent of empty policy-
speak, "find your own voice" can operate as a disingenuous mantra of diversity
that really "serves conformism to reigning social platitudes," so that "voice
does not equal cultural difference," according to Shivani.[50]

Patronage

Ayana Mathis did not suddenly appear on the porch of Oprah Winfrey's
media empire as some sort of literary foundling. Instead, she depended on
a series of vital connections provided by her Workshop mentor Marilynne

Robinson. Mathis has acknowledged that Robinson's "sort of encouragement and endorsement has meant everything," especially "in *career* kinds of ways, which is certainly not to be overlooked."[51] Two years after its launch in 2002, the Trident Media Group merged with the powerful literary agent Ellen Levine. Levine had served as Robinson's agent for decades, brokering the breakthrough deal with Farrar, Straus and Giroux in 2004 for *Gilead*, her Pulitzer Prize–winning second novel after a twenty-four-year hiatus from the genre. Robinson cemented her status as the most acclaimed living writer in the world with her next novel, *Home*, which won the Orange Prize for Fiction in 2009. So by 2011, the year of her pupil's graduation from the Workshop, Robinson's endorsement carried authority in the literary world matched only by Winfrey's in the popular realm. Levine therefore responded promptly when Robinson summoned her to represent her pupil.

Soon after its establishment in 1980, the Ellen Levine Literary Agency became one of the industry's most powerful promoters. Levine's clients have won virtually every conceivable literary accolade, including the Pulitzer Prize, the National Book Award, the National Book Critics Circle Award, the PEN/Faulkner Award, the PEN/Hemingway Award, and the Booker Award. The most well known of her clients' titles have been made into major motion pictures, such as *The English Patient, Holes, The Sweet Hereafter, Affliction, Ride with the Devil*, and *Housekeeping*, the adaptation of Robinson's debut novel from 1980. Levine has a record of representing Iowa Writers' Workshop faculty and graduates, such as Asali Solomon, for whom she landed a prestigious contract, also with Farrar, Straus and Giroux. Reluctant to accept first-time authors, Levine makes an exception for "Workshop grads" such as Solomon.[52] If the Workshop offered graduates connections to the publishing industry through the special fellowships Engle was continually negotiating during its earliest days, that tradition continues through the representation of Ellen Levine and the Trident Agency.

No single author of Levine's is more renowned than Robinson. Upon Robinson's retirement from the Workshop in the spring of 2016, Lan Samantha Chang declared her "the most distinguished writer in the United States right now."[53] With the backing of such a towering figure as Robinson, Mathis enjoyed a distinct advantage on the market as a first-time novelist. In an interview in 2013, Mathis mentioned that her agent, provided by a "well known author," functioned as "the best advocate and guide I could ever have hoped for."[54] On Robinson's advice, Levine offered Mathis guidance and representation typically reserved for established luminaries like Michael Ondaatje, the author of *The English Patient*.

The contract proffered by Knopf placed the book in the hands of the most influential arbiters of taste in the critical community, whose lists Winfrey had been scouring in search of a second title for her online book club. Formerly a teen mother, Winfrey identified immediately with Hattie Shepherd, the opening chapter's fifteen-year-old African American who names her newborn twins Philadelphia and Jubilee, much to the consternation of their father and grandmother. By chapter's end, the twins perish of pneumonia despite Hattie's efforts to save them. A moving scene depicts the young mother holding Philadelphia before her, the baby's head lolling despondently. " 'Fight . . . Like this,' she said and blew the air in and out of her own lungs, in solidarity with them, to show them it was possible."[55] The scene touched Winfrey, whose child also died in infancy.[56] Winfrey said, "beginning with Ayana's description of Hattie's desperate efforts to save her babies, Jubilee and Philadelphia, I was right with Hattie, in her house in Germantown, Philadelphia." She immediately wanted "to know Hattie, understand her and be introduced to everyone in her life."[57]

Mathis understood that her deal with Knopf, arranged by Levine, arose thanks to a combination of talent and to some extent institutional privilege, as she discussed in an interview with National Public Radio in 2014. The Workshop MFA, especially with Robinson as her thesis supervisor, was hard won through dedication necessary to contend with rancorous workshops and an austere mentor. Realizing the advantages Iowa offered her, she now dedicates herself as a faculty member to making "writers of color able to take advantage of that kind of access."[58]

Given this ardent advocacy for student publication, one might expect Mathis to foreground the importance of navigating the literary market in her current approach to teaching creative writing as a faculty member at the Workshop. Yet the Workshop's enduring anticommercial myth that sets literary culture at odds with mass culture is apparent in her claim during a video interview in 2013: "First novelists shouldn't think about publication or their careers. It's very dangerous to begin thinking, what will an editor like? What will people want to read?" she said, shifting her tone to a panicky whisper with her eyes wide in a sarcastic look of anxiety. Too much "tailoring of your writing in terms of the impact it has on one's career can make the writing inauthentic," she warned. The advice clearly suggests that she did not write *Hattie* with the intention of having it selected by Oprah for her new book club. "It's important to keep that off the table as much as possible."[59] Historian R. Jackson Wilson has likened the taboo of raising the question of capital with respect to literature as tantamount "to wondering who picked up the check after the last supper."[60]

As her incredulous reception of Winfrey's phone call shows, Oprah's Book Club members collectively did not make up Mathis's imagined audience. Instead, they consisted of her Workshop faculty and peers. In this sense, the Workshop's insularity means "essential feedback mechanisms" from audiences in the broader industry "are blocked, and the programs" like Iowa's "are indifferent to markets," as Shivani and McGurl note. However, for every instance in which first-time novelists like Mathis achieve acclaim without any attempt to promote themselves in the literary market, one can identify a T. C. Boyle among students, or a Kurt Vonnegut among faculty, who were acutely aware of markets and audiences, and deeply tapped into fluctuations of mass market tastes. Poetry remains a different case altogether, as that side of the program "has explicitly stated its disinterest in broad readership."[61]

The Workshop Author in Mass Culture

Without Torres's encouragement, Mathis is not likely to have applied to Iowa. Without Torres flagging her file for Chang, she might not have been admitted. Without Robinson, she would not have had access to her literary agent Levine; without Levine, no Knopf; no Knopf, no Oprah. This chain of delicate connections might have broken at any point. But powered by the endorsement of probably the most acclaimed living writer in the world, and credentialed by the foremost creative writing program in existence, she seemed destined for a publisher of Knopf's stature, if not a patron of Winfrey's command over mass culture. Robinson and Winfrey together backed *The Twelve Tribes of Hattie*, a rare instance of a "literary bestseller" in the publishing industry, and a feat of both popular and critical success that only Dickens was consistently able to achieve throughout his career. For all the pieces to fall into place so perfectly, it was "a kind of fluke," a "miracle for me," according to Mathis.[62]

The selection of *The Twelve Tribes of Hattie* for Oprah's Book Club 2.0 represents a milestone in Workshop history, like John Irving's novel *The World According to Garp* being made into a film that established the program as a vehicle for ushering literary culture into popular culture. The successes of Mathis and Irving suggest the profit potential of an Iowa MFA. To many authors, however, such as Jonathan Franzen, commercial success is mutually exclusive to literary excellence. Franzen feared that his novel *The Corrections* would be tainted if Winfrey adopted it, so he refused to allow it to be a book club selection. In 2004, he said, "I feel like I'm solidly in the high-art literary tradition. She's picked some good books, but she's picked enough schmaltzy, one-dimensional [ones] that I cringe, myself, even when I think she's really smart and she's really fighting the good fight."[63]

Interestingly, Mathis also does not approve of many of Winfrey's titles, noting how "she picks a wide range, some that I like, some that I don't like." But where she differs from Franzen is in her capacity to see that by blending genre fiction with literary works, "Oprah's Book Club breaks the barriers down . . . it breaks assumptions down, and that side of it is helpful."[64] In particular, she saw the benefits of enriching the reading of those who "normally say they only like to read mysteries or thrillers" and "may be intimidated by this strange 'literary fiction' label." With Winfrey's endorsement, these readers are more likely "to pick up a book" like hers "and enjoy it without worrying about the label," according to Mathis.[65] More than crossing boundaries, Winfrey's book club selections change the climate of the industry decidedly away from popular genre fiction toward the more challenging material she typically recommends. Winfrey is less interested in making bestsellers out of genre fiction than she is in turning literary novels into bestsellers, in the process bringing previously detached aesthetes—literary artisans toiling in anonymity—onto the center stage of popular culture.[66]

Franzen found no such progressive liberation from labels and mainstreaming of intellectual authors in the club, but instead saw it only as a tool of corporate media aligned with the malignant forces of capitalism. "I'm an independent writer and I didn't want that corporate logo on my book," he said, regarding it as a Faustian deal with commercial media's obsessing over "consumer advertising and consumer purchasing."[67] Franzen's rejection of Winfrey situates him as the white male humanist condemning the black female producer of mass media in a misogynistic rejection of both female and mass culture. In his phobia over commercial media, he overlooked the benefits that accrue to women and the black community from the spread of works like Mathis's. It is no small achievement—perhaps greater than the personal fame and wealth Mathis herself attained after her book's selection—that an online discussion of her novel on *Goodreads* among African-American women turned squarely to gender discrimination within their community. As forum contributors began to blame Hattie for the problems encountered by her children, others objected. "It's always easy to place more blame on the mother," a reader named Kisha argued. "That's the way society is set up, especially in the black community. We don't force our men to take responsibility, instead we make excuses for their actions and persecute the woman."[68]

The reach into the African-American community with a novel like Mathis's would not have been possible through the marketing engine of Knopf alone. When her book was adopted it literally became a new product, inside and out. The Oprah's Book Club logo appeared on the cover of all copies; a special digital version offered notes and a reading guide for clubbers to organize their discussions and meetings. Winfrey's notes on her favorite passages also appear in the digital editions, for the Amazon Kindle and Barnes and Noble's Nook devices, available for purchase on the iBookstore and online e-book venders. A host of video clips featuring brief interviews with Mathis appear on the Oprah website. When news of the novel's selection struck, Knopf swung into action, recalibrating the packaging of the literary commodity itself as well as the scope and scale of its production, print run, and distribution. "We obviously had to advance our on-sale date," Knopf spokesman Paul Bogaards reported. "This is a book that everyone at Knopf is completely enamored of. As a result of Oprah's endorsement we took our printing up to 125,000, from 50,000." Much to the company's delight, "All kinds of retail windows have opened."[69]

Reclaiming the airwaves from the National Football League and its predominantly male audience, Oprah devoted several hours worth of material to Mathis and her novel for a program titled "Super Soul Sunday." In 2013, a special edition of "Oprah's Soul Series" aired on Super Bowl Sunday, February 3, on Oprah's Sirius XM radio station, her Facebook page, and Oprah.com. Mathis answered reader questions on the VYou social video platform, as 13 million members converged on the official Oprah's Book Club 2.0 *Goodreads* forum. Still more splintered off into their own mobile networks for discussion of her book via GroupMe, in addition to Facebook, Instagram, and Twitter feeds (#OprahsBookClub). Print literary culture, and Knopf in particular, had never seen such a thorough multimedia campaign for a single novel. The greatest reach in all of this was of course the combined media of Winfrey's television network OWN (the Oprah Winfrey Network, which was formerly the Discovery Health Channel), which attracts 85 million viewers, and *O, The Oprah Magazine*, read by 15 million per month.[70]

The first ever title by a Workshop author endorsed by Winfrey, *The Twelve Tribes of Hattie* is also the program's first work to be embraced by ethnic women readers in the mass market. Workshop authors have in several cases courted broad female audiences through women's fiction with romantic themes. Anthony Swofford, for example, courted that market with his novel, *Exit A*, but was unsuccessful. Access to these and other lucrative markets, Workshop students have been aware, occurs through the program's internal system of privileges, dispensed from "certain übermasters" (Chang and Robinson in Mathis's case). As seen in Cisneros's comments on the system, many faculty "exercise disproportionate control over the distribution of rewards and honors" determining access to the most powerful publishers.[71] Defiance of that system, as many have discovered, can result in dropping out. Alumnus Joe Haldeman recalled that although he was not "harmed by a workshop, obviously some people are. Sometimes they're discouraged enough to quit writing."[72] To this end, "outright challenges to the authority of the masters," who have typically been program directors and the most distinguished authors among the faculty, "must be rare indeed," because the "system measures its success by the frequency of non-events" in this sense.[73] Mathis was precisely such a non-event. Her decision to meet rather than to challenge Robinson's authority paid rich dividends by providing her access to her agent Levine and the lucrative market beyond.

The impact on sales of an endorsement from Winfrey is enormous. After receiving her blessing, *A New Earth*, by Eckhart Tolle, sold 3,375,000 copies; James Frey's *A Million Little Pieces* sold 2,695,000; Elie Wiesel's *Night*, 2,021,000; and Cormac McCarthy's *The Road*, 1,385,000.[74] Now that Mathis has demonstrated that Workshop authors can reach this elite circle, the value of the Iowa MFA has risen. Winfrey's media corporation virtually eliminates dependence on publishers as the determining factor of authors' long-term prosperity.[75] For those fortunate enough to earn it, her endorsement takes away any concerns regarding publisher loyalty, such as those that consume authors like T. C. Boyle. "A first run of five hundred thousand copies, just like the record industry, may be great for a few authors," Boyle says, but he wonders "if they'll have sustained careers or not. Or are their expectations up too high after one success, which was orchestrated by the publisher? Will the publisher sustain you?" he asks. "Or you [publish] one or two books and you're gone?" Far more powerful than any one publisher, Winfrey-owned media can single-handedly sustain an author, as the sales figures of her selections illustrate.[76]

As the list of Winfrey's choices makes clear—with titles ranging from Tolstoy and Faulkner to Morrison and McCarthy—trade and romance genre fiction are not the staples of this system as many frustrated male Workshop students from the 1970s assumed. The "genteel tradition" of literature, one alumnus groused, "is being shoved rudely aside by our commodity-driven world" in New York publishing, where "demographics, gender, ethnicity and above all, marketability are the yardsticks by which literary talent is measured and presented to the American public." While Winfrey's club members fit the profile of "women over forty" who constitute "the overwhelming majority of novel readers," this does not mean they are all reading Danielle Steel, as evidenced by the challenging list of works they have devoured at Winfrey's behest.[77] Yet that stereotype of daytime drama TV viewers, precisely the time slot Winfrey's talk show occupied through 2011, persists in its association with Oprah's Book Club.

Although the number of voices like Franzen's openly deriding literary culture's movement into mass culture through Oprah's Book Club have diminished in the decades following his clash with Winfrey, the stigma of such highly commercialized broad appeal persists. "Thanks to Oprah," Hector Tobar of the *Los Angeles Times* wrote, "Mathis is now the beneficiary of the book world's most precious and rare commodity: buzz." Tobar claimed that readers anticipating her novel to be "a great work of narrative art are going to be disappointed." For him, the wall between mass culture and literary culture—despite overwhelming evidence to the contrary—still exists. Reviews like his vehemently oppose crossovers like Mathis, the author of what he calls "a competently written melodrama that only intermittently achieves anything resembling literary excellence."[78]

Yet new evidence points to the increasingly challenging nature of the works selected by Winfrey, and more importantly, the mass audience's eagerness to adopt them. While the club increased sales of its selected titles, in the twelve weeks following her nominations there were declines in sales for mystery and action-adventure novels, and also for romances. Because of the longer and more difficult nature of the book club selections, readers turned away from their usual lighter fare; weekly adult fiction book sales declined because readers were absorbed in month-long explorations of more challenging texts at a much deeper level, time extended also by the frequency of discussions both online and in person.[79] The club disrupts the consumer spending pattern of a steady diet of several Nora Roberts novels per week, for example, replacing it with immersion in a masterpiece like *Anna Karenina*. As for the therapeutic purpose of the reading promoted by the club, its medicine is hardly easy and coddling, but can prove quite caustic and disturbing, as seen in club selections such as Toni Morrison's *The Bluest Eye*.[80] Even Mathis herself underestimated Winfrey's literary acumen during their first conversation. The media mogul read lines from Morrison's *Sula* to illustrate similarities in tone and literary technique to passages in Mathis's novel. "It's clear that language really resonates with her, and that she's a very literary, passionate reader," Mathis gathered. She knew Winfrey had "read a lot of books," but "was surprised by the literariness of her viewpoints."[81]

Even if there was a grain of truth in Tobar's claim that melodrama intermittently takes over Mathis's narrative, her online presence as packaged by Harpo Productions appears to have a distinctly richer, more edifying purpose than that of the producers of *Days of Our Lives*, or sensual trade romances. If Mathis's critical reception is any indication—in a highly unusual achievement for a debut novel, *The Twelve Tribes of Hattie* graced the cover of the *New York Times Book Review* in 2013—she has proven herself worthy of the sales generated by Oprah's Book Club 2.0. The Oprah Effect is not just financial; it is also cultural. The club's educational mission "floats above commercial interests."[82] This in turn builds courage in readers to expand their understandings of these texts toward self-help/realization, a form of bibliotherapy that has always coursed through the lives of the most elite and respected of readers. The corrective emotional response of deep engagement with literature is epitomized by "6 Things Ayana Mathis Knows for Sure About Sticking With It," featured on Oprah.com. It mentions the poetry she read as consolation when "she was broke" and on the brink of homelessness, the way she sustained herself on inexpensive fare, and how she persisted in her efforts to find resources and cash—all foregrounding literature's capacity "to startle us out of a deep-sleep of death into a more capacious sense of life," as one avid reader said.[83]

As is clear from "Why Get an MFA?" a piece Mathis wrote for the *New York Times* in 2015, she is acutely aware of the need to diversify Workshop culture. With *The Twelve Tribes of Hattie*, she represents the Workshop's first step into the world of Harpo Productions. Her success demonstrates how the program can be allied with other commercial media powerhouses to awaken and mobilize new readerships. Her alliance with Winfrey offers a progressive twist—distinctly twenty-first century, radically diverse, and socially progressive—on Paul Engle's aggressive corporate enterprising of the Workshop's first era. With its peerless status, the Iowa Writers' Workshop continues to define contemporary literature. The program's privileged access to the publishing industry's most powerful agents, publishers, and promoters can now advance literature as an agent of social progress at the height of the digital revolution.

Before Mathis, no Workshop member had tapped into cross-platform resources for publicity on the scale of Winfrey's media empire. Through such unprecedented reach, the Workshop is now poised to realize the full potential of Mathis's credo that, in its most noble function, "literature is a triumph of radical empathy."[84]

Epilogue • No Monument

Engle's Legacy and the Workshop's Future

No monument stands in honor of Paul Engle in Iowa City. There is no bust of him in stone or bronze by the river next to the Iowa Memorial Union, where the old converted Quonset huts once housed the Iowa Writers' Workshop. Engle's name, however, does turn up among those of the many Workshop members, from Flannery O'Connor and Kurt Vonnegut to Marilynne Robinson, whose memorable words are set in brass on Iowa Avenue's Literary Walk connecting the heart of campus to town. Bearing a quote he penned in 1957 at the height of his poetic ambition, his inscription reads, "Poetry is boned with ideas nerved and blooded with emotions, all held together by the delicate, tough skin of words."[1] In 1990, over a decade before the Literary Walk was completed, Engle had already designed his own monument, a project he quite literally took to the grave. The epitaph on the tombstone where he was laid to rest in 1991 in Iowa City's Oakland Cemetery reads, " 'I can't move mountains. But I can make light.'—Paul Engle."[2]

In the absence of any road, scholarship, building, or academic chair bearing his name, Engle seems to have crafted his own public memory.[3] His indefatigable obsession with packaging and marketing the Iowa Writers' Workshop and International Writing Program—a lifelong dedication to winning countless donors, investors, publishers, corporations, governments, faculty, and students—culminated with his attempt to name his own legacy. By casting himself as a Promethean figure imbued with the power to "make light," he credited himself for illuminating the once culturally barren wasteland of Iowa with the literary world's most brilliant minds. Not even his most ardent detractors could deny his achievement of developing a fledgling creative writing program, consisting of "one little class" of eight "brilliantly untalented" students inherited from Wilbur Schramm, into the most influential force in contemporary literature.[4] The marker both triumphs and gloats in a final gesture intended as much for the gratification of his admirers as for the retribution of his rivals. This conspicuous self-designed memorial befits the young Rhodes scholar who arrived at Oxford with bits of Iowa manure still clinging to his shoes.[5] In defiance of New York publishers and Ivy League academics, Engle dared to make Iowa the literary capital of the world. With his signature delicate aggression, Engle made light by attracting literature's brightest minds since the 1940s.

Luminaries flocked to this otherwise unknown rural outpost in large part thanks to Engle's business acumen, promotional savvy, and relentless will. The Workshop transformed Iowa City into "a Rive Gauche, rising out of the infinite plains and truck stops of mid-America," in the words of his successor John Leggett.[6] Both town and university have recently been rebranded specifically to draw on this prestige. Engle's successor in the International Writing Program (IWP), Chris Merrill, spearheaded the movement for Iowa City's designation as a UNESCO City of Literature. Soon after that designation became official, the University of Iowa branded itself the "Writing University."[7] In conjunction with the City of Literature organization, the IWP, rather than the Workshop, is now the keeper of Engle's memory.

But deeper causes lurk behind his lack of lasting accolades. His undisguised competitive drive for capital built the economic foundation so crucial to attracting the world's most acclaimed literary talent. That strength in promotion and fund-raising, however, was considered unbecoming to many in the world of letters who saw him as an uncouth businessman. In the early 1990s, for example, Director Frank Conroy expressed a sentiment shared by many at the Workshop when he confessed to Leggett his disappointment that "the new [Michener] fellowships" would be "named, unfortunately, after Paul Engle."[8] Despite Engle's instrumental role in building the program into the powerhouse that it continues to be today, his memory has all but vanished from both Dey House (the program's headquarters) and the broader Workshop culture. "Few graduates know anything about him, and none read his poetry," as Loren Glass noted.[9] Yet the Workshop continues to bear his legacy of intense competition played out in a culture of triumph and shame in the workshop method he institutionalized.

Competition was fundamental to Engle's original vision for the program. "The Ivy League has had the past, the Big Ten will have the future," he predicted in the February 1957 issue of *Holiday* magazine, fighting words that were reprinted in the *Michigan Alumnus*. Members of the Ivy League retorted by alleging that Big Ten institutions such as Iowa were "educational rabbit warrens."[10] By the 1950s, the Workshop's reputation had already been established based on the names of such distinguished authors as Flannery O'Connor. Alumnus Robert Dana recalled how "the Workshop during the '50s was Paul Engle's homegrown, popcorn version of the Paris sidewalk café." Engle's homespun manner could pass for eccentric charm to some, or appear crude and off-putting to others. During a visit to the creative writing program at what was then called Arizona State College in Flagstaff, for example, the faculty treated him to a breakfast of "whole grain pancakes with real maple syrup." His hosts were shocked when Engle "licked the can" because "the syrup was so good he did not want to miss those drops." When the topic of conversation turned toward his extensive speaking tour on behalf of the Workshop, Engle sounded like the itinerant confidence man of Mark Twain's "The Man that Corrupted Hadleyburg," a charlatan who specializes in fleecing unlettered bumpkins. "In the boonies," he said with a smirk, "one can get away with the most outrageous statements, as long as one wears a jacket and tie."[11]

Publicity

In his role as the Workshop's impresario, Engle knew no bounds. In 1963 he wrote to First Lady Jacqueline Kennedy requesting that she appear on campus for a promotional event to support the program. A personal letter from the White House, signed "Arthur," from Arthur Schlesinger, Jr., special assistant to the president, noted that he "passed the letter from President Hancher and the Baudelaire pamphlet on to Mrs. Kennedy."[12] Engle had invited her to be Honorary Chairman of the Twenty-Fifth Fine Arts Festival to be held in Iowa City in the summer of 1963. Although the first lady demurred, she was just one of many world-famous celebrities he fearlessly courted; he was unafraid to ask for the world. Decades later the pattern reversed itself when the White House began reaching out to the Workshop, as President Barack Obama tapped Marilynne Robinson on several occasions for awards and visits.

Another major event during the early 1960s, billed as "A Day Celebrating the Friends of the Writing Program at The State University of Iowa," featured the "Special Guest: Bennett Cerf, *President*, RANDOM HOUSE," as the program read.[13] In 1961, the Workshop's influence over canon formation had reached the publishing industry, as seen in Random House's agreement to "publish a large anthology of poetry and fiction by the best writing talent from the Iowa writing program." Near that time a collection titled *New Poets of England and America* appeared. "Over one-third of the American poets were from the S.U.I. program in writing," the press reported. "A similar example would be the naming of one-third of the All-American players in football from one university," Engle boasted in one of the many sports analogies he favored to rationalize dominance and competition.[14]

The establishment of such a dominant position over the literary world required an unusual array of public relations tactics, many of which exploited Workshop students. The J. M. Hickerson advertising agency, for example, struck a deal with Engle for a "Portrait of Iowa campaign" proposed on March 28, 1960. The firm agreed to "create and run a series of 12 unusual, distinctive and 'logical' advertisements about Iowa during a period of 12 months, each advertisement to consist of illustrations by an Iowa artist, copy by a student in Paul Engle's creative workshop, and signatures of 12 sponsors." The ad broker offered to place the series in the *New York Times*, with its massive circulation at the time of 614,169 commanding a cost of $36,540 for twelve "Dominant ads." For access to the *Wall Street Journal*'s affluent 609,922 readers, the price was $68,400 for a dozen ads, and $101,232 for twelve full-page spreads.[15]

The power of the Workshop brand, particularly in leveraging promotion for Iowa businesses, was the cornerstone of Hickerson's plan. "Sponsors seeking out-of-Iowa business now could expect to profit rather quickly," he suggested, while others "seeking Iowa business from new citizens of Iowa could expect to profit later." "Promotional possibilities are tremendous!" according to the unctuous pitch, as companies "willing to shell out $400 or more per month for 12 months" included "the *Des Moines Register* and *Tribune*, Viking Pump, Boss Hotels, Electrical Companies of Iowa, Maytag, the Iowa Bar Association, Amana, Iowa Bankers Association, and Collins Radio." Hickerson suggested that "copy for this pattern advertisement can be written here, although the idea of the campaign is to have the copy written, at least drafted by a creative workshop student."[16] The main objective was of course commercial rather than pedagogical, as evidenced by the willingness to credit Workshop students for writing that was actually produced by the advertising agency. Ghostwritten ad copy bearing Workshop student bylines designed for salability meant the Workshop name, rather than the students' writing itself, carried the greatest value as a promotional tool in the advertising series. Language polished by ad agents bearing students' names presented a PR opportunity for the Workshop of the sort Engle had spent his career devising.[17]

The vast majority of Engle's time and energy was spent orchestrating such arrangements with advertising agents, publishers, business, and government agencies. He had little time for his own writing; his own teaching, by most accounts, was intermittent. Robert Dana, one of his greatest allies, even found his demeanor "enigmatic, and contradictory, and hard," recalling a man who cut an intimidating figure on campus. Engle often strode past his own faculty and students "in the university library without so much as a nod." His disdain for writers who "hadn't turned in any good work lately or published it anywhere" was notorious.[18] Yet faculty members were well aware that "graduate assistants write his books for him," as Vonnegut leaked in correspondence to the incoming instructor Richard Gehman, with the impish caveat to "burn this letter."[19]

Engle's use of graduate students often involved lucrative deals with magazine and newspaper publishers. Joan Rattner, special features editor of *This Week Magazine*, responded to Engle's pitch letter, suggesting he contribute to the series "Words to Live By." The journal, the editor notes, "has achieved enormous popularity and has had as contributors such people as Joseph Auslander, Somerset Maugham, Aldous Huxley and Frank Lloyd Wright." She offered $250 for 250 words on an inspiring quote, especially one offering affirmation "in these days of open cynicism about moral and spiritual beliefs." The reach was considerable: *This Week* was "distributed by 42 leading U.S. Sunday newspapers to a combined audience of over 13,000,000 families—the largest magazine audience in America."[20] Engle promptly spurred his charges.[21] Such activity remains hidden from view at Dey House today, largely because it threatens to undermine the program's current focus on maintaining its elite literary reputation.

The prevailing literary view of mass culture as a problem rather than an opportunity clashed severely with Engle's financial tactics. Resistance to commercial writing ran counter to the program's efforts to develop professional authors for whom writing could be the primary occupation and source of income, ideally without resorting to teaching for an added layer of financial security.[22] Some Workshop MFAs clearly deviated from the standardized literary writing of their training by venturing into genre fiction, as in the case of mystery novelist Max Allan Collins. Collins made his career at the heart of popular culture by scripting the Dick Tracy comic series. David Morrell, another Workshop graduate, also found success in popular culture. Working in a stairwell office on the third floor of the English-Philosophy Building, Morrell composed *First Blood* (the novel that spawned the *Rambo* films starring Sylvester Stallone) while enrolled in the MFA program. Unlike the vast majority of

English and Workshop faculty, former English department chair Brooks Landon considered the office sacred ground, claimed it as his own, and has occupied it for decades since.

Collins and Morrell, however, were exceptions to the anticommercial sentiment in the Workshop culture. Engle attempted to legitimate commercial writing in the program without sacrificing literary prestige, as seen in his promotion of lucrative literary journalism through deals such as *Esquire*'s sponsorship of the 1959 symposium "The Writer in Mass Culture." The magazine seemed to provide the solution to how "all widely-published writers have faced the constant issues of art and the marketplace." *Esquire* pursued literary prestige with its goal "to encourage fine writing at its source." By bridging the gap between "the huge circulation magazines [that] quite naturally want works which will be popular" and "the literary quarterlies [that] attract a very fine, but small and specialized audience," the journal represented the ideal publication to be associated with the Workshop as Engle envisioned it.[23] Through this middlebrow industrial logic, *Esquire* leveraged creative writing programs to recruit fresh literary talent for its pages.

The Workshop continues to show reluctance to embrace its growing visibility in mass culture. Iowa City UNESCO City of Literature staff attested to the ongoing resistance to its sanctioned efforts to publicize the program. Uncooperative Workshop faculty members have frustrated UNESCO's primary function, which is to celebrate and promote Iowa City's literary culture. One UNESCO staff member suggested that many affiliated with the program worry that UNESCO's promotional mission will eventuate in "tour buses full of visitors converging on Dey House," turning it into the American equivalent of Stratford-upon-Avon, the birthplace of Shakespeare, which has become a highly commercialized and popular tourist destination.[24]

The concern is that the ongoing function of the institution cannot sustain active tours and visitors coursing through the facilities. Most of the other nineteen cities bearing the City of Literature distinction, which include Dublin and Prague, have literary reputations not isolated to a single government-funded institution but spread more organically throughout various districts and local haunts unique to their civic cultures. These decentralized urban literary cultures contrast with that of Iowa City, which is highly concentrated in one exclusive academic unit. The city's underground press, to which UNESCO is blind, vanished in the late 1970s. In this sense, Iowa City is not so much a city of literature as an institution of literature housed in a midwestern Big Ten university, surrounded by corn fields and hog farms. Iowa City, the second

UNESCO City of Literature named in 2008, after Edinburgh, Scotland, in 2004, only has a literary history insofar as it is connected to the Workshop. On a civic level, the vast majority of literary lines of ascent run through the program. Workshop authors account for more than two-thirds of book readings and signings at Iowa City's famous Prairie Lights Bookstore, named after City Lights Bookstore in San Francisco, which served as the hub of the Beat Generation. Current data visualization projects on the Workshop suggest how future research might digitally map the constellation of its faculty and graduates who have helped establish the literary reputations of the other nineteen UNESCO Cities of Literature.[25] Most Cities of Literature in essence revolve around Iowa City, and more specifically, the Iowa Writers' Workshop.

Empire

The vast power and influence of the Workshop have recently come under the scrutiny of Workshop graduate Eric Bennett, who wrote an essay published in the *Chronicle of Higher Education* in February 2014 titled "How Iowa Flattened Literature." Bennett charges that the program systematically narrows the focus of literature, an argument that can be traced back to his animosity toward the former director Frank Conroy's teaching style, expressed through a powerful description of Conroy in his King Lear phase, flailing at his demons and snarling at invisible forces. But it generated the most serious controversy for discussing how Engle had accepted a financial contribution from a source funded by the CIA, when the International Writing Program received funds from the Farfield Foundation in 1967, although Bennett himself admits that there is no firm evidence that Engle was aware that the Congress for Cultural Freedom (CCF) was in fact a CIA front. "More than a few readers interpreted the *Chronicle* piece as evidence of conspiracies," Bennett says, but he "found no evidence that the CIA money influenced writing at Iowa."[26] Bennett insists that some readers unfairly characterized him as a conspiracy theorist.

Bennett may disavow the insinuation that "spies and spooks" shaped the writing in Engle's program, but he remains firm in his contention that the Workshop director's "vision . . . was both shaped and motivated by the Cold War." He takes a broad view of cultural assimilation of Cold War ideology, pointing out "the intellectual and ideological climate particular to two decades of American history, starting in 1945." That climate describes a pattern of values "both harder and more important to understand than a conspiracy theory."[27] This logic undermines Bennett's intent to peg the Workshop as a conspicuous participant in that intellectual and ideological climate. Hardly a factory of uniform doctrinaire Cold War cultural production, the Workshop was typical of the era's many cultural institutions that gathered funding from government sources. Engle's patriotism, more ordinary than extraordinary for its time, did not necessarily make him an ideologue. His internationalist bent and abiding conviction in free expression across cultures is evident in his indefatigable work on behalf of the International Writing Program. It is ironic indeed that during his lifetime he was accused by affiliates of the House Un-American Activities Committee of "connections with Communist front groups," whereas after his death others linked him to the CIA, each representing polar opposite factions in the Cold War.[28]

Enter John Leggett, Gentleman Publisher

Such sensationalistic—often contradictory—portraits of Engle's political identity stem from deeper resentment toward his ruthless pursuit of capital through the commercialization of the Workshop brand and willingness to commodify its unique artistic charisma. More than his politics, this commercial zeal made him a lightning rod for controversy during his lifetime. John Leggett, the director between the Engle and Conroy eras, from 1969 to 1987, likened Engle to a kind of P. T. Barnum, a "great literary showman" who was the antithesis of the English department chair John Gerber, "the consummate academic statesman" and "The Silver Fox."[29]

Engle and Gerber clashed severely when the Workshop moved in the 1960s from its Quonset huts in the parking lot of the Student Union to the English-Philosophy Building on Iowa Avenue. Leggett recalled how "Engle's success was not lost on the university," prompting the administration to offer the Workshop sought-after space in the English department's building. This set the stage for "a conflict between the two leaders with markedly different styles," tension that erupted over a faculty position offered while Engle was out of town. Engle's demand for complete administrative control was so uncompromising that he insisted the Workshop could not be run "under any management but his own."[30] He issued an ultimatum threatening to turn the program over to the auspices of the English department. When Gerber called his bluff by refusing to rescind the faculty offer, Engle resigned and soon after established the International Writing Program with his wife Hualing Engle. Leggett then took over the Workshop from the poet George Starbuck, who served as director in the interim.

The Workshop's current reluctance to commemorate and celebrate Engle seems entirely reasonable in light of his having abandoned the program that was the greatest achievement of his life. The rift with Gerber accounted for why, when Leggett "blew into town in 1969," Engle was "so indifferent to his extraordinarily successful creation." At the time Leggett could not fathom Engle's animosity toward the Workshop. It was not until Leggett invited him to attend the fiftieth anniversary of the Workshop that he fully understood how much Engle's relationship to the program had chilled. At first declining the invitation, Engle made a surprise appearance, supplying the most pithy and wry reading of his presence there. "His role to the convocation of a half century of Workshop graduates," Leggett recalled him saying, was "that of the corpse borne through Egyptian festivals to subdue unrestrained revelry."[31] Engle in effect provided his own epitaph, making light of his post-mortem directorship of the Workshop in another self-advertisement winning him instant acceptance at the gathering. Had Engle maintained that good-natured and self-effacing approach to the Workshop, it might have served as an olive branch to encourage greater recognition of his monumental achievements toward building the program.

The hiring of John Leggett extended Engle's institutional paradigm that was so deeply connected to the publishing industry. Leggett was "a book editor with a Maxwell Perkins role model" whose vision resonated with Engle's "scheme [that was] similar to that of a quality publisher, seeking the best young writers, hoping to nourish and launch them, yet without that inhibiting commercial risk." The surrogates for commercial risk and the rigors of the literary marketplace were the students themselves, in many cases more imposing than cantankerous naysayers like Conroy. Leggett stood by his belief in "the weekly exposures, humiliations, and occasional triumphs" as the avenue to success for building a "creative temperament" as the "core for any aspiring life." Salvation through suffering continues to be a keynote at the Workshop. In a *Des Moines Register* feature on the program in April 2016, Lan Samantha Chang noted that the workshop model was alive and well. Student Claire Lombardo described the shock of silently witnessing the dissection of one's work: "like waking up from a nap. You are in a weird stage, in a fugue state, a strange mood the rest of the night." Critical voices riot inside the heads of Workshop students. Michael Cunningham, an MFA graduate from 1980, admitted that he "perversely loved the agitation it engendered in me" to see "others mangled by the experience" of workshop bloodlettings in which he "often felt more than a little mauled myself." To the extent that the program continues to be

notoriously competitive, it is still Paul Engle's Workshop. Cunningham recalled one classmate "slapping a story of mine down on a tabletop and announcing to the members of our workshop, 'This is just *pornography.*' "
Although he "passed some bad nights in Iowa City, and some worse mornings," he felt "enlivened by the proximity of just under a hundred other people
ready to come to blows over questions involving the perfection or deficiency of
particular sentences."[32]

The Pedagogy and Commerce of Frank Conroy

Just as Engle's own career had been "a long slow slide from full-throated poetic aspiration into monochromatic administrative greatness," as Eric Bennett
aptly described it, Frank Conroy followed a similar course, abandoning his initial authorial vocation for his role as director of the Workshop. His first book,
Stop-Time, cemented his fame in 1967. Only decades later in 1993 did he produce his second major work, the novel *Body and Soul*. Conroy's tenure as director from 1987 to 2005 is marked by his intimidating presence in the classroom
and rigid enforcement of his beliefs about effective creative writing. By contrast,
Engle never played such an active role as an instructor. Disgruntled students
begrudge Conroy not for overzealous fund-raising and publicity of the sort
Engle indulged in, but on stopping innovation that strayed beyond what he
considered acceptable. "He shot down projects by shooting down their
influences," Bennett recalled. "He loathed Barth, Pynchon, Gaddis, Barthelme.
He had a thing against J. D. Salinger that was hard to explain." Melville and
Nabokov, the latter of whom many respected critics consider one of the best
prose stylists of all time, were "obnoxious" in his eyes. It is hard to imagine
the frustration of any student aspiring to write postmodern fiction or philosophical novels under the tutelage of a man who dismissed David Foster Wallace
with a growl and a wave of his hand: "he has this thing he does." Conroy saved
his most lavish diction for the destruction of these writers, and any manuscript
up for workshop bearing their influence was "Cockamamie," "bunk," "bun-
kum," or "balderdash," withering barbs that shattered many projects and egos.[33]

John Leggett could humiliate, but no director acculturated classes to habitual savagery more than Conroy. Brady Udall recalled his second showing at
workshop after an inauspicious debut dismissed by Conroy as "the worst kind
of amateurish yearnings." He explained how "for the first fifteen minutes of
class, Frank allowed my fellow writers to do what comes naturally in a Workshop class—they tore the story to bits." As Udall silently took his punishment

according to protocol, "Frank fidgeted, shook his head sadly, and finally, when he could take no more, held up his hands to halt the proceedings," proclaiming the story publishable as it stood. This, he insisted, was "a perfect story," without "a flaw or blemish in it, not even a comma out of place." He commanded Udall to "send this story off right away," because it was destined for publication.[34] Udall sent "Buckeye the Elder" to *Playboy*, whose editors proved Conroy right and accepted it at once without revision.

This was not the last of instances where mob rule conspired to undermine brilliant writing at the Workshop. During the previous generation, Leggett observed how difficult it was to find visiting professors capable of controlling this savage group impulse. His three requirements "of a good Workshop teacher" included "the prestige to attract students, an editorial sense that can foster talent . . . and a diplomacy that can keep student savagery from serious bloodletting." Perhaps most alarming in this schema is Leggett's unwillingness to reform this combative culture but instead fold it in a mantle of respectability, hoping it might prevent the volcano of envy and vengeance from erupting into a riot. One "tell-it-like-it-is apprentice," Leggett recalled, "summarized the worksheet of a shy classmate with, 'But this is just shit, terrible shit,' " an instance in a larger pattern of hostile abuse the director had neither inclination nor interest in stopping.[35]

Prior to Chang's directorship in the early 2000s, intervention by directors to alleviate hostility was intermittent and incident-specific, never program-wide. Conroy, for example, rescued several others besides Udall from the lynch mob of peer critics. In his homage to Conroy titled *Mentor: A Memoir*, Tom Grimes recounts the crucifixion of his best writing at the hands of his classmates. "Too many metaphors," one claimed; "I was lost," another sniffed; "Do people really talk this way?" someone asked; "If the narrator's a baseball player, how come he's intelligent?" Conroy leaped to his defense, but with such intensity that Grimes could not tell whether he "was defending *my* work, or *his* judgment?" At stake for Conroy was a symbolic defense of his power. Although he emerged with Conroy's blessing, Grimes found himself at his desk "the following morning [as] my classmates' voices rioted in my head. I couldn't hear my narrator, and if I lost his voice I'd lose the novel." Stultified, he "worked for six hours and composed two sentences." Grimes's great triumph lay in his capacity to "silence the other voices" so that they "never interfered with my work again."[36]

Conroy was both muse and antagonist, the object of praise and the subject of bitter derision. When he was a student at the Workshop, Bennett's desire to write philosophical fiction building toward a postmodern novel of ideas crashed on the rocks of Conroy's rigid disapproval. On closer examination, Conroy's disdain for postmodern writers appears to derive in part from his treatment at the hands of David Foster Wallace in a widely read *Harper's* cover story from 1996. Conroy's condemnation of his students' Wallace-inspired writing was apparently driven by more than just aesthetics. In the article, Conroy falls victim to the Workshop's own shame culture that vilified commercial writing as the great taboo. Wallace exposed that Conroy had published "a fawning puff piece about a cruise line for financial gain," as Kent Williams observed.[37] Wallace wrote, as the prelude to his onslaught: "Did I mention that famous writer and Iowa Writers' Workshop Chairperson Frank Conroy has his own experiential essay about cruising right there in Celebrity 7NC's [the cruise line's] brochure?"[38]

Conroy's piece, titled "My Celebrity Cruise or '*All This, and a Tan Too,*' " is "graceful and lapidary and persuasive," Wallace submits, but "it is also completely insidious and bad." The "real badness" is in its complicity with "Megaline's sale-to-sail agenda of micromanaging not only one's perceptions of a 7NC but even one's own interpretation and articulation of those perceptions." Still more troubling, according to Wallace, is that the project and placement of the piece "are sneaky and duplicitous and well beyond whatever eroded pales still exist in terms of literary ethics." By "appearing on an inset with skinnier pages and with different margins than the rest of the brochure," the "essay" creates "the impression that it has been excerpted from some large and objective thing Conroy wrote." Of course "it hasn't been." The cruise line's public relations liaison admitted that Celebrity had paid Conroy "whether he liked it or not." Conroy's own response to Wallace's questioning about the "essaymercial" was far more forthright. "With a small sigh that precedes a certain kind of weary candor," the director confessed, "I prostituted myself."[39]

By coincidence, Conroy had sailed on the same cruise Wallace reported on for his *Harper's* story. Conroy felt especially stung by Wallace's crucifixion of his "essaymercial" because he had been so forthright about discussing why he wrote the piece. Wallace even allowed that Conroy "answered [his] nosy questions" in a way that was "frank and forthcoming and in general totally decent about the whole thing." Yet Wallace followed through with the assault mainly because he felt betrayed by the author of the memoir that first inspired him to "try to be a writer." Wallace was particularly crestfallen to see Conroy's stagey and pretentious bio accompanying the essay showcasing him as the author of

Stop-Time. To Wallace's horror, the cultural prestige of this "classic" and "argu-ably the best literary memoir of the twentieth century," along with its author, had been repackaged into an elaborate celebrity endorsement for the cruise line.[40] Wallace's disillusioning moment is not unlike the many J. D. Salinger's Holden Caulfield experienced in *The Catcher in the Rye*. Holden sees through pretentious artists—from Ernie the piano player to his brother D.B. who pros-tituted his authorial career in Hollywood according to Holden—willing to compromise their talent to pander to the masses. Particularly appalling to him was the positioning of literature as an ad "in such a way that we come to it with the lowered guard and leading chin we reserve for something that is art" or at least something making a sincere effort to be art. That Conroy was no longer attempting art like *Stop-Time*, but instead using his talent to produce "an ad that pretends to be art," left Wallace feeling betrayed.[41] He found himself in the role of Nick Carraway realizing the artifice behind Gatsby's radiating smile that, in Fitzgerald's words, "understood you just so far as you wanted to be understood, believed in you as you would like to believe in yourself."[42] For Wallace, "an ad that pretends to be art is—at absolute best—like somebody who smiles at you only because he wants something from you."[43]

In *Mentor*, Tom Grimes sings Conroy's praises, despite cursing him on his first impression, following a speech the new Workshop director delivered in Key West in 1989. "I've applied to the Writers' Workshop," the young, ambi-tious Grimes said to Conroy, hopeful to receive some encouraging advice. "Yeah, you and eight hundred others," Conroy gruffly replied, excusing him-self to find a drink, then spotting an old friend to abandon Grimes for good. Furious, Grimes rushed home, ripped Conroy's *Stop-Time* off his shelf, and began yanking pages out of it "by the handful" until he had "gutted the thing." "Fuck Frank Conroy," he seethed through clenched teeth.[44] Grimes tells can-didly of his love for Conroy down to the anguish he felt during his mentor's nervous breakdown and eventual decline as colon cancer closed in during his final years.

Suppressed Evidence: The Conroy File

Paul Engle may have been a lightning rod of controversy at Iowa, but he had nothing to conceal in his official papers regarding his record as Workshop director. By contrast, Frank Conroy's file covering his directorship has been sealed until 2024, with access granted only through formal application and written permission of the Workshop director. In late August of 2016, nearly nine months after submitting multiple written requests—the first on December 2, 2015, met with four months of silence—I became the first non-affiliate of the program to be granted access to the Conroy file since its placement in Special Collections at the University of Iowa twelve years earlier in 2004. No Director's Files, from those of the early days of Schramm and Engle to Conroy's predecessor Leggett, have ever been restricted. Conroy's arrangement is neither customary nor routine, but instead marks an aberration in the archive. Thus the Workshop's decision to grant me access was also without precedent.

According to Lan Samantha Chang and her consultants, the reason for the protracted delay in their decision was the presence of material in the file of a sensitive nature, which, if disclosed, might have an adverse impact on the program's staff, faculty, students, and living writers. "Because we are an active, working writing program, we have important relationships with living writers, and for that reason, papers have been put under restricted access," Chang said.[45] Further, I later discovered that my request coincided with a crisis Chang had not mentioned, one that besieged the program, but had managed to avoid extensive scrutiny in the local media. The turmoil involved the alleged sexual misconduct of Workshop faculty member Thomas Sayers Ellis, who was dismissed from his position during the spring 2016 semester after eleven women testified against him in online statements describing a long history of alleged sexually inappropriate behavior ranging from harassment to predatory violence.[46] Whereas the full story appeared in *Jezebel*, it was buried in the *Iowa City Press-Citizen* under a headline concealing the cause of his dismissal. *Press-Citizen* readers had missed the truth, since a rather benign headline described the story as a tepid bureaucratic snafu that eventuated in the university continuing to pay a Workshop professor despite the cancellation of his course.[47] The financial injustice, however, paled in comparison to the suffering of Ellis's long list of victims, from those enduring the emotional discomfort of his alleged inappropriate classroom conduct, to his long-term intimacies in which alleged abuse was severe, chronic, and protracted.

Workshop administration determined to remove an undisclosed amount of material from the file before allowing me access. According to an agreement signed by Frank Conroy and university archivist David McCartney in January 2004, the Directors' Files series of the Iowa Writers' Workshop is to be closed to the public until January 1, 2024. However, in response to my request to the Workshop, access to the material was granted after a review by Workshop staff.[48] What was the nature of the evidence the Workshop carefully removed from the Conroy Director's File, a box of alphabetically sorted correspondence from the late 1980s through the early 1990s? Conroy's motives in sealing the document until 2024 of course were private. But the content of the file and the motives for keeping it from public view for such an extended period of twenty years after his death raise serious questions.

The pugnacious school of Norman Mailer, as Jane Smiley pointed out, developed through a boxing cult that took the blood sport as both a metaphor and an embodiment of creative writing. Sexism was rampant in the Workshop. Snodgrass and Vonnegut bore witness to the institutionally engrained gender bias of the veterans who defined the machismo climate, one that persisted throughout Leggett's era, making for a learning environment that clearly disadvantaged women. Snodgrass recalled not only avoiding John Berryman, but actively fleeing from him because his behavior in mixed company when alcohol was present was "too dangerous."[49]

Even in the thoroughly censored and sanitized file to which I was allowed access, evidence of Conroy's sexism abounded. In a letter to Norman Mailer dated April 19, 1990, Conroy thanked the famous author for visiting the Workshop and delivering a reading of his latest book, one that oozed masculinist gender politics in the vein of the retrograde backlashes against progressive feminism that marked the culture wars of the early 1990s. Conroy registered his allegiance with Mailer in direct opposition to the feminist movement, lauding his friend for his assault on the women, which he described as "a bravaro [sic] performance that has had everybody buzzing and talking." Conroy especially appreciated how the reading incited "a *lot* of discussion" that antagonized female students, sparking "a certain amount of feminist outrage at the selection from *Tough Guys* driving wonderful arguments in the bars where the students congregate." Far from showing any sympathy for their position, he was overjoyed that the women had been wounded so severely as to cause "a whole lot of energy released," which he characterized as "good energy, and I'm very grateful to you."[50]

Today, Workshop insiders such as Anthony Swofford concur that Lan Samantha Chang's "gentle leadership" marks a sea change in the gender and ethnic politics of the program. Her progressive influence highlights by contrast her predecessor Conroy's extension of the patriarchal dominance of the Engle era. The Ellis firing in spring 2016 therefore represented a major setback in this slow healing process. "The program has a history of male poets becoming involved with students; a repetition of that history—let alone a worse version of it—wouldn't do," according to the first published report of Ellis's dismissal. Therefore, immediately after the post by the advocacy organization VIDA disclosed the testimony of eleven of Ellis's victims, "classes were canceled, and by the time spring break was over, the week after the post went up, he'd been officially replaced."[51] Chang's leadership seemed to mark the end of the "important, inappropriate literary man" until Ellis arrived in Iowa City on a visiting professor appointment from his previous posts at Sarah Lawrence College and Case Western University, marking a grim return of the heyday of the "Saint" Ray Carver period that reached its zenith under Leggett, and whose legacy continued with Conroy.

"This book is the result of a vision," Engle proclaimed in his introduction to *Midland: Twenty-Five Years of Fiction and Poetry, Selected from the Writing Workshops of the State University of Iowa*.[52] That vision, he argued, was not intuitive. But for all his insistence that the success of the program was the result of careful planning rather than serendipitous whim, "a conscious thing [that] didn't just happen by chance," his subconscious reconfigured his work for the program into not so much a dream, but a nightmare he disclosed one drunken evening to a cluster of listeners that included Workshop student W. D. Snodgrass and world-famous poet Robert Penn Warren.[53]

In the dream, Engle was a prisoner of war frenetically performing for his captors "an especially degrading punishment" with more alacrity and agility than any of his fellow inmates. Placed naked clasping his ankles atop the camp's outer rock wall six feet off the ground, Engle was forced to step through a series of small depressions one foot at a time without losing hold of his ankles. The awkward and nearly impossible task exposed him in a debasing spectacle of absurd Kafkaesque struggle for the guards' amusement. Yet Engle's performance carried special power to assuage the enemy and improve conditions materially for his starving fellow inmates. Engle successfully transformed this one-man act in the theater of the absurd into a calculated deception, one richly symbolic of his speeches and engagements to promote the Workshop. This was not just a single nightmare, but a recurring dream, one that ended each time with the guards "no longer jeering" but looking on "with amazement and admiration" at his uncanny skill. The dream's Cold War allegory left Snodgrass "astonished not only by its horrors," but shocked that Engle "would recount it at a party where so many would understand," including the distinguished poet and southern gentleman Robert Penn Warren, who was serving as a visiting faculty member at the time. Stunned by the richness of this metaphorical self-disclosure, Snodgrass, who had been perfecting his own confessional poetry at the time that would eventually distinguish his career, lamented, "if only his poems had offered such revelations!"[54]

Like his dream—and galling confession thereof—Engle took a hard look in the mirror at the beginning of his 1996 autobiography, *A Lucky American Childhood*. "Ask Engle what he thinks of Paul, he'll say:/ I'm a real bastard in a beautiful way," he wrote in the poem titled "Paul Engle." Literature and violence are inextricably bound in this self-portrait, as his "hand gives you a poem or breaks your jaw." His willingness to lower himself into the dirt and place his hand in the fire to fuel its embers does not make him a miracle worker. "I can't move mountains" with mystical god-like force, "but I can make light" with unglamorous determination at his own peril. These final lines of the stanza encapsulate the enigma of his life he would inscribe on his tombstone.[55]

The embattled, frenetic "life-crammed, people-crowded" directorship of Engle, whom the *New York Times* described in 1961 as "everywhere at once, his shoulders hunched and his head poked forward like a running back," gave way to the cult of Raymond Carver under Leggett until 1987.[56] Conroy's acerbic command then yielded to Lan Samantha Chang's compassionate leadership, marking a significant advance from "the largely male, booted long-haired, laden with experience of war itself or of escaping it" Workshop of the 1970s, as Leggett described it. The effort now, which has had varying results, is to reverse the climate that alumni like Sandra Cisneros and Jane Smiley endured, in which "if one or two young women students turned up for a discussion of the worksheet, they rarely lasted the whole session," as Leggett attested.[57] Chang cites Tony Marra, Justin Torres, and Angela Flournoy as examples of successful students who have diversified the program.[58] Longtime staff member Connie Brothers, who has a vivid recollection of the Leggett and Conroy eras, pointed out that for the first time in the Workshop's history, gender balance has been achieved. Although it has been "extremely difficult" for women and ethnic students at the Workshop in the past, she said, it is "very encouraging" to see such progress.[59]

Despite that progress, some aspects of the Workshop still bear Engle's influence. Workshop sessions continue much in the way he originally designed them. There is little room for novels of ideas, as the institutionalization of creative writing threatens to homogenize student fiction and poetry.[60] Bennett's complaint that he was not allowed to pursue political allegory under Conroy is visible today in faculty member Ethan Canin's edict to "plot your way into an idea, don't idea your way into a plot," as he told one young woman whose story was up for workshop in April 2016.[61] Canin conducts workshop sessions with an almost scientific approach. Yet Canin himself, as a student in the program in August 1982, retreated from "the stultifying pressure of observation"—of the very sort he orchestrates today in workshop sessions—by ceasing writing "immediately and almost completely." Because he was so uncomfortable with the fact that "everything I wrote was going to be looked at" in such a highly contentious forum, "for a year and a half, I wrote nothing," he confessed, fulfilling assignments by handing in old stories he had written in college.[62] Even Canin, now one of the figureheads of the program who regularly delivers standing-room-only readings at Prairie Lights Bookstore, found the climate for literary production so unbearable that he wrote not a single word throughout three semesters of coursework as a Workshop student. As Canin's current teaching emphasis on the primacy of plot indicates, few Orwellian political allegories and Joyce-inspired experimental narratives have been produced at the Workshop, or are actively encouraged today. The primacy of character, Marilynne Robinson's mantra in the classroom, constrains Workshop pedagogy, which is surprisingly averse to experimentation and genre bending, as Cisneros's experience operating at the edge of prose and poetry attests.

Competition and survival, although rarely acknowledged explicitly, remain fixtures of Workshop culture. Writing in the late 1990s, faculty member R. V. Cassill, who witnessed the evolution of the program from its inception in the early 1940s, observed that "a constant urgency over all these years and among all groups was the articulated or barely hushed compulsion to publish." Publication continues to be the most universally recognized way for students "to justify themselves as part of the group, and to justify whatever anguish and effort might have brought them to the Workshop."[63] The Workshop in many ways still abides by what Conroy "said over and over": "the writing life is hard," a mantra that graduates such as Fritz McDonald "resented."[64]

From the Quonset huts of the early 1940s, the prevailing ethos of the program has suggested that the best writing occurs under duress. Engle embodied that principle in an incident that took place one summer at his country retreat in Stone City near his hometown of Cedar Rapids. This "tableau of rural serenity not much interrupted by Paul's weekly trips in to Iowa City to meet his summer class and interview potential students," as Cassill described it, came under serious threat in August 1959 when two criminal escapees from the nearby penitentiary held Engle and his family hostage.[65] When he returned home from Iowa City with his older daughter Mary, he discovered his wife and younger daughter Sara gagged and tied to chairs, and his refrigerator raided of its "cold drinks." Wielding large carving knives taken from the kitchen, the young men, twenty-five and twenty-one, warned Engle, "If you do exactly like we say, nobody will get hurt."[66]

Engle persuaded the men to untie his wife so she could make him dinner. As she prepared the meal, one of the captors responded to Mrs. Engle's question about what careers they wanted to pursue, mentioning he "would like to be a writer and had done some writing. He didn't have a typewriter anymore, though, because he had sold it to get money to escape," as she told reporters. Upon hearing that one of the men harbored literary aspirations, Engle sprang into character. He told them he had work to do, which they allowed. "So Engle sat down at his typewriter and tossed off two book reviews for the Chicago Tribune. He wrote about 800 words in all. The reviews were of 'The Buffalo Soldiers' and 'The Tender Shoot.' " Perhaps most telling was that Engle said he "had no trouble writing" under these circumstances, stalling the men until police arrived.[67] Threatening circumstances driven by a palpable sense of fear was the condition he created for aspiring young authors, which was supposed to teach them that writing is "accomplished only by the old and bitter way of sitting down in fear and trembling to confront the most terrifying thing in the world—a blank sheet of paper," filled only through the urgency to survive.[68]

Engle's vision for the Workshop traces back to his Gatsbyesque boyhood aspiration for outlaw fame, as seen in his well-thumbed copy of *Hopalong Cassidy*. As we learn at the conclusion of Fitzgerald's novel, the book is also a token of Gatsby's original ambition, whose raw authenticity bears a complex paradoxical relation to the revelation of his faux library after his death. In the process of creating and conditioning the world's most powerful creative writing program, Engle became the architect of his own plaguing nightmares and the scourge of his enemies. The Workshop, along with its vast array of imitators, created American literature, for better or worse, for more than three-quarters of a century. Careers depended on the program's prestige to take flight; signal moments in literary history—from O'Connor's *Wise Blood* and Snodgrass's *Heart's Needle* to Vonnegut's *Slaughterhouse-Five* and Robinson's *Gilead*—relied on this vital community and its powerful connections to the publishing industry. However, the perils of institutionalizing literary art into a systematic process of production surfaced in instances such as the creative block Rita Dove experienced upon graduation. For her, like many others, escaping the critical voices of workshop sessions was essential to carrying on a fruitful career as a professional writer. The influential workshop method and the program's celebrated legacy as the clearinghouse for contemporary literature and American culture thus come with a cautionary undercurrent checking the runaway dreams of professional authorship and literary fame. As Vonnegut's haunting warning from *Mother Night* inscribed on the Literary Walk on Iowa Avenue attests, "We are what we pretend to be. So we must be careful about what we pretend to be."[69]

NOTES

Introduction

1. Ed Dinger, ed., *Seems Like Old Times* (Iowa City: University of Iowa Press, 1986), 60.

2. Richard J. Kelly, ed., *We Dream of Honour: John Berryman's Letters to His Mother* (New York: W. W. Norton, 1988), 251–259.

3. Paul L. Mariani, *Dream Song: The Life of John Berryman* (Amherst: University of Massachusetts Press, 1996), 286.

4. Philip Levine, *The Bread of Time: Toward an Autobiography* (Ann Arbor: University of Michigan Press, 1993).

5. Philip Levine, "Mine Own John Berryman," in *A Community of Writers: Paul Engle and the Iowa Writers' Workshop*, ed. Robert Dana (Iowa City: University of Iowa Press, 1999), 164, 168, 185.

6. Dana, 226.

7. Eric Olsen and Glenn Schaeffer, eds., *We Wanted to Be Writers: Life, Love, and Literature at the Iowa Writers' Workshop* (New York: Skyhorse, 2011), 97–98.

8. Rosemary M. Magee, ed., *Conversations with Flannery O'Connor* (Jackson: University Press of Mississippi, 1987), 43.

9. Dana, 16.

10. Quoted in Zlatko Anguelov, "Tennessee Williams," *The Writing University* (10 January 2012), web.

11. Earl G. Ingersoll, ed., *Conversations with Rita Dove* (Jackson: University Press of Mississippi, 2003), 17.

12. Dinger, 123–124.

13. Olsen and Schaeffer, 259; Dana, 51.

14. F. Scott Fitzgerald, *The Great Gatsby* (New York: Charles Scribner's Sons, 1925), 173.

15. Papers of Paul Engle, Special Collections Department, University of Iowa Libraries, Iowa City, Iowa. Hereafter, PPE SCUI.

16. Paul Engle, ed., *Midland: Twenty-Five Years of Fiction and Poetry, Selected from the
Writing Workshops of the State University of Iowa* (New York: Random House, 1961), 1.

17. Dana, ix.

18. Engle, 2.

19. Dana, 38.

20. Dana, 39.

21. Engle, 4.

22. Stephen Wilbers, "Paul Engle: An Imaginative and Delicate Aggression," *Iowa
Alumni Review* 30 (1977): 8–13.

23. Dana, 39.

24. Dana, 46.

25. Dana, 29.

26. Edward J. Delaney, "Where Great Writers Are Made," *Atlantic Monthly*, 16 July
2007, web.

27. Delaney, 1.

28. D. G. Myers, *The Elephants Teach: Creative Writing Since 1880* (New Jersey: Pren-
tice Hall, 1996), 146. Records of the Iowa Writers' Workshop, Special Collections Department, University of Iowa Libraries, Iowa City, Iowa. Hereafter, RIWW SCUI.

29. Myers, 165.

30. RIWW SCUI.

31. Edmund Skellings to Stephen Wilbers, 10 May 1976, RIWW SCUI.

32. Crumley, whose *The Last Good Kiss* (1978) is regarded as one of the most influential crime novels of the late twentieth century, earned his MFA from the Workshop
in 1966, just one year before founding the creative writing program at Colorado State
University.

33. A sampling of the raw data from the 1976 survey conducted by Stephen Wilbers
illustrates the widespread influence of Iowa graduates and faculty on the development
of creative writing programs. Thomas Rabbitt (MFA, Iowa, 1972) founded the MFA
program at the University of Alabama, which was officially approved in November
1973. Rabbitt was the director with five faculty members, a total of twenty degree candidates, and four degrees awarded annually. William Harrison and James Whitehead,
both Iowa MFAs, were the key figures in the founding of the program at the University
of Arkansas in 1964. Philip O'Connor, Iowa MFA, helped establish the program at
Bowling Green State University in 1968. Mark Strand, Iowa MFA, was a co-founder of
the Brooklyn College program, established in 1974. The University of Massachusetts,
Amherst, was saturated with Iowa MFAs, including Joseph Langland, Andrew Fetler,
Richard Kim, and Robert Tucker, who made up half of its faculty in 1976. The University of Northern Iowa program (established 1961) was run by Loren Taylor, 1951 Iowa
MFA, whose professional standards learned at the Workshop seemed to eclipse

bureaucratic dysfunction. "I have had 3 students who have published in the last three years (two novels and poetry), but the result has not been because of any concentrated program of our department," he admitted. The effort, according to the Iowa model, was to professionalize, although there was not always a direct correlation between institutional cohesion and student publication toward professional careers. RIWW SCUI.

34. Myers, 146.

35. RIWW SCUI.

36. James L. West, III, *American Authors and the Literary Marketplace Since 1900* (Philadelphia: University of Pennsylvania Press, 2011).

37. Ben Harris McClary, "Washington Irving's Literary Pimpery," *American Notes and Queries* 10 (1972): 150–151. The pejorative diction of the title arises from McClary's discovery of Irving's proposal to aid a friend's career by attempting to place a manuscript, as if it were his friend's, with a publisher given to him several years earlier by a Boston businessman. It is "quite good," he assured his friend, and would go far to launch his career. Before the findings in this research, McClary was not so damning about the ethics of Irving's business dealings, tracing his promotion of several authors through archival letters in an earlier study titled "Washington Irving's Literary Midwifery: Five Unpublished Letters from the British Repository," *Philological Quarterly* 46 (1967): 277–283. McClary's finding, though provocative, is not typical of Irving's business practice that, however aggressive, was not so grossly unethical.

38. Stephen King, "Acceptance Speech: National Book Award for Distinguished Contribution to American Letters," The National Book Foundation (20 November 2003), web.

39. Tom Kealey, *The Creative Writing MFA Handbook: A Guide for Prospective Graduate Students* (New York: Bloomsbury, 2008), 22.

40. RIWW SCUI.

41. Jim Collins, *Bring on the Books for Everybody: How Literary Culture Became Popular Culture* (Durham, N.C.: Duke University Press, 2010).

42. Andrew Delbanco, *Melville: His World and Work* (New York: Knopf, 2005), 196.

43. RIWW SCUI.

44. Myers, 61.

45. Peter Elbow, *Writing Without Teachers* (Oxford: Oxford University Press, 1998 [1973]).

46. William Wallace Whitelock, *The Literary Guillotine* (New York: John Lane, 1903), 252.

47. Susan Coultrap-McQuin, *Doing Literary Business: American Women Authors in the Nineteenth Century* (Chapel Hill: University of North Carolina Press, 1990), 144.

48. Engle's income for his books *Poet's Choice* and *On Creative Writing* was $1,593.09 from E.P. Dutton and Company for a five-month period ending in April 1965. *An Old Fashioned Christmas* garnered steady royalty checks, yet scant earnings for

Poems in Praise are on record, with many checks like one for *American Child* from Dial Press dated June 30, 1959, worth as little as $11.09. Engle sold 29,268 Valentine cards for Hallmark Inc. in February 1967 (receipt dated March 31, 1967), securing a tidy $7,317 for his efforts; Hallmark had established a lucrative relationship with him several years earlier, with a steady stream of checks coming during the 1960s for more than $500. Christmas cards were his cash cow, as seen by his first Hallmark payday of $184.50 on January 20, 1961. Engle's creative writing fed greeting card and television industries. *The Golden Child* aired on television, was published in *Guideposts* (a white middle-class Protestant general interest magazine), and was rehashed into a greeting card by that journal. A letter dated October 14, 1960, from Glenn D. Kittler of *Guideposts* indicates a business relationship with Engle. Engle also dabbled in popular sports poetry, netting a substantial $2,000 advance for a poem on the Kentucky Derby for *Sports Illustrated*, as revealed in a letter from Percy Knauth dated April 23, 1961. Though considerable time and effort went into them, none of these publications are mentioned in Wilbers or Clarence A. Andrews, *A Literary History of Iowa* (Iowa City: University of Iowa Press, 1972). It is also worth noting that his Random House receipts are minuscule compared with those of his mass market productions. *Poems in Praise*, for example, earned him $20.16 in royalties on August 4, 1961 (as indicated in a letter from Jane Wilson of William Morris and Company, his agent). PPE SCUI.

49. Paul Engle to Sinclair Lewis, 27 February 1951, PPE SCUI.

50. Paul Engle, Response to draft chapter, "Engle Workshop," PPE SCUI.

51. Shirley Lim, "The Strangeness of Creative Writing: An Institutional History," *Pedagogy* 3.2 (2003), 157.

52. Quoted in Ron McFarland, "An Apologia for Creative Writing," *College English* 55 (1993), 28.

53. Dana Gioia, *Can Poetry Matter? Essays on Poetry and American Culture* (St. Paul, Minn.: Gray Wolf, 1992), 2.

54. For a skeptical approach toward the enterprise, see Dana Goodyear, "The Moneyed Muse," *New Yorker*, 19 February 2007, web.

55. Gioia, 13.

56. Edmund Skellings to Stephen Wilbers, 10 May 1976, RIWW SCUI.

57. All quotations in the paragraph are from Kiyohiro Miura, " 'I'll Make Your Career,' " in *A Community of Writers: Paul Engle and the Iowa Writers' Workshop*, ed. Robert Dana (Iowa City: University of Iowa Press, 1999), 57, 59.

58. Dinger, 15.

59. Ellison's point here has been underscored by recent theorists commenting on literature deliberately written for the masses, such as the serial fiction of the *New York Ledger*. Michael Denning's suggestion that "questions about the sincerity of [popular literature's] purported beliefs or the adequacy of their political proposals are less interesting than questions about the narrative embodiment of their political ideologies," a point which, I would argue, equally applies to self-conscious attempts at

serious literature for the elite market. Michael Denning, *Mechanic Accents: Dime Novels and Working-Class Culture in America* (New York: Verso, 1987), 103.

60. PPE SCUI.

61. Loren Glass, "Middle Man: Paul Engle and the Iowa Writers' Workshop," *The Minnesota Review* (Winter/Spring 2009), 2.

62. Lynn Neary, "In Elite MFA Programs, the Challenge of Writing While 'Other,' " *National Public Radio*, 19 August 2014, web.

63. Junot Díaz, "MFA vs. POC," *New Yorker*, 30 April 2014, 32.

64. Robert Sullivan, 2 February 1976, transcribed from audio cassette, RIWW SCUI.

65. Myers, 150.

66. Myers, 148–149.

67. Myers, 149.

68. Myers, 116.

69. Mearns's Dewey-influenced goal for writing instruction was "always of self-expression as a means of personal growth" to permeate every aspect of the student's life over and against mastering written expression in fiction, poetry, and drama. "The business of making professional poets" he disavowed entirely as "another matter—with which this writer has never had the least interest." Hughes Mearns, *Creative Power* (Garden City: Doubleday, Doran, 1929), 119–120.

70. Olsen and Schaeffer, 271. "The professional success rates for graduates in creative writing [based on the success rate for publication] is about one percent (compared with 90 percent for graduates of medical school)," according to Myers, 2.

71. Olsen and Schaeffer, 217–218.

72. Further signs of the difficulty of gaining entrance into the Workshop, even for a non-degree earning observer of a single class, appear in Frank Conroy's rejection of University of Iowa public relations representative Winston Barclay's offer "to sit in on one of the workshops for a semester" as a means of gaining a deeper understanding of the program to enhance future publicity. Winston Barclay to Frank Conroy, 26 February 1990, RIWW SCUI, Series V, Box 1, Director's Files, under permission of the Iowa Writers' Workshop. Directors of other programs would have welcomed such an opportunity for free publicity. Conroy instead demurred, citing high standards for admission, emphasizing that the "people who *didn't* make the cut include a medical doctor, numerous PhD's, Magnas and Summas from the best universities in the country, widely published fiction writers, people with very strong recommendations from current and past visiting staff, etc.," despite Barclay's desire to observe in a temporary capacity rather than formally apply. After regaling him with such daunting odds for admission, Conroy suggested to Barclay, "you can of course apply," an arch dismissal carrying considerable cruelty, especially since plenty of classroom space was available. The type of promotion Conroy did pursue was not free, as seen in his negotiations with private fund-raisers such as the Endowment Planning Group, who sent him an elaborate proposal for a

campaign titled "The Plan," a fifteen-page document sent via fax in 1990. In a letter to Michael Rea of the Dungannon Foundation, Conroy openly worried about accepting the offer because he was uncertain that the budget could withstand the high fees the private fund-raising consultant demanded. Roberta d'Estachio to Frank Conroy, 19 December 1990; Frank Conroy to Michael Rea, 14 December 1990, RIWW SCUI, Series V, Box 1, Director's Files, access under permission of the Iowa Writers' Workshop.

73. Olsen and Schaeffer, 61–62.

74. Olsen and Schaeffer, 60.

75. Paul Engle, ed., *On Creative Writing* (New York: E.P. Dutton, 1964), vii.

1. The Brilliant Misfit: Flannery O'Connor

1. Jean W. Cash, *Flannery O'Connor: A Life* (Knoxville: University of Tennessee Press, 2002), 93.

2. Flannery O'Connor, *The Habit of Being: Letters Edited and With an Introduction*, ed. Sally Fitzgerald (New York: Farrar, Straus and Giroux, 1979), 176.

3. Hajime Noguchi, *Criticism of Flannery O'Connor* (Tokyo: Bunkashobouhakubun-sha, 1985), 60–61.

4. Colman McCarthy, "The Servant of Literature in the Heart of Iowa: Paul Engle," *Washington Post*, 27 March 1983.

5. Cash, 81.

6. Jean Wylder, "Flannery O'Connor: A Reminiscence and Some Letters," *North American Review* 255.1 (Spring 1970), 60.

7. Brad Gooch, *Flannery: A Life of Flannery O'Connor* (New York: Little, Brown, 2009), 120.

8. Cash, 81.

9. James B. Hall to Jean Wylder, 6 January 1973, Jean Wylder Project, RIWW SCUI.

10. Gooch, 152.

11. Richard Gilman, "On Flannery O'Connor," *New York Review of Books*, 21 August 1969, 25.

12. James B. Hall to Jean Wylder, 6 January 1973, Jean Wylder Project, RIWW SCUI.

13. McCarthy.

14. Bob Fawcell, "William Porter's Writing Center: From Pulp to Post," *Daily Io-wan*, 26 January 1946.

15. Barbara Spargo to Stephen Wilbers, 2 February 1976, RIWW SCUI.

16. Wylder, 58. Tom Grimes notes that the GI Education Bill "accounted for the high percentage of men participating in the Workshop's early years," which placed O'Connor in a tiny minority of "one of only three women in the Workshop in the late 1940s"; *The Workshop: Seven Decades of the Iowa Writers' Workshop* (New York: Hyperion, 1999), 36.

17. Barbara Spargo to Stephen Wilbers, 2 February 1976, RIWW SCUI.

18. *Current Biography Yearbook: Who's News and Why, 1942* (New York: H.W. Wilson, 1942), 249.

19. Grimes, 35.

20. Gooch, 122.

21. Flannery O'Connor, *Mystery and Manners,* ed. Sally and Robert Fitzgerald (New York: Farrar, Straus and Giroux, 1969), 127.

22. O'Connor, *Mystery,* 127.

23. Cash, 39.

24. Flannery O'Connor, *Conversations,* ed. Rosemary Magee (Jackson: University Press of Mississippi, 1986), 99.

25. O'Connor, *Habit of Being,* 192.

26. Gooch, 123.

27. Hank Messick to Stephen Wilbers, 26 March 1976, RIWW SCUI.

28. Paul Engle, "How Creative Writing Is Taught at University of Iowa Workshop," *Des Moines Sunday Register,* 26 December 1947, 9E.

29. Wylder, 58.

30. Cash, 92.

31. Wylder, 58.

32. O'Connor, *Habit of Being,* 422.

33. O'Connor, *Habit of Being,* 74.

34. Paul Engle to Virgil Hancher, 31 October 1963, PPE SCUI.

35. Paul Engle, *A Lucky American Childhood* (Iowa City: University of Iowa Press, 1996), xiii.

36. Engle, *A Lucky American Childhood,* 23–24.

37. Engle, *A Lucky American Childhood,* 35.

38. Ben Ray Redman, Review of *Break the Heart's Anger* by Paul Engle, *New York Herald Tribune Books,* 22 March 1936.

39. PPE SCUI.

40. Engle, *A Lucky American Childhood,* 27.

41. In his vision, literature became a mechanism for what Henry Jenkins calls convergence culture, which in Engle's case marked the beginning of the current movement of literary culture into popular culture. The Workshop epitomizes an early embodiment of convergence culture, especially in the leveraging of diverse media merging at the intersection of technologies, industries, cultures, and audiences. Henry Jenkins, *Convergence Culture: Where Old and New Media Collide* (New York: New York University Press, 2006), 14.

42. Engle's process echoes what Jim Collins describes as the way "literary reading now comes with its own self-legitimating mythology that sanctifies the singularity of reading novels as an aesthetic experience, the way they *used* to be read, yet these same novels became global bestsellers only through the intervention of popular literary

culture." Jim Collins, *Bring on the Books for Everybody: How Literary Culture Became Popular Culture* (Durham, N.C.: Duke University Press, 2010), 225.

43. Cash, 81.

44. Gooch, 125–126.

45. Cash, 82.

46. Paul Engle, "Introduction" to *Midland*, manuscript draft, PPE SCUI.

47. See for example Mark McGurl's claim that Engle's sadism was a perfect match for O'Connor's masochism in *The Program Era: Postwar Fiction and the Rise of Creative Writing* (Cambridge: Harvard University Press, 2010). He argues that O'Connor was obsessed with "the necessary pleasures of the 'discipline' " of writing, especially "the discipline of narrative form . . . as a masochistic aesthetics of institutionalization," making "discipline itself a kind of religion" whereby institutions are reinforced by obedience to rules. Submitting to the authority of institutions such as Engle's Workshop and the Catholic Church, he claims, provided O'Connor with "a source of great pleasure, aesthetic or otherwise." McGurl, 135. The point is well taken, although it elides the very real stand O'Connor took against not only Engle's editorial feedback, but also that of the editor he arranged to publish her first novel, *Wise Blood*. Further, her willingness to satirize her mentor's zeal to market and advertise the program through business sponsorship also undermines this flat depiction of her as passively submitting to his will. The reality of their relationship was far more complex.

48. Engle, "How Creative Writing Is Taught."

49. Engle, "How Creative Writing Is Taught."

50. Engle, "How Creative Writing Is Taught."

51. Engle, "How Creative Writing Is Taught."

52. O'Connor, *Habit of Being*, 13.

53. Cash, 128.

54. O'Connor, *Habit of Being*, 14.

55. Flannery O'Connor, *The Complete Stories of Flannery O'Connor* (New York: Farrar, Straus and Giroux, 1946), ix.

56. O'Connor, *Complete Stories*, xi.

57. O'Connor, *Habit of Being*, 14.

58. Margaret Meaders, "Flannery O'Connor: Literary Witch," *Colorado Quarterly* (Spring 1962), 384.

59. Gooch, 136–137.

60. Robie Macauley to Stephen Wilbers, 16 April 1976, RIWW SCUI.

61. O'Connor, *Habit of Being*, 45.

62. Flannery O'Connor to Paul Engle, 14 February 1955, PPE SCUI.

63. Flannery O'Connor to Paul Engle, 3 April 1960, PPE SCUI.

64. Flannery O'Connor to Paul Engle, 7 June 1961, PPE SCUI.

65. Flannery O'Connor, *Wise Blood* (New York: Farrar, Straus and Giroux, 1949), 27.

66. O'Connor, *Complete Stories*, 132.

67. O'Connor, *Wise Blood*, 14.

68. O'Connor, *Wise Blood*, 15.

69. Wylder, 59.

2. The Star: W. D. Snodgrass

1. Donald J. Torchiana, "*Heart's Needle:* Snodgrass Strides Through the Universe," *Northwestern Tri-Quarterly* (Spring 1960), 18, RIWW SCUI.

2. Robert Bly, "When Literary Life Was Still Piled Up in a Few Places," in *A Community of Writers: Paul Engle and the Iowa Writers' Workshop*, ed. Robert Dana (Iowa City: University of Iowa Press, 1999), 39.

3. Peter Nelson quoted in Ed Dinger, ed., *Seems Like Old Times* (Iowa City: University of Iowa Press, 1986), 53.

4. Robert Dana, "De," in *The Poetry of W. D. Snodgrass: Everything Human*, ed. Stephen Haven (Ann Arbor: University of Michigan Press, 1993), 293.

5. W. D. Snodgrass, *After-Images: Autobiographical Sketches* (Rochester, N.Y.: BOA Editions, 1999), 9.

6. J. D. McClatchy, "W. D. Snodgrass: The Mild, Reflective Art," in *The Poetry of W. D. Snodgrass: Everything Human*, ed. Stephen Haven (Ann Arbor: University of Michigan Press, 1993), 118.

7. Dana, "De," 296.

8. Donald Hall, "Seasoned Wood," in *The Poetry of W. D. Snodgrass: Everything Human*, ed. Stephen Haven (Ann Arbor: University of Michigan Press, 1993), 285, 288.

9. Mark McGurl, *The Program Era: Postwar Fiction and the Rise of Creative Writing* (Cambridge: Harvard University Press, 2009), 130; James Joyce, *Portrait of the Artist as a Young Man* (New York: Signet, 1991), 217.

10. Paul Engle, "The Writer and the Place," in *Midland* (New York: Random House, 1961), xxv.

11. Suzanne McConnell quoted in *Seems Like Old Times*, ed. Ed Dinger (Iowa City: University of Iowa Press, 1986), 35.

12. R. W. Apple, "The Shaping of Writers on Campus" [reprint], *Des Moines Register*, 24 May 1963, 10.

13. Paul Engle, "How Creative Writing Is Taught at University of Iowa Workshop," *Des Moines Sunday Register*, 26 December 1947, 9G.

14. W. D. Snodgrass, "Mentors, Fomenters, and Tormentors," in *A Community of Writers: Paul Engle and the Iowa Writers' Workshop*, ed. Robert Dana (Iowa City: University of Iowa Press, 1999), 39.

15. Tom Grimes, ed., *The Workshop: Seven Decades of the Iowa Writers' Workshop* (New York: Hyperion, 1999), 724.

16. Jean Wylder, "Flannery O'Connor," in *A Community of Writers: Paul Engle and the Iowa Writers' Workshop*, ed. Robert Dana (Iowa City: University of Iowa Press, 1999), 234.

17. Snodgrass, "Mentors, Fomenters, and Tormentors," 119–120.

18. Stephen Wilbers, *The Iowa Writers' Workshop: Origins, Emergence, and Growth* (Iowa City: University of Iowa Press, 1980), 94.

19. Snodgrass, "Mentors, Fomenters, and Tormentors," 125.

20. Snodgrass, "Mentors, Fomenters, and Tormentors," 125.

21. Robert Boyers and W. D. Snodgrass, "W. D. Snodgrass: An Interview," *Salmagundi* 22–23 (Spring–Summer 1973): 165.

22. Boyers and Snodgrass, 165.

23. Snodgrass, "Mentors, Fomenters, and Tormentors," 131.

24. James B. Hall to Jean Wylder [n.d.], Jean Wylder Project, RIWW SCUI.

25. Snodgrass, "Mentors, Fomenters, and Tormentors," 129.

26. William Stafford to Jean Wylder, 8 January 1973, Jean Wylder Project, RIWW SCUI.

27. McClatchy, 117–118.

28. McClatchy, 114.

29. Snodgrass, "Mentors, Fomenters, and Tormentors," 133.

30. James B. Hall to Jean Wylder, 11 January 1973, Jean Wylder Project, RIWW SCUI.

31. W. D. Snodgrass, *Heart's Needle* (New York: Knopf, 1959), 52, 54, Iowa Authors Collection, SCUI.

32. Snodgrass, *Heart's Needle*, 47; Snodgrass, *Heart's Needle* [dust jacket], Iowa Authors Collection, SCUI.

33. Snodgrass, *Heart's Needle*, 47, Iowa Authors Collection, SCUI.

34. Snodgrass, *After-Images*, 194.

35. Richard Stern to Jean Wylder, 10 May 1973, Jean Wylder Project, RIWW SCUI.

36. Morgan Gibson to Jean Wylder, 4 January 1973, Jean Wylder Project, RIWW SCUI.

37. Snodgrass, *After-Images*, 194.

38. Snodgrass, *Heart's Needle* [dust jacket], Iowa Authors Collection, SCUI.

39. Snodgrass, *Heart's Needle*, 36–37, Iowa Authors Collection, SCUI.

40. Snodgrass, *Heart's Needle*, 34–35, Iowa Authors Collection, SCUI.

41. Snodgrass, *Heart's Needle*, 53, Iowa Writers Series, SCUI; Torchiana, "Snodgrass Strides Through the Universe," 18.

42. Ed Blaine to Stephen Wilbers, 14 June 1976, Stephen Wilbers Project, RIWW SCUI.

43. Ogden Plumb to Jean Wylder, 27 April 1973, Jean Wylder Project, RIWW SCUI.

44. Lewis Turco, "The Iowa Workshop: An Assenting View," *Prairie Schooner* (Spring 1965), 93–94, RIWW SCUI.

45. Marvin Bell, "He Made It Possible," in *A Community of Writers: Paul Engle and the Iowa Writers' Workshop*, ed. Robert Dana (Iowa City: University of Iowa Press, 1999), 74.

46. Snodgrass, "Mentors, Fomenters, and Tormentors," 123.

47. William Stafford to Jean Wylder, 8 January 1973, Jean Wylder Project, RIWW SCUI.

48. James Sunwall to Jean Wylder, 11 January 1973, Jean Wylder Project, RIWW SCUI.

49. Dana, "De," 293.

50. Dana, "De," 292.

51. McClatchy, 118.

52. Snodgrass, *Heart's Needle*, 62.

53. Philip L. Gerber and Robert J. Gemmett, eds., " 'No Voices Talk to Me': A Conversation with W. D. Snodgrass," *Western Humanities Review* 24.1 (Winter 1970), 71.

54. W. D. Snodgrass to Paul Engle, 30 December 1964; 11 January 1964; 21 June 1964; PPE SCUI.

55. John Gilgun to Jean Wylder, 2 January 1973, Jean Wylder Project, RIWW SCUI.

3. The Suicide: Robert Shelley

1. T. George Harris, "University of Iowa's Paul Engle: Poet-Grower of the World," *Look*, 1 June 1965, PPE SCUI.

2. Warren Carrier, "Some Recollections," in *A Community of Writers: Paul Engle and the Iowa Writers' Workshop*, ed. Robert Dana (Iowa City: University of Iowa Press, 1999), 23.

3. J. D. McClatchy, "W. D. Snodgrass: The Mild, Reflective Art," in *The Poetry of W. D. Snodgrass: Everything Human*, ed. Stephen Haven (Ann Arbor: University of Michigan Press, 1993), 114.

4. McClatchy, 114. See also Paul L. Gaston, *W. D. Snodgrass* (Boston: Twayne, 1978), 59.

5. Carrier, 23.

6. Vance Bourjaily describes how "one of [Kim's] manuscripts dealt in some way with suicide, and I may have said something about thinking suicide was too easy a solution for the problem in the story. It was at this point that Richard rose, looked to us for recognition, and on receiving it, said: 'We have a rather different attitude towards suicide in my culture.' He went on to describe people who thought of suicide as honorable, courageous, and ritually necessary in certain situations." Vance Bourjaily, "Dear Hualing," in *A Community of Writers: Paul Engle and the Iowa Writers' Workshop*, ed. Robert Dana (Iowa City: University of Iowa Press, 1999), 54.

7. Ray B. West, "COMMENT: The Boys in the Basement," *Western Review* 13.1 (Autumn 1948), 2.

8. Robert Shelley, "Le Lac des Cygnes," *Western Review* 13.1 (Autumn 1948), 34.

9. Student Applications, Robert Shelley, 1949, RIWW SCUI.

10. Robin Hemley, "A Critique of Postgraduate Workshops and a Case for Low-Residency MFAs," *Teaching Creative Writing*, ed. Heather Beck (New York: Palgrave, 2012), 104.

11. Harris, "University of Iowa's Paul Engle."

12. Paul Engle, "How Creative Writing Is Taught at University of Iowa Workshop," *Des Moines Sunday Register*, 26 December 1947, 9E.

13. Engle, "How Creative Writing Is Taught at University of Iowa Workshop."

14. Nancy C. Andreasen, "Creativity and Mental Illness," *American Journal of Psychiatry* 144.10 (1987): 1288–1292. Herbert Hendin, *Suicide in America: A New and Expanded Edition* (New York: W.W. Norton, 1995), 30. Also citing Andreasen's seminal 1987 study of mental illness at the Iowa Writers' Workshop is scientific research by Frederick K. Godwin and Kay Redfield Jamison in *Manic-Depressive Illness: Bipolar Disorders and Recurrent Depression* (Oxford: Oxford University Press, 2007), which concludes that a "predisposition to creativity" is significantly linked to suicides (394). Corroborating Andreasen's findings are those of Kay Jamison, whose "study of 47 British artists and writers found that 38 percent had sought treatment for mood disorders, compared to fewer than two percent in the general population." Significantly, "Half the poets in the group" sought treatment; Eric Maisel, *Creativity for Life: Practical Advice on the Artist's Personality and Career from America's Foremost Creativity Coach* (Novato, Calif.: New World Library, 2007), 47. The connection has been considered almost common knowledge among producers and insiders of creative media industries, as seen in Jimi Hendrix's autobiographical lyric lamenting that "Manic depression is a frustrating mess," and the more than five hundred paintings with unambiguous suicidal imagery, including Andy Warhol's *Suicide*, Edvard Munch's *The Suicide*, and Jackson Pollock's *Ten Ways of Killing Myself*. Former Workshop director Frank Conroy suffered a "nervous breakdown" that struck "as I finished my autobiography," *Stop-Time*. With no pharmaceutical or talking cure, he, like Shelley, was forced "out of shame and great effort, to hide the inner turmoil, put on a mask of normalcy and soldier through one day at a time"; Tom Grimes, *Mentor* (Portland, Ore.: Tin House, 2010), 223. For more on psychiatric issues among Workshop members, see chapter 7, "Mad Poets: Dylan Thomas and John Berryman."

15. Engle, "How Creative Writing Is Taught at University of Iowa Workshop."

16. E. A. Robinson, *The Poetry of E. A. Robinson*, ed. Robert Mezey (New York: Modern Library, 1999), 8.

17. Lorrie Goldensohn aptly warns, "any reader of Randall Jarrell ought to be careful not to make simplistic arguments about repressed homosexuality. It is as if Jarrell retreated to being a woman, or being maternal at any rate, not so much because he really wanted to be a woman, or give up any powerful prerogatives assigned to the male gender." Jarrell did not want to cancel male identity "but to enlarge it" by "appropriating

feminine character" and "poaching on emotions normally thought to belong to women alone." In this way he evaded falling into the "predictable binaries" that he believed restrained the creative process. Lorrie Goldensohn, *Dismantling Glory: Twentieth-Century Soldier Poetry* (New York: Columbia University Press, 2003), 213. Virginia Woolf similarly fueled her best writing, such as *Orlando*, by transcending the limitations of gender.

18. Richard Bode, *Beachcombing at Miramar: The Quest for an Authentic Life* (New York: Warner, 1996), 167. Others raising repressed homosexuality as the cause of the character Richard Cory's suicide include Scott Donaldson, Edwin Arlington Robinson's most recent biographer, who writes, "We are apt to look at a life as dependent upon male friendship as Robinson's and wonder if he did not live out his days as a closeted gay man (closeted against himself most of all)"; *Edwin Arlington Robinson: A Poet's Life* (New York: Columbia University Press, 2013), e-book.

19. James Sunwall, 11 January 1973, Jean Wylder Project, RIWW SCUI.

20. Harris, "University of Iowa's Paul Engle."

21. James B. Hall, "Our Workshops Remembered: The Heroic Phase" [n.d.], RIWW SCUI.

22. Quoted in Loren Glass, "Middle Man: Paul Engle and the Iowa Writers' Workshop," *Minnesota Review* 71–72 (Winter/Spring 2009), 4.

23. William Doreski, *The Years of Our Friendship: Robert Lowell and Allen Tate* (Oxford: University Press of Mississippi, 1990), 104.

24. Philip McGowan, *Anne Sexton and Middle Generation Poetry: The Geography of Grief* (Westport, Conn.: Greenwood, 2004), x.

25. Brewster Ghiselin, "Poets Learning," *Poetry* 79.5 (February 1952), 289.

26. Paul Engle, "Poet and Professor Overture," *Poetry* 79.5 (February 1952), 270.

27. Ghiselin, "Poets Learning," 289.

28. McClatchy, 115.

29. "Student Kills Self with Hunting Rifle," *Daily Iowan*, 26 April 1951: 1.

30. Robert Shelley, "Harvest," in *Midland: Twenty-Five Years of Fiction and Poetry, Selected from the Writing Workshops of the State University of Iowa*, ed. Paul Engle (New York: Random House, 1961), 538.

31. Carrier, 23.

32. James Sunwall, 11 January 1973, Jean Wylder Project, RIWW SCUI.

33. Shelley, "Harvest," 538.

34. Shelley, "Harvest," 538.

35. "Student Kills Self with Hunting Rifle," 1.

36. Quoted in Edward Brunner, *Cold War Poetry: The Social Text in the Fifties Poem* (Urbana and Chicago: University of Illinois Press, 2001), 274.

37. Robert Shelley, "On My Twenty-First Birthday," in *Midland: Twenty-Five Years of Fiction and Poetry, Selected from the Writing Workshops of the State University of Iowa*, ed. Paul Engle (New York: Random House, 1961), 539.

38. Quoted in Brunner, *Cold War Poetry*, 274.

39. "Go Way, Ya Bother Me!" *Daily Iowan*, 26 April 1951: 1.

40. Shelley, "Harvest," 538–539.

41. W. D. Snodgrass, "An Interview with Elizabeth Spires," *American Poetry Review* 15 (July–August 1990): 38–46.

42. Hall, "Our Workshops Remembered."

43. Engle, "Poet and Professor Overture," 268.

44. Donald Petersen, "The Stages of Narcissus," *Poetry* 83.3 (December 1953), 141–144.

45. Andreasen, 1288.

46. James Sunwall, 11 January 1973, Jean Wylder Project, RIWW SCUI.

47. Wylder-Leggett Addendum to James Sunwall, 11 January 1973, Jean Wylder Project, RIWW SCUI.

48. Richard Stern, 26 April 1973, Jean Wylder Project, RIWW SCUI.

49. Richard Stern, 26 April 1973, Jean Wylder Project, RIWW SCUI.

4. The Professional: R. V. Cassill

1. Jean Wylder, "R. V. Cassill," in *A Community of Writers: Paul Engle and the Iowa Writers' Workshop*, ed. Robert Dana (Iowa City: University of Iowa Press, 1999), 194–195.

2. Tom Grimes, ed., *The Workshop: Seven Decades of the Iowa Writers' Workshop* (New York: Hyperion, 1999), 36.

3. Edmund Skellings to Paul Engle, 17 May 1963, PPE SCUI.

4. Paul Engle, ed., *Midland* (New York: Random House, 1961), 583–584.

5. R. V. Cassill, *The Eagle on the Coin* (New York: Random House, 1950), 208–209.

6. R. V. Cassill, *Dormitory Women* (New York: Lion, 1954), 3.

7. Evan Thomas (Harper and Brothers Director, General Books Department) to Paul Engle, 10 March 1960, PPE SCUI.

8. Evan Thomas to Paul Engle, 10 March 1960, PPE SCUI.

9. William Oman to Paul Engle, 11 March 1960, PPE SCUI.

10. R. T. Bond to Paul Engle, 5 May 1960, PPE SCUI.

11. R. T. Bond to Paul Engle, 5 May 1960, PPE SCUI.

12. Paul Engle to John Gerber, 7 January 1963, PPE SCUI.

13. Paul Engle to Gordon G. Dupee, 26 November 1962, PPE SCUI.

14. Peter H. Huyck, "Cassill's Latest Book—A Treatment of the Mechanics," *Daily Iowan*, 19 March 1963.

15. Huyck, "Cassill's Latest Book."

16. Huyck, "Cassill's Latest Book."

17. Huyck, "Cassill's Latest Book."

18. Don Justice to Paul Engle, 4 April 1963, PPE SCUI.

19. David Roberts, Letter to the Editor, *Daily Iowan*, 22 March 1963.

20. Norman Peterson, Letter to the Editor, *Daily Iowan*, 23 March 1963.

21. Laird Addis, Jr., et al., Letter to the Editor, *Daily Iowan*, 26 March 1963.

22. Don Justice to Paul Engle, 4 April 1963, PPE SCUI.

23. Edmund Skellings to Paul Engle, 17 May 1963, PPE SCUI.

24. Don Justice to Paul Engle, 4 April 1963, PPE SCUI.

25. Edmund Skellings to Paul Engle, 17 May 1963, PPE SCUI.

26. Stephen Wilbers, *The Iowa Writers' Workshop: Origins, Emergence, and Growth* (Iowa City: University of Iowa Press, 1980), 96–97.

27. Edmund Skellings to Paul Engle, 17 May 1963, PPE SCUI.

28. R. V. Cassill to Paul Engle, 23 April 1963, PPE SCUI.

29. Gordon Dupee to Paul Engle, 26 July 1963, PPE SCUI.

30. Just as Cassill had dabbled in the market for erotic novels, Engle himself explored the seamy side of popular print culture. In 1962, for example, he ordered *The Housewife's Handbook on Selective Promiscuity*, only to discover that the United States Postal Service had refused delivery and impounded it. The publisher notified him that "Our attorneys are preparing a vigorous campaign to overcome this latest instance of Post Office censorship." To Paul Engle from Documentary Books, 31 December 1962, PPE SCUI.

31. One advertisement makes a particularly overt gesture at arguing that the man of letters is also a man of business by presenting facsimiles of two signed typewritten letters designed to look like evidence laid on a table. The letter taking up the left half of the advertisement on Cleveland's Western Reserve University letterhead certifies Engle's acumen as a speaker "both in the academic and the popular sense of setting up the criteria for judging American literature and following it through with appropriate and stimulating examples," a line underscored for emphasis. Next to it is a reference from Rochester Ad Club, Inc., a New York association of advertisers, lauding Engle's talk as "one of the most unique programs in the history of the Rochester Ad Club." In cursive above his name appears the heading, "To listen to him is an experience which should be enjoyed by more." W. Colston Leigh, Inc., Advertisement for Paul Engle, 1951, PPE SCUI.

32. R. V. Cassill to Paul Engle, n.d., 1962, PPE SCUI.

33. R. V. Cassill, "Why I Left the Midwest," in *In an Iron Time: Statements and Reiterations, Essays by R. V. Cassill* (West Lafayette, Ind.: Purdue University Press, 1969), 131.

34. Wilbers, 114.

35. Verlin Cassill to Stephen Wilbers, 26 August 1976, RIWW SCUI.

36. See the epilogue for more details and further discussion of how Engle's relationship with Gerber precipitated his resignation from the Workshop.

37. Cassill, "Why I Left the Midwest," 130.

38. "Biographical Note," R. Verlin Cassill Manuscripts, SCUI. See also Philip Roth's look back in anger at Iowa for comparison to Cassill's. After Roth's brief stint as a

faculty member, he fulminated against the campus and the town in the pages of *Esquire* so violently that its editors wrote President Virgil M. Hancher asking for a reply. He declined, explaining to Engle that "if I started a reply, I might say more than would be wise under the circumstances." Virgil Hancher to Paul Engle, 21 November 1962, PPE SCUI. Roth's piece, "Iowa: A Very Far Country Indeed," appeared in the December 1962 issue of *Esquire*.

39. Cassill, "Why I Left the Midwest," 131.

40. Mark McGurl, *The Program Era: Postwar Fiction and the Rise of Creative Writing* (Cambridge: Harvard University Press, 2009), 160–171.

41. R. V. Cassill, "The Killer Inside Me: Fear, Purgation, and the Sophoclean Light," in *Tough Guy Writers of the Thirties*, ed. David Madden (Carbondale: Southern Illinois University Press, 1968), 233.

42. Louis Menand, "Show or Tell: Should Creative Writing Be Taught?" *New Yorker*, 8 June 2009, web.

43. Verlin Cassill, "Associated Writing Programs," *ADE* [American Departments of English] *Bulletin* 17 (May 1968): 33–35.

44. Robert Day, "The Early Days of AWP," *Association of Writers and Writers Programs*, 11 September 2012, web.

45. R. V. Cassill, "Introduction," in *Fifteen by Three*, ed. James Laughlin (New York: New Directions, 1957), 7.

46. Clarence A. Andrews, *A Literary History of Iowa* (Iowa City: University of Iowa Press, 1972), 204–205.

47. R. V. Cassill, "And In My Heart," *Collected Stories* (University of Arkansas Press, 1989), 144. Among the many stories based on Cassill's experience teaching creative writing are "The Romanticizing of Dr. Fless," and "The Martyr." The former articulates the persistent theme in Cassill's stories of the struggle to write great literature in mass culture. Protagonist Dick Samson considers the case of Hart Crane's suicide and asks rhetorically, "what the hell good does it do you to write that well if nobody wants it? You may write the best poetry in the world, but the damned pigs force you to write prose to make a living." Cassill, "The Romaniticizing of Dr. Fless," *Collected Stories*, 555. "The Martyr" reprises another dominant theme in Cassill's work of romantic affairs in college settings, as his main character Professor Alleman in his mid-forties "was having an affair with a student named Lois." While lying in bed with her after a tryst, he inadvertently bursts into tears recalling "a pretty and rambunctious nun" he had as a student, a figure loosely based on Flannery O'Connor. Alleman inadvertently reveals he really loved the idealistic nun who "told him nothing was worth aiming for except sainthood," prompting the jealousy of Lois in an echo of Gretta Conroy, Gabriel's wife, in James Joyce's *The Dead*. Cassill, "The Martyr," *Collected Stories*, 570, 567. Cassill registered the significance of Gretta's revelation of her love for Michael Fury in his introduction to his first collection of stories, noting that how "Gabriel finds his wife's love at the instant of revelation when he learns it is irretrievably fixed to the memory of

the dead boy" is significantly linked to how "sometimes writers must hope no more of love from readers than that they may say, like Gabriel's wife, 'I can see his eyes as well as well! He was standing at the end of the wall where there was a tree.' " Cassill, "Introduction," 5.

48. Bernard Bergzorn, *New York Times Book Review*, 22 April 1965, 16.

49. James Laughlin, ed., *Fifteen by Three* (New York: New Directions, 1957), v.

50. Laughlin, *Fifteen by Three*, vi; Grimes, 35–36.

51. Cassill, "Why I Left the Midwest," 121.

52. Cassill, "And In My Heart," 145.

5. The Guru: Marguerite Young

1. Bruce Kellner, "Miss Young, My Darling," *Review of Contemporary Fiction* 20.2 (Summer 2000), 150.

2. Kellner, 160.

3. William Cotter Murray, "Marguerite Young: Trying on a Style," in *A Community of Writers: Paul Engle and the Iowa Writers' Workshop*, ed. Robert Dana (Iowa City: University of Iowa Press, 1999), 201.

4. Kellner, 160.

5. Murray, 205.

6. Murray, 204.

7. Murray, 202–203.

8. Murray, 204.

9. Barry Silesky, *John Gardner: Literary Outlaw* (Chapel Hill, N.C.: Algonquin, 2004), 62–63.

10. Murray, 203.

11. Kellner, 150.

12. Molly McQuade, "Famous Writers' School: Novelists and Poets Remember Their Student Days at the University of Chicago," *Chicago Tribune*, 4 June 1995, 2, web.

13. Quoted in Edna St. Vincent Millay, *Edna St. Vincent Millay: Collected Poems*, ed. Norma Millay (New York: HarperCollins, 2011), xxiii.

14. Charles Raus, *Conversations with American Writers* (New York: Knopf, 1985), 117.

15. McQuade, 2.

16. Raus, *Conversations*, 117.

17. McQuade, 2.

18. Kellner, 155.

19. Miriam Fuchs, "Interview with Marguerite Young," *Review of Contemporary Fiction* 23.1 (2003), 129.

20. Kellner, 155.

21. Charles E. Raus, "Marguerite Young: The Art of Fiction," *Paris Review* 66 (Fall 1977), 52.

22. Raus, "Art," 52.

23. Marguerite Young to Paul Engle, February 1947, PPE SCUI.

24. Raus, "Art," 52.

25. Kellner, 155.

26. Kellner, 152.

27. Virginia Woolf, *To the Lighthouse* (New York: Harcourt, 1981), 162–168, 48.

28. Marguerite Young, "Fictions Mystical and Epical," *Inviting the Muses: Stories, Essays, Reviews* (Normal, Ill.: Dalkey Archive, 1994), 162. In her 1975 *Harvard Advocate* essay "Feminine Sensibility," she claimed, "I do not think there is any difference between the works of men and women writers, and certainly do not think that women were limited, up to Virginia Woolf's time, to the literature of inter-human relationships." Marguerite Young, *Inviting the Muses: Stories, Essays, Reviews* (Normal, Ill.: Dalkey Archive, 1994), 144.

29. Ellen G. Friedman and Miriam Fuchs, "A Conversation with Marguerite Young," *Review of Contemporary Fiction* 9.3 (Fall 1989), 150.

30. "Congratulations to New York Book Critic Sam Anderson!" *New York Magazine*, 14 January 2008.

31. Nona Balakian, "Marguerite Young—A Celebration," 9 April 1983, Papers of Gustav Bergmann, SCUI.

32. Nona Balakian, "Marguerite Young, Innovator," in *Marguerite Young, Our Darling: Tributes and Essays*, ed. Miriam Fuchs (Normal, Ill.: Dalkey Archive, 1994), 4.

33. Quoted in Erika Duncan, "Marguerite Young: The Muse of Bleecker Street," in *Changes: A Journal of Arts and Entertainment* [n.d.], Papers of Gustav Bergmann, SCUI.

34. Quoted in Duncan, "Marguerite Young."

35. Vytas Valaitas, "A 1963 picture of Marguerite Young with the manuscript of her notably long novel, *Miss MacIntosh, My Darling*." First published in William Goyen, "A Fable of Illusion and Reality," *New York Times*, 12 September 1965, BR5.

36. Miriam Fuchs, ed., *Marguerite Young, Our Darling: Tributes and Essays* (Normal, Ill.: Dalkey Archive, 1994), xii.

37. Marguerite Young to Paul Engle, February 1945, PPE SCUI.

38. Marguerite Young to Paul Engle, February 1945, PPE SCUI.

39. Marguerite Young to Paul Engle, February 1945, PPE SCUI.

40. Marguerite Young to Paul Engle, 3 December 1947, PPE SCUI.

41. Marguerite Young to Paul Engle, February 1945, PPE SCUI.

42. Marguerite Young to Paul Engle, 11 April 1945, PPE SCUI.

43. Amy Clampitt, "Out of the Depressed Middle: The Imagination of Marguerite Young," in *Marguerite Young, Our Darling: Tributes and Essays*, ed. Miriam Fuchs (Normal, Ill.: Dalkey Archive, 1994), 5.

44. Marguerite Young to Paul Engle, October 1945, PPE SCUI.

45. As quoted in front matter of Marguerite Young, *Miss MacIntosh, My Darling*, vol. 2 (Normal, Ill.: Dalkey Archive, 1999).

46. Balakian, "Marguerite Young, Innovator," 4.

47. Marguerite Young to Paul Engle, 3 December 1947, PPE SCUI.

48. Andrew Levy, *The Culture and Commerce of the American Short Story* (Cambridge: Cambridge University Press, 1993), 128.

49. Levy, 129.

50. Peter Merchant, "My Marguerite Young," in *Marguerite Young, Our Darling: Tributes and Essays*, ed. Miriam Fuchs (Normal, Ill.: Dalkey Archive, 1994), 16.

51. Merchant, 14.

52. Merchant, 16.

53. Merchant, 15.

54. Merchant, 15.

55. Friedman and Fuchs, "A Conversation with Marguerite Young."

56. Merchant, 15.

57. Merchant, 15.

58. Marguerite Young, "Inviting the Muses," *Mademoiselle*, September 1965, 230.

59. Dennis Joseph Enright, *Signs and Wonders: Selected Essays* (Manchester: Carcanet, 2002), 35.

60. Marguerite Young, "On Teaching," *Review of Contemporary Fiction* 9.3 (Fall 1989), 164.

61. Marguerite Young, *Miss MacIntosh, My Darling* (New York: Scribner, 1965), 1.

62. Young, *Miss MacIntosh, My Darling*, 1.

63. Hardwick, the wife of Robert Lowell, penned the novel in Iowa City while Lowell was teaching at the Workshop. *The Simple Truth*'s exploration of academic life at Iowa at the time of a lurid murder trial captured her imagination.

64. Marguerite Young to Leola Bergmann, 4 December 1983, Papers of Gustav Bergmann, SCUI.

65. Clampitt, 5.

6. The Turncoat: Robert Lowell

1. James B. Hall, "Our Workshops Remembered: The Heroic Phase," 4, [n.d.], RIWW SCUI.

2. Robert Dana as quoted in Ed Dinger, ed., *Seems Like Old Times* (Iowa City: University of Iowa Press, 1986), 20.

3. Philip Levine, "Mine Own John Berryman," in *A Community of Writers: Paul Engle and the Iowa Writers' Workshop*, ed. Robert Dana (Iowa City: University of Iowa Press, 1999), 162–163.

4. Zlatko Anguelov, "Robert Lowell," *The Writing University*, 5 January 2012, web.

5. Isabelle Travis, " 'Is Getting Well Ever an Art': Psychopharmacology and Madness in Robert Lowell's *Day by Day*," *Journal of Medical Humanities* 32 (2011), 317; Richard Poirier, "Our Truest Historian," *New York Herald Tribune Book Week*, 11 October 1964: 1.

6. Robert Lowell, *The Letters of Robert Lowell*, ed. Saskia Hamilton (New York: Farrar, Straus and Giroux, 2005), 195.

7. Steven Gould Axelrod, *Robert Lowell: Life and Art* (Princeton, N.J.: Princeton University Press, 1978), 99.

8. Robert Lowell and Elizabeth Bishop, *Words in Air: The Complete Correspondence Between Elizabeth Bishop and Robert Lowell*, ed. Thomas Travisano and Saskia Hamilton (New York: Macmillan, 2008), 150.

9. Richard Tillinghast, *Robert Lowell's Life and Work: Damaged Grandeur* (Ann Arbor: University of Michigan Press, 1995), 29.

10. Lowell, *Letters*, 64.

11. Tillinghast, 52.

12. William Doreski, *The Years of Our Friendship: Robert Lowell and Allen Tate* (Oxford: University Press of Mississippi, 1990), 104.

13. Ian Hamilton, *Robert Lowell: A Biography* (New York: Faber and Faber, 2011), 167.

14. Paul Mariani, *Lost Puritan: A Life of Robert Lowell* (New York: W.W. Norton, 1994), 60-61.

15. Mariani, 56-57.

16. "Poet Robert Lowell Sentenced to Prison," *A&E Networks* (12 August 2015), web. See also Lowell, *Letters*, 683.

17. Lowell, *Letters*, 683.

18. David Laskin, *Partisans: Marriage, Politics, and Betrayal Among the New York Intellectuals* (Chicago: University of Chicago Press, 2000), 99.

19. After two trials, the evidence of which drew from the accident, Stafford was awarded $4,000; Lowell, *Letters*, 680.

20. W. D. Snodgrass, "Mentors, Fomenters, and Tormentors," in *A Community of Writers: Paul Engle and the Iowa Writers' Workshop*, ed. Robert Dana (Iowa City: University of Iowa Press, 1999), 125.

21. Snodgrass, 125.

22. Robert Dana, "Far From the Ocean," in *A Community of Writers: Paul Engle and the Iowa Writers' Workshop*, ed. Robert Dana (Iowa City: University of Iowa Press, 1999), 150.

23. Frank Bidart, *Harvard Advocate* 113.1-2 (November 1979), 12.

24. Tillinghast, 32.

25. Mariani, 88-89.

26. Mariani, 183.

27. Tillinghast, 52-51.

28. Axelrod, 23.

29. Snodgrass, 127-128.

30. Axelrod, 23.

31. Mariani, 190.

32. Lowell and Bishop, *Words in Air*, 97–98.

33. Mariani, 191.

34. Hamilton, 168.

35. Mariani, 188.

36. Mariani, 182.

37. Mariani, 189.

38. Lowell and Bishop, *Words in Air*, 98.

39. Lowell, *Letters*, 296.

40. Lowell and Bishop, *Words in Air*, 98.

41. Jane Howard, "Applause for a Poet," *Life*, 19 February 1965, 56.

42. Judith Baumel, "Robert Lowell: The Teacher," *Harvard Advocate* 113 (November 1979), 32.

43. Mariani, 192.

44. Levine, 165.

45. Levine, 163.

46. Joe Gould, an eccentric American writer during the 1940s whose ambition to write the longest book in history, called "The Oral History of the Contemporary World," inspired similar reactions toward his authorial madness. Ezra Pound read a fragment of the manuscript and commented on it; Marianne Moore had solicited chapters of it for the *Dial* in the 1920s, before the journal folded with the stock market crash of 1929. The mental illness Gould suffered from, likely hypergraphia as Jill Lepore conjectures, was "a mania, but seems more like something a writer might envy, which seems even rottener than envy usually does, because Gould was a . . . madman." Jill Lepore, "Joe Gould's Teeth," *New Yorker*, 27 July 2015, web.

47. Levine, 163.

48. Lowell's poetry was controversial for bringing his insanity into focus, particularly in his writings of the late 1950s in which he ridiculed his parents and revealed his multiple hospitalizations for bipolar disorder; Travis, 317.

49. Lowell and Bishop, *Words in Air*, 152.

50. Mariani, 191.

51. "Bednasek Says He's Not Guilty of Murdering Beauty 'I Loved,' " *Daily Iowan*, 13 December 1949, 1.

52. Elizabeth Hardwick, *The Simple Truth* (New York: Ecco, 1982), 17.

53. Hardwick, 16–17.

54. Hardwick, 78.

55. Lowell, *Letters*, 204.

56. Robert Lowell to Paul Engle, 8 February 1955, PPE SCUI.

57. Lowell and Bishop, *Words in Air*, 131.

58. Lowell and Bishop, *Words in Air*, 137.

59. Lowell and Bishop, *Words in Air*, 131.

60. Hamilton, 196.

61. Robert Lowell to Paul Engle, 30 March 1955, PPE SCUI.

62. Doreski, 104.

63. Robert Lowell to Paul Engle, 25 April 1952, PPE SCUI.

64. Hamilton, 196.

65. Robert Lowell to Paul Engle, 25 April 1952, PPE SCUI.

66. Mary Jane Baker, "Classes with a Poet," *Mademoiselle* 40 (1954), 106.

67. Jerome Mazzaro, *The Poetic Themes of Robert Lowell* (Ann Arbor: University of Michigan Press, 1965), 55.

68. Quoted in Louis J. Budd, ed., *Mark Twain: The Contemporary Reviews* (Cambridge: Cambridge University Press, 1999), 475.

69. Dana, "Far From the Ocean," 153.

70. Baker, 106.

71. Hamilton, 198.

72. Baker, 137.

73. Robert Lowell to Paul Engle, 7 May 1955, PPE SCUI.

74. Baker, 141.

75. Robert Lowell to Paul Engle, 25 April 1952, PPE SCUI.

76. Robert Lowell to Paul Engle, 8 February 1955, PPE SCUI.

77. Levine, 163–164.

78. Snodgrass, 139.

79. Mariani, 225.

80. Baker, 140.

81. Dinger, 22.

82. Robert Lowell to Paul Engle, 3 May 1957, PPE SCUI.

83. Dinger, 22.

84. Robert Lowell, *Life Studies and For the Union Dead* (New York: Farrar, Straus and Giroux, 2007), 87.

85. Lowell, *Life Studies and For the Union Dead*, 86.

86. Lowell, *Life Studies and For the Union Dead*, 89.

87. Lowell, *Life Studies and For the Union Dead*, 97.

88. Dana, "Far From the Ocean," 158.

7. Mad Poets: Dylan Thomas and John Berryman

1. Quoted in W. D. Snodgrass, "Mentors, Fomenters, and Tormentors," in *A Community of Writers: Paul Engle and the Iowa Writers' Workshop*, ed. Robert Dana (Iowa City: University of Iowa Press, 1999), 135.

2. Snodgrass, 135, Ray B. West, Jr., "Dylan Thomas at Iowa," in *A Community of Writers: Paul Engle and the Iowa Writers' Workshop*, ed. Robert Dana (Iowa City: University of Iowa Press, 1999), 244.

3. Quoted in Barry Silesky, *Ferlinghetti: The Artist in His Time* (New York: Warner, 1990), 25, 49.

4. Quoted in Paul Ferris, *Dylan Thomas: The Biography* (London: Phoenix Orion House, 2000), 279.

5. West, 244.

6. Silesky, 49.

7. Bill Read, *The Days of Dylan Thomas* (London: Weidenfeld and Nicolson, 1964), 140–141.

8. Clarence A. Andrews, *A Literary History of Iowa* (Iowa City: University of Iowa Press, 1972), 200.

9. Ray B. West to Stephen Wilbers, 20 July 1976, RIWW SCUI.

10. West, 242.

11. Dylan Thomas, *The Collected Letters of Dylan Thomas*, ed. Paul Ferris (London: J.M. Dent and Sons, 1985), 765.

12. Quoted in Read, 137.

13. Thomas, *Collected Letters*, 762.

14. Thomas, *Collected Letters*, 762–764.

15. Thomas, *Collected Letters*, 764.

16. Ed Glinert, *Literary London: A Street-by-Street Exploration of the Capital's Literary Heritage* (New York: Penguin, 2007), 83.

17. West, 235.

18. West, 257.

19. James Nashold and George Tremlett, *The Death of Dylan Thomas* (Edinburgh: Mainstream, 1997), 151.

20. Hilly Janes, *The Three Lives of Dylan Thomas* (London: Robson, 2014), e-book.

21. RIWW SCUI.

22. Quoted in Read, 150.

23. Quoted in Alan Norman Bold, ed., *Cambridge Book of English Verse, 1939–1975* (Cambridge: Cambridge University Press, 1976), 61.

24. Philip Levine, "Mine Own John Berryman," in *A Community of Writers: Paul Engle and the Iowa Writers' Workshop*, ed. Robert Dana (Iowa City: University of Iowa Press, 1999), 166.

25. Levine, 166.

26. Robert Penn Warren to Stephen Wilbers, 1 September 1976, RIWW SCUI.

27. Frances Jackson to Stephen Wilbers, 1 March 1976, RIWW SCUI.

28. Philip Levine to Stephen Wilbers, 19 February 1976, RIWW SCUI.

29. Philip Levine to Stephen Wilbers, 19 February 1976, RIWW SCUI.

30. John Berryman, *The Dream Songs* (New York: Farrar, Straus and Giroux, 2007), 40.

31. Quoted in Paul L. Mariani, *Dream Song: The Life of John Berryman* (Amherst: University of Massachusetts Press, 1990), 229.

32. Catherine Lacey, "Henry Doesn't Have Any Bats," *Paris Review*, 6 June 2013.

33. Emily Dickinson, *Final Harvest: Emily Dickinson's Poems*, ed. Thomas H. Johnson (Boston: Little, Brown, 1961), 111–112.

34. Richard J. Kelley, ed., *We Dream of Honour: John Berryman's Letters to His Mother* (New York: W.W. Norton, 1988), 251.

35. Lacey.

36. William Blake, *The Complete Poetry and Prose of William Blake*, ed. David Erdman (Berkeley: University of California Press, 2008), 412.

37. Kelley, 256.

38. Levine, 179.

39. Levine, 177.

40. Levine, 165.

41. Alan Golding, "American Poet-Teachers and the Academy," *A Concise Companion to Twentieth-Century American Poetry*, ed. Stephen Fredman (Malden, Mass.: Blackwell, 2005), 69.

42. Jack Kerouac, *On the Road* (New York: Penguin, 2005 [1957]), 5–6.

8. Celebrity Faculty: Kurt Vonnegut and John Irving

1. Kurt Vonnegut, "New World Symphony," in *A Community of Writers: Paul Engle and the Iowa Writers' Workshop*, ed. Robert Dana (Iowa City: University of Iowa Press, 1999), 115.

2. Kurt Vonnegut to Stephen Wilbers, January 1976, Stephen Wilbers Project, RIWW SCUI.

3. Kurt Vonnegut, *Mother Night* (New York: Dial, 2009 [1961]), v.

4. Vonnegut, "New World Symphony," 115.

5. Richard Rodriguez, *The Hunger of Memory: The Education of Richard Rodriguez* (New York: Random House, 1982).

6. Kurt Vonnegut, *Palm Sunday: An Autobiographical Collage* (New York: Random House, 2009), 85.

7. Thomas F. Marvin, *Kurt Vonnegut: A Critical Companion* (Westport, Conn.: Greenwood, 2002), 9.

8. John Irving, *The Imaginary Girlfriend* (New York: Arcade, 1996), n.p., e-book.

9. Kurt Vonnegut, *Letters*, ed. Dan Wakefield (New York: Delacorte, 2012), 78.

10. Marvin, 9.

11. William Rodney Allen, *Conversations with Kurt Vonnegut* (Jackson: University Press of Mississippi, 1988), 107.

12. Allen, 107.

13. Vonnegut, *Letters*, 123.

14. Kurt Vonnegut, *Slaughterhouse-Five* (New York: Dell, 1969), 200.

15. Vonnegut, *Slaughterhouse-Five*, 203.

16. Vonnegut, *Slaughterhouse-Five*, 201.

17. Kurt Vonnegut, Jr., "The Report on the Barnhouse Effect," in *Tomorrow, the Stars*, ed. Robert A. Heinlein (New York: Signet, 1953), 39–50; Kurt Vonnegut, Jr., "The Big Trip

Up Yonder," in *Assignment in Tomorrow*, ed. Frederik Pohl (New York: Hanover House, 1954), 123–138, Science Fiction Collection, Hevelin Science Fiction Collection, SCUI.

18. Vonnegut, *Letters*, 100.

19. Max McElwain, *Profiles in Communication: The Hall of Fame of the University of Iowa School of Journalism and Mass Communication* (Iowa City: Iowa Center for Communication Study, 1991), 161.

20. Paula Rabinowitz, *American Pulp: How Paperbacks Brought Modernism to Main Street* (Princeton: Princeton University Press, 2014), 25.

21. Rabinowitz, 59.

22. Rabinowitz, 222.

23. Vonnegut, *Letters* [n.p., photo caption].

24. Jerome Klinkowitz, *Kurt Vonnegut's America* (Columbia: University of South Carolina Press, 2009), 14.

25. Faculty Personnel Data Blank, Kurt Vonnegut, Jr., 22 September 1965, RIWW SCUI.

26. Kurt Vonnegut, "Have I Got a Car For You!" *In These Times*, 24 November 2004, web.

27. Klinkowitz, 15.

28. Eric Olsen and Glenn Schaeffer, eds., *We Wanted to Be Writers: Life, Love, and Literature at the Iowa Writers' Workshop* (New York: Skyhorse, 2011), 190.

29. Olsen and Schaeffer, 222.

30. Irving, *Imaginary Girlfriend*, [n.p., e-book].

31. Irving, *Imaginary Girlfriend*.

32. Vonnegut, *Letters*, 122–123.

33. Olsen and Schaeffer, 41.

34. Olsen and Schaeffer, 189.

35. Olsen and Schaeffer, 189.

36. Vonnegut, *Letters*, 106.

37. Richard Schickel, "Black Comedy with Purifying Laughter," *Harper's* [1st proof, galley 3062], May 1966, RIWW SCUI.

38. John C. Gerber to Mr. Kurt Vonnegut, 15 April 1966, RIWW SCUI.

39. Vonnegut, *Letters*, 132.

40. Vonnegut, *Letters*, 106.

41. Vonnegut, *Palm Sunday*, 90.

42. Vonnegut, *Palm Sunday*, 91.

43. Vonnegut, *Letters*, 74.

44. Vonnegut, *Palm Sunday*, 288.

45. Vonnegut, *Letters*, 131.

46. Vonnegut, *Letters*, 119.

47. Rinehart had supported the Workshop since the 1940s with its fellowship, engineered by Engle, granting the publisher first rights to student and faculty works. The

first of these works was Flannery O'Connor's *Wise Blood*, which eventually landed with Farrar, Straus and Giroux.

48. Vonnegut, *Letters*, 129.

49. Quoted in Robert Scholes, " 'Mithridates, He Died Old': Black Humor and Kurt Vonnegut, Jr.," *The Hollins Critic* 3.4 (October 1966), 8.

50. John C. Gerber to Mr. Kurt Vonnegut, 2 July 1965, RIWW SCUI; John C. Gerber to Mr. Kurt Vonnegut, 14 March 1966, RIWW SCUI.

51. Kurt Vonnegut to Stephen Wilbers, January 1976, Stephen Wilbers Project, RIWW SCUI.

52. Vance Bourjaily to John C. Gerber, 17 January 1966, RIWW SCUI.

53. Jerome Klinkowitz, *The Vonnegut Statement* (New York: Panther, 1975), 15.

54. Kurt Vonnegut, Jr., to John C. Gerber, 11 July 1965, RIWW SCUI.

55. Vonnegut, *Letters*, 116.

56. Vonnegut, *Slaughterhouse-Five*, 28.

57. Schaeffer and Olsen, 182.

58. Schaeffer and Olsen, 190.

59. Kurt Vonnegut to Stephen Wilbers, January 1976, Stephen Wilbers Project, RIWW SCUI.

60. Kurt Vonnegut to John C. Gerber, 11 July 1965, RIWW SCUI.

61. Vonnegut, *Letters*, 116.

62. Kurt Vonnegut, *A Man Without a Country*, ed. Daniel Simon (New York: Seven Stories, 2005), 41.

63. Vonnegut, *Letters*, 78.

64. Schaeffer and Olsen, 196.

65. Vonnegut, *Letters*, 398.

66. Vonnegut, *Slaughterhouse-Five*, 18.

67. Vonnegut, *Letters*, 121.

68. Vonnegut, *Letters*, 73.

69. W. D. Snodgrass, "Mentors, Fomenters, and Tormenters," in *A Community of Writers: Paul Engle and the Iowa Writers' Workshop*, ed. Robert Dana (Iowa City: University of Iowa Press, 1999), 144.

70. Vonnegut, *Letters*, 132.

71. Schaeffer and Olsen, 218–219.

72. Schaeffer and Olsen, 199–200.

73. Schaeffer and Olsen, 121.

74. Connie Brothers, interview by David Dowling, Iowa City, Iowa, 2 December 2015.

75. Schaeffer and Olsen, 121.

76. Schaeffer and Olsen, 196.

77. Vonnegut, *Letters*, 117.

78. Vonnegut, *Letters*, 82.

79. His agent with the Cosby Bureau International sent a letter saying, "At Kurt Vonnegut's request, I am returning $2,000 to you" as repayment for his late 1960s loan drawn from Workshop funds; Janet L. Cosby to Frank Conroy, 14 April 1989, RIWW SCUI, Series V, Box 1, Director's Files, access under permission of the Iowa Writers' Workshop.

80. Vonnegut, *Letters*, 124.

81. Vonnegut, *Letters*, 139–140.

82. David H. Lynn, "Editor's Notes," *Kenyon Review* 18.3–4 (Summer–Autumn 1996), 1.

83. Vonnegut, *Letters*, 130.

84. Vonnegut, *Letters*, 119.

85. Gail Godwin, "Kurt Vonnegut: Waltzing with the Black Crayon," in *A Community of Writers: Paul Engle and the Iowa Writers' Workshop*, ed. Robert Dana (Iowa City: University of Iowa Press, 1999), 219–220.

86. Schaeffer and Olsen, 155.

87. Schaeffer and Olsen, 236.

88. Anis Shivani, "Iowa Writers' Workshop Graduate Spills It All: Interview with John McNally, Author of *After the Workshop*," *Huffington Post*, 25 May 2011, web.

89. Schaeffer and Olsen, 155.

90. Schaeffer and Olsen, 190.

91. Godwin, 222.

92. The only extant version of Vonnegut's profile of Conroy is a fax he sent to the Workshop in 1990, which reads as follows.

FRANK CONROY I have known for a long time (having tried so hard to play the clarinet and the piano that musicians are in some way radically different from the rest of us). My friend Frank Conroy is a jazz pianist. (And a good one.) It was once explained to me (by a man who talks through his hat even more than I do) that musicians process music with that part of their brain meant to be used for ordinary language (for routine blah, blah, blah, Chinese, or French, or English, or whatnot). Witness Mozart (as fluent in music when a toddler as other toddlers in Salzburg were in German). If that isn't true about musicians, I don't want to hear so. It is too pretty a piece of information for me to do without. Which brings us to Conroy and Fats Waller. (Where else could we be at this point?) Conroy is as arch and dainty at a keyboard as Waller was. He also writes that way. (And also mentions Waller.)

Which brings us to dealing with unhappy memories by means of art. (Where else could we be at this point?) One can safely assume (I assume) that Waller (being both fat and black in America) had many unhappy memories. (Some of them probably are no more than five minutes old). So does Frank Conroy, although he is tall and white and skinny. I know this from what he chooses to write about. (Peace be to Philip Roth and Erica Jong, et al. who waste so much time denying that they are characters in their fictions.)

Yes, and Conroy, whether writing or playing the piano, by force of will and talent review bad memories in tones and cadences which I said before are arch and dainty. (Why shouldn't I repeat myself if something I've said is good and true?) One thinks (I think) of all the jazz musicians who let agony show through the rips in their otherwise seamless performances, or even played nothing but rips and never mind the fabric. (Rips? Riffs? The same?) Some say that was what made them great. But Waller achieved greatness without doing that. (Not even when playing and singing "Black and Blue.")

Miracle.

I am entitled to call Conroy childlike, since he is eleven years my junior. But I would call him that even if he were my great-grandfather. You should see him when he plays the piano. He is like a child (Waller as a toddler?), amazed by the enchanting sounds he makes so easily. I have never watched him write. (Has anybody?) But he must be similarly amazed. (Almost goofy with delight).

Kurt Vonnegut to Frank Conroy, 23 April 1990, RIWW SCUI, Series V, Box 1, Director's Files, access under permission of the Iowa Writers' Workshop.

93. Correspondence of Kurt Vonnegut, 20 May 1988, RIWW SCUI.

94. Vonnegut, *Slaughterhouse-Five*, 122.

9. Infidels: Sandra Cisneros and Joy Harjo

1. "Sandra Cisneros and Joy Harjo," *Literary Friendships*, 17 May 2005, American Public Media.

2. Renee H. Shea, "A Conversation with Sandra Cisneros," in *Sandra Cisneros in the Classroom: "Do Not Forget to Reach,"* ed. Carol Jago (Urbana, Ill.: National Council of Teachers of English, 2002), 33.

3. Eric Olsen and Glen Schaeffer, eds., *We Wanted to Be Writers* (New York: Skyhorse, 2011), 178.

4. Olsen and Schaeffer, 230–231.

5. Wolfgang Binder, ed., "Sandra Cisneros," *Partial Autobiographies: Interviews with Twenty Chicano Poets* (Erlangen: Verlag, Palm & Enke, 1985), 64.

6. Tom Grimes, ed., *The Workshop: Seven Decades of the Iowa Writers' Workshop* (New York: Hyperion, 1999), 149–150.

7. Grimes, 149–150; Bruce Dick and Amritjit Singh, eds., *Conversations with Ishmael Reed* (Jackson: University Press of Mississippi, 1995), 59.

8. Binder, 64.

9. Ramola D., "An Interview with Sandra Cisneros," *Writer's Chronicle* 38.6 (Summer 2006), 6.

10. Brooks Landon, conversation with David Dowling, 18 September 2015, Iowa City, Iowa.

11. Olsen and Schaeffer, 188.

12. Connie Brothers, interview with David Dowling, 18 September 2015, Iowa City, Iowa.

13. Olsen and Schaeffer, 188.

14. Carmen Haydee Rivera, *Border Crossings and Beyond: The Life and Works of Sandra Cisneros* (Santa Barbara, Calif.: ABC-CLIO, 2009), 24.

15. Joy Harjo, *The Last Song* (Albuquerque: Puerto del Sol, 1975).

16. Joy Harjo, *The Spiral of Memory: Interviews*, ed. Laura Coltelli (Ann Arbor: University Press of Michigan, 1996), 114.

17. Olsen and Schaeffer, 152.

18. Harjo, *Spiral*, 114.

19. Ed Dinger, ed., *Seems Like Old Times* (Iowa City: University of Iowa Press, 1986), 50.

20. Dinger, 47.

21. Dinger, 47.

22. Dinger, 41.

23. Dinger, 48.

24. Dinger, 42.

25. Olsen and Schaeffer, 153.

26. Rita Dove, *Conversations with Rita Dove*, ed. Earl G. Ingersoll (Jackson: University Press of Mississippi, 2003), 16.

27. Olsen and Schaeffer, 153.

28. "Joy Harjo," in *The Poet's Notebook: Excerpts from the Notebooks of Contemporary American Poets*, ed. Stephen Kuusisto et al. (New York: W.W. Norton, 1995), 84.

29. Joy Harjo, "My Sister, Myself: Two Paths to Survival," *Ms.*, September/October 1995, 73.

30. Rhonda Pettit, *Joy Harjo* (Boise: Boise State University Press, 1988), 9; Harjo, "My Sister," 71.

31. Joy Harjo, *She Had Some Horses* (New York: Thunder's Mouth, 2006), 64.

32. Olsen and Schaeffer, 54.

33. "Joy Harjo's 'Crazy Brave' Path to Finding Her Voice," *National Public Radio*, 9 July 2012, web.

34. Olsen and Schaeffer, 64.

35. Olsen and Schaeffer, 64.

36. "Sandra Cisneros and Joy Harjo," *Literary Friendships*.

37. Joy Harjo, "Poems from 'What Drove Me to This' and from 'She Had Some Horses,'" MFA thesis, University of Iowa, May 1978, 20.

38. "Sandra Cisneros and Joy Harjo," *Literary Friendships*.

39. Harjo, MFA thesis, 17.

40. Harjo, MFA thesis, 29.

41. Harjo, *Spiral*, 70.

42. Emily Dickinson, *Final Harvest: Emily Dickinson's Poems*, ed. Thomas H. Johnson (Boston: Little, Brown, 1961), 211.

43. Joy Harjo, *Crazy Brave: A Memoir* (New York: W.W. Norton, 2012), 35; Rivera, 63.

44. Harjo, *Spiral*, 70.

45. Sandra Cisneros, *The House on Mango Street* (New York: Vintage, 2009), 97.

46. Cisneros, *The House on Mango Street*, 100.

47. Rivera, 22.

48. "Sandra Cisneros and Joy Harjo," *Literary Friendships*.

49. Sandra Cisneros, Foreword, *Holler If You Hear Me: The Education of a Teacher and His Students*, Gregory Michie (New York: Teachers College Press, 1999), ix.

50. Penelope Mesic, "Sandra Cisneros," *Contemporary Literary Criticism*, vol. 69, ed. Roger Matuz (Detroit: Gale Research, 1992), 144.

51. Olsen and Schaeffer, 239.

52. Olsen and Schaeffer, 62.

53. Olsen and Schaeffer, 187.

54. Olsen and Schaeffer, 230.

55. Olsen and Schaeffer, 190.

56. "Sandra Cisneros and Joy Harjo," *Literary Friendships*.

57. "Sandra Cisneros and Joy Harjo," *Literary Friendships*.

58. Olsen and Schaeffer, 191–192.

59. Stephanie Vanderslice, "Once More to the Workshop: A Myth Caught in Time," in *Does the Writing Workshop Still Work?* ed. Dianne Donnelly (Bristol, U.K.: Multilingual Matters, 2010), 32.

60. "Sandra Cisneros and Joy Harjo," *Literary Friendships*.

61. Olsen and Schaeffer, 106.

62. Tracy Kidder, interview with David Dowling, 24 November 2015, Iowa City, Iowa.

63. Sandra Cisneros, *A House of My Own: Stories From My Life* (New York: Knopf, 2015), e-book.

64. Cisneros, "Introduction: A House of My Own," in *The House on Mango Street*, xvi.

65. Cisneros, *A House of My Own*.

66. Olsen and Schaeffer, 171, 98.

67. Olsen and Schaeffer, 217.

68. Olsen and Schaeffer, 222.

69. "Sandra Cisneros: I Hate the Iowa Writers' Workshop," WNYC interview, 23 April 2009, web.

70. Olsen and Schaeffer, 219.

71. "Sandra Cisneros," WNYC interview.

72. "Sandra Cisneros and Joy Harjo," *Literary Friendships*.

73. "Sandra Cisneros and Joy Harjo," *Literary Friendships*.

10. The Crossover: Rita Dove

1. Zlatko Anguelov, "Marvin Bell," *The Writing University*, web.

2. Charles Bullard, "U of I Writers' Workshop Graduate Appointed to be U.S. Poet Laureate," *Des Moines Register*, 19 May 1993, [n.p.], Student Records: Rita Dove, RIWW.

3. "Sandra Cisneros and Joy Harjo," *Literary Friendships*, American Public Media, 17 May 2005.

4. Rita Dove, *Conversations with Rita Dove*, ed. Earl G. Ingersoll (Jackson: University Press of Mississippi, 2003), 15–16.

5. Barbara Yost, "Memories and Magic: Dove's Pulitzer," July/August 1987, 18, Student Records: Rita Dove, RIWW.

6. Dove, *Conversations*, 16.

7. Yost, 18, Student Records: Rita Dove, RIWW.

8. Dove, *Conversations*, 16.

9. Dove, *Conversations*, 16.

10. Renee H. Shea, "American Smooth: A Profile of Rita Dove," *Poets and Writers*, September/October 2004, 41.

11. Dove, *Conversations*, 16.

12. Yost, 19, Student Records: Rita Dove, RIWW.

13. Robert McDowell, "The Assembling Vision of Rita Dove," *Callaloo* 9.1 (1986), 61.

14. Rita Dove, "The Discovery of Oranges," MFA thesis, University of Iowa, May 1977, 18–19.

15. Dove, *Conversations*, 98.

16. Max McElwain, *Profiles in Communication* (Iowa City: Iowa Center for Communication Study, 1991), 164.

17. Dove, *Conversations*, 17.

18. Dove, *Conversations*, 72.

19. Dove, *Conversations*, 16–17.

20. Dove, *Conversations*, 15.

21. Dove, *Conversations*, 17.

22. Dove, *Conversations*, 18.

23. Conversation with Fred Viebahn, 18 October 2016, University of Iowa, Iowa City, Iowa.

24. Yost, 18–19, Student Records: Rita Dove, RIWW.

25. Connie Brothers, interview with David Dowling, 2 December 2015, Iowa City, Iowa.

26. Dove, *Conversations*, 28.

27. Rita Dove, *Through the Ivory Gate* (New York: Pantheon, 1992), 1.

28. William Walsh, "Isn't Reality Magic? An Interview with Rita Dove," *Kenyon Review* 16.3 (1994), 150.

29. Dove, *Conversations*, 165.

30. Malin Pereira, *Rita Dove's Cosmopolitanism* (Urbana: University of Illinois Press, 2003), 74; see also Trey Ellis, "The New Black Aesthetic," *Callaloo* 12 (Winter 1989): 233–243.

31. Dove, MFA thesis, 29.

32. Pereira, 75.

33. Dove, *Conversations*, 98.

34. Dove, *Conversations*, 98.

35. Therese Steffen, *Crossing Color: Transcultural Space and Place in Rita Dove's Poetry, Fiction, and Drama* (Oxford: Oxford University Press, 2001), 10.

36. Theodore O. Mason, "African-American Theory and Criticism," *The Johns Hopkins Guide to Literary Theory and Criticism* (Baltimore: Johns Hopkins University Press, 1994), 15–16.

37. Dove, *Conversations*, 21.

38. Dove, MFA thesis, 26.

39. Walsh, 149.

40. Dove, *Conversations*, 22.

41. Dove, *Conversations*, 22–23.

42. Quoted in Elizabeth Alexander, *The Power of Possibility: Essays, Reviews, and Interviews* (Ann Arbor: University of Michigan Press, 2007), 52.

43. Steffen, 169.

44. Steffen, 12–13.

45. Steffen, 171.

46. Mohamed B. Taleb-Khyar, "An Interview with Maryse Condé and Rita Dove," *Callaloo* 14.2 (1991): 234. See also Pat Righelato, *Understanding Rita Dove* (Columbia: University of South Carolina Press, 2006), 7.

47. Patricia Kirkpatrick, "The Throne of Blues: An Interview with Rita Dove," *Hungry Mind Review* 35 (1995), 57.

48. Steffen, 7.

49. Dove, MFA thesis, 5.

50. Dove, *Conversations*, 27.

51. Steffen, 169.

52. The strong current of German literature and culture that runs through the heart of Dove's corpus began in Iowa with a poem called "The Bird Frau." In it, she portrays a German mother awaiting the return of her son from war. The wait grows torturous, claiming her sanity; she "fed the parakeet,/ broke its neck." She then resolves to "Let everything go wild," losing herself among the trees, floating about them and singing "like an old rag bird" herself. "She ate less, grew lighter, air tunneling/ through bone, singing." Passing children flee as she hauntingly beckons them with her small song, "Ein Liedchen, Kinder!" (a little tune, children!). The poem's arresting denouement appears in a moving tableau of her "Rudi, come home on crutches," his birdlike "thin

legs balancing this atom of life." Dove, MFA thesis, 42. This lyrical portrait of a mother driven mad by the prospect of the loss of her son in battle extends beyond the inner angst that transforms her life into a birdlike existence. Her modernist Imagism in this case is imbued with subtle yet powerful political commentary on the larger devastating effects of war that extend beyond its soldiers and reach deep into the hearts and minds of their loved ones on the home front. Indeed, the bird lady is a casualty of war here, as her love for her son eerily transforms her into the birdlike form that he himself embodies when he arrives on thin legs propped up by crutches.

53. Steffen, 171.

54. Righelato, 13.

55. McElwain, 163.

56. Eric Bennett writes, "After 1967, there is no trace in the public archives of CIA funding for writing at Iowa, either for the Iowa Writers' Workshop or the International Writing Program," although Engle had accepted funds from the Congress for Cultural Freedom, which was proven to be a CIA front. Bennett points out that although many have suspected this as evidence of "conspiracies lurking behind the façade of American reality," he found "no evidence that the CIA money influenced writing at Iowa," and that such "relatively benign activity" instead fits into the broader historical pattern of the cultural cold war." Eric Bennett, *Workshops of Empire: Stegner, Engle, and American Creative Writing During the Cold War* (Iowa City: University of Iowa Press, 2015), 113; Mark McGurl, *The Program Era: Postwar Fiction and the Rise of Creative Writing* (Cambridge: Harvard University Press, 2009).

57. McElwain, 164.

58. Bennett, 113.

59. Ekaterini Georgoudaki, "Rita Dove: Crossing Boundaries," *Callaloo* 14.2 (1991), 420.

60. Righelato, 13.

61. Dove, *Conversations*, 159.

62. Steffen, 170.

63. Steffen, 170.

64. Steffen, 14–15.

65. Rita Dove, *The Yellow House on the Corner* (Pittsburgh: Carnegie Mellon Press, 1980), 64.

66. Dove, *Conversations*, 112.

11. The Genius: Jane Smiley

1. Quoted in Neil Nakadate, *Understanding Jane Smiley* (Columbia: University of South Carolina Press, 2010), 6.

2. Nakadate, 7.

3. Eric Olsen and Glen Schaeffer, eds., *We Wanted To Be Writers: Life, Love, and Literature at the Iowa Writers' Workshop* (New York: Skyhorse, 2011), 186.

4. Jane Smiley, *Thirteen Ways of Looking at the Novel* (New York: Random House, 2005), 3.

5. Jane Smiley, "Iowa City, 1974," *Mentors, Muses, and Monsters: 30 Writers on the People Who Changed Their Lives*, ed. Elizabeth Benedict (New York: Simon and Schuster, 2009), 261.

6. Olsen and Schaeffer, 185.

7. Olsen and Schaeffer, 185.

8. Olsen and Schaeffer, 185.

9. Stephen King, *On Writing: A Memoir of the Craft* (New York: Scribner, 2000), 87.

10. One scene particularly captured how these volatile ingredients funneled into male authorial ambition. As Glen Schaeffer recalled, "At the time, not a weekend went by that Mailer wasn't in the news for punching someone in an expensive Manhattan restaurant." Literature and boxing became seamless, since Mailer's most recent book, *The Fight*, detailed the "rumble in the jungle" featuring Muhammad Ali and George Foreman. Schaeffer's Workshop instructor, Vance Bourjaily, claimed that Mailer had trained for his public altercations. At a pig roast he was hosting for the graduate students, Bourjaily suggested only half-jokingly that Schaeffer challenge Mailer to a fight. "We were all drunk," Schaeffer explained, "and I believe John Falsey egged it on." Bourjaily's suggestion was not entirely in jest, since he was a long-standing friend of Mailer's from his early days in New York City. The aging Mailer, then in his early fifties like Bourjaily, might represent the older generation at the bout billed as "an exhibition at Iowa." There he could prove "that *theirs* was the baddest generation." Schaeffer proposed that he could write up the event as a participatory MFA thesis in the spirit of Frederick Exley's *Fighting Norman Mailer*. They abandoned the idea, however, when Schaeffer realized that if he was to trounce Mailer in the ring, he would be maligned for destroying a beloved icon, and if he lost, he and his generation would suffer total humiliation. Olsen and Schaeffer, 182–183.

11. Olsen and Schaeffer, 218.

12. Smiley, "Iowa City, 1974," 261.

13. Smiley's revelation of the abuse endured by her female classmate behind closed doors points to a pattern of patriarchal control over burgeoning female creativity that traces back to the nineteenth century. In Fanny Fern's fictional autobiography *Ruth Hall*, from 1855, we hear of the entrapment of the young, precocious female writer at the hands of an aggressive editor who attempts to seize and monopolize her talent as his own. "Stay!" exclaimed her editor, "placing his hand on the latch," the symbol of his attempt to lock her into exclusive publishing rights. She eludes him, to his frustration, while he shouts, "I'll have my revenge" as "the last folds of her dress fluttered out the door." Fanny Fern, *Ruth Hall and Other Writings* (New Brunswick, N.J.: Rutgers University Press, 1986), 157.

14. Smiley, "Iowa City, 1974," 261.

15. Mary Ann Cain, " 'A Space of Radical Openness': Re-Visioning the Creative Writing Workshop," *Does the Writing Workshop Still Work?* ed. Dianne Donnelly (Bristol, U.K.: Multilingual Matters, 2010), 220.

16. Cain, 221.

17. Gaston Bachelard, *The Poetics of Space* (New York: Penguin, 2014), 54.

18. Carmen Haydee Rivera, *Border Crossings and Beyond: The Life and Works of Sandra Cisneros* (Santa Barbara, Calif.: Praeger, 2009), 22.

19. Olsen and Schaeffer, 227.

20. Olsen and Schaeffer, 200.

21. Smiley, "Iowa City, 1974," 261.

22. T. Coraghessan Boyle, "This Monkey, My Back," in *The Eleventh Draft: Craft and the Writing Life from the Iowa Writers' Workshop*, ed. Frank Conroy (New York: HarperCollins, 1999), 9.

23. Nakadate, 6–7.

24. Smiley, "Iowa City, 1974," 265.

25. Jane Smiley, "Swiss Family Schaeffer," *Nation*, 15 October 2007, 32–36.

26. Olsen and Schaeffer, 78.

27. Olsen and Schaeffer, 99.

28. Josh O'Leary, "Smiley Discusses 'Prophetic' Book," *Iowa City Press Citizen*, 27 October 2015, 1A-8A, Alumni Files, RIWW SCUI.

29. Smiley, "Iowa City, 1974," 264.

30. Jane Howard, *Families* (New Brunswick, N.J.: Transaction, 1978), 247.

31. Howard, 256.

32. Howard, 254.

33. Howard, 222.

34. Philip Roth, "Iowa: A Very Far Country Indeed," *Esquire*, December 1962, 132.

35. Howard, 253.

36. Smiley, "Iowa City, 1974," 267.

37. Smiley, "Iowa City, 1974," 264.

38. Howard, 17.

39. Olsen and Schaeffer, 186.

40. Dwight Garner, "Allan Gurganus," *Salon*, 8 December 1997, web.

41. Smiley, "Iowa City, 1974," 263.

42. Smiley, "Iowa City, 1974," 262–263.

43. In *Good Prose*, Kidder recalls how he "said harsh, dismissive things about other students' stories, precisely because they were no worse than my own, and sometimes even better." He resolved to "submit as little as possible to workshops" to avoid the abuse he witnessed, such as that of a woman who "after her story had been pummeled a while, stood up and declared to the class, 'This is a story about a lot of beautiful people, and a lot of beautiful things *going down!*' and stalked out of the room." Kidder recalled his classmates attacking one another's writing through withering slights that

included " 'pretentious, sentimental, boring, and Budweiser writing.' " Tracy Kidder and Richard Todd, *Good Prose: The Art of Nonfiction* (New York: Random House, 2013), 137–138.

44. Smiley, "Iowa City, 1974," 263.

45. Smiley, "Iowa City, 1974," 263.

46. Smiley, "Iowa City, 1974," 264.

47. Stephanie Vanderslice, "Once More to the Workshop: A Myth Caught in Time," in *Does the Workshop Still Work?* ed. Dianne Donnelly (Bristol, U.K.: Multilingual Matters, 2010), 31.

48. Olsen and Schaeffer, 100.

49. Quoted in Garner.

50. Jane Smiley, "Jeffrey, Believe Me," in *The Age of Grief: A Novella and Stories by Jane Smiley* (New York: Knopf, 1987), 64.

51. Smiley, "Jeffrey, Believe Me," 65.

52. Jane Smiley, Note to "Long Distance," in *The Workshop: Seven Decades of the Iowa Writers' Workshop*, ed. Tom Grimes (New York: Hyperion, 1999), 377.

53. Jane Smiley, "A Reluctant Muse Embraces His Task, and Everything Changes," in *Writers on Writing: Collected Essays from the New York Times*, ed. John Darnton (New York: Times Books, 2001), 222.

54. Smiley, "Iowa City, 1974," 267.

55. On December 15, 1973, just two years before Smiley's composition of "Jeffrey, Believe Me," the American Psychological Association removed homosexuality from its list of mental disorders in the DSM-II Diagnostic and Statistical Manual of Mental Disorders. "LGBT Rights Milestones," *CNN Library*, 30 October 2015, web. This helps contextualize the gender ideology deployed in the story as far more progressive than it appears from a twenty-first-century vantage point.

56. Connie Brothers, interview by David Dowling, 2 November 2015.

57. Jane Smiley, "Curriculum Vita," Coffee House Press Records, SCUI.

58. Robert McPhillips, "Jane Smiley's People," *Washington Post*, 19 November 1989, 8, Coffee House Press Records, SCUI.

59. Jay Schaefer, "Dentist, Bombs, and a Seducer," *San Francisco Chronicle* [n.d.], Coffee House Press Records, SCUI.

60. Michiko Kakutani, "Books of the Times: *The Age of Grief*, by Jane Smiley," *New York Times*, 26 August 1987, C21, Coffee House Press Records, SCUI.

61. Olsen and Schaeffer, 78.

62. Smiley, *Thirteen Ways of Looking at the Novel*, 372–373.

63. Jane Smiley, "Say It Ain't So, Huck: Second Thoughts on Mark Twain's 'Masterpiece,' " *Harper's*, January 1996, 61. This article pioneered the alternative feminist approaches to the American male literary canon, paving the way for recent journalism that has called into question monuments like Henry David Thoreau, as in Kathryn Schulz's "Pond Scum," *New Yorker*, 29 October 2015, web.

64. For a defense of Twain arguing that he should not be held to the standard of "Smiley's modern political sophistication," see Doug Underwood, *Journalism and the Novel: Truth and Fiction, 1700–2000* (Cambridge: Cambridge University Press, 2008), 196. Underwood points out that since Twain "is certainly no contemporary liberal," he should not be expected to be a "model of contemporary political correctness," especially given "his sentimental view of his Missouri upbringing, his brief service with the Missouri troops opposing the Union Army, and his insulting statements about Native Americans in his other works" (196).

65. Underwood, 197.

12. Red High-Tops for Life: T. C. Boyle

1. Eric Olsen and Glenn Schaeffer, eds., *We Wanted to Be Writers: Life, Love, and Literature at the Iowa Writers' Workshop* (New York: Skyhorse, 2011), 230.

2. Olsen and Schaeffer, 230.

3. Jef Tombeur, "An Unpublished Interview with T. Coraghessan Boyle," Auteurs .net, April 1989, web.

4. T. C. Boyle, *World's End* (New York: Viking Penguin, 1988), ix.

5. Elizabeth E. Adams, "T. Coraghessan Boyle: The Art of Fiction," *Paris Review* 161 (2012), web.

6. Sandra Cisneros and Joy Harjo, *Literary Friendships*, American Public Media, 17 May 2005.

7. Paul Gleason, *Understanding T. C. Boyle* (Columbia: University of South Carolina Press, 2009), 1.

8. Gleason, 1–2.

9. T. C. Boyle, "This Monkey, My Back," in *The Eleventh Draft: Craft and the Writing Life from the Iowa Writers' Workshop*, ed. Frank Conroy (New York: HarperCollins, 1999), 7.

10. T. Coraghessan Boyle, "Greasy Lake," in *Greasy Lake and Other Stories* (New York: Penguin, 1986), 2.

11. Tombeur.

12. Anthony DeCurtis, "T. Coraghessan Boyle: A Punk's Past Recaptured," *Rolling Stone*, 14 January 1988, web.

13. Boyle, "This Monkey, My Back," 8.

14. Allen Ginsberg, "Howl, For Carl Solomon," in *Howl and Other Poems* (San Francisco: City Lights, 1959), 9.

15. Boyle, "This Monkey, My Back," 8.

16. Boyle, "This Monkey, My Back," 8.

17. Adams.

18. Boyle, "This Monkey, My Back," 8.

19. Adams.

20. Boyle, "This Monkey, My Back," 7–11.

21. Adams.

22. Olsen and Schaeffer, 231.

23. Gleason, 2.

24. Nelson Algren, *The Last Carousel* (New York: G.P. Putnam's Sons, 1973), 77.

25. Olsen and Schaeffer, 79.

26. Scott Rettberg, "Scott Rettberg Interviews T. C. Boyle," Auteurs.net, 23 November 1998.

27. Connie Brothers, interview with David Dowling, 2 December 2015.

28. Adams.

29. Rettberg.

30. Rettberg.

31. Boyle, "This Monkey, My Back," 11.

32. Olsen and Schaeffer, 232.

33. Adams.

34. Adams.

35. Judith Handschuh, "T. Coraghessan Boyle," *Bookreporter*, 1998–2000, accessed 26 January 2016, web.

36. Adams.

37. Algren, 77.

38. Ernest Hemingway, *A Moveable Feast* (New York: Scribner, 2009), 65.

39. Algren, 77.

40. Tombeur.

41. Boyle, "This Monkey, My Back," 10.

42. Olsen and Schaeffer, 169.

43. Olsen and Schaeffer, 227.

44. Rettberg.

45. Cameron Martin, "T. C. Boyle: An Email Dialogue with Cameron Martin," *Barnes and Noble Review*, 9 February 2009, web.

46. Olsen and Schaeffer, 239, 118.

47. Martin, "T. C. Boyle: An Email Dialogue."

48. Adams.

49. Mark Mittlestadt, "Grace and Rubies 'Not Private,' " *Daily Iowan*, 27 February 1976, 3.

50. Diane Friedman, "City Holds Keys to Grace and Rubies," *Daily Iowan*, 31 August 1976, 6.

51. Mittlestadt, 3.

52. Boyle, *Descent of Man*, 95.

53. Boyle, *Descent of Man*, 84.

54. Boyle, *Descent of Man*, 98.

55. Boyle, *Descent of Man*, 97–98.

56. Patricia Lamberti, "Interview with T. C. Boyle," *Other Voices* 33 (Fall–Winter 2000), web.

57. T. Coraghessan Boyle, Preface to "A Women's Restaurant," in *The Workshop: Seven Decades of the Iowa Writers' Workshop*, ed. Tom Grimes (New York: Hyperion, 1999), 306–307. In addition to Irving's inspiration, Dickens provided Boyle's model for simultaneously reaching highbrow readers and a mass audience, in a piece flush with literary allusions—"Lysistrata, Gertrude Stein, Carrie Nation" along with Melville and Dickens—but with unmistakable appeal to readers of *Penthouse* who would delight in a scenario involving an obsessed, Ahab-like monomaniac's mission to infiltrate the women-only restaurant. Boyle, *Descent of Man*, 85.

58. Friedman, 6.

59. Boyle, Preface to "A Women's Restaurant," 306.

60. Boyle, *Descent of Man*, 85.

61. A closer examination of Boyle's stories in the collection *Descent of Man* reveals a pattern of brutality and sexist attitudes toward women, though thoroughly satirized and obviously not condoned. The title story, "Descent of Man," for example, begins with the line, "I was living with a woman who suddenly began to stink" (3). It goes on to tell a surreal tale of sexual competition according to the magical realist plot of a love triangle between the jealous narrator, his anthropologist wife, and her chimpanzee subject, who becomes her lover. The story features hilarious instances of the protagonist measuring himself against an ape, a rival who bests him physically and intellectually. Aghast that the creature has cleaned out their provisions, the narrator demands an explanation from his wife, who says he is "a big, active male and that she can attest for his need for so many calories" (14).

Other instances give pause, such as the widely anthologized "Greasy Lake," in which Boyle's alarmingly sympathetic narrator nearly commits the act. Set on an empty beach, his story "Drowning" depicts a random act of violence evocative of Camus's *The Stranger*. Lacking the humor of "Descent of Man" and the madcap antics of "A Women's Restaurant," it evokes the nadir of man's regression to primitive impulsive violence. The story portrays the violation of a sole sunbather not only by the fat social misfit who encounters her while combing the beach, but a group of fishermen who are the woman's would-be rescuers. Yet another figure who might save her drowns at sea. The dark view of humanity impinges directly on the violation of the female body, as with so many of the stories in *Descent of Man*.

62. Boyle, Preface to "A Women's Restaurant," 306–307.

63. The piece stands along with Iowa graduate Robert Bly's men's counter-movement—yet hardly so pious and self-righteous—as another backlash against first-wave feminism from the Workshop. Like Burgess in *A Clockwork Orange*, Boyle glories in the physical kinetic ballet of fight scenes—the "Greasy Lake" narrator takes a kick to the face described like a high-stepping majorette—among characters whose motives for brawling are as absurd as they are comic, and often impulsive to the point of social deviance glimpsing a dark nihilistic universe.

64. "Grace and Rubies Restaurant," *Lost Womyn's Space*, 16 December 2011, web.

65. Lynne Cherry, "Grace and Rubies: A Women's Haven," *Daily Iowan*, 31 May 1977.

66. "Our Correspondents: Iowa City," *Dyke: A Quarterly* 2 (1977), 86.

67. Olsen and Schaeffer, 310.

13. The Mystic: Marilynne Robinson

1. "Courses," *Iowa Student Information System*, University of Iowa, web.

2. Bryan Appleyard, "Marilynne Robinson, Word's Best Writer of Prose," *Times* (London), 21 September 2008, web.

3. Wyatt Mason, "The Revelations of Marilynne Robinson," *New York Times Magazine*, 1 October 2014, web.

4. Marilynne Robinson, interview with David Dowling, 13 April 2016, email.

5. "Marilynne Robinson," *The Daily Show with Jon Stewart* (Comedy Central), 8 July 2010, web video; "UI Professor on 'The Daily Show,' " *Iowa City Press Citizen*, 10 July 2010, RIWW UISC.

6. President Barack Obama and Marilynne Robinson, "President Barack Obama and Marilynne Robinson: A Conversation in Iowa," *New York Review of Books*, 5 November 2015.

7. Joe Fassler, "Marilynne Robinson on Democracy, Reading, and Religion in America," *Atlantic*, 16 May 2012.

8. Abby Aguirre, "The Story Behind President Obama's Interview with Marilynne Robinson," *Vogue*, 14 October 2015, web.

9. Ross Posnock, ed., *The Cambridge Companion to Ralph Ellison* (Cambridge: Cambridge University Press, 2005), xiv. Ellison wrote more than two thousand pages of his second novel but never finished it, perhaps the most bizarre quagmire following a famous first novel according to Wil Haygood, "The Invisible Manuscript," *Washington Post*, 19 August 2007, web.

10. Emma Brockes, "A Life in Writing: Marilynne Robinson," *Guardian*, 29 May 2009, web.

11. Jonathan Lee, "Interview with Marilynne Robinson, 2014 National Book Award Finalist, Fiction," *National Book Foundation*, [n.d.], retrieved 1 March 2016, web.

12. Brockes.

13. Marilynne Robinson, "Being Here," University of Iowa Presidential Lecture, 14 February 2010, web [video].

14. Although the film adaptation of Robinson's *Housekeeping* received positive reviews, she objected to Columbia Pictures and director Bill Forsyth's deviation from her novel's conclusion. Jason W. Stevens, ed., *This Life, This World: New Essays on Marilynne Robinson's* Housekeeping, Gilead, *and* Home (Leiden, The Netherlands: Brill, 2014), xii.

15. Quoted in Chad Wriglesworth, "Becoming a Creature of Artful Existence: Theological Perception and Ecological Design in Marilynne Robinson's *Gilead*," in *This Life, This World: New Essays on Marilynne Robinson's* Housekeeping, Gilead, *and* Home, ed. Jason W. Stevens (Leiden, The Netherlands: Brill, 2014), 101.

16. Jason Stevens, "Marilynne Robinson: A Chronology," in *This Life, This World: New Essays on Marilynne Robinson's* Housekeeping, Gilead, *and* Home, ed. Jason W. Stevens (Leiden, The Netherlands: Brill, 2014), xiii.

17. James H. Maguire, *Reading Marilynne Robinson's* Housekeeping (Boise: Boise State University Press, 2003), 11.

18. Maguire, 11.

19. Wriglesworth, 102.

20. Sarah Fay, "Marilynne Robinson: The Art of Fiction No. 198," *Paris Review* 186 (2008), 60.

21. Susan Sontag to Frank Conroy, 6 April 1992, RIWW SCUI, Series V, Box 1, Director's Files, access under permission of the Iowa Writers' Workshop.

22. Frank Conroy to Susan Sontag, 6 April 1992, RIWW SCUI, Series V, Box 1, Director's Files, access under permission of the Iowa Writers' Workshop.

23. Brockes.

24. Karen Armstrong, "Marilynne Robinson's 'The Givenness of Things,' " *New York Times*, 7 December 2015, web.

25. Stevens, xi.

26. Lisa Durose, "Marilynne Robinson: A Bibliography," *American Notes and Queries* 10.1 (Winter 1997): 31–46.

27. "Writers' Workshop Professor Wins $250,000 Prize," *Iowa City Press-Citizen*, 5 February 1998, RIWW SCUI.

28. Mason.

29. Gigi Wood, "Local Author in National Spotlight," *Iowa City Press-Citizen*, 20 November 2004, web.

30. Bob Abernethy, "Marilynne Robinson, Extended Interview," *Religion and Ethics Newsweekly*, 18 September 2009, web.

31. For an excellent example of her holograph manuscripts, see pinterest.com, https://s-media-cache-ako.pinimg.com/736x/c7/2a/45/c72a45fcc1e6aff26b6a 35f8a60fc3c3.jpg.

32. Emily Bobrow, "Meeting Marilynne Robinson," *Economist*, 21 May 2011, web.

33. Mason.

34. Marilynne Robinson, "By the Book," *New York Times*, 7 March 2013, web.

35. Marilynne Robinson, *The Givenness of Things* (New York: Farrar, Straus and Giroux, 2015), 133–134.

36. Jane Mulkerrins, "Marilynne Robinson: The Pulitzer Prize Winning Author on Her New Book," *Telegraph*, 18 October 2014, web.

37. For more on the social commentary describing "intense interior lives" in Robinson's fiction, especially about the "transition from domesticity to indigence," see Maggie Galehouse, "Their Own Private Idaho: Transience in Marilynne Robinson's *Housekeeping*," *Contemporary Literature* 41.1 (Spring 2000): 117–137.

38. Mason.

39. Allen Ginsberg, *Howl and Other Poems* (San Francisco: City Lights, 1959), 30.

40. Marilynne Robinson, *Gilead* (New York: Farrar, Straus and Giroux, 2004), 7.

41. Stevens, xi.

42. Robinson, *Gilead*, 19.

43. For more on Emerson's appreciation of Humboldt and the astronomer's adoption by New England transcendentalist intellectuals, see Laura Dassow Walls, *The Passage to Cosmos: Alexander von Humboldt and the Shaping of America* (Chicago: University of Chicago Press, 2009).

44. Abernethy.

45. Abernethy.

46. Mason.

47. Ralph Waldo Emerson, *The Collected Works of Ralph Waldo Emerson*, 10 vols., ed. Alfred R. Ferguson et al. (Cambridge: Harvard University Press, 1959–1972), 1:10.

48. David Dowling, *Emerson's Protégés: Mentoring and Marketing Transcendentalism's Future* (New Haven: Yale University Press, 2014), 20, 255.

49. Robinson, *Gilead*, 246.

50. Henry David Thoreau, *Walden*, ed. J. Lyndon Shanley (Princeton: Princeton University Press, 1971), 329.

51. Robinson, *Gilead*, 246.

52. Robinson, *Gilead*, 247.

53. Mason.

54. Abernethy.

55. Richard Lanham, *The Economics of Attention: Style and Substance in the Age of Information* (Chicago: University of Chicago Press, 2006), 3.

56. Abernethy.

57. "President Obama and Marilynne Robinson: A Conversation in Iowa," *New York Review of Books*, 19 November 2015, 6.

58. Marilynne Robinson, "Save Our Public Universities: In Defense of America's Best Idea," *Harper's*, March 2016, 30; Jeff Charis-Carlson, "Marilynne Robinson to Lecture on Crisis in Higher Education," *Des Moines Register*, 16 November 2016, web.

59. Jeff Charis-Carlson, "Graduate Employee Union Rips UI President Choice," *Iowa City Press-Citizen*, 4 September 2015, web.

60. Robinson, "Save Our Public Universities," 37.

61. Robinson, *The Givenness of Things*, 3–4.

62. Robinson, "Save Our Public Universities," 37.

63. Ralph Waldo Emerson, "The American Scholar," in *The American Transcendentalists: Essential Writings*, ed. Lawrence Buell (New York: Modern Library, 2006), 93.

64. Robinson, "Save Our Public Universities," 30.

65. Emerson, "The American Scholar," 92.

66. Emerson, "The American Scholar," 84.

67. Emerson, "The American Scholar," 99.

68. Fay, 38.

69. Meghan O'Rourke, "A Moralist of the Midwest," *New York Times Magazine*, 24 October 2004, web.

70. O'Rourke.

71. Thessaly Le Force, "A Teacher and Her Student," *Vice*, 18 June 2013, web.

72. Le Force.

73. Marilynne Robinson, "Diminished Creatures," in *The Eleventh Draft: Craft and the Writing Life from the Iowa Writers' Workshop*, ed. Frank Conroy (New York: HarperCollins, 1999), 157.

74. Julia Shriver, "Robinson to Receive Award," *Daily Iowan*, 10 July 2013, RIWW SCUI.

75. Le Force.

76. Dowling, 86.

77. Lee, "Interview with Marilynne Robinson."

78. Robinson, "Fear," *New York Review of Books*, 24 September 2014, web.

79. Fay, 39.

80. Robinson, "Diminished Creatures," 159.

81. Robinson, "By the Book."

82. Robinson, "Diminished Creatures," 159.

14. The Warrior: Anthony Swofford

1. Anthony Swofford, *Jarhead: A Marine's Chronicle of the Gulf War and Other Battles* (New York: Scribner, 2003), 70; Anne Sexton, "Wanting to Die," in *Selected Poems of Anne Sexton*, ed. Dianne Wood Middlebrook (Boston: Houghton Mifflin, 1988), 98.

2. Swofford, *Jarhead*, 71.

3. Swofford, *Jarhead*, 71.

4. Anthony Swofford, *Hotels, Hospitals, and Jails: A Memoir* (New York: Hachette, 2012), 204.

5. Swofford, *Hotels*, 234.

6. Jeffrey M. Anderson, "Interview with Anthony Swofford: Unscrewing *Jarhead*," *Combustible Celluloid*, 24 October 2004, web.

7. Anderson.

8. Swofford, *Jarhead*, 1.

9. Swofford, *Jarhead*, 1.

10. Anthony Swofford, interview with David Dowling, 24 May 2016.

11. Kurt Vonnegut, *Slaughterhouse-Five* (New York: Dell, 1969), 3.

12. Jon Robert Adams, *Male Armor: The Soldier-Hero in Contemporary American Literature* (Charlottesville: University of Virginia Press, 2008), 124.

13. Swofford, *Jarhead*, 11, 254.

14. Anthony Swofford, "Foreword," in *Home to War: A History of the Vietnam Veterans Movement*, ed. Gerald Nicosia (New York: Carroll and Graf, 2004), xxi–xxiii.

15. Erich Maria Remarque, *All Quiet on the Western Front* (New York: Random House, 2013 [1929]), 32.

16. Lyne Gabriel, "A Soldier from a Familiar Part of Town," *Daily Iowan*, 29 January 2004, p. 4C.

17. Swofford, *Jarhead*, 10, 11.

18. Nathaniel Fick, "How Accurate Is Jarhead? What One Marine Makes of the Gulf War Movie," *Slate*, 9 November 2005, web.

19. Anthony Swofford, "Escape and Evasion (Stories)," MFA thesis, University of Iowa, Iowa Writers' Workshop, May 2001, iii.

20. *Jarhead*, directed by Sam Mendes, Universal Pictures, 2005, DVD, supplementary material.

21. Swofford, *Jarhead*, 247.

22. Samuel Beckett, *Waiting for Godot* (New York: Grove, 1982), 54.

23. Swofford, *Jarhead*, dust jacket.

24. William T. Vollmann, "Military Brats in Love," *New York Times Book Review*, 14 January 2007, web.

25. As quoted in Fick.

26. Vollman.

27. Swofford, *Jarhead*, 34, 36.

28. Elisabeth Piedmont-Marton, "Gulf War Memoir Syndrome," *Texas Observer*, 12 September 2003, web.

29. Adams, 116.

30. Mark Bowden, "The Things They Carried," *New York Times*, 2 March 2003, web.

31. Michiko Kakutani, "Books of the Times: A Warrior Haunted by Ghosts of Battle," *New York Times*, 19 February 2003, web.

32. Matt Schudel, "Frank Conroy; Author and Iowa Writers' Workshop Director," *Washington Post*, 7 April 2005, web.

33. Anthony Swofford, interview with David Dowling, 24 May 2016.

34. Anthony Swofford, interview with David Dowling, 24 May 2016.

35. William L. Hamilton, "At Home with Chris Offutt: Learning Not to Trespass on the Gently Rolling Past," *New York Times*, 18 April 2002, web.

36. Chris Offutt, "My Dad, the Pornographer," *New York Times Magazine*, 5 February 2015, web.

37. Swofford, "Escape and Evasion (Stories)," 32.

38. Swofford, "Escape and Evasion (Stories)," 56–57.

39. "Interview with Anthony Swofford," *Iowa Review*, April 2015, web.

40. Anthony Swofford, interview with David Dowling, 6 April 2016, email.

41. Connie Brothers, interview with David Dowling, 2 November 2015.

42. Stephen Bloom, "He Was Tough and Generous," *Chicago Tribune*, 10 April 2005, Sect. 2, pp. 1–4.

43. Connie Brothers, interview with David Dowling, 2 November 2015.

44. Anthony Swofford, interview with David Dowling, 7 April 2016, email.

45. Stephen Elliott, "Interview with Anthony Swofford," *Believer*, February 2007, web.

46. Reza Aslan, "Reza Aslan Reading, Live from Prairie Lights," 7 April 2005, University of Iowa Libraries Special Collections, Iowa Digital Library.

47. Frank Conroy to Pinckney Benedict, 25 May 1988, RIWW SCUI, Series V, Box 1, Director's Files, access under permission of the Iowa Writers' Workshop.

48. James Michener to Frank Conroy, 26 September 1989, RIWW SCUI, Series V, Box 1, Director's Files, access under permission of the Iowa Writers' Workshop.

49. Frank Conroy to Erik Nelson, 22 September 1989, RIWW SCUI, Series V, Box 1, Director's Files, access under permission of the Iowa Writers' Workshop.

50. James Michener to Frank Conroy, 26 September 1989, RIWW SCUI, Series V, Box 1, Director's Files, access under permission of the Iowa Writers' Workshop.

51. Paul Sorenson, "Stuck in the Desert of Romance," *Daily Iowan*, 24 January 2007, 7A.

52. Anthony Swofford, interview with David Dowling, 6 April 2016, email.

53. In collaboration with director Sam Mendes, Swofford narrated and co-produced *Semper Fi* and *Jarhead Diaries*, documentary material bundled with the DVD of *Jarhead* released in 2005. *Jarhead Diaries* focuses on the making of the film, and *Semper Fi* was designed to acknowledge and respect the American troops who were still on the front lines of battle in Iraq. It profiles the homecoming experience of several Marine combatants. Swofford was a co-presenter and fellow memoirist with his wife Christa Parravani at several events in and around New York City. "Book Launch: *Her* by Christa Parravani with Anthony Swofford," *The Powerhouse Arena*, 5 March 2013.

54. Swofford, *Hotels*, i.

15. The Voice: Ayana Mathis and Mass Culture

1. Kathleen Rooney, *Reading with Oprah: The Book Club That Changed America* (Fayatteville: University of Arkansas Press, 2005), 118; David Pesci, "The Oprah Effect: Texts, Readers, and the Dialectic of Signification," *Communications Review* 5.2 (2002): 143–178.

2. Hardy Green, "Why Oprah Opens Readers' Wallets," *Business Week*, 9 October 2005, web.

3. David Daley, "Ayana Mathis: Oprah Winfrey Is on the Phone and a Career Is Born," *Salon*, 16 December 2012, web.

4. Patricia Sellers, "The Business of Being Oprah," *Fortune*, 1 April 2002, web.

5. Daley.

6. Daley.

7. Jonathan Lee, "A Question of Faith," *Guernica: A Magazine of Art and Politics*, 15 May 2013, web.

8. Daley.

9. Matthew Salesses, "When Defending Your Writing Becomes Defending Yourself," *NPR: Code Switch, Frontiers of Race, Culture, and Identity*, 20 July 2014, web.

10. Lynn Neary, "In Elite MFA Programs, the Challenge of Writing While 'Other,' " *NPR: Code Switch, Frontiers of Race, Culture, and Identity*, 19 August 2014, web.

11. Sheryl McCarthy, "One to One: Ayana Mathis, Author, *The Twelve Tribes of Hattie*," CUNYtv, 22 January 2013, web video.

12. McCarthy.

13. Daley.

14. McCarthy.

15. Julie Mannell, "University of Iowa Fail," *Community on BuzzFeed*, 24 March 2015, web.

16. Minnesota's Mayo Medical School, the educational counterpart of the Mayo Medical Clinic, had a 2.1 percent acceptance rate in 2018; Alyssa Rege, "10 Medical Schools with the Lowest Acceptance Rates," *Becker's Medical Review*, 3 April 2018, web. The Iowa Writers' Workshop's admission of 25 students out of 1,026 applicants for fall 2015 yielded an acceptance rate of 2.4 percent. Yale Law School's acceptance rate was 8.4 percent in 2017.

17. Neary.

18. Neena Andrews, "Oprah Talks to Ayana Mathis," *O, The Oprah Magazine, South Africa*, March 2013, web.

19. Daley.

20. Daley.

21. Daley.

22. Ayana Mathis, "The Twelve Tribes of Hattie" [excerpt], MFA thesis, Iowa Writers' Workshop, 2011, 18–20.

23. Mathis, "Twelve Tribes," 21.

24. Mathis, "Twelve Tribes," 22.

25. Werner Huber et al., *Self-Reflexivity in Literature* (Wiesbaden, Germany: Konigshausen & Neumann, 2005).

26. Ayana Mathis, "What Will Happen to All of That Beauty," *Guernica: A Magazine of Art and Politics*, 15 December 2014, web.

27. Oprah Winfrey and Ayana Mathis, "Exclusive Webisode: Author Ayana Mathis' Three Greatest Lessons," Oprah.com, February 2013, web.

28. Winfrey and Mathis, "Three Greatest Lessons."

29. Ayana Mathis, *The Twelve Tribes of Hattie* (New York: Knopf, 2012).

30. Mark McGurl, *The Program Era: Postwar Fiction and the Rise of Creative Writing* (Cambridge: Harvard University Press, 2009), 131, 135.

31. Christopher Clair, " 'It Still Doesn't Quite Seem Real': Writers' Workshop Alumna Mathis Experiencing Post-Oprah Whirlwind," *Iowa Now*, 1 February 2013, web.

32. Dan Barden, "Workshop: A Rant Against Creative Writing Classes," *Poets and Writers* (March/April 2008), 87.

33. As quoted in Michael Parks, "On the Write Track: A University of Arkansas Program Has Trained Students in the Nuts and Bolts of Producing Good Fiction and Poetry for 40 Years," *Arkansas Democrat-Gazette*, 3 April 2008, E6.

34. Torres's own fame, driven mainly by his memoir, is immediately visible in mass culture in *Salon*'s selection of him among the sexiest men of 2011, the year he graduated from the Workshop. "Salon's Sexiest Men of 2011," *Salon*, 17 November 2011, web.

35. Ramin Setoodeh, " 'Girls' Finale: Director of Iowa Writers' Workshop Weighs In," *Variety*, 24 March 2014, web.

36. Daley.

37. McGurl, 301.

38. Anis Shivani, *Against the Workshop: Provocations, Polemics, Controversies* (Huntsville: Texas Review Press, 2011), 170.

39. McGurl, 301.

40. Shivani, 172.

41. McGurl, 229.

42. Clair.

43. Siddhartha Deb and Ayana Mathis, "Why Get an MFA?" *New York Times*, 18 August 2015, web.

44. Shivani, 153–155.

45. Junot Díaz, "MFA vs. POC," *New Yorker*, 30 April 2014, 32.

46. Deb and Mathis.

47. Neary.

48. Anthony Swofford, interview by David Dowling, 24 May 2016.

49. Deb and Mathis.

50. Shivani, 172.

51. Daley.

52. E. I. Johnson, "Famous Literary Agent: Ellen Levine," *The View from the Top: Interviews with Industry Experts*, 7 June 2007, web.

53. Jeff Charis-Carlson and Zach Berg, "Marilynne Robinson Retiring from Iowa Writers' Workshop," *Iowa City Press-Citizen*, 27 April 2016, web.

54. McCarthy.

55. Mathis, *Twelve Tribes*, 9.

56. Nicole Mowbray, "Oprah's Path to Power," *Guardian*, 3 March 2003, web.

57. Andrews.

58. Neary.

59. McCarthy.

60. R. Jackson Wilson, "Emerson as Lecturer: Man Thinking, Man Saying," in *The Cambridge Companion to Ralph Waldo Emerson*, ed. Joel Porte and Saundra Morris (Cambridge: Cambridge University Press, 1999), 79.

61. Shivani, 170; also see McGurl on professionalism in MFA programs, 55, 95, 409.

62. Lee.

63. Jim Collins, *Bring on the Books for Everybody: How Literary Culture Became Popular Culture* (Durham, N.C.: Duke University Press, 2010), 105.

64. Lee.

65. Lee.

66. Craig L. Garthwaite, *You Get a Book! Demand Spillovers, Combative Advertising, and Celebrity Endorsements*, National Bureau of Economic Research, no. w17915, 2012.

67. Collins, 105.

68. Kisha, "African-American Historical Fiction Discussion: Ayana Mathis's 'Twelve Tribes of Hattie,'" *Goodreads*, 19 March 2014, 10:39 A.M., web.

69. Felicia R. Lee, "Novelist's Debut Is Newest Pick for Oprah's Book Club," *New York Times*, 5 December 2012, web.

70. Nicole Nichols and Wendy Luckenbill, "Oprah's Book Club 2.0 Announces Its Second Selection, 'The Twelve Tribes of Hattie' by Ayana Mathis," *Discovery Press Web*, 5 December 2012, web.

71. Shivani, 290.

72. Eric Olsen and Glenn Schaeffer, eds., *We Wanted to Be Writers: Life, Love, and Literature at the Iowa Writers' Workshop* (New York: Skyhorse, 2011), 219.

73. Shivani, 290.

74. Jason Boog, "Top 10 Bestselling Books in Oprah's Book Club," *GalleyCat*, 23 May 2011, web.

75. Mathis did not comment in response to my questions as to whether she would actively pursue a mass audience such as Oprah's Book Club readers again with her next project. Ayana Mathis, correspondence with David Dowling, 30 April 2016.

76. Olsen and Schaeffer, 294.

77. Olsen and Schaeffer, 185.

78. Hector Tobar, "Melodrama Overtakes Mathis' 'Twelve Tribes of Hattie,'" *Los Angeles Times*, 20 December 2012, web.

79. Garthwaite, 60.

80. Communications scholar Janice Radway explains how participation in book clubs can function as "narrative therapy," especially through immersion in story worlds that leave the reader "earless, eyeless, motionless for hours." Such deep reading

provides "the cure of interlocking dreams" to counter anxiety, fear, and loneliness. Janice A. Radway, *A Feeling for Books: The Book-of-the-Month-Club, Literary Taste, and Middle-Class Desire* (Chapel Hill: University of North Carolina Press, 1997), 15. For more on the culture and gender politics of audience in popular literature, see Janice Radway, *Reading the Romance: Women, Patriarchy, and Popular Culture* (Chapel Hill: University of North Carolina Press, 1984).

81. Lee.

82. Collins, 103.

83. Harold Bloom, *How to Read and Why* (New York: Simon and Schuster, 2001), 142.

84. "Ayana Mathis: 2013 National Book Festival," *Library of Congress National Book Festival*, Library of Congress, 14 January 2014, web video.

Epilogue

1. Plaque Dedicated to Paul Engle, Literary Walk, Iowa Avenue, Iowa City, Iowa.

2. Paul Engle's Plot, Oakland Cemetery, Iowa City, Iowa (Photo by Travis Vogan).

3. Loren Glass, "Middle Man: Paul Engle and the Iowa Writers' Workshop," *Minnesota Review* (Winter/Spring 2009), 10.

4. Zlatko Anguelov, "Paul Engle," *The Writing University*, web.

5. Paul Engle, *A Lucky American Childhood* (Iowa City: University of Iowa Press, 1996), ix.

6. Tom Grimes, ed., *The Workshop: Seven Decades of the Iowa Writers' Workshop* (New York: Hyperion, 1999), 707.

7. In 2000, then governor Tom Vilsack designated October 12, Engle's birthday, as "Paul Engle Day," naming him "Iowa's Poet of the Century." Merrill persuaded UNESCO to establish two projects that bear Engle's name, the Paul Engle Prize, an annual literary award first given to Workshop faculty member James Alan McPherson in 2011, and the Glory of the Senses high school essay contest.

8. Frank Conroy to Jack Leggett, 10 May 1990, RIWW SCUI, Series V, Box 1, Director's Files, access under permission of the Iowa Writers' Workshop. The stigma of Engle was behind Conroy's refusal of an offer from highly acclaimed poet and Workshop alumnus Robert Dana to provide a one-day workshop and reading from his latest book. Dana had been a longtime Engle ally, making his otherwise reasonable bid unconscionable to Conroy, who disingenuously alluded to "the sad news of the current budget crunch" despite the Workshop's flush financial situation. The Workshop, as he reported to former director John Leggett, in fact "was in fine shape" financially, enjoying "four years of the highest salary increases in the College of Liberal Arts." Frank Conroy to Robert Dana, 7 October 1991; Frank Conroy to Jack Leggett, 10 May 1990, RIWW SCUI, Series V, Box 1, Director's Files, access under permission of the Iowa Writers' Workshop.

9. Glass, 10.

10. "The Mighty Big Ten Versus the Ivy League" [Advertisement for *Holiday*] *Michigan Alumnus* 73.13 (16 February 1957), 230.

11. Ed Dinger, ed., *Seems Like Old Times* (Iowa City: University of Iowa Press, 1986), 21–22.

12. Arthur Schlesinger, Jr., to Paul Engle, 6 November 1962, PPE SCUI, Box 8.

13. "A Day Celebrating the Friends of the Writing Program at The State University of Iowa," 18 September 1962, PPE SCUI, Box 8.

14. "11 Students at S.U.I. Win Industries' Writing Grants," *Des Moines Register*, 24 November 1960, PPE SCUI, Box 8.

15. J. M. Hickerson to Paul Engle, 28 March 1960, PPE SCUI, Box 8.

16. J. M. Hickerson to Paul Engle, 28 March 1960, PPE SCUI, Box 8.

17. Another emblematic instance of Engle's use of Workshop student writing for public relations appeared in a promotional piece published in the magazine *Transmission: Northern Gas Company*. The full-page advertisement for the Workshop trumpeted, "Writers with the creative urge find fertile ground for literary development at the State University of Iowa's . . . [in large letters below] *WRITERS' WORKSHOP.*" The text below continues the pitch: "In the Workshop a writer is exposed to intensive discussion and demonstration of all elements of writing as well as to an extensive sampling of the literature of all times and all countries." Following the advertisement is a short story titled "Beany" credited to Workshop student Andy Fetler. Northern Gas Company was of course one of Engle's many corporate sponsors. In this case, as with the agreement contracted with advertising agent J. M. Hickerson, Inc., students' writing functions as advertising. [Advertisement for Iowa Writers' Workshop], *Transmission: Northern Gas Company* 10.1 (1962), 15, PPE SCUI.

18. Robert Dana, ed., *A Community of Writers: Paul Engle and the Iowa Writers' Workshop* (Iowa City: University of Iowa Press, 1999), ix.

19. Kurt Vonnegut, *Kurt Vonnegut Letters*, ed. Dan Wakefield (New York: Delacorte Press, 2012), 132.

20. Joan Rattner to Paul Engle, 16 March 1960, PPE SCUI, Box 8.

21. Popular audiences with literary or high cultural pretensions formed Engle's target market for publicity, as seen in the libretto of an opera he wrote for Hallmark's *Hall of Fame* television program. In bringing high culture to the masses, Engle worked closely with Webster Schott at Hallmark, who also read the manuscript of his book *Western Child* and offered suggestions. Webster Schott to Paul Engle, 28 March 1960, PPE SCUI, Box 8.

22. The prospect of teaching creative writing as the primary means of living presumably supplemented by royalties from one's publications, according to Workshop MFA Geoffrey Wolff, suggests that the employment of creative writers by the academy is corrupt. Real authors, he argues, need no institutional shelter from the market. "Those who can't, teach; those who can, sell to Dreamworks and Disney," he

urges, noting "it's always risky to accuse others of selling out," typically novelists such as Workshop graduates Max Allan Collins and David Morrell brokering deals with movie producers for their work. Geoffrey Wolff, "Communal Solitude," in *The Eleventh Draft: Craft and the Writing Life from the Iowa Writers' Workshop*, ed. Frank Conroy (New York: HarperCollins, 1999), 107. The justification of selling to Disney as validation of one's literary worth is evident in Director Frank Conroy's promotion of his students for the Disney Studios' Apprenticeship Writers' Program with Walt Disney Pictures and Television. Judy Weinstein to Frank Conroy, 18 January 1990, RIWW SCUI, Series V, Box 1, Director's Files, access under permission of the Iowa Writers' Workshop.

23. "The Writer in Mass Culture," Transcript, SCUI; Dorothy Collin, "Four Writers Will Speak at 2-Day Session," *Daily Iowan*, 4 December 1959.

24. Iowa City UNESCO City of Literature Staff, in conversation with David Dowling, Iowa City, Iowa, 13 October 2015.

25. Nicholas M. Kelley, "Mapping the Program Era: Sample Data Visualizations," *The Program Era Project*, 31 May 2016, web.

26. Eric Bennett, *Workshops of Empire: Stegner, Engle, and American Creative Writing During the Cold War* (Iowa City: University of Iowa Press, 2015), 112, 196 n. 114.

27. Bennett, 112.

28. "Engle Denies Charges of Red Ties," Tuxedo, N.Y., 9 November, A.P. "Paul Engle Denies He Has Un-American Committee Listing" [newspaper clippings, n.d., no journal titles], PPE SCUI.

29. Grimes, *The Workshop*, 708.

30. Grimes, *The Workshop*, 708.

31. Grimes, *The Workshop*, 709.

32. Grimes, *The Workshop*, 707, 710, 714.

33. Eric Bennett, "How Iowa Flattened Literature," *Chronicle of Higher Education*, 10 February 2014, web.

34. Grimes, *The Workshop*, 654.

35. Grimes, *The Workshop*, 709.

36. Tom Grimes, *Mentor: A Memoir* (Portland, Ore.: Tin House, 2010), 31.

37. Kent Williams, "Workshop Woes: A Supposedly Bad Thing the Iowa Writers' Workshop Did to Literature," *Little Village*, 20 February 2014, web.

38. David Foster Wallace, "Shipping Out: On the (Nearly Lethal) Comforts of a Luxury Cruise," *Harper's* (January 1996), 41.

39. Wallace, 42.

40. Wallace, 42–43.

41. Wallace, 43.

42. F. Scott Fitzgerald, *The Great Gatsby* (New York: Charles Scribner's Sons, 1925 [2004]), 54.

43. Wallace, 43.

44. Grimes, *Mentor*, 8–9. As described in chapter 15, Reza Aslan similarly was appalled at the deceptive bait-switch tactic by which Conroy lured him into thinking he was a "pet" only to blindside him with a humiliating vivisection in his first showing at workshop. Aslan swears by Conroy's teaching, insisting that all the knowledge necessary for his authorial career he acquired in the director's seminar. Reza Aslan, "Reza Aslan Reading, Live from Prairie Lights," 7 April 2005, University of Iowa Libraries Special Collections, Iowa Digital Library.

45. Email correspondence, Lan Samantha Chang to David Dowling, 8 June 2016.

46. Ellis is an African American, which complicates the racial dynamics of the narrative of what Joy Harjo characterized as a predatory atmosphere in the program between male faculty, most of whom where white, and their female students, one that traces back at least to the 1950s. Eric Olsen and Glen Schaeffer, eds. *We Wanted to Be Writers: Life, Love, and Literature at the Iowa Writers' Workshop* (New York: Skyhorse, 2011), 64.

47. Jia Tolentino, "Is This the End of the Era of the Important, Inappropriate Literary Man?" *Jezebel*, 28 March 2016, web; Jeff Charis-Carlson, "Writers' Workshop Professor Still Employed After Classes Canceled, Reassigned," *Iowa City Press-Citizen*, 11 May 2016, web. For the testimony of the eleven women alleging sexual misconduct perpetrated by Workshop faculty member Thomas Sayers Ellis, see "Reports from the Field: Statements Against Violence," *VIDA: Women in Literary Arts*, 6 March 2016, web.

48. David McCartney, email correspondence with author, 11 November 2017.

49. W. D. Snodgrass, "Mentors, Fomenters, and Tormentors," in *A Community of Writers: Paul Engle and the Iowa Writers' Workshop*, ed. Robert Dana (Iowa City: University of Iowa Press, 1999), 144.

50. Frank Conroy to Norman Mailer, 19 April 1990, RIWW SCUI, Series V, Box 1, Director's Files, access under permission of the Iowa Writers' Workshop.

51. Tolentino.

52. Paul Engle, ed., *Midland: Twenty-Five Years of Fiction and Poetry, Selected from the Writing Workshops of the State University of Iowa* (New York: Random House, 1961), xxii.

53. Anguelov.

54. Snodgrass, 124.

55. Paul Engle, *A Lucky American Childhood* (Iowa City: University of Iowa Press, 1996), xxiii.

56. Engle, *A Lucky American Childhood*, xxi; " 'Yes' Is the Basic Attitude at S.U.I., Atkinson Finds," *Des Moines Register*, 12 May 1961, PPE SCUI. Atkinson was the *New York Times* reporter who had published a feature story on the Workshop in 1961.

57. Grimes, *The Workshop*, 707.

58. Mike Klein, "This Place in Iowa Makes World Famous Writers," *Des Moines Register*, 13 April 2016, web.

59. Connie Brothers, interview with David Dowling, 2 December 2015.

60. A number of strenuous arguments to the contrary have arisen in defense of the Workshop on the issue of uniformity of writing in an institutionalized setting. Frank Conroy, for example, denied these allegations in a two-page typed statement apparently intended for public relations purposes that appears in his Director's file. In it, he objects to the charge—perhaps most visibly made by Nelson Algren in 1973 in *The Last Carousel*—that "first novels of short-stories are shallow, naïve, slick, and jejune, so the argument goes, because they were written in Workshops made up of graduate students who know nothing about life and hence have nothing to write about." Conroy insists, "its [*sic*] a facile argument that sounds okay until one examines the rather arrogant assumptions that lie behind it," namely that "some other environment exists—a garret, perhaps, with attendant poverty, loneliness and despair—that would turn out better writers." He debunks the idea that "a Golden Age" existed "before workshops, when people learned in the school of hard knocks and produced great stuff." His points are compelling until he overextends himself with the claim that "most first novels of fifty years ago are forgotten now, and weren't any better than contemporary work. I dare say they were worse."

In justifying contemporary literature, Conroy of course is defending his own dual role as contemporary author and facilitator of contemporary literary production as director of the Iowa Writers' Workshop. But he contradicts his sweeping defense of contemporary literature in his attempt to refute the assertion that "Conformism! Writing by committee!" lurks behind the system of weekly meetings, presided over by an older writer, of young writers reading and responding to each other's work. Conroy alludes to his experience as reviewer for the National Endowment for the Arts in Washington, "in which I read thousands of manuscripts"—all contemporary—"from all over the country and noticed more conformity, and especially conformity to the aesthetics of the marketplace," posited as a far more pernicious source than a creative writing program, "in non-workshop writers than I did in those writers attending the numerous MFA programs spread out over the nation." A litany of Iowa Writers' Workshop authors then follows as evidence of the eclectic nature of such programs, yet not successfully disproving the allegation of conformist writing since each was trained in a radically different era: "its [*sic*] hard for me to connect people like Flannery O'Connor, John Irving, Tracy Kidder, Jayne Anne Phillips, Ethan Canin, or T.C. Boyle, except that they're all fine writers." Frank Conroy, circa 1989 [n.d.], RIWW SCUI, Series V, Box 1, Director's Files, access under permission of the Iowa Writers' Workshop.

61. Klein.

62. Ethan Canin, "Smallness and Invention; or, What I Learned at the Iowa Writers' Workshop," in *The Eleventh Draft: Craft and the Writing Life from the Iowa Writers' Workshop*, ed. Frank Conroy (New York: HarperCollins, 1999), 26.

63. Grimes, *The Workshop*, 716.

64. Grimes, *Mentor*, 220.

65. Grimes, *The Workshop*, 717.

66. Laurie Van Dyke, "Both Engle Captors Nabbed," 4 August 1959, *Cedar Rapids Gazette;* Laurie Van Dyke, "Paul Engles Tell Gazette of Ordeal," 2 August 1959, *Cedar Rapids Gazette*, PPE SCUI.

67. Van Dyke, "Both Engle Captors Nabbed"; Van Dyke, "Paul Engles Tell Gazette of Ordeal."

68. Paul Engle, "Introduction" to *Midland*, manuscript draft, PPE SCUI.

69. Kurt Vonnegut, *Mother Night* (New York: Random House, 1969), v.

INDEX